studysync®

Reading & Writing Companion

GRADE 12 UNITS

Epic Heroes • The Human Condition
An Exchange of Ideas • Emotional Currents

88studysync

studysync.com

2015 G12

studysync®

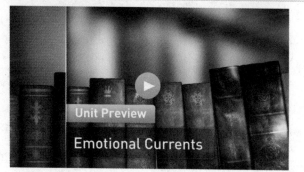
Reading & Writing Companion   iii

STUDENT GUIDE

GETTING STARTED

Welcome to the StudySync Reading and Writing Companion! In this booklet, you will find a collection of readings based on the theme of the unit you are studying. As you work through the readings, you will be asked to answer questions and perform a variety of tasks designed to help you closely analyze and understand each text selection. Read on for an explanation of

1 INTRODUCTION

An Introduction to each text provides historical context for your reading as well as information about the author. You will also learn about the genre of the excerpt and the year in which it was written.

2 FIRST READ

During your first reading of each excerpt, you should just try to get a general idea of the content and message of the reading. Don't worry if there are parts you don't understand or words that are unfamiliar to you. You'll have an opportunity later to dive deeper into the text.

Many times, while working through the Think Questions after your first read, you will be asked to **annotate** or **make annotations** about what you are reading. This means that you should use the "Notes" column to make comments or jot down any questions you may have about the text. You may also want to note any unfamiliar vocabulary words here.

3 THINK QUESTIONS

These questions will ask you to start thinking critically about the text, asking specific questions about its purpose, and making connections to your prior knowledge and reading experiences. To answer these questions, you should go back to the text and draw upon specific evidence that you find there to support your responses. You will also begin to explore some of the more challenging vocabulary words used in the excerpt.

4   CLOSE READ & FOCUS QUESTIONS

After you have completed the First Read, you will then be asked to go back and read the excerpt more closely and critically. Before you begin your Close Read, you should read through the Focus Questions to get an idea of the concepts you will want to focus on during your second reading. You should work through the Focus Questions by making annotations, highlighting important concepts, and writing notes or questions in the "Notes" column. Depending on instructions from your teacher, you may need to respond online or use a separate piece of paper to start expanding on your thoughts and ideas.

5   WRITING PROMPT

Your study of each excerpt or selection will end with a writing assignment. To complete this assignment, you should use your notes, annotations, and answers to both the Think and Focus Questions. Be sure to read the prompt carefully and address each part of it in your writing assignment.

6   EXTENDED WRITING PROJECT

After you have read and worked through all of the unit text selections, you will move on to a writing project. This project will walk you through steps to plan, draft, revise, edit, and finally publish an essay or other piece of writing about one or more of the texts you have studied in the unit. Student models and graphic organizers will provide guidance and help you organize your thoughts as you plan and write your essay. Throughout the project, you will also study and work on specific writing skills to help you develop different portions of your writing.

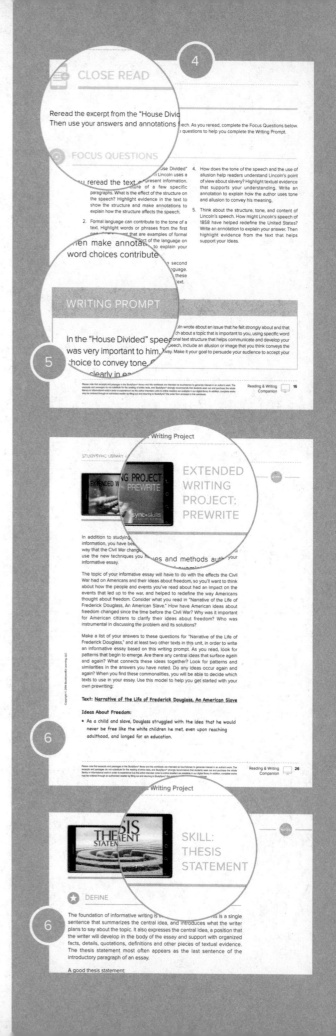

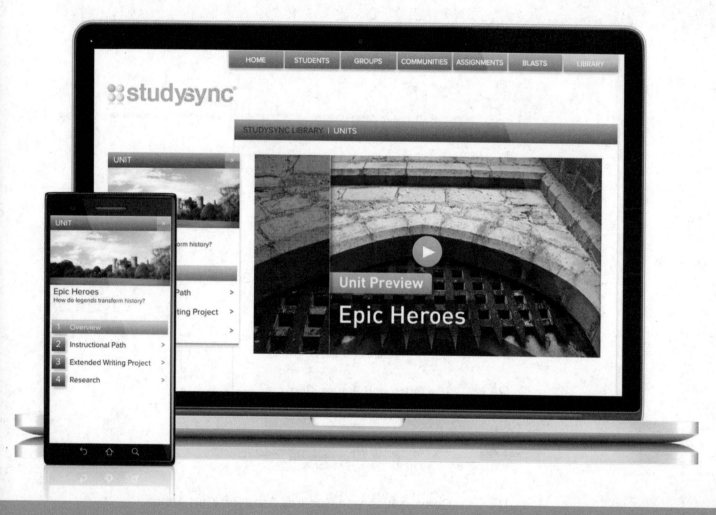

studysync®

Reading & Writing Companion

How do legends transform history?

Epic Heroes

Epic Heroes

TEXTS

TEXTS

EXTENDED WRITING PROJECT

453

Text Fulfillment
through
StudySync

BEOWULF

(LINES 1325–1477)

POETRY
Anglo-Saxon Tradition
8th to 11th Century

INTRODUCTION

The author, date of composition, and inspiration of "Beowulf" are unknown, but its place as an archetypal Anglo-Saxon text and oldest surviving epic poem in English is indisputable. For 12 years the people of Denmark under the leadership of King Hrothgar are terrorized by a brutal monster named Grendel. When Beowulf, hero of the Geats, learns of this, he decides to repay a favor to Hrothgar by slaying the beast. Little does he know that he will also have to contend

"Ride we anon, and mark the trail of the mother of Grendel."

FIRST READ

XX

1325. HROTHGAR spake, helmet-of-Scyldings:—
1326. "Ask not of pleasure! Pain is renewed
1327. to Danish folk. Dead is Aeschere,
1328. of Yrmenlaf the elder brother,
1329. my sage adviser and stay in council,
1330. shoulder-comrade in stress of fight
1331. when warriors clashed and we warded our heads,
1332. hewed the helm-boars; hero famed
1333. should be every earl as Aeschere was!
1334. But here in Heorot a hand hath slain him
1335. of wandering death-sprite. I wot not whither,
1336. proud of the prey, her path she took,
1337. fain of her fill. The feud she **avenged**
1338. that yesternight, unyieldingly,
1339. Grendel in grimmest grasp thou killedst,—
1340. seeing how long these liegemen mine
1341. he ruined and **ravaged.** Reft of life,
1342. in arms he fell. Now another comes,
1343. keen and cruel, her kin to avenge,
1344. faring far in feud of blood:
1345. so that many a thane shall think, who e'er
1346. sorrows in soul for that sharer of rings,
1347. this is hardest of heart-bales. The hand lies low
1348. that once was willing each wish to please.
1349. Land-dwellers here and liegemen mine,
1350. who house by those parts, I have heard relate
1351. that such a pair they have sometimes seen,
1352. march-stalkers mighty the moorland haunting,
1353. wandering spirits: one of them seemed,

1354. so far as my folk could fairly judge,

1355. of womankind; and one, accursed,

1356. in man's guise trod the misery-track

1357. of exile, though huger than human bulk.

1358. Grendel in days long gone they named him,

1359. folk of the land; his father they knew not,

1360. nor any brood that was born to him

1361. of **treacherous** spirits. Untrod is their home;

1362. by wolf-cliffs haunt they and windy headlands,

1363. fenways fearful, where flows the stream

1364. from mountains gliding to gloom of the rocks,

1365. underground flood. Not far is it hence

1366. in measure of miles that the mere expands,

1367. and o'er it the frost-bound forest hanging,

1368. sturdily rooted, shadows the wave.

1369. By night is a wonder weird to see,

1370. fire on the waters. So wise lived none

1371. of the sons of men, to search those depths!

1372. Nay, though the heath-rover, harried by dogs,

1373. the horn-proud hart, this holt should seek,

1374. long distance driven, his dear life first

1375. on the brink he yields ere he brave the plunge

1376. to hide his head: 'tis no happy place!

1377. Thence the welter of waters washes up

1378. wan to welkin when winds bestir

1379. evil storms, and air grows dusk,

1380. and the heavens weep. Now is help once more

1381. with thee alone! The land thou knowst not,

1382. place of fear, where thou findest out

1383. that sin-flecked being. Seek if thou dare!

1384. I will reward thee, for waging this fight,

1385. with ancient treasure, as erst I did,

1386. with winding gold, if thou winnest back."

XXI

1387. BEOWULF spake, bairn of Ecgtheow:

1388. "Sorrow not, sage! It beseems us better

1389. friends to avenge than **fruitlessly** mourn them.

1390. Each of us all must his end abide

1391. in the ways of the world; so win who may

1392. glory ere death! When his days are told,

1393. that is the warrior's worthiest doom.

1394. Rise, O realm-warder! Ride we anon,

1395. and mark the trail of the mother of Grendel.

1396. No harbor shall hide her—heed my promise!—
1397. enfolding of field or forested mountain
1398. or floor of the flood, let her flee where she will!
1399. But thou this day endure in patience,
1400. as I ween thou wilt, thy woes each one."
1401. Leaped up the graybeard: God he thanked,
1402. mighty Lord, for the man's brave words.
1403. For Hrothgar soon a horse was saddled
1404. wave-maned steed. The sovran wise
1405. stately rode on; his shield-armed men
1406. followed in force. The footprints led
1407. along the woodland, widely seen,
1408. a path o'er the plain, where she passed, and trod
1409. the murky moor; of men-at-arms
1410. she bore the bravest and best one, dead,
1411. him who with Hrothgar the homestead ruled.
1412. On then went the atheling-born
1413. o'er stone-cliffs steep and strait defiles,
1414. narrow passes and unknown ways,
1415. headlands sheer, and the haunts of the Nicors.
1416. Foremost he fared, a few at his side
1417. of the wiser men, the ways to scan,
1418. till he found in a flash the forested hill
1419. hanging over the hoary rock,
1420. a woful wood: the waves below
1421. were dyed in blood. The Danish men
1422. had sorrow of soul, and for Scyldings all,
1423. for many a hero, 'twas hard to bear,
1424. ill for earls, when Aeschere's head
1425. they found by the flood on the foreland there.
1426. Waves were welling, the warriors saw,
1427. hot with blood; but the horn sang oft
1428. battle-song bold. The band sat down,
1429. and watched on the water worm-like things,
1430. sea-dragons strange that sounded the deep,
1431. and nicors that lay on the ledge of the ness—
1432. such as oft essay at hour of morn
1433. on the road-of-sails their ruthless quest,—
1434. and sea-snakes and monsters. These started away,
1435. swollen and savage that song to hear,
1436. that war-horn's blast. The warden of Geats,
1437. with bolt from bow, then balked of life,
1438. of wave-work, one monster, amid its heart
1439. went the keen war-shaft; in water it seemed
1440. less doughty in swimming whom death had seized.

1441. Swift on the billows, with boar-spears well

1442. hooked and barbed, it was hard beset,

1443. done to death and dragged on the headland,

1444. wave-roamer wondrous. Warriors viewed

1445. the grisly guest.

1446. Then girt him Beowulf

1447. in martial mail, nor mourned for his life.

1448. His breastplate broad and bright of hues,

1449. woven by hand, should the waters try;

1450. well could it ward the warrior's body

1451. that battle should break on his breast in vain

1452. nor harm his heart by the hand of a foe.

1453. And the helmet white that his head protected

1454. was destined to dare the deeps of the flood,

1455. through wave-whirl win: 'twas wound with chains,

1456. decked with gold, as in days of yore

1457. the weapon-smith worked it wondrously,

1458. with swine-forms set it, that swords nowise,

1459. **brandished** in battle, could bite that helm.

1460. Nor was that the meanest of mighty helps

1461. which Hrothgar's orator offered at need:

1462. "Hrunting" they named the hilted sword,

1463. of old-time heirlooms easily first;

1464. iron was its edge, all etched with poison,

1465. with battle-blood hardened, nor blenched it at fight

1466. in hero's hand who held it ever,

1467. on paths of peril prepared to go

1468. to folkstead of foes. Not first time this

1469. it was destined to do a daring task.

1470. For he bore not in mind, the bairn of Ecglaf

1471. sturdy and strong, that speech he had made,

1472. drunk with wine, now this weapon he lent

1473. to a stouter swordsman. Himself, though, durst not

1474. under welter of waters wager his life

1475. as loyal liegeman. So lost he his glory,

1476. honor of earls. With the other not so,

1477. who girded him now for the grim encounter.

THINK QUESTIONS

1. Note in chronological order the two acts of revenge that Hrothgar describes in section XX. For each act, explain who killed whom and why they did it, and supply the textual evidence from Hrothgar's speech that confirms the event.

2. Supply three examples of imagery from section XX that support the inference that the region where Grendel and his mother live is a sinister place.

3. Explain what Beowulf is preparing to do at the end of section XXI, and describe what values underlie his decision. Cite textual evidence in your response.

4. Review lines 1387 to 1398. Use context to determine the meaning of the word **avenge.** Explain how context helped you determine the meaning of the word.

5. Use the context clue provided in the passage to guess at the meaning of **ravaged.** Verify your preliminary determination of the meaning by checking in a dictionary. Then write the definition of *ravaged,* identify the part of speech used in the text, and describe the context clue in the text.

CLOSE READ

Reread the lines from the poem *Beowulf*. As you reread, complete the Focus Questions below. Then use your answers and annotations from the questions to help you complete the Writing Prompt.

FOCUS QUESTIONS

1. Describe how the setting affects plot development in the scenes in which Beowulf, Hrothgar, and the search party hunt for the home of Grendel and his mother. Highlight and annotate textual evidence to explain your ideas.

2. How would you describe Beowulf's code of behavior? How does the character of Beowulf affect the plot? Highlight and annotate textual evidence to explain your ideas.

3. Highlight a word that is unfamiliar to you and that is interfering with your comprehension of the text. Then use one or more strategies to determine the meaning of the word. Write a definition of the word, describe how you determined the word's meaning, and explain how knowing the definition helps you better understand the text. Use annotations to write your response to these questions.

4. Find an example of hyperbole associated with Beowulf's sword. Highlight evidence in the text and use annotations to explain how the passages you've chosen propel the plot forward.

5. Recall the unit's Essential Question: Where does history end and legend begin? *Beowulf* features both historical and mythical elements. What inferences can you make about medieval Scandinavia based on the poem? In the poem, where does history end and legend begin? Highlight textual evidence and make annotations to explain your ideas.

WRITING PROMPT

How does a combination of character, plot, and setting in this excerpt from *Beowulf* help you understand the Anglo-Saxon worldview and culture? Use your understanding of story elements to analyze the passage and describe what the literary elements suggest about the underlying beliefs, values, and concerns of the culture *Beowulf* originated from.

GRENDEL

FICTION
John Gardner
1971

INTRODUCTION

Grendel is a modern retelling of *Beowulf* from the monster's point of view. In this excerpt, King Hrothgar has built a giant meadhall (a large building with a single room for feasting and entertainment) and is hosting a celebration. As the outcast Grendel observes the festivities, bemoaning his brutish nature, he notes the irony of the humans' heroic perception of themselves—a perception created through the power of art and imagination, as represented by the character of the Shaper, the poet bard of Hrothgar's court.

"I backed away, crablike, further into darkness..."

FIRST READ

Excerpt from Chapter 4

1   Inspired by winds (or whatever you please), the old man sang of a glorious meadhall whose light would shine to the ends of the ragged world. The thought took seed in Hrothgar's mind. It grew. He called all his people together and told them his daring scheme. He would build a magnificent meadhall high on a hill, with a view of the western sea, a victory-seat near the giants' work, old ruined fortress from the world's first war, to stand forever as a sign of the glory and justice of Hrothgar's Danes. There he would sit and give treasures out, all wealth but the lives of men and the people's land. And so his sons would do after him, and his sons' sons, to the final generation.

2   I listened, huddled in the darkness, tormented, mistrustful. I knew them, had watched them; yet the things he said seemed true. He sent to far kingdoms for woodsmen, carpenters, metalsmiths, goldsmiths—also carters, victualers, clothiers to attend to the workmen—and for weeks their uproar filled the days and nights. I watched from the vines and boulders of the giants' ruin, two miles off. Then word went out to the races of men that Hrothgar's hall was finished. He gave it its name. From neighboring realms and from across the sea came men to the great celebration. The harper sang.

3   I listened, felt myself swept up. I knew very well that all he said was ridiculous, not light for their darkness but flattery, illusion, a **vortex** pulling them from sunlight to heat, a kind of midsummer **burgeoning,** waltz to the sickle. Yet I was swept up. "Ridiculous!" I hissed in the black of the forest. I snatched up a snake from beside my foot and whispered to it, "I knew him when!" But I couldn't bring out a wicked cackle, as I'd meant to do. My heart was light with Hrothgar's goodness, and leaden with grief at my own bloodthirsty ways. I backed away, crablike, further into darkness—like a crab retreating in pain when you strike two stones at the mouth of his underwater den. I backed away till the honeysweet lure of the harp no longer mocked me. Yet even

NOTES

now my mind was tormented by images. Thanes filled the hall and a great silent crowd of them spilled out over the surrounding hill, smiling, peaceable, hearing the harper as if not a man in all that lot had ever twisted a knife in his neighbor's chest.

4 "Well then he's changed them," I said, and stumbled and fell on the root of a tree. "Why not?

5 Why not? the forest whispered back—yet not the forest, something deeper, an impression from another mind, some live thing old and terrible.

6 I listened, tensed.

7 Not a sound.

8 "He reshapes the world," I whispered, **belligerent.** "So his name implies. He stares strange-eyed at the mindless world and turns dry sticks to gold."

9 A little poetic, I would readily admit. His manner of speaking was infecting me, making me **pompous.** "Nevertheless," I whispered crossly—but I couldn't go on, too conscious all at once of my whispering, my eternal posturing, always transforming the world with words—changing nothing. I still had the snake in my fist. I set it down. It fled.

10 "He takes what he finds," I said stubbornly, trying again, "And by changing men's minds he makes the best of it. Why not?" But it sounded **petulant;** and it wasn't true, I knew. He sang for pay, for the praise of women—one in particular—and for the honor of a famous king's hand on his arm. If the ideas of art were beautiful, that was art's fault, not the Shaper's. A blind selector, almost mindless: a bird. Did they murder each other more gently because in the woods sweet songbirds sang?

...

11 Men and women stood talking in the light of the meadhall door and on the narrow streets below; on the lower hillside boys and girls played near the sheep pens, shyly holding hands. A few lay touching each other in the forest eaves. I thought how they'd shriek if I suddenly showed my face, and it made me smile, but I held myself back. They talked nothing, stupidities, their soft voices groping like hands. I felt myself tightening, cross, growing restless for no clear reason, and I made myself move more slowly. Then, circling the clearing, I stepped on something fleshy, and jerked away. It was a man. They'd cut his throat. His clothes had been stolen. I stared up at the hall, baffled, beginning to shake. They went on talking softly, touching hands, their hair full of light. I lifted up the body and slung it across my shoulder.

12   Then the harp began to play. The crowd grew still.

13   The harp sighed, the old man sang, as sweet-voiced as a child.

14   He told how the earth was first built, long ago: said that the greatest gods made the world, every wonder-bright plain and the turning seas, and set out as signs of his victory the sun and moon, great lamps for light to land-dwellers, kingdom torches, and **adorned** the fields with all colors and shapes, made limbs and leaves and gave life to every creature that moves on land.

15   The harp turned solemn. He told of an ancient feud between two brothers which split all the world between darkness and light. And I, Grendel, was the dark side, he said in effect. The terrible race God cursed.

16   I believed him. Such was the power of the Shaper's harp! Stood wriggling my face, letting tears down my nose, grinding my fists into my streaming eyes, even though to do it I had to squeeze with my elbow the corpse of the proof that both of us were cursed, or neither, that the brothers had never lived, nor the god who judged them. "Waaa!" I bawled.

17   Oh what a conversion!

18   I staggered out into the open and up toward the hall with my burden, groaning out, "Mercy! Peace!" The harper broke off, the people screamed. (They have their own versions, but this is the truth.) Drunken men rushed me with battle-axes. I sank to my knees, crying. "Friend! Friend!" They hacked at me, yipping like dogs. I held up the body for protection. Their spears came through it and one of them nicked me, a tiny scratch high on my left breast, but I knew by the sting it had venom on it and I understood, as shocked as I'd been the first time, that they could kill me—eventually would if I gave them a chance. I struck at them, holding the body as a shield, and two fell bleeding from my nails at the first little swipe. The others backed off. I crushed the body in my hug, then hurled it in their faces, turned, and fled. They didn't follow.

Excerpted from *Grendel* by John Gardner, published by Vintage Books.

THINK QUESTIONS

1. Where are the Danes during most of this excerpt? Where is Grendel? What do the two different settings suggest about their different places in society? Cite textual evidence to support your answer.

2. Find two words or phrases in the text that best describe Grendel, and explain why you chose them. Use evidence from the text to support your explanations.

3. How does Grendel react to the harp player? Support your answer using evidence from the text.

4. Identify a context clue in the text that suggests the meaning of the word **vortex** as it is used in *Grendel*. Using that context clue, write your definition of *vortex*.

5. Identify a context clue in the text that suggests the meaning of the word **adorned** as it is used in *Grendel*. Using that context clue, write your definition of *adorned*.

Please note that excerpts and passages in the StudySync® library and this workbook are intended as touchstones to generate interest in an author's work. The excerpts and passages do not substitute for the reading of entire texts, and StudySync® strongly recommends that students seek out and purchase the whole literary or informational work in order to experience it as the author intended. Links to online resellers are available in our digital library. In addition, complete works may be ordered through an authorized reseller by filling out and returning to StudySync® the order form enclosed in this workbook.

Reading & Writing Companion

15

CLOSE READ

Reread the excerpt from *Grendel*. As you reread, complete the Focus Questions below. Then use your answers and annotations from the questions to help you complete the Writing Prompt.

FOCUS QUESTIONS

1. How does the excerpt from *Grendel* introduce the theme of human sinfulness? How does Grendel's discovery of the corpse further develop this theme? Highlight textual evidence, and use annotations to explain how the text you've highlighted helps you answer these questions.

2. Themes of good versus evil and the power of song are introduced in the excerpt from *Grendel*. How do these two themes interact and build on one another to produce a complex account? Highlight textual evidence, and use annotations to explain how the text you've highlighted helps you answer this question.

3. How is Hrothgar described in the excerpts from *Beowulf* and *Grendel?* How is the relationship between Hrothgar and Grendel different in the two works? What is the connection between the relationship depicted in each work and the theme of good versus evil? Highlight textual evidence in both selections, and use annotations to explain how the text you've highlighted helps you answer these questions.

4. Highlight a word in *Grendel* whose precise meaning you do not know. Then use one or more strategies to determine the word's meaning. Write a definition of the word, describe how you determined the word's meaning, and explain how knowing the definition helps you better understand the text. Use annotations to write your response to these questions.

5. Recall that **hyperbole** is a figure of speech that uses exaggeration to express a strong emotion, make a point, or evoke humor. Identify and highlight an example of hyperbole in the first paragraph from *Grendel*. Make annotations to explain the figure of speech and how it develops theme.

6. The Essential Question of this unit asks, "Where does history end and legend begin?" Written in 1971, *Grendel* depicts a creature that is both similar to and different from the monster of the same name in the early medieval text *Beowulf*. Where does the historical conception of Grendel end and a new legend begin in the updated version of the story? Highlight textual evidence in both selections, and make annotations to support your response.

WRITING PROMPT

Many works of literature explore the position of "outsiders" in society, and the character Grendel is one of the most well-known literary outsiders. What comment does the novel *Grendel* make about being an outsider? How does Grendel's outsider status relate to the themes of the pain of isolation, good versus evil, and the power of art to misrepresent reality? Refer to textual evidence from both the novel and the poem to analyze what Gardner expresses about outsiders through his portrayal of the monster Grendel.

Copyright © BookheadEd Learning, LLC

THE ECCLESIASTICAL HISTORY OF THE ENGLISH PEOPLE

NON-FICTION
Venerable Bede
731

INTRODUCTION

The Venerable Bede was a monk who lived in England during the Anglo-Saxon period. He was a skilled linguist whose translation of the Greek and Latin works of early Church fathers helped pave the way for Christianity in England. He was also a prolific author and earned the title "The Father of English History" with his masterpiece, *The Ecclesiastical History of the English People*, which documents the influence of the church on the development of English civilization. In this excerpt, King Edwin converts to Christianity after being encouraged by the religious counselor Paulinus and conferring with his trusted chiefs.

"...receive the faith and keep the commandments of Him who rescued you from your earthly foes..."

FIRST READ

The Anglo-Saxons Embrace Christianity

1   King Edwin hesitated to accept the word of God which Paulinus preached but, as we have said, used to sit alone for hours at a time, earnestly debating within himself what he ought to do and what religion he should follow. One day Paulinus came to him and, placing his right hand on the king's head, asked him if he recognized this sign.

2   The king began to tremble and would have thrown himself at the bishop's feet but Paulinus raised him up and said in a voice that seemed familiar, "First you have escaped with God's help from the hands of the foes you feared; secondly you have acquired by His gift the kingdom you desired; do not delay in fulfilling it but receive the faith and keep the commandments of Him who rescued you from your earthly foes and raised you to the honor of an earthly kingdom. If from henceforth you are willing to follow His will which is made known to you through me, He will also rescue you from the everlasting torments of the wicked and make you a partaker with Him of His eternal kingdom of heaven."

3   When the king had heard his words, he answered that he was both willing and bound to accept the faith which Paulinus taught. He said, however, that he would confer about this with his loyal chief men and his counsellors so that, if they agreed with him, they might all be **consecrated** together in the waters of life. Paulinus agreed, and the king did as he had said. A meeting of his council was held, and each one was asked in turn what he thought of this **doctrine** hitherto unknown to them and this new worship of God which was being proclaimed.

4   Coifi, the chief of the priests, answered at once, "Notice carefully, King, this doctrine which is now being **expounded** to us. I frankly admit that, for my part, I have found that the religion which we have hitherto held has no virtue nor

profit in it. None of your followers has devoted himself more earnestly than I have to the worship of our gods, but nevertheless there are many who receive greater benefits and greater honor from you than I do and are more successful in all their undertakings. If the gods had any power, they would have helped me more readily, seeing that I have always served them with greater zeal. So it follows that if, on examination, these new doctrines which have now been explained to us are found to be better and more effectual, let us accept them at once without any delay."

5   Another of the king's chief men agreed with this advice and with these wise words and then added, "This is how the present life of man on earth, King, appears to me in comparison with that time which is unknown to us. You are sitting feasting with your eldermen and thanes in winter time; the fire is burning on the hearth in the middle of the hall and all inside is warm, while outside the wintry storms of rain and snow are raging; and a sparrow flies swiftly through the hall. It enters in at one door and quickly flies out through the other. For the few moments it is inside, the storm and wintry tempest cannot touch it, but after the briefest moment of calm, it flits from your sight, out of the wintry storm and into it again. So this life of man appears but for a moment; what follows or indeed what went before, we know not at all. If this new doctrine brings us more certain information, it seems right that we should accept it." Other elders and counsellors of the king continued in the same manner, being divinely prompted to do so.

6   Coifi added that he would like to listen still more carefully to what Paulinus himself had to say about God. The king ordered Paulinus to speak, and when he had said his say, Coifi exclaimed, "For a long time now I have realized that our religion is worthless; for the more diligently I sought the truth in our cult, the less I found it. Now I confess openly that the truth shines out clearly in this teaching which can bestow on us the gift of life, salvation, and eternal happiness. Therefore, I advise your Majesty that we should promptly abandon and commit to the flames the temples and the altars which we have held sacred without reaping any benefit." Why need I say more? The king publicly accepted the gospel which Paulinus preached, renounced idolatry, and confessed his faith in Christ. When he asked the high priest of their religion which of them should be the first to **profane** the altars and the shrines of the idols, together with their precincts, Coifi answered, "I will; for through the wisdom the true God has given me no one can more suitably destroy those things which I once foolishly worshipped, and so set an example to all." And at once, casting aside his vain superstitions, he asked the king to provide him with arms and a stallion; and mounting it, he set out to destroy the idols. Now a high priest of their religion was not allowed to carry arms or to ride except on a mare. So, girded with a sword, he took a spear in his hand, and mounting the king's stallion, he set off to where the idols were. The common people who saw him thought he was mad. But as soon as he approached the shrine,

NOTES

without any hesitation he profaned it by casting the spear which he held into it; and greatly rejoicing in the knowledge of the worship of the true God, he ordered his companions to destroy and set fire to the shrine and all the enclosures. The place where the idols once stood is still shown, not far from York, to the east, over the river Derwent. Today it is called Goodmanham, the place where the high priest, through the inspiration of the true God, profaned and destroyed the altars which he himself had consecrated.

THINK QUESTIONS

1. Describe the order of events in the selection. What does King Edwin decide to do, and why does he call his council? What is the result of these events? Support your answer with evidence from the text.

2. Who is Coifi? What reasons does he give for converting to Christianity? Why is his support of the King's conversion especially important? Cite textual evidence to support your responses.

3. What is the author's point of view on the conversion of King Edwin and his council? What words and phrases does he use that provide clues to his point of view? What does the author's point of view reveal about the role of religion in Anglo-Saxon England? Cite specific examples in your answer.

4. Use context to determine the meaning of the word **profane** as it is used in *The Ecclesiastical History of the English People*. Note the term is used more than once. Write your definition of profane and explain how context helped you determine the definition.

5. Use context to determine the meaning of the word **doctrine** as it is used in *The Ecclesiastical History of the English People*. Note the term is used more than once. Write your definition of doctrine and explain how context helped you determine the definition.

CLOSE READ

Reread the excerpt from *The Ecclesiastical History of the English People*. As you reread, complete the Focus Questions below. Then use your answers and annotations from the questions to help you complete the Writing Prompt.

FOCUS QUESTIONS

1. In paragraph 1, what conflict is Edwin facing? How do you know that he is struggling internally with this conflict? Highlight evidence in the text and make annotations to explain how the passages you've chosen help you respond to the questions.

2. In paragraph 3, how does Edwin respond when Paulinus tries to convince him to convert to Christianity? What does this reaction reveal about him as a ruler? Highlight evidence in the text and make annotations to explain how the passages you've chosen help you respond to the questions.

3. In paragraph 5, one of King Edwin's councilmen uses an analogy. What two things are being compared? What is the purpose of this analogy? Highlight evidence in the text and make annotations to explain how the passages you've chosen help you respond to the questions.

4. In the last paragraph, how and why does Coifi's role change? Highlight evidence in the text and make annotations to explain how the passages you've chosen help you respond to the question.

5. Find and highlight the word *idol* in the text. Then find and highlight the other form of *idol* used in the text. What is the part of speech and meaning of *idol?* How does the suffix added to the second form affect the part of speech and meaning? Make annotations to respond to these questions.

6. Recall the Essential Question for this unit: Where does history end and legend begin? *The Ecclesiastical History of the English People* is a non-fiction text, but the line between historical fact and legend was not as important when Bede was writing as it is today. In what ways does Bede's account seem more legendary than fact based? Consider the details Bede includes and what you know about how political and religious conflicts were solved during the time period. Highlight evidence in the text to support your response.

WRITING PROMPT

How do individuals, events, and ideas interact and develop over the course of the excerpt from *The Ecclesiastical History of the English People?* What do these interactions and developments reveal about the Anglo-Saxons and the history of Christianity? Use your understanding of informational text elements to support your response. Cite textual evidence to support your analysis.

THE CANTERBURY TALES

POETRY
Geoffrey Chaucer
1470

INTRODUCTION

In Geoffrey Chaucer's 14th Century poem, the narrator joins 29 travelers on a pilgrimage from London to Canterbury Cathedral to pay homage to St. Thomas Becket. Telling stories along their journey, with the best tale winning a prize of a free dinner, the pilgrims compete with colorful characters and magical plots. The Wife of Bath, a prosperous widow married five times, tells the tale of a young knight who commits a heinous crime and is sentenced to death. If, by the end of a year and a day, the knight can name the one thing that women truly want, the queen will commute his sentence. On his quest, the knight meets an old woman who holds the answer to the riddle. Accepting her conditions to ensure his

"I'll grant you life if you can tell to me What thing it is that women most desire."

 FIRST READ

NOTES

FROM THE PROLOGUE

1   Here begins the Book of the Tales of Canterbury

2   When April with his showers sweet with fruit
3   The drought of March has pierced unto the root
4   And bathed each vein with liquor that has power
5   To generate therein and sire the flower;
6   When Zephyr also has, with his sweet breath,
7   Quickened again, in every holt and heath,
8   The tender shoots and buds, and the young sun
9   Into the Ram one half his course has run,
10   And many little birds make melody
11   That sleep through all the night with open eye
12   (So Nature pricks them on to ramp and rage)—
13   Then do folk long to go on pilgrimage,
14   And palmers to go seeking out strange strands,
15   To distant shrines well known in sundry lands.
16   And specially from every shire's end
17   Of England they to Canterbury wend,
18   The holy blessed martyr there to seek
19   Who help ed them when they lay so ill and weak
20   Befell that, in that season, on a day
21   In Southwark, at the Tabard, as I lay
22   Ready to start upon my pilgrimage
23   To Canterbury, full of devout **homage,**
24   There came at nightfall to that hostelry
25   Some nine and twenty in a company
26   Of **sundry** persons who had chanced to fall
27   In fellowship, and pilgrims were they all
28   That toward Canterbury town would ride.

NOTES

29 The rooms and stables spacious were and wide,
30 And well we there were eased, and of the best.
31 And briefly, when the sun had gone to rest,
32 So had I spoken with them, every one,
33 That I was of their fellowship anon,
34 And made agreement that we'd early rise
35 To take the road, as you I will **apprise.**
36 But none the less, whilst I have time and space,
37 Before yet farther in this tale I pace,
38 It seems to me accordant with reason
39 To inform you of the state of every one
40 Of all of these, as it appeared to me,
41 And who they were, and what was their degree,
42 And even how arrayed there at the inn;
43 And with a knight thus will I first begin.

FROM THE WIFE OF BATH'S TALE

44 And so befell it that this King Arthur
45 Had at his court a lusty bachelor
46 Who, on a day, came riding from river;
47 And happened that, alone as she was born,
48 He saw a maiden walking through the corn,
49 From whom, in spite of all she did and said,
50 Straightway by force he took her maidenhead;
51 For which violation was there such clamour,
52 And such appealing unto King Arthur,
53 That soon condemned was this knight to be dead
54 By course of law, and should have lost his head,
55 Peradventure, such being the statute then;
56 But that the other ladies and the queen
57 So long prayed of the king to show him grace,
58 He granted life, at last, in the law's place,
59 And gave him to the queen, as she should will,
60 Whether she'd save him, or his blood should spill.
61 The queen she thanked the king with all her might,
62 And after this, thus spoke she to the knight,
63 When she'd an opportunity, one day:
64 "You stand yet," said she, "in such poor a way
65 That for your life you've no security.
66 I'll grant you life if you can tell to me
67 What thing it is that women most desire.
68 Be wise, and keep your neck from iron dire!
69 And if you cannot tell it me anon,
70 Then will I give you license to be gone

NOTES

71 A twelvemonth and a day, to search and learn

72 Sufficient answer in this grave concern.

73 And your knight's word I'll have, ere forth you pace,

74 To yield your body to me in this place."

...

75 This knight my tale is chiefly told about

76 When what he went for he could not find out,

77 That is, the thing that women love the best,

78 Most saddened was the spirit in his breast;

79 But home he goes, he could no more delay.

80 The day was come when home he turned his way;

81 And on his way it chanced that he should ride

82 In all his care, beneath a forest's side,

83 And there he saw, a-dancing him before,

84 Full four and twenty ladies, maybe more;

85 Toward which dance eagerly did he turn

86 In hope that there some wisdom he should learn.

87 But truly, ere he came upon them there,

88 The dancers vanished all, he knew not where.

89 No creature saw he that gave sign of life,

90 Save, on the greensward sitting, an old wife;

91 A fouler person could no man devise.

92 Before the knight this old wife did arise,

93 And said: "Sir knight, hence lies no travelled way.

94 Tell me what thing you seek, and by your fay.

95 Perchance you'll find it may the better be;

96 These ancient folk know many things," said she.

97 "Dear mother," said this knight assuredly,

98 "I am but dead, save I can tell, truly,

99 What thing it is that women most desire;

100 Could you inform me, I'd pay well your hire."

101 "Plight me your troth here, hand in hand," said she,

102 "That you will do, whatever it may be,

103 The thing I ask if it lie in your might;

104 And I'll give you your answer ere the night."

105 "Have here my word," said he. "That thing I grant."

106 "Then," said the crone, "of this I make my vaunt,

107 Your life is safe; and I will stand thereby,

108 Upon my life, the queen will say as I.

109 Let's see which is the proudest of them all

110 That wears upon her hair kerchief or caul,

111 Shall dare say no to that which I shall teach;

112 Let us go now and without longer speech."

NOTES

113 Then whispered she a sentence in his ear,
114 And bade him to be glad and have no fear.

115 When they were come unto the court, this knight
116 Said he had kept his promise as was right,
117 And ready was his answer, as he said.
118 Full many a noble wife, and many a maid,
119 And many a widow, since they are so wise,
120 The queen herself sitting as high justice,
121 Assembled were, his answer there to hear;
122 And then the knight was bidden to appear.

123 Command was given for silence in the hall,
124 And that the knight should tell before them all
125 What thing all worldly women love the best.
126 This knight did not stand dumb, as does a beast,
127 But to this question promptly answered
128 With manly voice, so that the whole court heard

129 "My liege lady, generally," said he,
130 "Women desire to have the sovereignty
131 As well upon their husband as their love,
132 And to have mastery their man above;
133 This thing you most desire, though me you kill
134 Do as you please, I am here at your will."
135 In all the court there was no wife or maid
136 Or widow that denied the thing he said,
137 But all held, he was worthy to have life.
138 And with that word up started the old wife
139 Whom he had seen a-sitting on the green.
140 "Mercy," cried she, "my sovereign lady queen!
141 Before the court's dismissed, give me my right.
142 'Twas I who taught the answer to this knight;
143 For which he did gave his word to me, out there,
144 That the first thing I should of him require
145 He would do that, if it lay in his might.
146 Before the court, now, pray I you, sir knight,"
147 Said she, "that you will take me for your wife;
148 For well you know that I have saved your life.
149 If this be false, say nay, upon your fay!"
150 This knight replied: "Alas and welaway!
151 That I so promised I will not protest.
152 But for God's love pray make a new request.
153 Take all my wealth and let my body go."

154 "Nay then," said she, "beshrew us if I do!
155 For though I may be foul and old and poor,
156 I will not, for all metal and all ore
157 That from the earth is dug or lies above,
158 Be aught except your wife and your true love."

159 "My love?" cried he, "nay, rather my damnation!
160 Alas! that any of my race and station
161 Should ever so dishonoured foully be!"
162 But all for naught; the end was this, that he
163 Was so **constrained** he needs must go and wed,
164 And take his ancient wife and go to bed.

165 Now, peradventure, would some men say here,
166 That, of my negligence, I take no care
167 To tell you of the joy and all the array
168 That at the wedding feast were seen that day.
169 Make a brief answer to this thing I shall;
170 I say, there was no joy or feast at all;
171 There was but heaviness and grievous sorrow;
172 For privately he wedded on the morrow,
173 And all day, then, he hid him like an owl;
174 So sad he was, his old wife looked so foul.

175 Great was the woe the knight had in his thought
176 When he, with her, to marriage bed was brought;
177 He rolled about and turned him to and fro.
178 His old wife lay there, always smiling so,
179 And said: "O my dear husband, ben'cite!
180 Fares every knight with wife as you with me?
181 Is this the custom in King Arthur's house?
182 Are knights of his all so fastidious?
183 I am your own true love and, more, your wife;
184 And I am she who saved your very life;
185 And truly, since I've never done you wrong,
186 Why do you treat me so, this first night long?
187 You act as does a man who's lost his wit;
188 What is my fault? For God's love tell me it,
189 And it shall be amended, if I may."

190 "Amended!" cried this knight, "Alas, nay, nay!
191 It will not be amended ever, no!
192 You are so loathsome, and so old also,
193 And therewith of so low a race were born,
194 It's little wonder that I toss and turn.
195 Would God my heart would break within my breast!"

196 "Is this," asked she, "the cause of your unrest?"

197 "Yes, truly," said he, "and no wonder 'tis."

...

198 "Now, sir, with age you have **upbraided** me;

199 And truly, sir, though no authority

200 Were in a book, you gentles of honour

201 Say that men should the aged show favour,

202 And call him father, of your gentleness;

203 And authors could I find for this, I guess.

204 Now since you say that I am foul and old,

205 Then fear you not to be made a cuckold;

206 For dirt and age, as prosperous I may be,

207 Are mighty wardens over chastity.

208 Nevertheless, since I know your delight,

209 I'll satisfy your worldly appetite.

210 "Two choices," said she, "which one will you try,

211 To have me foul and old until I die,

212 And be to you a true and humble wife,

213 And never anger you in all my life;

214 Or else to have me young and very fair

215 And take your chance with those who will repair

216 Unto your house, and all because of me,

217 Or in some other place, as well may be.

218 Now choose which you like better and reply."

219 This knight considered, and did sorely sigh,

220 But at the last replied as you shall hear:

221 "My lady and my love, and wife so dear,

222 I put myself in your wise governing;

223 Do you choose which may be the more pleasing,

224 And bring most honour to you, and me also.

225 I care not which it be of these things two;

226 For if you like it, that suffices me."

227 "Then have I got of you the mastery,

228 Since I may choose and govern, in earnest?"

229 "Yes, truly, wife," said he, "I hold that best."

230 "Kiss me," said she, "we'll be no longer wroth,

231 For by my truth, to you I will be both;

232 That is to say, I'll be both good and fair.

233 I pray God I go mad, and so declare,

234 If I be not to you as good and true
235 As ever wife was since the world was new.
236 And, save I be, at dawn, as fairly seen
237 As any lady, empress, or great queen
238 That is between the east and the far west,
239 Do with my life and death as you like best.
240 Throw back the curtain and see how it is."

241 And when the knight saw verily all this,
242 That she so very fair was, and young too,
243 For joy he clasped her in his strong arms two,
244 His heart bathed in a bath of utter bliss;
245 A thousand times, all in a row, he'd kiss.
246 And she obeyed his wish in everything
247 That might give pleasure to his love-liking.

248 And thus they lived unto their lives' fair end,
249 In perfect joy; and Jesus to us send
250 Meek husbands, and young ones, and fresh in bed,
251 And good luck to outlive them that we wed.
252 And I pray Jesus to cut short the lives
253 Of those who'll not be governed by their wives;
254 And old and **querulous** niggards with their pence,
255 And send them soon a mortal pestilence!

THINK QUESTIONS

1. Why might the time of year that the pilgrims are traveling, as identified in the Prologue, be meaningful? Use textual evidence to support your answer.

2. An antihero is a main character who lacks traditional heroic qualities such as being noble and courageous. In what way is the knight in the Wife of Bath's tale an antihero? Refer to one or more details from the text to support your answer.

3. In what way does the last part of the Wife of Bath's tale deal with the concept of beauty? Use textual evidence to support your answer.

4. Use context to determine the meaning of the word **apprise** as it is used in *The Canterbury Tales*. Explain how context helps you determine the word's meaning. Write your definition of *apprise*.

5. Use context to determine the meaning of the word **upbraided** as it is used in *The Canterbury Tales*. Explain how context helps you determine the word's meaning. Write your definition of *upbraid*.

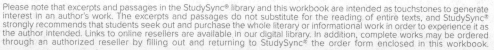
Please note that excerpts and passages in the StudySync® library and this workbook are intended as touchstones to generate interest in an author's work. The excerpts and passages do not substitute for the reading of entire texts, and StudySync® strongly recommends that students seek out and purchase the whole literary or informational work in order to experience it as the author intended. Links to online resellers are available in our digital library. In addition, complete works may be ordered through an authorized reseller by filling out and returning to StudySync® the order form enclosed in this workbook.

Reading & Writing Companion   29

CLOSE READ

Reread the excerpt from the poem *The Canterbury Tales*. As you reread, complete the Focus Questions below. Then use your answers and annotations from the questions to help you complete the Writing Prompt.

FOCUS QUESTIONS

1. Highlight a word in the Prologue to *The Canterbury Tales* that you did not know before reading the text. Then use one or more strategies to determine the word's meaning. Write the definitions of the word, describe the steps you took to learn the word's meaning, and explain how knowing the word's meaning helps you better understand the text. Use annotations to write your response to these questions.

2. Chaucer uses strong modifiers to show the anger and frustration the knight feels when he must marry the old woman. What motivates these emotions? Highlight some of these adjectives and adverbs in the seventh and eighth stanzas and write annotations to explain how they reflect the knight's unhappiness. Study context to gain a greater understanding of the words you choose.

3. One theme of the Wife of Bath's tale involves true love. What can you infer about her attitude toward true love? Highlight evidence from the text that will help support your ideas. Choose one piece of evidence from the middle of the excerpt and one from near the end.

4. Another theme of the Wife of Bath's tale involves the role of a woman's physical beauty in male-female relationships. Use textual evidence to infer what the knight's attitude is toward beauty, or the lack thereof. Highlight in the eighth and tenth stanzas and make annotations to explain your choices.

5. In the Wife of Bath's tale, what can you infer about the Wife's attitude toward the connection between people's social rank and how well they behave and how wise they are? Highlight evidence from different parts of the excerpt and make annotations to explain your choices.

6. As you reread the excerpt from the Prologue of *The Canterbury Tales,* think about how such pilgrimages to Canterbury might have contributed to national unity in medieval England. Keep in mind that, at the time, St. Thomas Becket was considered a national hero. Then apply the unit's Essential Question to the text. In *The Canterbury Tales,* where does history end and legend begin? Highlight evidence from the excerpt and make annotations to explain your response.

WRITING PROMPT

Chaucer's tales include many examples of magic and witchcraft. Think about some of the traditional qualities associated with witches in legends. How is magic used to bring about justice and redemption? Write a response in which you compare and contrast the descriptions and actions of the old woman in the Wife of Bath's tale with those of a witch. How does her "magic" redeem the knight's behavior? Use textual evidence to support your position, including inferences.

THE ONCE AND FUTURE KING

FICTION
T.H. White
1958

INTRODUCTION

T.H. White's Arthurian novel *The Once and Future King* is considered a masterpiece of modern fantasy literature. In writing the novel, White altered the source material about King Arthur to reflect on power and justice from a decidedly modern perspective. In White's version, Merlyn is an anachronistic character who has existed for centuries, living backwards in time. Merlyn uses his knowledge of future history to help shape King Arthur's ideas about "might

"...now he was to see for certain whether he had lived in vain."

FIRST READ

Excerpt from Book II Chapter VI

1   The King of England painfully climbed the two hundred and eight steps which led to Merlyn's tower room, and knocked on the door. The magician was inside, with Archimedes sitting on the back of his chair, busily trying to find the square root of minus one. He had forgotten how to do it.

2   "Merlyn," said the King, panting, "I want to talk to you."

3   He closed his book with a bang, leaped to his feet, seized his wand of lignum vitae, and rushed at Arthur as if he were trying to shoo away a stray chicken.

4   "Go away!" he shouted. "What are you doing here? What do you mean by it? Aren't you the King of England? Go away and send for me! Get out of my room! I never heard of such a thing! Go away at once and send for me!"

5   "But I am here."

6   "No, you're not," retorted the old man resourcefully. And he pushed the King out of the door, slamming it in his face.

7   "Well!" said Arthur, and he went off sadly down the two hundred and eight stairs.

8   An hour later, Merlyn presented himself in the Royal Chamber, in answer to a summons which had been delivered by a page.

9   "That's better," he said, and sat down comfortably on a carpet chest.

10   "Stand up," said Arthur, and he clapped his hands for a page to take away the seat.

11   Merlyn stood up, boiling with **indignation.** The whites of his knuckles **blanched** as he clenched them.

12 "About our conversation on the subject of **chivalry,**" began the King in an airy tone.

....

13 Merlyn was immediately watching him with a sharp eye. His knobbed fingers fluttered among the stars and secret signs of his gown, but he would not help the speaker. You might say that this moment was the critical one in his career—the moment towards which he had been living backward for heaven knows how many centuries, and now he was to see for certain whether he had lived in vain.

14 "I have been thinking," said Arthur, "about Might and Right. I don't think things ought to be done because you are able to do them. I think they should be done because you ought to do them. After all, a penny is a penny in any case, however much Might is exerted on either side, to prove that it is or not. Is that plain?"

15 Nobody answered.

16 "Well, I was talking to Merlyn on the battlements one day, and he mentioned that the last battle we had—in which seven hundred kerns were killed—was not so much fun as I had thought it was. Of course, battles are not fun when you come to think about them. I mean, people ought not to be killed, ought they? It is better to be alive."

17 "Very well. But the funny thing is that Merlyn was helping me to win battles. He is still helping me, for that matter, and we hope to win the battle of Bedegraine together, when it comes off."

18 "We will," said Sir Ector, who was in the secret.

19 "That seems to me to be inconsistent. Why does he help me to fight wars, if they are bad things?"

20 There was no answer from anybody, and the King began to speak with agitation.

21 "I could only think," said he, beginning to blush, "I could only think that I—that we—that he—that he wanted me to win them for a reason."

22 He paused and looked at Merlyn, who turned his head away.

23 "The reason was—was it?—the reason was that if I could be the master of my kingdom by winning these two battles, I could stop them afterwards and then do something about the business of Might. Have I guessed? Was I right?"

24 The magician did not turn his head, and his hands lay still in his lap.

25 "I was!" exclaimed Arthur.

26 And he began talking so quickly that he could hardly keep up with himself. "You see," he said, "Might is not Right. But there is a lot of Might knocking about in this world, and something has to be done about it. It is as if people were half horrible and half nice. Perhaps they are even more than half horrible, and when they are left to themselves they run wild. You get the average baron that we see nowadays, people like Sir Bruce Sans Pitié, who simply go clod-hopping round the country dressed in steel, and doing exactly what they please, for sport. It is our Norman idea about the upper classes having a **monopoly** of power, without reference to justice. Then the horrible side gets uppermost, and there is thieving and rape and plunder and torture. The people become beasts.

27 "But, you see, Merlyn is helping me to win my two battles so that I can stop this. He wants me to put things right.

28 "Lot and Uriens and Anguish and those—they are the old world, the old-fashioned order who want to have their private will. I have got to vanquish them with their own weapons—they force it upon me, because they live by force—and then the real work will begin. This battle at Bedegraine is the preliminary, you see. It is after the battle that Merlyn is wanting me to think about."

29 Arthur paused again for comment or encouragement, but the magician's face was turned away. It was only Sir Ector, sitting next to him, who could see his eyes.

30 "Now what have I thought," said Arthur, "is this. Why can't you harness Might so that it works for Right? I know it sounds nonsense, but, I mean, you can't just say there is no such thing. The Might is there, in the bad half of people, and you can't neglect it. You can't cut it out, but you might be able to direct it, if you see what I mean, so that it was useful instead of bad."

Excerpt from Book II Chapter VIII

31 Kay looked up, with his tongue between his teeth, and remarked:

32 "By the way. You remember that argument we were having about aggression? Well, I have thought of a good reason for starting a war."

33 Merlyn froze.

34 "I would like to hear it."

35 "A good reason for starting a war is simply to have a good reason! For instance, there might be a king who had discovered a new way of life for human beings—you know, something which would be good for them. It might even be the only way of saving them from destruction. Well, if the human beings were too wicked or too stupid to accept his way, he might have to force it on them, in their own interests, by the sword."

36   The magician clenched his fists, twisted his gown into screws, and began to shake all over.

37   "Very interesting," he said in a trembling voice. "Very interesting. There was just such a man when I was young—an Austrian who invented a new way of life and convinced himself that he was the chap to make it work. He tried to **impose** his reformation by the sword, and plunged the civilized world into misery and chaos. But the thing which this fellow had overlooked, my friend, was that he had had a predecessor in the reformation business, called Jesus Christ. Perhaps we may assume that Jesus knew as much as the Austrian did about saving people. But the odd thing is that Jesus did not turn the disciples into storm troopers, burn down the Temple at Jerusalem, and fix the blame on Pontius Pilate. On the contrary, he made it clear that the business of the philosopher was to make ideas *available,* and not to impose them on people."

38   Kay looked pale but obstinate.

39   "Arthur is fighting the present war," he said, "to impose his ideas on King Lot."

Excerpted from The Once and Future King *by T.H. White, published by the Penguin Group.*

 THINK QUESTIONS

1.   What is the central conflict of the excerpt? Is it resolved over the course of the passage? If so, how? Use evidence from the text to support your interpretation.

2.   From the evidence presented in the text, how might you characterize the relationship between Merlyn and Arthur?

3.   What inference can you make about the following exchange between Arthur and Merlyn?

   "That's better," he said, and sat down comfortably on a carpet chest. "Stand up," said Arthur, and he clapped his hands for a page to take away the seat. Merlyn stood up, boiling with indignation. The whites of his knuckles blanched as he clenched them. "About our conversation on the subject of chivalry," began the King in an airy voice.

4.   Use context to determine the meaning of the word **indignation** as it is used in *The Once and Future King*. Write your definition of *indignation*.

5.   The Latin root of the word **impose** means "to put upon." Write definitions for the following related words: *impose* (verb), *imposition* (noun), *imposing* (adjective), and *impostor* (noun). Identify how the meaning of the root shifts across each word. Use a dictionary for help, if needed.

CLOSE READ

Reread the excerpt from *The Once and Future King*. As you reread, complete the Focus Questions below. Then use your answers and annotations from the questions to help you complete the Writing Prompt.

FOCUS QUESTIONS

1. As you reread the text of *The Once and Future King*, remember that rhetoric refers to the use of language in a text. A study of the rhetoric used in this excerpt involves understanding the characters' points of view and the language used to describe the characters' behavior. In the first section of the excerpt from Chapter VI, what can you infer about the characters' behavior and personalities? Highlight evidence in the text and make annotations to explain how the language used in the passages you've chosen reveals this information about the characters.

2. The second part of the excerpt from Chapter VI begins with "the moment towards which [Merlyn] had been living backward for heaven knows how many centuries, and now he was to see for certain whether he had lived in vain" (paragraph 13). What happens during the rest of this Chapter VI excerpt? What does Merlyn do? How does his behavior compare or contrast with this strong statement about the importance of this event? Highlight sections and language from the text to support your ideas.

3. How do the exchanges between Arthur and Merlyn and between Merlyn and Kay interact to create a complex story? What evidence from the text supports your ideas? How does the author use language to distinguish the characters' points of view?

4. Use your understanding of theme, tone, connotation, biased language, point of view, and explicit versus implicit meaning to give an overview of the rhetoric used in the excerpt. Highlight evidence from the text to support your analysis.

5. The Essential Question for this unit asks, "Where does history end and legend begin?" Consider *The Once and Future King* not only as a work of historical fiction but also as an allegory for World War II. An allegory is a story in which the characters and events are symbols for ideas or events outside the text. Which characters, details, and events from the excerpt might allude to historical events instead of Arthurian legend? Why might the author have chosen to comment on the events of World War II in this way? Highlight textual evidence to support your response.

WRITING PROMPT

In *The Once and Future King,* the narrator indicates that Arthur's speech about might and right was the "critical one of his career." Why is this event so important? Does this excerpt make clear whether Merlyn's goals are achieved? Why or why not? State your claim and use your understanding of point of view, tone, connotation, biased language, and rhetoric to support your analysis. Use evidence from the text as you support your claim.

LE MORTE D'ARTHUR

FICTION
Sir Thomas Malory
1485

INTRODUCTION

In the 15th century, Sir Thomas Malory translated and organized the diverse body of existing Arthurian romance tales that had developed in England and France since Anglo-Saxon times. Malory's retelling of the heroic adventures of King Arthur and the knights of the Round Table, *Le Morte d'Arthur*, became the first prose masterpiece of the English language. In this excerpt, King Arthur engages in his final battle, waged against an army commanded by his illegitimate son, Mordred.

"The king cried out as he lay in his bed and slept, 'Help, help!'"

FIRST READ

Part Eight: The Death of Arthur
IV: The Day of Destiny

From 3

1   Upon Trinity Sunday at night King Arthur dreamed a wonderful dream, and that was this: it seemed that he saw upon a platform a chair and the chair was fastened to a wheel; thereupon King Arthur sat in the richest cloth of gold that might be made. And the king thought that under him, far from him, was hideous deep black water; therein were all manner of serpents and worms and wild beasts, foul and horrible. Suddenly the king thought that the wheel turned upside-down and he fell among the serpents, and every beast caught him by a limb. The king cried out as he lay in his bed and slept, "Help, help!"

2   Then knights, squires, and yeomen awakened the king, and he was so dazed that he knew not where he was. He stayed awake until it was nigh day and then he fell to slumbering again, not sleeping but not thoroughly awake. Then it seemed to the king that Sir Gawain actually came unto him with a number of fair ladies.

3   When King Arthur saw him he cried, "Welcome, my sister's son; I thought that ye were dead. And now that I see thee alive, much am I beholden unto almighty Jesus. Ah, fair nephew, what are these ladies that have come hither with you?"

4   "Sir," said Sir Gawain, "all those are ladies for whom I have fought when I was a living man. And all these are those whom I did battle for in righteous quarrels; at their devout prayer, because I did battle for them righteously, God hath given them the grace to bring me hither unto you. Thus God hath given me leave to warn you away from your death: for if ye fight to-morn with Sir Mordred, as ye have both agreed, doubt ye not that ye shall be slain, and the most part of your people on both sides. Through the great grace and

NOTES

goodness that almighty Jesus hath unto you, and through pity for you and many other good men who would be slain there, God in His special grace hath sent me to you to give you warning that in no wise should ye do battle to-morn; but ye should make a treaty for a month. And make this offer generously to-morn so as to assure the delay, for within a month Sir Lancelot shall come with all his noble knights and rescue you worshipfully and slay Sir Mordred and all who ever will hold with him."

5   Then Sir Gawain and all the ladies vanished; at once the king called upon his knights, squires, and yeomen and charged them quickly to fetch his noble lords and wise bishops unto him. When they had come the king told them of his vision and what Sir Gawain had said to him: that if he fought on the morn, he would be slain. Then the king commanded and charged Sir Lucan le Butler, his brother Sir Bedivere, and two bishops to make a treaty in any way for a month with Sir Mordred: "And spare not; offer him lands and goods, as much as ye think best."

6   They departed and came to Sir Mordred, where he had a grim host of a hundred thousand men. There they entreated Sir Mordred a long time, and at last it was agreed for Sir Mordred to have Cornwall and Kent during King Arthur's days and all England after the king's days.

4

7   Then they agreed that King Arthur and Sir Mordred should meet between their two hosts, and that each of them should bring fourteen persons with him. They came back with this word to King Arthur.

8   Then he said, "I am glad that this is done." So he went into the field.

9   When King Arthur prepared to depart for the meeting in the field he warned all his host that if they should see any sword drawn, "see that ye come on fiercely and slay that traitor Sir Mordred, for I in no wise trust him."

10   In like wise Sir Mordred warned his host: "If ye see any sword drawn, see that ye come on fiercely and then slay all who stand before you, for in no way will I trust this treaty; I know well that my father wishes to be avenged upon me."

11   So they met for their appointment and were thoroughly agreed and accorded; wine was fetched and they drank together. Just then an **adder** came out of a little heath-bush and stung a knight on the foot. When the knight felt the sting, he looked down and saw the adder; at once he drew his sword to slay the adder, and thought to cause no harm. But when the hosts on both sides saw that sword drawn, they blew trumpets and horns and shouted grimly, and the two hosts rushed toward each other.

NOTES

12   Then King Arthur mounted his horse and said, "Alas, this unhappy day!" So he rode to join his party, and Sir Mordred did in like wise. And never since was there seen a more **doleful** battle in any Christian land, for there was great rushing and riding, thrusting and striking, and many a grim word was spoken by each side, and many a deadly stroke was dealt. But King Arthur rode steadily throughout the army of Sir Mordred many times and did full nobly, as a noble king should; never at any time did he weaken. And Sir Mordred did his duty that day and put himself in great peril. Thus they fought all the long day, and no knight ever stinted till he was laid to the cold earth. So they fought on till it was near night, and by that time there were a hundred thousand who lay dead upon the ground. Then King Arthur was madly wroth out of measure, when he saw that so many of his people were slain. When the king looked about him he was aware that of all his host and of all his good knights no more were left alive but two: one was Sir Lucan le Butler, and the other his brother Sir Bedivere; and they were both sorely wounded.

13   "Jesus, mercy!" said the king. "Where are all my noble knights? Alas, that ever I should see this doleful day! For now I have come to my end. But would to God that I knew where that traitor Sir Mordred, who hath caused all this mischief, is."

14   Then King Arthur looked about and saw where Sir Mordred stood leaning upon his sword among a great heap of dead men. "Now give me my spear," said King Arthur to Sir Lucan, "for yonder I have spied the traitor who hath wrought all this woe."

15   "Sir, let him be," said Sir Lucan, "for he brings ill fortune, And if ye can pass through this unlucky day, ye shall be right well revenged upon him. Good lord, remember your night's dream and what the spirit of Sir Gawain told you last night. God in His great goodness hath preserved you so far. Therefore for God's sake, my lord, leave off now; for, blessed be God, ye have won the field: here we three are alive, but with Sir Mordred no one is alive. Therefore if ye leave off now, this wicked day of destiny is over."

16   "Now betide me death, betide me life," said the king, "now that I see him yonder alone, he shall never escape my hands! For I shall never have him at better avail."

17   "God speed you well!" said Sir Bedivere.

18   Then the king got his spear in both his hands and ran toward Sir Mordred, crying, "Traitor, now has thy death-day come!"

19   When Sir Mordred heard King Arthur he ran toward him with his sword drawn in his hand. Then King Arthur **smote** Sir Mordred under the shield with a

thrust of his spear on through the body more than a fathom. When Sir Mordred felt that he had his death-wound, he thrust himself with all his might up to the handguard of King Arthur's spear; and right so, holding his sword in both his hands, he smote his father King Arthur upon the side of the head so that the sword pierced the helmet and the brain-pan. Therewith Sir Mordred fell stark dead to the earth; and the noble King Arthur fell to the earth and there he **swooned** often, and Sir Lucan and Sir Bedivere lifted him up each time. So they led him, weak between them, to a little chapel not far from the sea, and when the king was there he seemed reasonably comfortable.

20 Then they heard people cry out in the field.

21 "Now go thou, Sir Lucan," said the king, "and let me know what that noise in the field betokens."

22 So Sir Lucan departed slowly, for he was grievously wounded in many places; as he went he saw and noticed by the moonlight how plunderers and robbers had come into the field to plunder and to rob many a full noble knight of brooches and beads, of many a good ring, and of many a rich jewel. And whoever was not fully dead, the robbers slew them for their armor and their riches. When Sir Lucan understood this work, he came back to the king as quickly as he could and told him all that he had heard and seen.

23 "Therefore, by my counsel," said Sir Lucan, "it is best that we bring you to some town."

5

24 "I would it could be so," said the king, "but I cannot stand, my head aches so. Ah, Sir Lancelot, this day have I sorely missed thee! And alas, that ever I was against thee! For now I have my death, whereof Sir Gawain warned me in my dream."

25 Then Sir Lucan took up the king on one side and Sir Bedivere did so on the other side, and in the lifting the king swooned. Also with the lifting, Sir Lucan fell into a swoon and part of his guts fell out of his body, and therewith the noble knight's heart burst. When the king awoke he beheld Sir Lucan, how he lay foaming at the mouth, and how part of his guts lay at his feet.

26 "Alas," said the king, "this is to me a full heavy sight to see this noble duke die so for my sake; for he wished to help me, he who had more need of help than I. Alas, he would not complain, his heart was so set upon helping me. Now Jesus have mercy upon his soul!"

27 Then Sir Bedivere wept for the death of his brother.

28   "Leave this mourning and weeping," said the king, "for all this will not avail me. For wit thou well, if I might live myself the death of Sir Lucan would grieve me evermore, but my time passeth on fast. Therefore take though here Excalibur, my good sword, and go with it to yonder water's side; when thou comest there, I charge thee to throw my sword into that water and come again and tell me what thou saw there."

29   "My lord," said Sir Bedivere, "your command shall be done, and quickly I shall bring you word back."

30   So Sir Bedivere departed. And along the way he beheld that noble sword, that the pommel and the haft were all of precious stones. Then he said to himself, "If I throw this rich sword into the water, thereof shall never come good, but only harm and loss." Then Sir Bedivere hid Excalibur under a tree, and as soon as he might he came again unto the king and said that he had been at the water and had thrown the sword into the water.

31   "What saw thou there?" said the king.

32   "Sir," he said, "I saw nothing but waves and winds."

33   "That is untruly said by thee," said the king."Therefore go thou quickly again and do my command. As thou art dear to me, spare not but throw it in."

34   Then Sir Bedivere returned again and took the sword in his hand, and again he thought it a sin and a shame to throw away that noble sword. So once more he hid the sword and returned again and told the king that he had been at the water and done his command.

35   "What saw thou there?" said the king.

36   "Sir," he said, "I saw nothing but waves and winds."

37   "Ah, traitor untrue," said King Arthur, "now hast thou betrayed me twice! Who would have thought that thou who hast been to me so lief and dear and thou who art called a noble knight would betray me for the richness of this sword? But now go again quickly; thy long **tarrying** putteth me in great jeopardy of my life, for I have taken cold. And unless thou do now as I bid thee, if ever I may see thee again I shall slay thee with my own hands; for thou would for my rich sword see me dead."

38   Then Sir Bedivere departed and went to the sword and quickly took it up and went to the water's side, and there he bound the girdle around the hilt; then he threw the sword as far into the water as he might. And there came an arm and a hand above the water which caught it and shook and **brandished** it

thrice and then vanished with the sword into the water. So Sir Bedivere came back to the king and told him what he saw.

39   "Alas," said the king, "help me hence, for I fear that I have tarried over-long."

40   Then Sir Bedivere took the king upon his back and so went with him to the water's side. When they reached there they saw a little barge which waited fast by the bank with many fair ladies in it. Among them all was a queen, and they all had black hoods; they all wept and shrieked when they saw King Arthur.

41   "Now put me into that barge," said the king.

42   Sir Bedivere did so gently, and three queens received him there with great mourning and put him down; in one of their laps King Arthur laid his head. Then that queen said, "Ah, dear brother, why have ye tarried so long from me? Alas, this wound on your head hath caught over-much cold."

43   So they rowed from the land and Sir Bedivere beheld all those ladies go from him. Then Sir Bedivere cried, "Ah, my lord Arthur, what shall become of me, now that ye go from me and leave me here alone among my enemies?"

44   "Comfort thyself," said the king, "and do as well as thou may, for in me is no more trust to trust in. I must go into the Vale of Avalon to heal me of my grievous wound. And if thou hear nevermore of me, pray for my soul!"

45   But ever the queens and ladies wept and shrieked, so that it was a pity to hear. As soon as Sir Bedivere had lost sight of the barge, he wept and wailed and then took to the forest and walked all night. And in the morning he was aware of a chapel and a hermitage between two ancient woods.

...

From 7

46   Yet some men say in many parts of England that King Arthur is not dead, but was taken by the will of our Lord Jesus into another place. And men say that he shall come again and shall win the Holy Cross. Yet I will not say that it shall be so; rather, I would say that here in this world he changed his form of life. But many men say that there is written upon his tomb this line:

47   HERE LIES ARTHUR
         THE ONCE AND FUTURE KING

THINK QUESTIONS

1. At the end of the selection, the author says that King Arthur gets on a barge and goes "into the Vale of Avalon." What is really happening in this scene? How do you know? Cite textual evidence to support your inference.

2. Describe the character of King Arthur. What character traits does he show in this selection? Support your response with evidence from the text.

3. Describe the battle scene. How does the author use details to describe the fight? On what or on whom does the author focus in the scene? Cite textual evidence to support your answer.

4. Use context to determine the meaning of the word **doleful** as it is used in *Le Morte d'Arthur*. How do the words following its use suggest its meaning? Note that the term is used more than once. Write your definition of *doleful*.

5. Use the context clues provided in the passage to determine the meaning of **tarrying.** Write your definition of *tarrying*. How do nearby words help convey its meaning? Check your definition in a print or online dictionary.

CLOSE READ

Reread the excerpts from *Le Morte d'Arthur*. Then use your answers and annotations from the questions to help you complete the Writing Prompt.

FOCUS QUESTIONS

1. As you reread *Le Morte d'Arthur*, pay close attention to how the author develops the character of Arthur. What words and phrases does he use? What tone does he create with his word choices? Highlight evidence in the text and make annotations to analyze the development of Arthur's character.

2. In paragraphs 6 and 7, what do Arthur and Mordred tell their hosts, or armies? What happens as a result? What impact does this event have on the rest of the plot? Make annotations to explain your response. Support your response with textual evidence.

3. King Arthur and his knights make repeated references to the Christian God and religion. What can you infer about the role of religion in England during the fifteenth century based on these references? Highlight examples of religious connections and make annotations to note what these references reveal about England. Support your response with textual evidence.

4. King Arthur asks Sir Bedivere to do something three times. What does Arthur ask Sir Bedivere to do? What does Sir Bedivere do, and what is the final result? Why is this action important to Arthur, and what might it symbolize? Highlight your evidence and annotate to explain your ideas. Support your response with textual evidence.

5. At the end of the selection, what happens to Arthur? What does this ending say about Arthur's character and the Arthurian legend? How does this ending help you determine the theme? Highlight evidence from the text that will help support your ideas.

6. Recall the unit's Essential Question: Where does history end and legend begin? Which parts of *Le Morte d'Arthur* sound like history? Which sound like legend? What conclusion can you draw based on your ideas? Highlight evidence from the text to support your ideas.

WRITING PROMPT

Analyze the character of King Arthur as presented in this selection from *Le Morte d'Arthur*. What words and phrases does the author use to describe his words and actions? In what way do his actions reflect heroes from other stories? Then make a claim as to which traits make Arthur an archetypal hero. Use your understanding of story elements to build your analysis. Cite textual evidence to support your response.

CONVERSATION WITH GEOFFREY ASHE
RE: KING ARTHUR

NON-FICTION

Geoffrey Ashe
1999

INTRODUCTION

British cultural historian Geoffrey Ashe has written numerous books and articles centering on the factual analysis of the King Arthur legend. Ashe has advanced the theory that a King Arthur figure did exist, and that Riothamus, a British military leader from the 5th century, is likely the man behind the legend. This excerpt from an interview of Ashe by Britannia.com provides

"It may be factual. We must face the possibility that it isn't."

 FIRST READ

1 *Since the twelfth century, a lot of creative effort has been expended on Arthur, and, in recent years, that creativity has taken the form of film, video, TV games, comic books, music and scholarly research. How do you account for the amazing persistence of these stories over the centuries?*

2 The versions that are most familiar, bringing in the Round Table and Merlin and Guinevere and Lancelot, took shape in medieval Europe. One reason for their becoming popular was that they appealed to a wide variety of interests, in an age when there wasn't much in the way of imaginative fiction. They offered stories of adventure and war and love and magic and religion. They had something for everybody who reads such things at all, and that included women, whose tastes in literature were becoming influential.

3 Of course that's not the whole of it. As you point out, Arthur isn't purely a medieval character. He keeps fading out and coming back, and he has been pictured differently in different periods. I think there is a constant factor that has a great deal to do with his vitality. One way or another, his legend embodies the dream of a golden age which is found in many societies and mythologies. It's a haunting, persistent dream. Even modern novelists, well aware that there never was a real golden age, have pictured Arthur's reign as a time when people of vision and courage were on top for a while, surviving against the odds, and going down gloriously. It's something we would like to believe in.

...

4 *Prior to Geoffrey of Monmouth, in the twelfth century, there were oral and written traditions concerning Arthur, but most of what we "know" of him is due to Geoffrey, who published his highly imaginative History of the Kings of Britain in the late 1130s. Without him, would we have even heard of Arthur?*

Would the subsequent developers of the story, Wace, Chretien de Troyes, Layamon, Malory, and others, have written about him? Does Geoffrey, ultimately, deserve all the credit?

5   It's always risky to guess at what would have happened if things had gone otherwise. But Arthur's fame before Geoffrey was strictly among the Welsh, Cornish and Bretons, the Celtic peoples of the west, descended from Britons of his own time or apparent time. If Geoffrey hadn't expanded the saga into a "history" that was read throughout most of Europe, it might have stayed regional and never inspired authors outside. The Irish had a hero something like Arthur, Finn MacCool, and stories of Finn spread to Scotland, but that's as far as they went. No one like Geoffrey took him up, and he never attained international renown as Arthur did.

     ...

6   *We know that, over the years, King Arthur has proven to be a mother lode of source material for writers and other artists, and it has been said that even some reigning English monarchs found ways to put the "King" to work for them. Can you explain?*

7   English kings during the Middle Ages definitely believed in Arthur. It was good for their morale and good for the Crown's **mystique** that they should be heirs of such a famous monarch. Practical politics were involved. Edward I claimed to rule Scotland on the ground that Arthur had ruled Scotland! Later, propagandists for the Tudor sovereigns, who were part Welsh, made much of their **alleged** Arthurian ancestry, and it enhanced the prestige of the greatest of them, Elizabeth I. Later again, Tennyson's best-selling Idylls of the King, a poetic evocation of Arthur in terms of Victorian ideals, helped to revive the glamour of the Crown when dissatisfaction with the actual Victoria had laid it open to attack.

     ...

8   *The evidence for Arthur before Geoffrey of Monmouth seems to consist mostly of sketchy entries in ancient chronicles, obscure battle poems, and credulity-straining episodes from various saints' lives. Shouldn't someone who had been so successful in conquest and who was the center of a glorious court have left more of a trail behind, with better documentary support?*

9   In Dark Age Britain we have to recognize various **adverse** factors, such as the loss and destruction of manuscripts by invading armies; the character of the early material, oral rather than written; the decline of learning and even literacy among the Welsh monks who might have

kept reliable records. The whole period is plunged in obscurity from the same causes. People who were certainly real and important are no better attested.

10   An old Welsh text with some historical pretensions says Arthur was the leader of a national counter offensive against encroaching Saxons and won twelve battles in widely separated parts of the country. The passage is fairly circumstantial, and there is at least something in it, since counter action did happen, sporadically over four or five decades. I think it likely that Arthur played a conspicuous part in it at some stage. But his status as a long-term supremo could be a **retroactive** promotion inspired later by the growth of his legend. It may be factual. We must face the possibility that it isn't. Insufficient data!

11   *When did Arthur actually live . . . if he did live?*

12   He's usually imagined as living in the Middle Ages, and going around in castles with knights in armour and magnificently dressed ladies. But he certainly didn't. As I said, his legend in its best known form was a medieval creation, and authors in those days didn't care about authenticity like a modern historical novelist. When they handled a traditional story they updated it, putting things in terms of their own time, irrespective of when it was supposed to have happened. This shows in art as well, in illustrations to the Bible, for instance. You'll see a painting of the angel appearing to Mary, and a window at the back looks out on a French chateau that couldn't possibly have existed in Nazareth. So, with the Arthur story, characters in a **milieu** which the authors knew quite well to be ancient were still dressed up as knights and ladies appropriate to the twelfth or thirteenth century. Neither Arthur nor any of his circle would have been like that. To answer the question, he really belongs in the late fifth century or the early sixth, a mysterious phase after Britain broke away from the Roman Empire. He may indeed have been a king, but it's hard to say what kingship amounted to.

13   *The study of Arthur seems to be becoming a literary pursuit rather than a historical one, and perhaps with some justification, given the scarcity of hard evidence. What about archaeology... do you think that can ever tell us anything about Arthur, or is it a dead end?*

14   Archaeology may never prove anything about Arthur personally. Something might turn up: his name on a memorial stone previously overlooked, or even a coin, though no British coins for the period have been found. It's probably too much to hope for. What archaeology can do, and certainly will, is tell us more about the Dark Age Britain where his legend originated. In doing so, it can shed light on the literary process itself.

Please note that excerpts and passages in the StudySync® library and this workbook are intended as touchstones to generate interest in an author's work. The excerpts and passages do not substitute for the reading of entire texts, and StudySync® strongly recommends that students seek out and purchase the whole literary or informational work in order to experience it as the author intended. Links to online resellers are available in our digital library. In addition, complete works may be ordered through an authorized reseller by filling out and returning to StudySync® the order form enclosed in this workbook.

Reading & Writing
Companion   **49**

15   For instance, recent excavations have shown that Tintagel in Cornwall was a major community during the fifth century, very likely a regional centre of government. Now Geoffrey of Monmouth says a Cornish overlord had a stronghold at Tintagel, and Arthur was begotten there. Archaeology doesn't prove the story, but it does prove that Geoffrey chose an appropriate location. It points to a tradition of Tintagel's importance at the right time, an authentic tradition, which Geoffrey drew upon. He wasn't inventing irresponsibly, out of nothing. And that must affect our assessment of him. It encourages belief in a factual basis for at least some of his account, however wildly he exaggerates and fantasizes.

16   *You had something to do with the excavations at Cadbury Castle, probably the leading candidate for being the location of "King Arthur's Camelot." Could you tell us about your involvement in that project and the results?*

17   This is another case like Tintagel, where archaeology has shed light in its own way. Cadbury is a large isolated hill in Somerset. During the last centuries B.C., its summit area was inhabited, with a protection of earthwork ramparts. There was never a castle here in the medieval sense; the fortified hill itself was the "castle," as elsewhere in southern and southwest England. The Romans captured it and evicted the people.

18   A writer in the time of Henry VIII, John Leland, said this was Camelot. The Camelot of romance is a dream city which it would be futile to look for, but it has an aspect that may be significant. It's not the capital of Britain, it's Arthur's personal headquarters. Cadbury could have become the headquarters of a real Arthur, and a dim recollection of that reality could have conjured up the fiction.

19   Believing there was evidence to support such a view, Dr. Ralegh Radford, the pioneer of British Dark Age archaeology, formed an excavation committee with Leslie Alcock as director and myself as secretary. We carried out work in 1966–70 which showed, among much else, that the hill was re-occupied in the latter part of the fifth century and refortified on a massive scale, with a new encircling rampart of stone and timber and a gate house. Whoever was in charge was clearly a chief or king with impressive resources of manpower, at any rate an "Arthur-type figure," as Alcock put it. No complete parallel for the Cadbury fortification has been found anywhere else in post-Roman Britain. It remains special and unique.

20   When Leland picked out this hill as Camelot, he picked what seems to be the most plausible candidate (as, by the way, several novelists have agreed). How did he do it? Even a modern archaeologist couldn't have

guessed that the fifth century fortification was there, embedded in the old earthworks, just by looking without digging. I would say there must have been a tradition about the hill and its powerful overlord, handed down from the Dark Ages. The overlord may have been Arthur or he may not, but as at Tintagel, archaeology shows that people who spoke of Arthur here were not talking in a void. They knew something.

21   In the film of the musical *Camelot,* you have a brief glimpse of a map of Britain, and Camelot is in Somerset. It's there because I told Warner Brothers to put it there. That is my one contribution to Hollywood.

22   *There have been various attempts to identify Arthur with someone who is well-documented. Some investigators have argued that he was a Scottish prince, others, that he was a minor Welsh king. Still others have claimed that Arthur is elusive only because he has been improperly dated, and that he is "really" Caratacus, the first century leader of British resistance to Rome, or Lucius Artorius Castus, a Roman commander of the second century. Do any of these identifications appeal to you?*

23   As full identifications, no. They tend to cancel each other out. But the Arthur of legend may well be a composite, a superhero created by **grafting** deeds of other men on to the saga of the original, and some of these figures may have gone into the making of him. That might account for Arthurian echoes which their advocates have detected. And I suspect that the basic idea is sound, only they haven't looked in the right place.

24   *Ambrosius Aurelianus, a genuine, historical character who flourished at about the right time, was a heroic figure who could be a credible original for Arthur. What disqualifies him from consideration?*

25   Nothing absolutely disqualifies him. But why should storytellers have invented another name for him when he had a perfectly good one? Early authors are quite clear that Arthur and Ambrosius were different people.

26   *That brings us to the next question. In April 1981, you published an article in Speculum, the journal of the Medieval Academy of America, in which you detailed the research that you did to identify a genuine historical figure of Arthur, who fits all the known facts. Could you summarize your conclusions as presented in that article?*

27   The discussion has gone further since 1981. You can follow it in my book *The Discovery of King Arthur* and in various articles. My new idea was to scrutinize Arthur's foreign warfare in Geoffrey of Monmouth and take it seriously. Historians had assumed that any original Arthur would never have gone outside Britain: in that respect, Geoffrey's narrative was pure fancy, and it was useless looking for clues overseas. I did look overseas

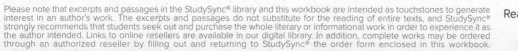

and found trustworthy records of a "king of the Britons" who took an army to Gaul toward the year 470. We even have a letter to him. He is referred to as Riothamus, which means "supreme king" or "supremely royal" and may be a sort of honorific applied to a man who had another name. His career seems to underlie at least a major portion of Geoffrey's account, and passages in a Breton text and several chronicles suggest that he was in fact the original Arthur. One or two previous writers have thought the same.

Excerpted from *Conversation with Geoffrey Ashe re: King Arthur* by Geoffrey Ashe and britannia.com, published by britannia.com.

 THINK QUESTIONS

1. According to Geoffrey Ashe, why did the Arthurian legends become popular? Why do people continue to tell them? Cite textual evidence to support your response.

2. Who does Geoffrey Ashe credit for the Arthurian story gaining popularity outside of Britain? What is his response to the interviewer's question about the lack of solid evidence surrounding Arthur? Support your response with evidence from the text.

3. What contributions can archaeology make to the study of Arthur? What contributions have Geoffrey Ashe and his colleagues made? Cite textual evidence to support your answer.

4. Identify context clues in the text that suggest the meaning of the word **adverse** as it is used in *Conversation with Geoffrey Ashe*. Using those context clues, write your definition of *adverse*.

5. Use the context clues provided in the passage to determine the meaning of **retroactive.** Write your definition of *retroactive*. Then check your definition in a print or online dictionary and write the dictionary definition.

CLOSE READ

Reread the excerpt from *Conversation with Geoffrey Ashe re: King Arthur*. As you reread, complete the Focus Questions below. Then use your answers and annotations from the questions to help you complete the Writing Prompt.

FOCUS QUESTIONS

1. How does Ashe's work at Cadbury Castle support his ideas about history and Arthur? Based on that work, what answer would Ashe likely give to the unit's Essential Question: Where does history end and legend begin? Support your answer with textual evidence.

2. Examine the historical figures mentioned by the interviewer and Ashe. What do they have in common? What does Ashe think of each suggestion of the figures as "real" Arthurs? How do these figures continue to develop Ashe's central idea? Highlight evidence from the text that will help support your ideas.

3. After discussing Arthur as a literary creation, the interview switches to discussing archaeology. How does Ashe support this switch? How is Ashe's archaeological work related to his answer to the fourth question? Highlight your evidence and annotate to explain your ideas. Support your answer with textual evidence.

4. Examine the historical figures mentioned by the interviewer and Ashe. What do they have in common? What does Ashe think of each suggestion of the figures as "real" Arthurs? How do these figures continue to develop Ashe's central idea? Highlight evidence from the text that will help support your ideas.

5. How does Ashe's work at Cadbury Castle support his ideas about history and Arthur? Based on that work, what answer would Ashe likely give to the unit's Essential Question: Where does history end and legend begin? Support your answer with textual evidence.

WRITING PROMPT

Analyze the development of Geoffrey Ashe's ideas as presented in this interview. How does he introduce his ideas? What is the role of the interviewer in the building of ideas? What support does Ashe offer and how does he build his central idea over the course of the interview? Use your understanding of informational text elements as you write your response. Support your writing with evidence from the text.

UNSOLVED MYSTERIES OF HISTORY:

AN EYE-OPENING INVESTIGATION INTO THE MOST BAFFLING EVENTS OF ALL TIME

NON-FICTION
Paul Aron
2000

INTRODUCTION

Author Paul Aron has said that "history makes for great detective stories." This excerpt from his book *Unsolved Mysteries of Histories* traces evidence of King Arthur throughout history and explains how various historical chronicles and literary works contributed to the King Arthur legend.

"...there weren't as many kingdoms in the world as Geoffrey had Arthur conquering."

FIRST READ

NOTES

Excerpt from Chapter 8: Who Was King Arthur?

1   The legend of King Arthur—in stark contrast to the actual man—is easy to track back to its origins. Much of the credit goes to an obscure Welsh **cleric** named Geoffrey of Monmouth, who taught at Oxford during the first half of the twelfth century. In about 1138 Geoffrey produced *The History of the Kings of Britain*.

2   The story, as Geoffrey tells it, moves toward its climax in the fifth century. **Heathen** Saxons, led by the brothers Hengist and Horsa, have invaded and destroyed much of the country. A young wizard, Merlin, arrives on the scene with prophecies of a king who will save Britain.

3   Meanwhile, King Uther falls hopelessly in love with Ygerna. Unfortunately, she's already married—to Gorlois, the duke of Cornwall. Merlin steps in to help out. He transforms Uther into an exact likeness of Gorlois, so the king can slip by the duke's guards and sleep with Ygerna. Thus is Arthur conceived.

4   Fast forward about fifteen years, when the young Arthur ascends to the throne. He routs the Saxons, confining them to a small section of Britain. Later he conquers the Picts, the Scots, the Irish, and among many others, the Icelanders. When Roman ambassadors demand he pay tribute to the emperor, Arthur crosses the English Channel and defeats their armies in France.

5   While Arthur is abroad, his nephew, Mordred, crowns himself king and lives in adultery with Arthur's queen, Guinevere. Arthur returns and slays the traitor but is himself seriously wounded. He's last seen as he's carried off to the "isle of Avalon."

6   So goes the tale, as told by Geoffrey of Monmouth. Arthur's victory is only temporary, since the Anglo-Saxons eventually do conquer Arthur's Britons

NOTES

(thus making Britain into Angle-land, or England). But this only added to the story's appeal to the Britons, who yearned for a return to a golden age when they ruled the land. For them, Arthur was not dead; he was waiting for the right moment to return from Avalon.

7   That yearned-for golden age became even more golden in the imaginations of later medieval writers, who enhanced Geoffrey's legend. The French author Robert Wace introduced the Round Table, so that Arthur's knights could sit as equals. Another Frenchman, Chretien de Troyes, brought to the fore Lancelot, Arthur's loyal knight (and Guinevere's passionate lover). The German Wolfram von Eschenbach added Parzival. By the end of the Middle Ages, Arthur's fifth-century foot soldiers had become knights on horses; his fortified hills had become grand castles; and his court had become Camelot, a chivalric **utopia.**

8   It was an Englishman, Thomas Malory, whose fifteenth-century *Morte d'Arthur* combined all these elements, giving his countrymen a mythic tradition to match any nation's. There was a certain irony to this, since the original story pitted Arthur's Britons against the Anglo-Saxon ancestors of the English, but such is the nature of classic myths. They can **transcend** almost any sort of border; witness the revival of the legend in the twentieth century in variations ranging from the feminist (most notably, in the novels of Marion Zimmer Bradley) to the musical (starring Richard Burton, in the Broadway version).

9   The yearning for a return to a golden age, it seems, is eternal. When journalist Theodore H. White, quoting from the musical, referred to the Kennedy years as "one brief, shining moment," the president's administration was quickly labeled "Camelot."

10   Yet lost amid his legend was Arthur himself. Even in Geoffrey of Monmouth's own lifetime, it was clear that his *History* was anything but. In about 1197, William of Newburgh called Geoffrey's work a "laughable web of fiction" and calculated that there weren't as many kingdoms in the world as Geoffrey had Arthur conquering.

11   Since then, historians following in William's footsteps have attempted to sift from the legend the "historical" Arthur—if, indeed, he really existed.

12   Above all, that meant turning to the (very few) sources that preceded Geoffrey of Monmouth and were thus both closer to Arthur's time and less likely to have been corrupted by later mythologizing. These were mostly Welsh writings, since it was the Welsh who were descendants of the ancient Britons.

13   These Britons came to power after the fall of the Roman Empire, early in the fifth century. They had wielded considerable power under the empire, so it seemed natural (to them) that they take over after the Roman legions left.

That was unlike other areas of the former empire, where the invaders who drove out the Romans seized power. Independent Britain was therefore still in many ways Roman; the Britons, or at least their upper class, saw themselves as the heirs to the imperial culture and civilization.

14   Unfortunately for them, they also inherited the Roman enemies. The Britons immediately found themselves under attack from groups they thought of as barbarians: the Irish from the west, the Picts from the north, and the Anglo-Saxons from across the North Sea. The invaders saw no reason to withdraw just because the Britons had replaced the Romans.

15   The situation the Welsh bards described was desperate—every bit as much as that faced by the British in Geoffrey of Monmouth's account. But if we can believe a Welsh monk named Gildas, in about the year 500 the Britons won a great victory at a spot called Mount Badon. In *The Ruin of Britain,* written only about fifty years after that, Gildas described the battle and the two generations of relative peace and prosperity that followed.

16   Was this **interregnum** of Gildas the brief, shining moment of Camelot? Perhaps. But, as skeptics have been quick to point out, nowhere does Gildas mention the name of Arthur. Frustratingly, Gildas never says who commanded the Britons.

17   This was left to Nennius, another Welsh cleric. In the *History of the Britons,* which Nennius compiled sometime early in the ninth century, there's no doubt about the identity of the hero: it is "the warrior Arthur." According to Nennius, Arthur defeated the Saxons in twelve battles, at one point slaying 960 of the enemy in a single charge.

18   But can Nennius be trusted? Such obviously impossible deeds as single-handedly killing 960 of the enemy clearly belong to the traditions of epic poetry, not history. His **notoriously** disorganized material didn't help, either; the cleric himself described his approach as "making one heap" of all he found. Some historians found comfort in that, arguing that someone unable to organize anything probably also couldn't invent anything, but others just found it frustrating.

19   Welsh writers who followed Nennius also credited Arthur with the victory at Mount Badon. But, like Nennius, they were all writing at least three hundred years after the actual events. It was impossible to tell whether the oral tradition they recounted was the actual history of fifth-century Britain.

Excerpted from *Unsolved Mysteries of History: An Eye-Opening Investigation into the Most Baffling Events of All Time* by Paul Aron, published by John Wiley & Sons.

 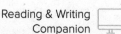

THINK QUESTIONS

1. The author refers to Welsh and British people and histories in the text. What is the historic relationship between the Welsh and the British? Who wrote the early histories of Arthur and why did the written accounts differ so widely? Cite textual evidence to support your answer.

2. What main question is the author trying to answer with this text? How does he try to answer that question? Does he come to a conclusion? Support your answer with evidence from the text.

3. Who does the author cite as sources in this excerpt? Why did he choose to cite these people? Support your response with evidence from the text.

4. Use context to determine the meaning of the word **transcend** as it is used in *Unsolved Mysteries of History*. Write your definition of *transcend*.

5. Use context to determine the meaning of the word **notoriously** as it is used in *Unsolved Mysteries of History*. Write your definition of *notoriously*.

CLOSE READ

Reread the excerpt from *Unsolved Mysteries of History.* As you reread, complete the Focus Questions below. Then use your answers and annotations from the questions to help you complete the Writing Prompt.

FOCUS QUESTIONS

1. Reread the text and focus on the Arthurian writers named by the author. What do almost all of them have in common? What did each contribute to the Arthurian legend? What inference can you draw about the time period based on this information? Highlight textual evidence to support your response.

2. In paragraph 7, the author mentions non-British writers. What do these writers have to do with the Arthurian legend? What inference can you draw about the legends based on this information? Write your inference using annotations and highlight textual evidence to support your inference.

3. Reread Geoffrey of Monmouth's version of the Arthurian legend. In which way is this story similar to the stories you've read in this unit? In which way is it different? What does that tell you about the legend? Highlight your evidence and make annotations to explain your choices.

4. Using the annotations you've done so far, what inference can you draw about history in the time of the Britons and Anglo-Saxons? Highlight evidence from the text that supports your inference.

5. How much of the story of King Arthur as relayed by Aron is legend, and how much is history? How do you know? Highlight evidence from the text that supports your ideas.

WRITING PROMPT

What conclusion about early British history and literature can you draw based on the information presented in *Unsolved Mysteries of History?* In what way does this conclusion enhance or enrich your understanding of the Arthurian legend and its origins? Support your response with textual evidence.

THE LORD OF THE RINGS

FICTION
J.R.R. Tolkien
1954

INTRODUCTION

J. R. R. Tolkien's epic trilogy tells a classic tale of good versus evil played out in the world of Middle-earth, a setting strongly influenced by Tolkien's familiarity with Anglo-Saxon mythology. In this excerpt from the first book, "The Fellowship of the Ring," the wizard Gandalf is explaining the history of a ring that has come into the possession of the young hobbit Frodo Baggins. Crafted by the evil wizard, Sauron, as the most powerful of nine series of rings, it has had several owners, including the murderous Gollum and Frodo's adoptive elder cousin, Bilbo Baggins. Now the forces of evil are determined to get it back, which would have devastating consequences for hobbits, elves, dwarves, and humans alike.

"Many that live deserve death. And some that die deserve life."

FIRST READ

NOTES

Excerpt from The Fellowship of the Ring
Book One, Chapter II: The Shadow of the Past

1 "[The Enemy] knows that it is not one of the Seven, or the Nine, for they are accounted for. He knows that it is the One. And he has at last heard, I think, of *hobbits* and the Shire.

2 "The Shire— he may be seeking for it now, if he has not already found out where it lies. Indeed, Frodo, I fear that he may even think that the long-unnoticed name of *Baggins* has become important."

3 "But this is terrible!" cried Frodo. "Far worse than the worst that I imagined from your hints and warnings. O Gandalf, best of friends, what am I to do? For now I am really afraid. What am I to do? What a pity that Bilbo did not stab that vile creature, when he had a chance!"

4 "Pity? It was Pity that **stayed** his hand. Pity, and Mercy: not to strike without need. And he has been well rewarded, Frodo. Be sure that he took so little hurt from the evil, and escaped in the end, because he began his ownership of the Ring so. With Pity."

5 "I am sorry," said Frodo. "But I am frightened; and I do not feel any pity for Gollum."

6 "You have not seen him," Gandalf broke in.

7 "No, and I don't want to," said Frodo. "I can't understand you. Do you mean to say that you, and the Elves, have let him live on after all those horrible deeds? Now at any rate he is as bad as an Orc, and just an enemy. He deserves death."

8   "Deserves it! I daresay he does. Many that live deserve death. And some that die deserve life. Can you give it to them? Then do not be too eager to deal out death in judgment. For even the very wise cannot see all ends. I have not much hope that Gollum can be cured before he dies, but there is a chance of it. And he is bound up with the fate of the Ring. My heart tells me that he has some part to play yet, for good or ill, before the end; and when that comes, the pity of Bilbo may rule the fate of many, yours not least. In any case we did not kill him: he is very old and very wretched. The Wood-elves have him in prison, but they treat him with such kindness as they can find in their wise hearts."

9   "All the same," said Frodo, "even if Bilbo could not kill Gollum, I wish he had not kept the Ring. I wish he had never found it, and that I had not got it! Why did you let me keep it? Why didn't you make me throw it away, or, or destroy it?"

10 "Let you? Make you?" said the wizard. "Haven't you been listening to all that I have said? You are not thinking of what you are saying. But as for throwing it away, that was obviously wrong. These Rings have a way of being found. In evil hands it might have done great evil. Worst of all, it might have fallen into the hands of the Enemy. Indeed it certainly would; for this is the One, and he is exerting all his power to find it or draw it to himself.

11 "Of course, my dear Frodo, it was dangerous for you; and that has troubled me deeply. But there was so much at stake that I had to take some risk, though even when I was far away there has never been a day when the Shire has not been guarded by watchful eyes. As long as you never used it, I did not think that the Ring would have any lasting effect on you, not for evil, not at any rate for a very long time. And you must remember that nine years ago, when I last saw you, I still knew little for certain."

12 "But why not destroy it, as you say should have been done long ago?" cried Frodo again. "If you had warned me, or even sent me a message, I would have done away with it."

13 "Would you? How would you do that? Have you ever tried?"

14 "No. But I suppose one could hammer it or melt it."

15 "Try!" said Gandalf. "Try now!"

16 Frodo drew the Ring out of his pocket again and looked at it. It now appeared plain and smooth, without mark or device that he could see. The gold looked very fair and pure, and Frodo thought how rich and beautiful was its colour, how perfect was its roundness. It was an admirable thing and altogether precious. When he took it out he had intended to fling it from him into the very

NOTES

hottest part of the fire. But he found now that he could not do so, not without a great struggle. He weighed the Ring in his hand, hesitating, and forcing himself to remember all that Gandalf had told him; and then with an effort of will he made a movement, as if to cast it away, but he found that he had put it back in his pocket.

17   Gandalf laughed grimly. "You see? Already you too, Frodo, cannot easily let it go, nor will to damage it. And I could not 'make' you, except by force, which would break your mind. But as for breaking the Ring, force is useless. Even if you took it and struck it with a heavy sledge-hammer, it would make no dent in it. It cannot be unmade by your hands, or by mine.

18   "Your small fire, of course, would not melt even ordinary gold. This Ring has already passed through it **unscathed,** and even unheated. But there is no smith's **forge** in this Shire that could change it at all. Not even the anvils and furnaces of the Dwarves could do that. It has been said that dragon-fire could melt and consume the Rings of Power, but there is not now any dragon left on earth in which the old fire is hot enough; nor was there ever any dragon, not even Ancalagon the Black, who could have harmed the One Ring, the Ruling Ring, for that was made by Sauron himself. There is only one way: to find the Cracks of Doom in the depths of Orodruin, the Fire-mountain, and cast the Ring in there, if you really wish to destroy it, to put it beyond the grasp of the Enemy for ever."

19   "I do really wish to destroy it!" cried Frodo. "Or, well, to have it destroyed. I am not made for **perilous** quests. I wish I had never seen the Ring! Why did it come to me? Why was I chosen?"

20   "Such questions cannot be answered," said Gandalf. "You may be sure that it was not for any merit that others do not possess: not for power or wisdom, at any rate. But you have been chosen, and you must therefore use such strength and heart and wits as you have."

21   "But I have so little of any of these things! You are wise and powerful. Will you not take the Ring?"

22   "No!" cried Gandalf, springing to his feet. "With that power I should have power too great and terrible. And over me the Ring would gain a power still greater and more deadly." His eyes flashed and his face was lit as by a fire within. "Do not tempt me! For I do not wish to become like the Dark Lord himself. Yet the way of the Ring to my heart is by pity, pity for weakness and the desire of strength to do good. Do not tempt me! I dare not take it, not even to keep it safe, unused. The wish to **wield** it would be too great, for my strength. I shall have such need of it. Great perils lie before me."

NOTES

23 He went to the window and drew aside the curtains and the shutters. Sunlight streamed back again into the room. Sam passed along the path outside whistling. "And now," said the wizard, turning back to Frodo, "the decision lies with you. But I will always help you." He laid his hand on Frodo's shoulder. "I will help you bear this burden, as long as it is yours to bear. But we must do something, soon. The Enemy is moving."

Excerpted from *The Lord of the Rings* by J. R. R. Tolkien, published by Houghton Mifflin Company.

THINK QUESTIONS

1. Provide three pieces of textual evidence that show Frodo and Gandalf are living in an imaginary world and not the real world.

2. Provide two pieces of textual evidence showing that Frodo is in danger.

3. What evidence can you find to support the inference that the hobbit, Frodo, is similar to a human being?

4. Remembering that the Middle English prefix *un-* means "not," use the context clues provided in the passage to determine the meaning of **unscathed.** Write your definition of *unscathed*.

5. Remembering that the Latin suffix *-ous* means "full of," use the context clues provided in the passage to determine the meaning of **perilous.** Write your definition of *perilous*.

CLOSE READ

Reread the excerpt from *The Lord of the Rings*. As you reread, complete the Focus Questions below. Then use your answers and annotations from the questions to help you complete the Writing Prompt.

FOCUS QUESTIONS

1. As you reread the text of *The Lord of the Rings*, remember that the excerpt consists of a conversation between Frodo and Gandalf. Readers have to use inference to gather details about the setting. In the first two paragraphs of the excerpt, why can you infer that the Shire is a place?

2. Middle-Earth is a place that bears some similarities to the real world. What evidence is there in the third and fourth paragraphs that some of the creatures in Middle-Earth have humanlike qualities?

3. Tolkien enriches his story with figurative language. In paragraph 8, what poetic device does he use in the first six sentences? Make annotations to show examples. How does the use of this poetic device give weight to what Gandalf says about Gollum?

4. Paragraph 18 mentions the Cracks of Doom. Make an inference about what kind of place this is, and provide textual evidence to support this inference.

5. Recall the Essential Question for the unit: Where does history end and legend begin? Tolkien's *The Lord of the Rings* is a timeless fantasy, but it has themes that can be applied to the real world. Identify such a theme that relates to the real world and explain how Tolkien uses fantastic elements to develop it. Highlight textual evidence from the excerpt to support your response.

WRITING PROMPT

Think about how the conversation between Frodo and Gandalf provides you with information about the setting of the first part of *The Lord of the Rings*. Imagine that the next morning Frodo panics and flings the ring out his window. Write a short narrative summarizing what happens during the next few days. Include details describing the Shire and the creatures there based on textual evidence from the selection. Also include figurative language in your narrative.

DC COMICS:

SIXTY YEARS OF THE WORLD'S FAVORITE COMIC BOOK HEROES

NON-FICTION

Les Daniels

1995

INTRODUCTION

In the late 1930's, DC Comics introduced Superman and Batman, ushering in a new era of superheroes in American popular culture. Competitors immediately followed suit with their own comic book heroes—such as Wonder Man, Captain Marvel, Captain America, The Human Torch, Sub-Mariner, Plasticman, Blackhawk, and Blue Beetle—launching what became known as the Golden Age of Comics

"...publishers large and small were flooding the newsstands with a cascade of costumed characters."

FIRST READ

DC Inspires a Horde of Heroes

1   By 1939, the double-barreled triumph of Superman and Batman had knocked the infant comic book industry on its ear. The idea that heroes nobody had heard of a few months before could suddenly sell hundreds of thousands of copies was just too tempting to resist, and before long publishers large and small were flooding the newsstands with a cascade of costumed characters. DC had established a new genre with its super heroes, and the competition would be fast and furious.

2   A rival might come from anywhere, even the same building. Victor Fox, an accountant for DC, saw the sales figures and promptly opened his own office just a few floors away. He hired Will Eisner, later one of the most respected talents in comics, to write and draw a deliberate imitation of Superman called Wonder Man for *Wonder Comics* (May 1939). Eisner never suspected this might be illegal, but DC did and promptly sued Fox for **plagiarism.** "We beat him," says DC's Jack Liebowitz, but Fox didn't even wait for the 1940 judgment and canceled Wonder Man after his first appearance. Fox had some success later in 1939 with Blue Beetle, who got his strength from vitamins.

3   Considerably more creativity was shown in the first issue of *Marvel Comics* (October 1939), which later gave its name to its fledgling publisher. Deriving their powers respectively from fire and water, the Human Torch and the Sub-Mariner were guys with a gimmick. From the same firm in 1941 came the patriotic Captain America, created by Joe Simon and Jack Kirby; after a dispute with the publisher, the innovative team went to work at DC in 1942.

4   The toughest competitor of all was Captain Marvel, who got his start in *Whiz Comics* (February 1940). The product of a large, established firm called Fawcett Publications, Captain Marvel in his heyday was the biggest seller in the business, but in some ways he seemed suspiciously close to Superman. DC decided to sue. "It took a long time," says Jack Liebowitz. The legal battle

Please note that excerpts and passages in the StudySync® library and this workbook are intended as touchstones to generate interest in an author's work. The excerpts and passages do not substitute for the reading of entire texts, and StudySync® strongly recommends that students seek out and purchase the whole literary or informational work in order to experience it as the author intended. Links to online resellers are available in our digital library. In addition, complete works may be ordered through an authorized reseller by filling out and returning to StudySync® the order form enclosed in this workbook.

Reading & Writing Companion   **67**

dragged on for years as the two corporations duked it out like super heroes, and the dust didn't settle until 1953. DC editor Jack Schiff compiled a scrapbook documenting similarities, but the district court dismissed DC's complaint. DC appealed, and the case was heard by no less a jurist than Judge Learned Hand, who reversed the dismissal and **remanded** the case back to the lower court. At this point Fawcett finally decided to settle, and agreed to stop publishing Captain Marvel.

5   For all of that, Captain Marvel is a great character. Created by artist C. C. Beck and writer Bill Parker, the scripts developed a humorous slant in scripts provided by Otto Binder. The often **obtuse** hero was a "Big Red Cheese" to his brilliant enemy Dr. Sivana, and was nearly defeated by an intellectually advanced earthworm called Mr. Mind. Beck's simple artwork had real appeal, and kids loved the idea that young Billy Batson could turn into the "World's Mightiest Mortal" simply by uttering the magic word "Shazam!" In 1973, events came full circle when DC acquired the rights from Fawcett to revive the character with a comic book called *Shazam!*, and a successful TV series followed in 1974.

6   Captain Marvel wasn't the only hero who eventually became part of the DC family after getting his start elsewhere. When the Quality Comics Group folded during an industry slump in 1956, DC picked up two major features that had first appeared in August 1941: Plastic Man and Blackhawk. The bizarre brainchild of cartoonist Jack Cole, Plastic Man got some acid in an open wound and ended up "stretchin' like a rubber band." Cole had a surreal imagination and the convoluted **contortions** of his character were a joy to behold. Decked out in dark goggles, Plastic Man was perhaps the hippest hero in comics. All his counterparts had jealously guarded secret identities, but "Plas," a reformed criminal, just couldn't be bothered; his sidekick wasn't a kid, but a fat guy in a polka dot shirt. There has never been a funnier crime-fighter.

7   Blackhawk, by contrast, was born on the bloody battlefields of World War II. A Polish flier shot down by the Nazis, he established a **guerrilla** unit on an uninhabited island and recruited six aviators from allied nations: Andre, Chuck, Chop Chop, Olaf, Stanislaus, and Hendrickson. They had no special powers, but they did have matching uniforms and great planes. One of the first hero teams in comics, the Blackhawks flourished even after the war ended. Created by the prolific Will Eisner, the series would later benefit from the impeccable draftsmanship of Red Crandall. It began a long run at DC in 1957.

8   The acquisition over the years of characters like Captain Marvel, Plastic Man and Blackhawk strengthened DC's stable, and confirmed the company's status as the home of the most famous super heroes in the world.

Excerpted from *DC Comics: Sixty Years of the World's Favorite Comic Book Heroes* by Les Daniels, published by Bullfinch.

 THINK QUESTIONS

1. Describe two competitors to DC Comics in the late 1930s to early 1940s. How did DC Comics respond to these new companies? Cite textual evidence to support your response.

2. Who was Captain Marvel? What happened to the character and why? Support your response with evidence from the text.

3. Which two popular heroes were revived by DC Comics when Quality Comics Group folded? Compare and contrast the two heroes. Support your comparison with evidence from the text.

4. Use context to determine the meaning of the word **plagiarism** as it is used in *DC Comics: Sixty Years of the World's Favorite Comic Book Heroes*. Write your definition of *plagiarism*.

5. Use context to determine the meaning of **contortions.** Imagining the character of Plastic Man may help. Write your definition of *contortions*.

CLOSE READ

Reread the excerpt from *DC Comics: Sixty Years of the World's Favorite Comic Book Heroes.* As you reread, complete the Focus Questions below. Then use your answers and annotations from the questions to help you complete the Writing Prompt.

FOCUS QUESTIONS

1. According to the author, what events launched the demand for superheroes? How did the comic book industry respond? Highlight evidence in the text and use annotations to note the relationship between the events you highlighted.

2. In paragraph 4, the author introduces Captain Marvel. Who was this character, and how was he related to DC Comics? How did DC respond to Captain Marvel, and what was the ultimate result? Highlight your evidence and annotate to explain your ideas.

3. What conclusion can you draw about DC Comics in the middle of the twentieth century based on their response to Wonder Man and Captain Marvel? What does that conclusion tell you about comic books at the time in general? Highlight your evidence and annotate to explain your ideas.

4. What was DC Comics's response to other comics companies going out of business? In what two ways did this help DC Comics? Highlight your evidence and make annotations to explain your choices.

5. Recall the unit's Essential Question: Where does history end and legend begin? How did comic book creators draw on history in the middle of the 20th century to create new superheroes? Support your response with evidence from the text.

WRITING PROMPT

Analyze the author's choices regarding the sequence of events. How does the author present the events in this history of a comic book company? Does the structure effectively convey the relationships between the events described? Why or why not? Use your understanding of signal words and phrases to support your response. Cite textual evidence to support your analysis.

ysync®

WRITE

Extended Writing Project Prompt and Directions:
You have been reading and learning about stories of h
literary terms as theme and story elements. Now you
your own narrative. You will learn skills in the writer's
Prewrite, Plan, Draft, and Revise, before the final step o

Think about the heroes in the selections you have read. W
how does a legendary hero help shape the history of a nation
assignment will be to write a narrative about a hero (or heroine) mo
Morte d'Arthur or Beowulf. You can write about a real, heroic person you know, or you can
write about a fictional character. You can set your narrative in a real or imagined world.

ED WRITING PROJECT
NARRATIVE WRITING

Extended Writing Project:
Narrative Writing
by StudySync

1 | WRITE

Font | Size | B I I_x A U

EXTENDED WRITING PROJECT

NARRATIVE WRITING

WRITING PROMPT

Think about the heroes in the selections you have read. What qualities define a hero, and how does a legendary hero help shape the history of a nation? Write a narrative about a hero (or heroine) modeled on the style of *Le Morte d'Arthur* or *Beowulf.* You can write about a real, heroic person you know, or you can write about a fictional character. You can set your narrative in a real or imagined world.

Your narrative should include:

- An engaging opening that introduces the characters and setting
- Vivid descriptions of the setting and characters
- A logically organized sequence of events
- An ending that effectively wraps up the story
- An underlying theme or message

Narrative writing tells a story of real or imagined experiences or events. Narratives can be fiction or non-fiction. Fictional narratives can take the form of novels, short stories, poems, or plays. Non-fiction narratives are true stories, often expressed in memoirs or diary entries, personal essays or letters, autobiographies or biographies, or histories. Many narratives have a clearly identified narrator who tells the story as it unfolds. In non-fiction narratives, the author usually tells the story. In fictional narratives, the narrator can be a character in the story or someone outside of the story. Effective narrative writing uses storytelling techniques, relevant descriptive details, and well-structured event sequences to convey a story to readers. The features of narrative writing include:

- Setting
- Characters
- Plot

- Conflict
- Theme
- Point of view

As you actively participate in this extended writing project, you will receive more instructions and practice to help you craft each of the elements of narrative writing.

 STUDENT MODEL

Before you get started on your own narrative, begin by reading this narrative that one student wrote in response to the writing prompt. As you read this student model, highlight and annotate the features of narrative writing that the student included in her story.

Lady Letha, Knight of Mordred

It is a day of destiny. My lord Mordred's army is to meet with the forces of the unspeakable tyrant, Arthur. I feel strong, and my brothers-in-arms are showing great courage as they prepare to face the enemy this morning. We are to meet on the field at Camlann. It is said that Sir Mordred is to sign a treaty with his father, the villain. But my lord has told us that if any of the enemy draws his sword, we are to attack without mercy.

. . .

There was no easy path for me to become a knight. I was a servant of my lady Morgan Le Fay. At first men laughed when they learned of my intention and told me the only sword I'd ever swing was a bread knife. Yet the knights who were devoted to my lady were not like the other men. Though perhaps at first they thought it amusing to instruct me in the skills of swordplay, as I practiced, I became strong and skilled. They grew impressed. When I told my lady of my intentions, she smiled and gave her blessing to my undertaking. More importantly, she supplied me with a sword that she said had special powers only for me. The sword was called Nightshade. She also ordered a suit of armor to be crafted for me by the finest smith in Rheged.

During my first battle, Nightshade moved as if it had a mind of its own. Some fierce opponents who sneered at me found themselves without heads. I fought near Sir Mordred to make sure he was safe. When I saw an enemy try to sneak up, I showed no pity. By the end of the battle, I had men running from me like mice fleeing a cat.

. . .

As we muster in the field in the morning mist at Camlann, the enemy appears out of the fog like evil ghosts. We drink a toast to each other, and all seems well at first. But suddenly one of Arthur's knights draws a sword, and we quickly fall into battle formation. Bloodcurdling screams arise as the armies charge at each other with great determination.

My brothers and I embrace our leader's command and show our foes no mercy. Yet they too fight with great power, and no side can gain the advantage. I position myself near dear Sir Mordred and watch for any potential threats. While the sun rises, the fog vanishes and the glint of sunlight off the warriors' armor is like the lightning that accompanies the thunder of hundreds of sword-strikes.

The deaths and terrible injuries mount. The shouts of despair rise to a level nearly even to that of the shouts of rage as warriors charge at new opponent after new opponent. My lord calls out encouragement to his noble warriors, but at times I think I can hear him choke back tears as he watches much of his army wilting along with that of the enemy.

As the sun reaches the midpoint of its afternoon descent, several of Arthur's knights begin to make steady progress toward my beloved leader. I rally some of my friends who still have their strength. Sir Mordred's favorite knight, Sir Lewis, nudges me and points at an enemy with his sword. "We must stop Sir Lucan. He is a mighty knight who can do our lord great harm."

We struggle in hand-to-hand combat with those knights till twilight. Though we have been keeping Sir Mordred safe, Sir Lucan is edging closer and closer to him. As I see him deal Sir Lewis an awful clout to the helm, I step forward and swing Nightshade with all my might at a gap in his armor near the hip. I expect to cleave him in two, yet he is able to thrust his dagger at me even as he limps away, badly hurt. His dagger slices my neck, and I cry out.

I feel my life force slipping away. Through the haze of fatigue and pain I see the approach of the enemy king, one of the few men still able to fight. He charges hard at my Lord Mordred, who turns to face his father with grim resolve. With great skill and effort, the cursed monarch runs my lord through with a spear, but with the last of his strength, my lord lashes out with a mighty blow of his sword at Arthur's head, and I know neither man will live to see the morning.

I die. I die content that I have given my best service to my lord and that the tyranny of Arthur has died with me.

 THINK QUESTIONS

1. What is the setting of this narrative? Refer to two or more details from the text to support your understanding of why this student has included certain details to convey the setting of the story to readers.

2. Describe the conflict of this story. Explain which details this student has chosen to include in this story and why.

3. Write two or three sentences explaining the point of view this student chose for this narrative and the details that reveal the narrator's point of view.

4. Thinking about the writing prompt, which selections or other resources would you like to use to create your own narrative? What are some ideas that you may want to develop into your own narrative?

5. Based on what you have read, listened to, or researched, how would you answer the question "Where does history end and legend begin?" What are some ways in which you might include special qualities in the hero in the narrative you'll be developing?

Please note that excerpts and passages in the StudySync® library and this workbook are intended as touchstones to generate interest in an author's work. The excerpts and passages do not substitute for the reading of entire texts, and StudySync® strongly recommends that students seek out and purchase the whole literary or informational work in order to experience it as the author intended. Links to online resellers are available in our digital library. In addition, complete works may be ordered through an authorized reseller by filling out and returning to StudySync® the order form enclosed in this workbook.

Reading & Writing Companion

75

PREWRITE

WRITING PROMPT

Think about the heroes in the selections you have read. What qualities define a hero, and how does a legendary hero help shape the history of a nation? Write a narrative about a hero (or heroine) modeled on the style of *Le Morte d'Arthur* or *Beowulf*. You can write about a real, heroic person you know, or you can write about a fictional character. You can set your narrative in a real or imagined world.

Your narrative should include:

- An engaging opening that introduces the characters and setting
- Vivid descriptions of the setting and characters
- A logically organized sequence of events
- An ending that effectively wraps up the story
- An underlying theme or message

You have been reading and learning about stories that feature heroes. In the extended writing project, you will use those narratives as models to compose your own narrative essay.

Since the topic of your narrative will be a hero story, you'll want to think about how heroes were developed in the selections you've read. Consider the elements of narrative writing that the authors of the student model narrative and *Le Morte d'Arthur* included in their narratives. What makes the main character a hero? What problem or conflict does each author create? How does the story's point of view enhance the narrative?

Make a list of the answers to these questions for the model or *Le Morte d'Arthur* and your own hero. As you write down your ideas, look for patterns that begin to emerge. How are your hero's characteristics similar to or different

from Arthur's or Letha's? How do heroes in these stories react to conflict? Looking for these patterns may help you solidify the ideas you want to explore in your narrative. Use this model to help you get started with your own prewriting:

Hero: Lady Letha, a knight of Mordred who is fighting against King Arthur

Characters: Letha, Morgan le Fay, Mordred, Sir Lewis

Setting: Battlefield of Camlann

Conflict: The final battle of Arthur and Mordred

Plot: Lady Letha, a knight, is on the battlefield. She flashes back to her training as a knight and the hardships she faced. Then the story returns to the battle. Letha is killed protecting Mordred, who also dies along with King Arthur.

Point of View: First person, from Letha's perspective

Theme: Female knights can be as capable as male ones, but good still conquers evil.

Please note that excerpts and passages in the StudySync® library and this workbook are intended as touchstones to generate interest in an author's work. The excerpts and passages do not substitute for the reading of entire texts, and StudySync® strongly recommends that students seek out and purchase the whole literary or informational work in order to experience it as the author intended. Links to online resellers are available in our digital library. In addition, complete works may be ordered through an authorized reseller by filling out and returning to StudySync® the order form enclosed in this workbook.

Reading & Writing Companion   77

SKILL: ORGANIZE NARRATIVE WRITING

 DEFINE

Every **narrative,** be it a novel or a seven-word story, revolves around a **conflict,** or a problem that the characters must face or overcome. A conflict can be external—a knight fighting a dragon, or internal—a teenager struggling with the death of a friend.

To describe the events, a narrative needs a **narrator.** The narrator can be a character in the story, telling the story from the **first-person point of view.** Or the narrator can be outside the story, telling it from the **third-person point of view.** If the narrator knows the thoughts and the actions of all of the characters, then that point of view is called **third-person omniscient.** When the narrator knows the thoughts and actions of only one character, then the point of view is called **third-person limited.** Whichever type of narrator you choose, make sure you are consistent throughout the story.

In a narrative, **characters** need to be introduced and developed. If they aren't, your audience will be confused. Details about the characters can be revealed slowly or all at once, but characters typically develop and change over the course of the narrative.

IDENTIFICATION AND APPLICATION

• Present the conflict, or problem, early in the story to engage readers and keep them reading.

  › Explain the conflict's significance to the characters. Why is this conflict worth reading about?

• Establish a clear and consistent point of view.

  › Effective narratives can use first-person, third-person, or third-person omniscient point of view.

  › First-person point of view uses first-person pronouns, such as *I, me,* and *my.*

> Third-person point of view uses third-person pronouns, such as *he, they,* and *hers.*

- Introduce and develop your characters.

  › As a writer, know your characters' motivations. Ask yourself: Why do they act the way they do? Does the reader need more background to understand this character?

  › Characters can be introduced all at once or over the course of the narrative.

  › In most narratives, the main character should grow or change in some way by the end of the story.

- Create a smooth progression of events.

  › Use clear transitions and signal words.

 MODEL

The student model narrative "Lady Letha, Knight of Mordred" presents the **main character** and **narrator** right in the title. Many hero stories and legends are named for their main character, including *Beowulf* and *Le Morte d'Arthur* ("The Death of Arthur," in French).

The **point of view** is established in the opening lines of the narrative.

> *It is a day of destiny.* **My** *lord Mordred's army is to meet with the forces of the unspeakable tyrant, Arthur. I feel strong, and* **my** *brothers-in-arms are showing great courage as they prepare to face the enemy this morning.*

The narrator uses **first-person** pronouns, including *I* and *my.* That means that the narrator is speaking from first-person point of view and that the narrator is also part of the story. In this case, the narrator is the hero, Lady Letha.

In the first paragraph, the author presents the **conflict,** or problem, of the story: "My lord Mordred's army is to meet with the forces of the unspeakable tyrant, Arthur." This conflict covers the same time period as the selection from *Le Morte d'Arthur*—Arthur's final battle, at Camlann.

In the next paragraph, the student writer develops the character of Lady Letha.

> *There was no easy path for me to become a knight.* **I was a servant of my lady Morgan Le Fay.** *At first men laughed when they learned of* **my intention** *and told me the only sword I'd ever swing was a bread knife. Yet the knights who were devoted to my lady were not like the other men. Though perhaps*

Please note that excerpts and passages in the StudySync® library and this workbook are intended as touchstones to generate interest in an author's work. The excerpts and passages do not substitute for the reading of entire texts, and StudySync® strongly recommends that students seek out and purchase the whole literary or informational work in order to experience it as the author intended. Links to online resellers are available in our digital library. In addition, complete works may be ordered through an authorized reseller by filling out and returning to StudySync® the order form enclosed in this workbook.

Reading & Writing
Companion

79

at first they thought it amusing to instruct me in the skills of swordplay, as I practiced, **I became strong and skilled.**

This paragraph is a flashback, because the verb tense changes from present to past. As readers, we learn Letha's background from her memory: "I was a servant." She dreamed of being a knight, calling it "my intention," but most men did not want to teach her to fight. Eventually, she impressed her teachers and "became strong and skilled." In this short paragraph, the writer shows readers that Letha is determined, hardworking, and a skilled knight.

NOTES

SKILL:
NARRATIVE
SEQUENCING

 DEFINE

A writer carefully crafts the **sequence of events** in a narrative—**exposition, rising action, climax, falling action,** and **resolution.** The events in a story build toward a specific **outcome,** whether that's a full resolution of the story's conflict, the main character's growth over the course of the story, or a pervading sense of foreboding, danger, or suspense.

The sequence of events also has to make sense. The writer has to provide details—or else deliberately leave them out—to make the story thought-provoking and entertaining. To effectively build to the outcome of the narrative, the writer also carefully crafts his or her language to achieve the perfect **tone,** such as suspense, humor, hatred, or contentment.

The author thinks about his or her audience and the purpose for writing when he or she is deciding which events to include in the story and what tone to use. For instance, a mystery writer will sequence events leading toward the resolution of the mystery and will use words that help create that sense of suspense.

 IDENTIFICATION AND APPLICATION

- A narrative outline, especially in the form of a plot diagram, can help writers organize a sequence of events before they begin writing a story.
  › A narrative outline should follow this framework: exposition, rising action (conflict), climax, falling action, resolution.
- The exposition contains essential information for the reader, such as characters, setting, and the problem or conflict the characters will face.
- In the rising action, a writer begins to develop plot and character.
- The climax is the turning point in the story, often where the most exciting action takes place.

Please note that excerpts and passages in the StudySync® library and this workbook are intended as touchstones to generate interest in an author's work. The excerpts and passages do not substitute for the reading of entire texts, and StudySync® strongly recommends that students seek out and purchase the whole literary or informational work in order to experience it as the author intended. Links to online resellers are available in our digital library. In addition, complete works may be ordered through an authorized reseller by filling out and returning to StudySync® the order form enclosed in this workbook.

Reading & Writing
Companion

81

 NOTES

- The details and events that follow the climax make up the falling action.
- The story must end in resolution of the conflict.
- The story's tone is achieved by careful word choice as well as the events of the narrative.
  - › Use a thesaurus to replace general words (*sad*) with specific, vivid synonyms (*despondent*).
- An author's audience and purpose dictate the sequence of events as well as the tone the author uses.

 MODEL

The author of the student model narrative "Lady Letha, Knight of Mordred" used a story plot diagram to outline and organize his ideas. This student's story was based on *Le Morte d'Arthur*. Look at the outline and think about how you will outline and organize the sequence of events in your story.

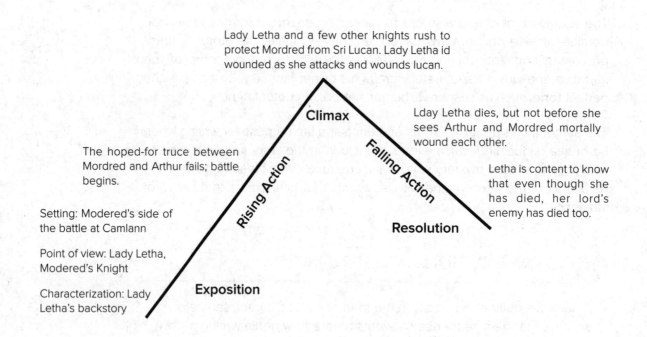

Lady Letha and a few other knights rush to protect Mordred from Sri Lucan. Lady Letha id wounded as she attacks and wounds lucan.

Climax

Lday Letha dies, but not before she sees Arthur and Mordred mortally wound each other.

The hoped-for truce between Mordred and Arthur fails; battle begins.

Rising Action

Falling Action

Letha is content to know that even though she has died, her lord's enemy has died too.

Setting: Modered's side of the battle at Camlann

Resolution

Point of view: Lady Letha, Modered's Knight

Characterization: Lady Letha's backstory

Exposition

PRACTICE

Complete a plot diagram for your narrative that follows the model. When you are finished, trade with a partner and offer each other feedback. Does your partner offer enough exposition? How does the rising action lead to the climax? Do the falling action and resolution follow logically from what came before? Offer each other suggestions, and remember that they are most helpful when they are constructive.

PLAN

WRITING PROMPT

Think about the heroes in the selections you have read. What qualities define a hero, and how does a legendary hero help shape the history of a nation? Write a narrative about a hero (or heroine) modeled on the style of *Le Morte d'Arthur* or *Beowulf.* You can write about a real, heroic person you know, or you can write about a fictional character. You can set your narrative in a real or imagined world.

Your narrative should include:

- An engaging opening that introduces the characters and setting
- Vivid descriptions of the setting and characters
- A logically organized sequence of events
- An ending that effectively wraps up the story
- An underlying theme or message

Use the information you included in your Narrative Sequencing Plot Diagram to write a one-paragraph summary that tells what will happen in your narrative. Do not worry about including all of the details now. Your summary should focus on developing the sequence of events for your narrative. Note places where the features of narrative writing would be most effective. You will use this short summary as a jumping off point when you write a full draft of your narrative.

Consider the following questions as you write your summary:

- What details and events are most important in the rising action of a story?
- What is the purpose of a story's climax?
- How will you lead readers toward a resolution of a story?
- Is there anything you want to withhold from the reader? What purpose would that serve?
- What do you hope readers will take away from your story?

NOTES

SKILL:
INTRODUCTIONS

  DEFINE

The **introduction** is the opening to a story. An introduction needs to grab readers' attention and entice them to keep reading. In a short narrative, the introduction should introduce the problem, or conflict.

Some introductions reveal hints of an internal conflict, as these famous opening lines from *Anna Karenina* do: "All happy families are alike; each unhappy family is unhappy in its own way."

Others may use sensory language to throw readers right into the thick of an external conflict, as these lines from "An Occurrence at Owl Creek Bridge" by Ambrose Bierce:

> A man stood upon a railroad bridge in northern Alabama, looking down into the swift water twenty feet below. The man's hands were behind his back, the wrists bound with a cord. A rope closely encircled his neck. It was attached to a stout cross-timber above his head and the slack fell to the level of his knees. Some loose boards laid upon the ties supporting the rails of the railway supplied a footing for him and his executioners— two private soldiers of the Federal army, directed by a sergeant who in civil life may have been a deputy sheriff.

An introduction can present something unexpected to the reader, who will then want to read more: "It was a bright cold day in April, and the clocks were striking thirteen" (*1984*, George Orwell).

All these examples engage the reader and pique his or her curiosity about the story.

Please note that excerpts and passages in the StudySync® library and this workbook are intended as touchstones to generate interest in an author's work. The excerpts and passages do not substitute for the reading of entire texts, and StudySync® strongly recommends that students seek out and purchase the whole literary or informational work in order to experience it as the author intended. Links to online resellers are available in our digital library. In addition, complete works may be ordered through an authorized reseller by filling out and returning to StudySync® the order form enclosed in this workbook.

Reading & Writing
Companion

85

IDENTIFICATION AND APPLICATION

- The introduction and conclusion frame the events of a narrative.
- The introduction is the author's way of inviting readers into a story.
- The introduction usually provides information about characters, setting, and conflict.
- Use the introduction to orient the reader in the fictional world you are creating in your narrative. Make sure that you are able to answer the following questions with your introduction:
  › Who are the characters? What is the setting? What is the conflict?
- Include sensory details (e.g., sights, sounds, smells, tastes, etc.) to capture readers' attention and draw them into the narrative.

MODEL

The author of the student model narrative "Lady Letha, Knight of Mordred" begins the narrative *in media res*, in the middle of the action.

> It is a day of destiny. **My lord Mordred's army is to meet with the forces of the unspeakable tyrant, Arthur.** I feel strong, and my brothers-in-arms are showing great courage as they prepare to face the enemy this morning. We are to meet on **the field at Camlann.** It is said that Sir Mordred is to sign a treaty with his father, **the villain.** But my lord has told us that if any of the enemy draws his sword, we are to attack without mercy.

The writer uses the first sentence to grab the reader's attention. The readers are left wondering why this day is so important. In the second sentence, the writer introduces the conflict, or problem: "My lord Mordred's army is to meet with the forces of the unspeakable tyrant, Arthur." The **introduction** goes on to provide the setting, the "field at Camlann."

The author describes King Arthur, the popular hero, as "the unspeakable tyrant" and "the villain." This provides clues to the reader of the perspective of the narrator and creates interest in the character. While the introduction provides a lot of the basic *who, what, where* answers, it also leaves enough mystery to engage the reader in the story.

PRACTICE

Write an introduction for your narrative essay that invites the reader into the story. You may want to introduce the main characters, setting, or conflict. When you are finished, trade with a partner and offer each other feedback. Did your partner create an interesting world with interesting characters? Were you engaged? Did you want to keep reading and learn more? Offer each other suggestions, and remember that they are most helpful when they are constructive.

Please note that excerpts and passages in the StudySync® library and this workbook are intended as touchstones to generate interest in an author's work. The excerpts and passages do not substitute for the reading of entire texts, and StudySync® strongly recommends that students seek out and purchase the whole literary or informational work in order to experience it as the author intended. Links to online resellers are available in our digital library. In addition, complete works may be ordered through an authorized reseller by filling out and returning to StudySync® the order form enclosed in this workbook.

Reading & Writing
Companion

87

NOTES

SKILL: NARRATIVE TECHNIQUES

⭐ DEFINE

To write a story, authors use a variety of techniques to develop the plot and characters. Narrative techniques include dialogue, description, pacing, reflection, and multiple plot lines.

Most narratives have **dialogue,** or the conversation between two or more characters. Dialogue can be used to develop characters or to move the plot forward. Writers use **description** outside of dialogue to describe the setting, characters, and events. Strong description often includes figurative language.

Pacing is the speed at which a story is told. A writer can play with pacing. For example, a writer might speed up the pace as the story nears a climax or slow down the pace to reflect a character's indecision.

During a story, the author or narrator might want to comment on the action. This technique is called **reflection.** Reflection is effective in a personal narrative, especially in the introduction or conclusion.

While most stories have one plot, some have **multiple plot lines.** To create multiple plot lines, a narrator might spend one chapter or section following one character and then jump to another character who is doing a separate, but related, task.

••• IDENTIFICATION AND APPLICATION

- Rather than always having your narrator tell the reader what has happened, use dialogue to allow the characters to do the explaining.
  › Set all dialogue off in quotation marks and clearly note who is speaking.
- Use vivid description to engage the reader and help them visualize the characters, setting, and other elements in the narrative.
  › Only include descriptions relevant to the reader's understanding of the element being described.

- Use pacing effectively to convey a sense of urgency or calm in a narrative.
- Consider using reflection to show the reader how the author feels about the topic.
- Multiple plot lines can be an effective way to show how multiple characters interact when they aren't together.
  › When using multiple plot lines, clearly convey to the reader which plot line they're reading at that moment.
  › Keep transitions clear.
- Use any combination of the above narrative techniques to develop experiences, events, and/or characters.

 MODEL

The author of *Le Morte d'Arthur* uses a combination of **narrative techniques** to develop the events leading up to Arthur's death.

Rather than telling the reader everything that happens, the author uses **dialogue** to move the plot forward.

> Then they heard people cry out in the field.
> "Now go thou, Sir Lucan," said the king, "and let me know what that noise in the field betokens."
> So Sir Lucan departed slowly, for he was grievously wounded in many places;...

The author could have written: *Arthur was concerned about the people in the field, so he sent Sir Lucan out to check on them.* Instead, the author used a line of dialogue to express the same feeling without needing to say everything outright. The author uses effective **description** of the activities in the field:

> So Sir Lucan departed slowly, for he was grievously wounded in many places; as he went he saw and noticed by the moonlight how plunderers and robbers had come into the field to plunder and to rob many a full noble knight of brooches and beads, of many a good ring, and of many a rich jewel. And whoever was not fully dead, the robbers slew them for their armor and their riches.

The reader can easily picture what is happening in the field that is causing a commotion.

Please note that excerpts and passages in the StudySync® library and this workbook are intended as touchstones to generate interest in an author's work. The excerpts and passages do not substitute for the reading of entire texts, and StudySync® strongly recommends that students seek out and purchase the whole literary or informational work in order to experience it as the author intended. Links to online resellers are available in our digital library. In addition, complete works may be ordered through an authorized reseller by filling out and returning to StudySync® the order form enclosed in this workbook.

Reading & Writing Companion   **89**

Sometimes, to increase the **pacing,** the author did describe a conversation quickly:

> When Sir Lucan understood this work, he came back to the king as quickly as he could and told him all that he had heard and seen.

> "Therefore, by my counsel," said Sir Lucan, "it is best that we bring you to some town."

In this example, the author is able to jump over the conversation to keep the plot moving along. The actual words that Sir Lucan uses to describe the events in the field are not important, only his conclusion that King Arthur is not safe in the chapel.

SKILL: CONCLUSIONS

 DEFINE

The **conclusion** is the end of a narrative. The conclusion is the reader's final experience with a narrative. It should resolve the events of the story and provide a sense of closure.

A strong conclusion follows logically from what the characters have experienced over the course of the narrative. It may also reflect on the happenings of the story.

IDENTIFICATION AND APPLICATION

- Along with the introduction, a conclusion frames the events of a narrative.
- The conclusion is the author's farewell to the reader, after the reader has experienced the events of the story.
- The conclusion must provide the resolution of the conflict (how the problem is solved).
  › The conclusion may reflect on the events in the story.
- Writers may include descriptive details to arouse an emotional response in a reader as the story ends.

 MODEL

The author of the student model narrative "Lady Letha, Knight of Mordred" ends the story with a dramatic **conclusion:**

> I feel my life-force slipping away. Through the haze of fatigue and pain I see the approach of the enemy king, one of the few men still able to fight. He charges hard at my Lord Mordred, who turns to face his father with grim resolve. With great skill and effort, the cursed monarch runs my lord through

with a spear, but with the last of his strength, my lord lashes out with a mighty blow of his sword at Arthur's head, and I know neither man will live to see the morning.

I die. I die content that I have given my best service to my lord and that the tyranny of Arthur has died with me.

Epics and legends often conclude with the death of the hero—including Arthur (in this unit's excerpt from *Le Morte d'Arthur*) and Beowulf (at the end of the complete poem). These heroes often succumb to death while sacrificing themselves for others. Lady Letha follows this pattern, dying to protect her lord, Sir Mordred. Her role as narrator continues as she reveals that despite her efforts, Mordred dies too—though she is consoled with the knowledge that Arthur perished as well because of her heroic efforts.

⚡ PRACTICE

Write a conclusion for your narrative essay. When you are finished, trade with a partner and offer each other feedback. How effectively did the writer wrap up the story? What final thought did the writer leave you with? Offer each other suggestions, and remember that they are most helpful when they are constructive.

DRAFT

WRITING PROMPT

Think about the heroes in the selections you have read. What qualities define a hero, and how does a legendary hero help shape the history of a nation? Write a narrative about a hero (or heroine) modeled on the style of *Le Morte d'Arthur* or *Beowulf.* You can write about a real, heroic person you know, or you can write about a fictional character. You can set your narrative in a real or imagined world.

Your narrative should include:

- An engaging opening that introduces the characters and setting
- Vivid descriptions of the setting and characters
- A logically organized sequence of events
- An ending that effectively wraps up the story
- An underlying theme or message

You've already made progress toward writing your own narrative. You've thought about your purpose, audience, and topic. You've decided on what your narrative techniques will be and have sequenced out the plot. You've started your introduction and conclusion. Now it's time to write a draft of your narrative.

Use your sequence of events and your other prewriting materials to help you as you write. Remember that narrative writing begins with an introduction that introduces the characters, setting, and conflict. Body paragraphs develop the plot with events and descriptive details. Transitions help the reader follow the sequence of events. A concluding paragraph resolves the conflict and wraps up the story. An effective conclusion should leave a lasting impression on your readers.

Please note that excerpts and passages in the StudySync® library and this workbook are intended as touchstones to generate interest in an author's work. The excerpts and passages do not substitute for the reading of entire texts, and StudySync® strongly recommends that students seek out and purchase the whole literary or informational work in order to experience it as the author intended. Links to online resellers are available in our digital library. In addition, complete works may be ordered through an authorized reseller by filling out and returning to StudySync® the order form enclosed in this workbook.

Reading & Writing Companion **93**

When drafting, ask yourself these questions:

- How can I improve my introduction to make it more appealing?
- What can I do to make my hero come alive?
- What descriptive details—about setting, character, or events—can I add to make the story more interesting?
- Would dialogue or a different point of view make the characters or story more vivid?
- How well have I communicated my overall message, or theme?
- What final thought do I want to leave with my readers?
- Before you submit your draft, read it over carefully. You want to be sure that you've responded to all aspects of the prompt.

SKILL:
DESCRIPTIVE
DETAILS

Descriptive details make writing more specific and help readers visualize a narrative. They convey a vivid picture of the experiences, events, setting, and characters in a narrative using **sensory language,** which appeals to one or more of the five senses (sight, hearing, touch, taste, and smell).

 ## IDENTIFICATION AND APPLICATION

- Descriptive details help readers visualize key story elements:
  - › Characters (what they look like and how they act)
  - › **Direct characterization:** The writer makes explicit statements about a character and what that character experiences.
  - › **Indirect characterization:** The writer reveals a character through his or her words, thoughts, and actions and through what other characters think and say about the character.
  - › Setting (the time, location, and culture the narrative is set in)
  - › Plot events (including plot development and conflict)
- Writers use strong adjectives to clarify descriptions and to help readers better understand and visualize the story.
- Sensory language engages readers and helps them better understand the experiences described in a narrative. It creates **imagery, the "word pictures"** that writers create to evoke an emotional response.

MODEL

In the excerpt from *Le Morte d'Arthur,* Thomas Malory creates a vivid scene:

> Upon Trinity Sunday at night **King Arthur dreamed a wonderful dream,** and that was this: it seemed that he saw **upon a platform a chair and the chair was fastened to a wheel;** thereupon King Arthur sat in **the richest cloth of gold that might be made.** And the king thought that under him, far from him was **hideous deep black water;** therein were all manner of **serpents and worms and wild beasts, foul and horrible.**

Suddenly **the king thought that the wheel turned upside-down and he fell among the serpents, and every beast caught him by a limb.** The king cried out as he lay in his bed and slept, "Help, help!"

The **event** is made clear at the start of this passage, "King Arthur dreamed a wonderful dream." Malory's use of the adjective *wonderful* suggests that this dream is important.

In this description of the dream, Malory says that King Arthur is seated "upon a platform a chair and the chair was fastened to a wheel." Below him is "hideous deep black water" and "serpents and worms and wild beasts, foul and horrible." This provides the reader with a strong image of the **setting.**

Arthur is described to be wearing "the richest cloth of gold that might be made," and this description serves to directly **characterize** him, showing that Arthur is very powerful and wealthy.

He **experiences** trauma in this dream, and Malory uses strong descriptive details and sensory language to convey it to the reader: "the king thought that the wheel turned upside-down and he fell among the serpents and every beast caught him by a limb." This description is rich with detail and sensory language, notably the sense of touch shown through the beasts grabbing Arthur's arms and legs. (Imagine how much less powerful this scene would be if Malory had just written, "Arthur had a nightmare about snakes"!)

REVISE

WRITING PROMPT

Think about the heroes in the selections you have read. What qualities define a hero, and how does a legendary hero help shape the history of a nation? Write a narrative about a hero (or heroine) modeled on the style of *Le Morte d'Arthur* or *Beowulf*. You can write about a real, heroic person you know, or you can write about a fictional character. You can set your narrative in a real or imagined world.

Your narrative should include:

- An engaging opening that introduces the characters and setting
- Vivid descriptions of the setting and characters
- A logically organized sequence of events
- An ending that effectively wraps up the story
- An underlying theme or message

You have written a draft of your narrative. You have also received input from your peers about how to improve it. Now you are going to revise your draft.

Here are some recommendations to help you revise.

- Review the suggestions made by your peers.
- Focus on the big picture first. Smaller details will be overlooked if readers are confused about the plot or the relationships between characters.
  - › Revise your introduction if it isn't engaging or if it doesn't orient readers with the characters and setting and properly introduce the conflict.
  - › Check that the sequence of your narrative is clear and that the tone is appropriate. Add transition or time-order words to clarify any sections.

Please note that excerpts and passages in the StudySync® library and this workbook are intended as touchstones to generate interest in an author's work. The excerpts and passages do not substitute for the reading of entire texts, and StudySync® strongly recommends that students seek out and purchase the whole literary or informational work in order to experience it as the author intended. Links to online resellers are available in our digital library. In addition, complete works may be ordered through an authorized reseller by filling out and returning to StudySync® the order form enclosed in this workbook.

Reading & Writing
Companion

97

> › Ensure that your conclusion reflects on the narrative and neatly wraps it up.
> › Make sure your narrative has a theme or message.

- After you have revised elements of plot, think about descriptive details that will better help your readers visualize the story.

  > › Do you need to add any descriptive details? For example, is there a detail about the setting that could help convey the mood?
  > › Would adding dialogue help flesh out your characters? Dialogue can add life to your narrative.
  > › Consider your narrator. Does the narrator have a clear voice? Is there anything additional he or she could share with the reader?

EDIT, PROOFREAD AND PUBLISH

WRITING PROMPT

Think about the heroes in the selections you have read. What qualities define a hero, and how does a legendary hero help shape the history of a nation? Write a narrative about a hero (or heroine) modeled on the style of *Le Morte d'Arthur* or *Beowulf.* You can write about a real, heroic person you know, or you can write about a fictional character. You can set your narrative in a real or imagined world.

Your narrative should include:

- An engaging opening that introduces the characters and setting
- Vivid descriptions of the setting and characters
- A logically organized sequence of events
- An ending that effectively wraps up the story
- An underlying theme or message

You have revised your narrative essay and received input from your peers on that revision. Now it's time to edit and proofread your essay to produce a final version. Have you included all of the valuable suggestions from your peers? Ask yourself: Is my writing clear and coherent (does it make sense as you intend it)? Have I used descriptive details and precise language? What more can I do to improve my narrative's structure and organization?

When you are satisfied with your work, move on to proofread it for errors. For example, check that you have used correct punctuation for dialogue and have used all hyphens correctly. Be sure to correct any misspelled words.

Once you have made all your corrections, you are ready to submit and publish your work. You can distribute your writing to family and friends, hang it on a bulletin board, or post it on your blog. If you publish online, consider including art or images to illustrate your narrative.

studysync®

Reading & Writing Companion

How do we express the complexities of being human?

The Human Condition

UNIT 2   How do we express the complexities of being human?

The Human Condition

TEXTS

TEXTS

EXTENDED WRITING PROJECT

453

Text Fulfillment
through
StudySync

SONNET 29

POETRY
William Shakespeare
1609

INTRODUCTION

Widely considered the world's greatest playwright, William Shakespeare was also an accomplished poet. A deep thinker and learned man, Shakespeare composed over 150 sonnets, which generally consists of fourteen lines organized into three rhyming quatrains and a rhyming couplet, written in iambic pentameter. As you read Sonnet 29, ask yourself how Shakespeare uses the form of the sonnet to express his ideas about love.

"For thy sweet love remember'd such wealth brings..."

FIRST READ

1 When, in disgrace with fortune and men's eyes,
2 I all alone **beweep** my outcast state,
3 And trouble deaf heaven with my **bootless** cries,
4 And look upon myself, and curse my fate,
5 Wishing me like to one more rich in hope,
6 Featur'd like him, like him with friends possess'd,
7 Desiring this man's art and that man's **scope,**
8 With what I most enjoy **contented** least;
9 Yet in these thoughts myself almost despising,
10 Haply I think on thee, and then my state,
11 Like to the lark at break of day arising
12 From sullen earth, sings hymns at heaven's gate;
13 For thy sweet love remember'd such wealth brings
14 That then I **scorn** to change my state with kings.

THINK QUESTIONS

1. What is the speaker's state of mind at the beginning of the poem? Support your response with evidence from the poem.

2. Who is the "him" referred to in lines 6 and 7? How do you know? What is the speaker's attitude toward "him"? Support your answer with textual evidence.

3. Where in the poem does the speaker's mood change? What causes this change? Support your response with evidence from the text.

4. Use word parts and context to determine the meaning of the word **beweep** as it is used in "Sonnet 29" and explain how you found it. Based on this definition, what is the meaning of the prefix *be-*?

5. Use context to determine the meaning of the word **bootless** as it is used in "Sonnet 29." Write your definition of *bootless* and explain how you got it.

CLOSE READ

Reread the poem "Sonnet 29." As you reread, complete the Focus Questions below. Then use your answers and annotations from the questions to help you complete the Writing Prompt.

FOCUS QUESTIONS

1. Reread "Sonnet 29" and focus on the poem's tone. What is the tone at the beginning of the poem, and how is it expressed? How does the tone change over the course of the poem? What is the effect of this change on the meaning of the poem? Highlight evidence in the text, and use the annotation tool to explain how the lines you've chosen reveal the tone.

2. Shakespeare breaks from traditional Elizabethan sonnet form by repeating the same rhyming word in the first quatrain and the third quatrain. What effect does this repetition have? Where else is that word repeated? Highlight evidence to support your ideas and write annotations to explain your response.

3. The sonnet makes two mentions of heaven in different figures of speech. Identify and explain each instance. Then analyze the role of "heaven" in the poem. Highlight your evidence and annotate to explain your ideas.

4. What role does the second quatrain play in the overall sonnet? In what ways is it similar to or different from the rest of the poem? Highlight evidence from the text that will help support your ideas.

5. Provide a close reading of the sonnet's final couplet. How does the speaker use figures of speech to sum up the poem? Explain the two figures of speech used in your response. Highlight your evidence and make annotations to explain your ideas.

6. Recall the unit's Essential Question: How do we express the complexities of being human? How does Shakespeare use figures of speech to express the speaker's complex feelings? What makes this strategy effective? Highlight evidence from the text and make annotations to explain your ideas.

WRITING PROMPT

In "Sonnet 29," explain how Shakespeare uses poetic structure, tone, and figurative language to show the speaker's emotions. What is each element's role, and how do the elements work together? Base your analysis on your understanding of tone, sonnet structure, and figures of speech. Support your writing with evidence from the text.

HAMLET
(SCENES FROM ACTS I, II AND III)

DRAMA
William Shakespeare
1601

INTRODUCTION

The *Tragedy of Hamlet, Prince of Denmark*, by William Shakespeare, is a vivid portrayal of madness, rich with themes of treachery and revenge. His father the King's death and his mother's virtually immediate remarriage to his uncle throws Hamlet into existential turmoil—a struggle for personal meaning and grueling internal strife that threatens to consume him. In this state a ghost, a character once played in Globe productions by Shakespeare himself in around 1602, visits the Prince. Hamlet's soliloquies, exemplifying the best of Shakespeare's eloquent and clever language, raise unanswerable questions and explore the reality of being human in one of the greatest plays ever written.

"To be, or not to be, that is the question..."

FIRST READ

1 *Hamlet has returned home from studying in Wittenberg to attend his father's funeral. Still in deep mourning, Hamlet is appalled by his mother's hasty remarriage to the dead King's brother, who has assumed the throne and persists in calling him "son." The circumstances drive Hamlet to voice his first passionate soliloquy.*

From Act I, Scene ii:

Hamlet: son to the late King Hamlet, and nephew to the present King
Claudius: King of Denmark
Gertrude: Queen of Denmark, and mother to Hamlet
Polonius: Lord Chamberlain
Laertes: son to Polonius

Location: Elsinore, the castle

2 KING: Take thy fair hour, Laertes, time be thine,
3 And thy best graces spend it at thy will!
4 But now, my cousin Hamlet, and my son—

5 HAMLET: *[Aside]* A little more than kin, and less than kind.

6 KING: How is it that the clouds still hang on you?

7 HAMLET: Not so, my lord, I am too much in the sun.

8 QUEEN: Good Hamlet, cast thy nighted color off,
9 And let thine eye look like a friend on Denmark.
10 Do not for ever with thy vailed lids
11 Seek for thy noble father in the dust.
12 Thou know'st 'tis common, all that lives must die,
13 Passing through nature to eternity.

NOTES

14 HAMLET: Ay, madam, it is common.

15 QUEEN: If it be,
16 Why seems it so particular with thee?

17 HAMLET: Seems, madam? Nay, it is, I know not "seems."
18 'Tis not alone my inky cloak, good mother,
19 Nor customary suits of solemn black,
20 Nor windy suspiration of forc'd breath,
21 No, nor the fruitful river in the eye,
22 Nor the dejected havior of the visage,
23 Together with all forms, moods, shapes of grief,
24 That can denote me truly. These indeed seem,
25 For they are actions that a man might play,
26 But I have that within which passes show,
27 These but the **trappings** and the suits of woe.

28 KING: 'Tis sweet and commendable in your nature, Hamlet,
29 To give these mourning duties to your father.
30 But you must know your father lost a father,
31 That father lost, lost his, and the survivor bound
32 In **filial** obligation for some term
33 To do obsequious sorrow. But to persever
34 In **obstinate** condolement is a course
35 Of **impious** stubbornness, 'tis unmanly grief,
36 It shows a will most incorrect to heaven,
37 A heart unfortified, or mind impatient,
38 An understanding simple and unschool'd:
39 For what we know must be, and is as common
40 As any the most vulgar thing to sense,
41 Why should we in our peevish opposition
42 Take it to heart? Fie, 'tis a fault to heaven,
43 A fault against the dead, a fault to nature,
44 To reason most absurd, whose common theme
45 Is death of fathers, and who still hath cried,
46 From the first corse till he that died to-day,
47 "This must be so." We pray you, throw to earth
48 This unprevailing woe, and think of us
49 As of a father, for let the world take note
50 You are the most immediate to our throne,
51 And with no less nobility of love
52 Than that which dearest father bears his son
53 Do I impart toward you. For your intent
54 In going back to school in Wittenberg,
55 It is most **retrograde** to our desire,

Please note that excerpts and passages in the StudySync® library and this workbook are intended as touchstones to generate interest in an author's work. The excerpts and passages do not substitute for the reading of entire texts, and StudySync® strongly recommends that students seek out and purchase the whole literary or informational work in order to experience it as the author intended. Links to online resellers are available in our digital library. In addition, complete works may be ordered through an authorized reseller by filling out and returning to StudySync® the order form enclosed in this workbook.

Reading & Writing
Companion   **109**

NOTES

56 And we beseech you, bend you to remain
57 Here in the cheer and comfort of our eye,
58 Our chiefest courtier, cousin, and our son.

59 QUEEN: Let not thy mother lose her prayers, Hamlet,
60 I pray thee stay with us, go not to Wittenberg.

61 HAMLET: I shall in all my best obey you, madam.

62 KING: Why, 'tis a loving and a fair reply.
63 Be as ourself in Denmark. Madam, come.
64 This gentle and unforc'd accord of Hamlet
65 Sits smiling to my heart, in grace whereof,
66 No jocund health that Denmark drinks to-day,
67 But the great cannon to the clouds shall tell,
68 And the King's rouse the heaven shall bruit again,
69 Respeaking earthly thunder. Come away.

70 *[Flourish. Exeunt all but HAMLET.]*

71 HAMLET: O that this too too solid flesh would melt,
72 Thaw and resolve itself into a dew!
73 Or that the Everlasting had not fix'd
74 His canon 'gainst self-slaughter! O God, God,
75 How weary, stale, flat and unprofitable
76 Seem to me all the uses of this world!
77 Fie on't, ah fie! 'tis an unweeded garden
78 That grows to seed, things rank and gross in nature
79 Possess it merely. That it should come to this!
80 But two months dead, nay, not so much, not two.
81 So excellent a king, that was to this
82 Hyperion—to a satyr, so loving to my mother
83 That he might not beteem the winds of heaven
84 Visit her face too roughly. Heaven and earth,
85 Must I remember? Why, she would hang on him
86 As if increase of appetite had grown
87 By what it fed on, and yet, within a month—
88 Let me not think on't! Frailty, thy name is woman!—
89 A little month, or ere those shoes were old
90 With which she followed my poor father's body,
91 Like Niobe, all tears—why, she, even she—
92 O, God, a beast that wants discourse of reason
93 Would have mourn'd longer—married with my uncle,
94 My father's brother, but no more like my father
95 Than I to Hercules. Within a month,

96   Ere yet the salt of most unrighteous tears
97   Had left the flushing in her **galled** eyes,
98   She married—O most wicked speed: to post
99   With such **dexterity** to incestuous sheets,
100 It is not, nor it cannot come to good,
101 But break my heart, for I must hold my tongue.

<u>From Act II, Scene ii</u>

102 *Hamlet has been visited by an apparition claiming to be the ghost of his*
     father, who urges Hamlet to avenge his father's murder. Hamlet swears he
     will obey, but hesitates. Watching a group of traveling players perform the
     murder of Priam, king of Troy, Hamlet compares one actor's passionate
     portrayal of Hecuba, Priam's grieving widow, to his own inaction.

103 HAMLET: O, what a rogue and peasant slave am I!
104 Is it not monstrous that this player here,
105 But in a fiction, in a dream of passion,
106 Could force his soul so to his own conceit
107 That from her working all his visage wann'd,
108 Tears in his eyes, distraction in his aspect,
109 A broken voice, an' his whole function suiting
110 With forms to his conceit? And all for nothing,
111 For Hecuba!
112 What's Hecuba to him, or he to Hecuba,
113 That he should weep for her? What would he do
114 Had he the motive and the cue for passion
115 That I have? He would drown the stage with tears,
116 And cleave the general ear with horrid speech,
117 Make mad the guilty, and appall the free,
118 Confound the ignorant, and amaze indeed
119 The very faculties of eyes and ears. Yet I,
120 A dull and muddy-mettled rascal, peak
121 Like John-a-dreams, unpregnant of my cause,
122 And can say nothing; no, not for a king,
123 Upon whose property and most dear life
124 A damn'd defeat was made. Am I a coward?
125 Who calls me villain, breaks my pate across,
126 Plucks off my beard, and blows it in my face,
127 Tweaks me by the nose, gives me the lie i' the throat
128 As deep as to the lungs? Who does me this?
129 Hah, 'swounds, I should take it; for it cannot be
130 But I am pigeon-liver'd, and lack gall
131 To make oppression bitter, or ere this
132 I should 'a' fatted all the region kites

Copyright © BookheadEd Learning, LLC

NOTES

133   With this slave's offal. Bloody, bawdy villain!

134   Remorseless, treacherous, lecherous, kindless villain!

135   Why, what an ass am I! This is most brave,

136   That I, the son of a dear father murthered,

137   Prompted to my revenge by heaven and hell,

138   Must, like a whore unpack my heart with words,

139   And fall a-cursing like a very drab,

140   A stallion. Fie upon't, foh!

141   About, my brains! Hum—I have heard

142   That guilty creatures sitting at a play

143   Have by the very cunning of the scene

144   Been struck so to the soul, that presently

145   They have proclaim'd their malefactions:

146   For murther, though it have no tongue, will speak

147   With most miraculous organ. I'll have these players

148   Play something like the murther of my father

149   Before mine uncle. I'll observe his looks,

150   I'll tent him to the quick. If 'a do blench,

151   I know my course. The spirit that I have seen

152   May be the dev'l, and the dev'l hath power

153   T' assume a pleasing shape, yea, and perhaps,

154   Out of my weakness and my melancholy,

155   As he is very potent with such spirits,

156   Abuses me to damn me. I'll have grounds

157   More relative than this—the play's the thing

158   Wherein I'll catch the conscience of the King.

From Act III, Scene i

159   *Hamlet has been acting mad in front of his family and the court. The King and Polonius hope that Hamlet's strange behavior stems from his love for Polonius's daughter, Ophelia, and they spy on the young couple in order to confirm their suspicions. While hidden, they catch Hamlet in a private moment of anguished contemplation.*

160   HAMLET: To be, or not to be, that is the question:

161   Whether 'tis nobler in the mind to suffer

162   The slings and arrows of outrageous fortune,

163   Or to take arms against a sea of troubles,

164   And by opposing, end them. To die, to sleep—

165   No more, and by a sleep to say we end

166   The heart-ache and the thousand natural shocks

167   That flesh is heir to; 'tis a consummation

168   Devoutly to be wish'd. To die, to sleep—

169   To sleep, perchance to dream—ay, there's the rub,

170 For in that sleep of death what dreams may come,

171 When we have shuffled off this mortal coil,

172 Must give us pause; there's the respect

173 That makes **calamity** of so long life:

174 For who would bear the whips and scorns of time,

175 Th' oppressor's wrong, the proud man's contumely,

176 The pangs of despis'd love, the law's delay,

177 The **insolence** of office, and the spurns

178 That patient merit of th' unworthy takes,

179 When he himself might his quietus make

180 With a bare bodkin; who would fardels bear,

181 To grunt and sweat under a weary life,

182 But that the dread of something after death,

183 The undiscover'd country, from whose bourn

184 No traveller returns, puzzles the will,

185 And makes us rather bear those ills we have,

186 Than fly to others that we know not of?

187 Thus conscience does make cowards of us all,

188 And thus the native hue of resolution

189 Is sicklied o'er with the pale cast of thought,

190 And enterprises of great pith and moment

191 With this regard their currents turn awry,

192 And lose the name of action.

Act III, Scene iii

A room in the Castle.

193 *[Enter KING, ROSENCRANTZ, and GUILDENSTERN.]*

194 KING: I like him not; nor stands it safe with us

195 To let his madness range. Therefore prepare you;

196 I your commission will forthwith dispatch,

197 And he to England shall along with you:

198 The terms of our estate may not endure

199 Hazard so near us as doth hourly grow

200 Out of his lunacies.

201 GULIDENSTERN: We will ourselves provide:

202 Most holy and religious fear it is

203 To keep those many many bodies safe

204 That live and feed upon your majesty.

205 ROSENCRANTZ: The single and peculiar life is bound,

206 With all the strength and armour of the mind,

207 To keep itself from 'noyance; but much more

Copyright © BookheadEd Learning, LLC

NOTES

208 That spirit upon whose weal depend and rest
209 The lives of many. The cease of majesty
210 Dies not alone; but like a gulf doth draw
211 What's near it with it: it is a massy wheel,
212 Fix'd on the summit of the highest mount,
213 To whose huge spokes ten thousand lesser things
214 Are mortis'd and adjoin'd; which, when it falls,
215 Each small annexment, petty consequence,
216 Attends the **boisterous** ruin. Never alone
217 Did the king sigh, but with a general groan.

218 KING: Arm you, I pray you, to this speedy voyage;
219 For we will fetters put upon this fear,
220 Which now goes too free-footed.

221 ROSENCRANTZ and GULIDENSTERN: We will haste us.

222 *[Exeunt ROSENCRANTZ and GULIDENSTERN.]*

223 *[Enter POLONIUS.]*

224 POLONIUS: My lord, he's going to his mother's closet:
225 Behind the arras I'll convey myself
226 To hear the process; I'll warrant she'll tax him home:
227 And, as you said, and wisely was it said,
228 'Tis meet that some more audience than a mother,
229 Since nature makes them partial, should o'erhear
230 The speech, of vantage. Fare you well, my liege:
231 I'll call upon you ere you go to bed,
232 And tell you what I know.

233 KING: Thanks, dear my lord.

234 [Exit POLONIUS.]

235 O, my offence is rank, it smells to heaven;
236 It hath the primal eldest curse upon't,—
237 A brother's murder!—Pray can I not,
238 Though inclination be as sharp as will:
239 My stronger guilt defeats my strong intent;
240 And, like a man to double business bound,
241 I stand in pause where I shall first begin,
242 And both neglect. What if this cursed hand
243 Were thicker than itself with brother's blood,—
244 Is there not rain enough in the sweet heavens
245 To wash it white as snow? Whereto serves mercy

246   But to confront the visage of offence?
247   And what's in prayer but this twofold force,—
248   To be forestalled ere we come to fall,
249   Or pardon'd being down? Then I'll look up;
250   My fault is past. But, O, what form of prayer
251   Can serve my turn? Forgive me my foul murder!—
252   That cannot be; since I am still possess'd
253   Of those effects for which I did the murder,—
254   My crown, mine own ambition, and my queen.
255   May one be pardon'd and retain the offence?
256   In the corrupted currents of this world
257   Offence's gilded hand may shove by justice;
258   And oft 'tis seen the wicked prize itself
259   Buys out the law; but 'tis not so above;
260   There is no shuffling;—there the action lies
261   In his true nature; and we ourselves compell'd,
262   Even to the teeth and forehead of our faults,
263   To give in evidence. What then? what rests?
264   Try what repentance can: what can it not?
265   Yet what can it when one cannot repent?
266   O wretched state! O bosom black as death!
267   O limed soul, that, struggling to be free,
268   Art more engag'd! Help, angels! Make assay:
269   Bow, stubborn knees; and, heart, with strings of steel,
270   Be soft as sinews of the new-born babe!
271   All may be well.

272   *[Retires and kneels.]*

273   *[Enter Hamlet.]*

274   HAMLET: Now might I do it pat, now he is praying;
275   And now I'll do't;—and so he goes to heaven;
276   And so am I reveng'd.—that would be scann'd:
277   A villain kills my father; and for that,
278   I, his sole son, do this same villain send
279   To heaven.
280   O, this is hire and salary, not revenge.
281   He took my father grossly, full of bread;
282   With all his crimes broad blown, as flush as May;
283   And how his audit stands, who knows save heaven?
284   But in our circumstance and course of thought,
285   'Tis heavy with him: and am I, then, reveng'd,
286   To take him in the purging of his soul,
287   When he is fit and season'd for his passage?

288   No.

289   Up, sword, and know thou a more horrid hent:

290   When he is drunk asleep; or in his rage;

291   Or in the incestuous pleasure of his bed;

292   At gaming, swearing; or about some act

293   That has no relish of salvation in't;—

294   Then trip him, that his heels may kick at heaven;

295   And that his soul may be as damn'd and black

296   As hell, whereto it goes. My mother stays:

297   This physic but prolongs thy sickly days.

298   *[Exit.]*

299   *[The King rises and advances.]*

300   KING: My words fly up, my thoughts remain below:

301   Words without thoughts never to heaven go.

302   *[Exit.]*

THINK QUESTIONS

1. In Act I, how do King Claudius and Queen Gertrude try to reason with Hamlet? What does Hamlet's soliloquy suggest about his response to their reasoning? Cite textual evidence in your response.

2. In Act II, what key comparison does Hamlet draw between himself and the players confirming that he is a coward? What inference can you make about the power of words versus actions from this comparison? Cite evidence from the text.

3. In Act III, Scene i, what does Hamlet mean when he says "to be, or not to be, that is the question"? Citing textual evidence from his soliloquy, explain the determination Hamlet makes on this question. What can you infer about the human condition from this speech?

4. Review the King's lines in Act I, scene ii that begin with "'Tis sweet and commendable..." Use context to determine the meaning of the word **filial** as used in the fifth line. Explain how context helped you determine the meaning of the word.

5. Use context clues to determine a preliminary definition of **trappings** as used in Act I, scene ii. Verify your preliminary definition by checking a dictionary. Write down the definition of *trappings*, identify the part of speech used in the text, and describe the context clue in the text.

CLOSE READ

Reread the scenes from *Hamlet*. As you reread, complete the Focus Questions below. Then use your answers and annotations from the questions to help you complete the Writing Prompt.

FOCUS QUESTIONS

1. How does Hamlet's soliloquy in Act I develop his attitude toward the world? How does Hamlet's soliloquy in Act II compare or contrast with his speech in Act I? What character development does this show? Highlight and explain textual evidence, noting how the evidence relates to both the specific situation at hand and to Hamlet's overall outlook on humanity.

2. What does Hamlet do in Act III, scene iii, when he encounters the king? What positive and negative traits does it reveal, and how does this develop his character? How does it relate to his role as an archetypal character? Highlight textual evidence and make annotations to explain your choices.

3. In Act I, what does Hamlet mean when he describes the "trappings and the suits of woe"? Provide textual evidence that supports the idea that the "trappings" he describes are only the so-called tip of the iceberg for him.

4. In the final excerpt from Act III, the king kneels in prayer. He says:

   O wretched state! O bosom black as death!
   O limed soul, that, struggling to be free,
   Art more engag'd! Help, angels! Make assay:
   Bow, stubborn knees; and, heart, with strings of steel,
   Be soft as sinews of the new-born babe!

   Knowing that *limed* refers to a bird trapped with a lime-based paste, what do you think Shakespeare suggests, denotatively and connotatively, through the phrase "limed soul" in this passage?

5. What words with a similar denotation could Shakespeare have used in place of *question* in the line "To be or not to be, that is the question"? Describe three such words and explain how each would change the meaning of the line.

6. How does Hamlet's "To be or not to be" soliloquy in Act III, scene i reveal the complexities of being human? Highlight textual evidence and make annotations to explain your choices.

WRITING PROMPT

Recall from the Unit 2 Introduction "The English Renaissance" that the intellectual currents behind humanism brought the focus of literature away from the afterlife and toward the affairs of earthly life—including politics, love, and philosophy. In Hamlet's "To be or not to be" soliloquy in Act II, scene i, how does Hamlet blend a discussion of the afterlife with introspection that reflects Renaissance humanism? Look closely at how Hamlet describes the challenges of life with the type of deep thought that marked Renaissance humanism. In your response, provide a summary of Renaissance humanism as you understand it from the Unit 2 Introduction, and provide an inference about Hamlet's attitude toward such deep thought and his interest in human affairs. Provide textual evidence to support your response.

SHAKESPEARE: THE WORLD AS STAGE

NON-FICTION
Bill Bryson
2007

INTRODUCTION

Known for his distinctly humorous writing style, Bill Bryson is a highly regarded American author of various non-fiction books on travel, science, language, and other topics. Bryson's biography of William Shakespeare, *Shakespeare: The World As Stage*, focuses on what little is known conclusively about the famous playwright and poet. The excerpt here discusses the Shakespeare authorship debate.

"...the writer might just as well have suggested that Shakespeare never owned a pair of shoes or pants."

 FIRST READ

Excerpt from Chapter 9: Claimants

1   There is an extraordinary—seemingly an **insatiable**—urge on the part of quite a number of people to believe that the plays of William Shakespeare were written by someone other than William Shakespeare. The number of published books suggesting—or more often insisting—as much is estimated now to be well over five thousand.

2   Shakespeare's plays, it is held, so brim with expertise—on law, medicine, statesmanship, court life, military affairs, the bounding main, antiquity, life abroad—that they cannot possibly be the work of a single lightly educated **provincial**. The presumption is that William Shakespeare of Stratford was, at best, an amiable **stooge,** an actor who lent his name as cover for someone of greater talent, someone who could not, for one reason or another, be publicly identified as a playwright.

3   The controversy has been given respectful airing in the highest quarters. PBS, the American television network, in 1996 produced an hour-long documentary **unequivocally** suggesting that Shakespeare probably wasn't Shakespeare. *Harper's Magazine* and the *New York Times* have both devoted generous amounts of space to sympathetically considering the anti-Stratford arguments. The Smithsonian Institution in 2002 held a seminar titled "Who Wrote Shakespeare?" The best-read article in the British magazine *History Today* was one examining the authorship question. Even *Scientific American* entered the fray with an article proposing that the person portrayed in the famous Martin Droeshout engraving might actually be—I weep to say it— Elizabeth I. Perhaps the most extraordinary development of all is that Shakespeare's Globe Theater in London—built as a monument for his plays and with aspirations to be a world-class study center—became, under the stewardship of the artistic director Mark Rylance, a kind of clearinghouse for anti-Stratford sentiment.

Copyright © Bookheaded Learning, LLC

NOTES

4   So it needs to be said that nearly all of the anti-Shakespeare sentiment—actually all of it, every bit—involves manipulative scholarship or sweeping misstatements of fact. Shakespeare "never owned a book," a writer for the *New York Times* gravely informed readers in one doubting article in 2002. The statement cannot actually be refuted, for we know nothing about his incidental possessions. But the writer might just as well have suggested that Shakespeare never owned a pair of shoes or pants. For all the evidence tells us, he spent his life unclothed as well as bookless, but it is probable that what is lacking is the evidence, not the apparel or the books.

5   Daniel Wright, a professor at Concordia University in Portland, Oregon, and an active anti-Stratfordian, wrote in *Harper's Magazine* that Shakespeare was "a simple, untutored wool and grain merchant" and "a rather ordinary man who had no connection to the literary world." Such statements can only be characterized as wildly imaginative. Similarly, in the normally **unimpeachable** *History Today,* William D. Rubinstein, a professor at the University of Wales at Aberystwyth, stated in the opening paragraph of his anti-Shakespeare survey: "Of the seventy-five known contemporary documents in which Shakespeare is named, not one concerns his career as an author."

6   That is not even close to being so. In the Master of the Revels' accounts for 1604–1605—that is, the record of plays performed before the king, about as official a record as a record can be—Shakespeare is named seven times as the author of plays performed before James I. He is identified on the title pages as the author of the sonnets and in the dedications of two poems. He is named as author on several quarto editions of his plays, by Francis Meres in *Palladis Tamia,* and by Robert Greene in the *Groat's-Worth of Wit.* John Webster identifies him as one of the great playwrights of the age in his preface to *The White Devil.*

7   The only absence among contemporary records is not of documents connecting Shakespeare to his works but of documents connecting any other human being to them. As the Shakespeare scholar Jonathan Bate has pointed out, virtually no one "in Shakespeare's lifetime or for the first two hundred years after his death expressed the slightest doubt about his authorship."

Excerpted from Shakespeare: The World As Stage by Bill Bryson, published by HarperCollins Publishers.

THINK QUESTIONS

1. For what purpose does the author list sources of media coverage of the authorship controversy at the beginning of the selection? Cite textual evidence to support your answer.

2. What is the author's response to the claim that Shakespeare "never owned a book"? What tone does he use in his response? Support your response with evidence from the text.

3. How does the author conclude this excerpt? What does that tell you about Bryson's view of the authorship debate? Support your inference with textual evidence.

4. Use context to determine the meaning of the word **insatiable** as it is used in *Shakespeare: The World as Stage*. Write your definition of *insatiable* and tell how you found it.

5. Use your knowledge of word parts and the context clues provided in the passage to determine the meaning of **unimpeachable**. Write your definition of *unimpeachable* and tell how you got it.

CLOSE READ

Reread the excerpt from *Shakespeare: The World as Stage*. As you reread, complete the Focus Questions below. Then use your answers and annotations from the questions to help you complete the Writing Prompt.

FOCUS QUESTIONS

1. In the second paragraph, what does Bryson mean when he refers to Shakespeare as a "lightly educated provincial"? What connotation does that phrase have, and what does it tell you about Bryson's viewpoint? Highlight evidence in the text and make annotations to explain the phrase.

2. Why does Bryson list the professions of Daniel Wright and William D. Rubinstein in Paragraph 5? What is his purpose for including the long list of media outlets in Paragraph 3? How do these details support his central idea? Highlight evidence from the text and make annotations to support your ideas.

3. What is Bryson's central idea in Paragraph 4? How does Bryson's tone in the paragraph help develop the central idea? Highlight evidence to support your ideas and use annotations to help you write your response.

4. Use your understanding of tone and supporting details to determine the central idea of the excerpt. Highlight evidence from the text to support your ideas.

5. Recall the unit's Essential Question: How do we express the complexities of being human? What does the Shakespearean authorship debate reveal about human nature? What does it say about Shakespeare's critics? Support your response with evidence from the text.

WRITING PROMPT

What is Bill Bryson's central idea in the excerpt from *Shakespeare: The World as Stage*? How does Bryson's tone or bias contribute to the development of this central idea? Which key details support the central idea? Cite textual evidence to support your response.

THE LOVE SONG OF J. ALFRED PRUFROCK

POETRY
T.S. Eliot
1915

INTRODUCTION

T.S. Eliot's pedigree is impeccable. Born in St. Louis to an old New England family, he was educated at Harvard, the Sorbonne, and Oxford, and received the Nobel Prize for Literature in 1948 for his boldly innovative and influential style. "Prufrock" demonstrates Eliot's characteristic stream of consciousness and versatility with diction. His narrator seems to be struggling with middle age, but Eliot was only 22 when he wrote the poem.

"And would it have been worth it, after all...?"

FIRST READ

"The Love Song of J. Alfred Prufrock"

1 *S'io credesse che mia risposta fosse*
2 *A persona che mai tornasse al mondo,*
3 *Questa fiamma staria senza piu scosse.*
4 *Ma perciocche giammai di questo fondo*
5 *Non torno vivo alcun, s'l'odo il vero,*
6 *Senza tema d'infamia ti rispondo.*

7 Let us go then, you and I,
8 When the evening is spread out against the sky
9 Like a patient **etherized** upon a table;
10 Let us go, through certain half-deserted streets,
11 The muttering retreats
12 Of restless nights in one-night cheap hotels
13 And sawdust restaurants with oyster-shells:
14 Streets that follow like a **tedious** argument
15 Of **insidious** intent
16 To lead you to an overwhelming question....
17 Oh, do not ask, "What is it?"
18 Let us go and make our visit.

19 In the room the women come and go
20 Talking of Michelangelo.

21 The yellow fog that rubs its back upon the window-panes,
22 The yellow smoke that rubs its muzzle on the window-panes
23 Licked its tongue into the corners of the evening,
24 Lingered upon the pools that stand in drains,
25 Let fall upon its back the soot that falls from chimneys,
26 Slipped by the terrace, made a sudden leap,

27   And seeing that it was a soft October night,

28   Curled once about the house, and fell asleep.

29   And indeed there will be time

30   For the yellow smoke that slides along the street,

31   Rubbing its back upon the window panes;

32   There will be time, there will be time

33   To prepare a face to meet the faces that you meet

34   There will be time to murder and create,

35   And time for all the works and days of hands

36   That lift and drop a question on your plate;

37   Time for you and time for me,

38   And time yet for a hundred indecisions,

39   And for a hundred visions and revisions,

40   Before the taking of a toast and tea.

41   In the room the women come and go

42   Talking of Michelangelo.

43   And indeed there will be time

44   To wonder, "Do I dare?" and, "Do I dare?"

45   Time to turn back and descend the stair,

46   With a bald spot in the middle of my hair—

47   (They will say: "How his hair is growing thin!")

48   My morning coat, my collar mounting firmly to the chin,

49   My necktie rich and modest, but asserted by a simple pin—

50   (They will say: "But how his arms and legs are thin!")

51   Do I dare

52   Disturb the universe?

53   In a minute there is time

54   For decisions and revisions which a minute will reverse.

55   For I have known them all already, known them all:

56   Have known the evenings, mornings, afternoons,

57   I have measured out my life with coffee spoons;

58   I know the voices dying with a dying fall

59   Beneath the music from a farther room.

60   So how should I presume?

61   And I have known the eyes already, known them all—

62   The eyes that fix you in a formulated phrase,

63   And when I am formulated, sprawling on a pin,

64   When I am pinned and wriggling on the wall,

65   Then how should I begin

66   To spit out all the butt-ends of my days and ways?

67   And how should I presume?

NOTES

68 And I have known the arms already, known them all—

69 Arms that are braceleted and white and bare

70 (But in the lamplight, downed with light brown hair!)

71 Is it perfume from a dress

72 That makes me so digress?

73 Arms that lie along a table, or wrap about a shawl.

74   And should I then presume?

75   And how should I begin?

    ...

76 Shall I say, I have gone at dusk through narrow streets

77 And watched the smoke that rises from the pipes

78 Of lonely men in shirt-sleeves, leaning out of windows?

79 I should have been a pair of ragged claws

80 Scuttling across the floors of silent seas.

    ...

81 And the afternoon, the evening, sleeps so peacefully!

82 Smoothed by long fingers,

83 Asleep... tired... or it **malingers**.

84 Stretched on the floor, here beside you and me.

85 Should I, after tea and cakes and ices,

86 Have the strength to force the moment to its crisis?

87 But though I have wept and fasted, wept and prayed,

88 Though I have seen my head (grown slightly bald) brought in upon a platter,

89 I am no prophet—and here's no great matter;

90 I have seen the moment of my greatness flicker,

91 And I have seen the eternal Footman hold my coat, and snicker,

92 And in short, I was afraid.

93 And would it have been worth it, after all,

94 After the cups, the marmalade, the tea,

95 Among the porcelain, among some talk of you and me,

96 Would it have been worth while,

97 To have bitten off the matter with a smile,

98 To have squeezed the universe into a ball

99 To roll it toward some overwhelming question,

100 To say: "I am Lazarus, come from the dead,

101 Come back to tell you all, I shall tell you all"—

102 If one, settling a pillow by her head,

103   Should say: "That is not what I meant at all;

104   That is not it, at all."

NOTES

105 And would it have been worth it, after all,
106 Would it have been worth while,
107 After the sunsets and the dooryards and the sprinkled streets,
108 After the novels, after the teacups, after the skirts that trail along the
109   floor—
110 And this, and so much more?—
111 It is impossible to say just what I mean!
112 But as if a magic lantern threw the nerves in patterns on a screen:
113 Would it have been worth while
114 If one, settling a pillow or throwing off a shawl,
115 And turning toward the window, should say:
116   "That is not it at all,
117   That is not what I meant, at all."

    ...

118 No! I am not Prince Hamlet, nor was meant to be;
119 Am an attendant lord, one that will do
120 To swell a progress, start a scene or two,
121 Advise the prince; no doubt, an easy tool,
122 **Deferential,** glad to be of use,
123 Politic, cautious, and meticulous;
124 Full of high sentence, but a bit obtuse;
125 At times, indeed, almost ridiculous—
126 Almost, at times, the Fool.

127 I grow old... I grow old...
128 I shall wear the bottoms of my trousers rolled.

129 Shall I part my hair behind? Do I dare to eat a peach?
130 I shall wear white flannel trousers, and walk upon the beach.
131 I have heard the mermaids singing, each to each.

132 I do not think that they will sing to me.

133 I have seen them riding seaward on the waves
134 Combing the white hair of the waves blown back
135 When the wind blows the water white and black.

136 We have lingered in the chambers of the sea
137 By sea-girls wreathed with seaweed red and brown
138 Till human voices wake us, and we drown.

THINK QUESTIONS

1. What phrases or lines are repeated in the poem? What do these repetitions tell you about the speaker of the poem? Cite textual evidence to support your answer.

2. What physical descriptions of the speaker does "The Love Song of J. Alfred Prufrock" provide? What inferences can you make about Prufrock using the direct descriptions and his actions? Support your response with textual evidence.

3. Write two or three sentences summarizing the events of the poem. What is the speaker's goal or purpose in the poem? Does he achieve his purpose? What seems to occur in the time span of the poem? Use textual evidence to support your response.

4. Use context to determine the meaning of the word **deferential** as it is used in "The Love Song of J. Alfred Prufrock." Write your definition of *deferential* and explain how you arrived at this definition.

5. Use context to determine the meaning of the word **malingers** as it is used in "The Love Song of J. Alfred Prufrock." Write your definition of *malingers* and explain how you arrived at this definition.

CLOSE READ

Reread the poem "The Love Song of Alfred J. Prufrock." As you reread, complete the Focus Questions below. Then use your answers and annotations from the questions to help you complete the Writing Prompt.

FOCUS QUESTIONS

1. In the first stanza, Prufrock tells his audience that this poem is leading to "an overwhelming question." Highlight the questions Prufrock asks in the text. Are any of these questions likely to be the "overwhelming question" he promised? Write annotations to draw conclusions about Prufrock from the questions you identified.

2. The title tells a reader that this poem is a "love song." What is the role of women in the poem? What seems to be Prufrock's relationship to them? How does the author use figures of speech to describe women, and how do those choices imply a theme? Highlight evidence to support your ideas and write annotations to explain your responses.

3. What is the role of the ocean imagery in "The Love Song of J. Alfred Prufrock"? How does it relate to other figures of speech in the poem? Highlight examples of ocean imagery and annotate to explain how this imagery might contribute to theme.

4. What is the speaker's tone in the first four stanzas of the poem? What kinds of words and phrases does the speaker use, and what connotations do those words have? What effect does the tone have on the reader? Highlight textual evidence and write annotations to explain your ideas.

5. Choose one allusion in the poem and explain its meaning. What is the role of the allusion in the poem? What inferences about theme can be made from the allusion? Highlight textual evidence to support your answer.

6. Throughout "The Love Song of J. Alfred Prufrock," there are repeated references to food and eating and drinking. What do these references say about Prufrock? What might they say about the complexity of human lives in general, and how do these ideas contribute to a theme of the poem? Highlight your evidence and make annotations to explain your response.

WRITING PROMPT

Determine two or more themes in "The Love Song of J. Alfred Prufrock" and analyze how they are developed over the course of the text. How does T. S. Eliot use figures of speech—including hyperbole, understatement, metaphors, and allusions—to develop theme in the poem? How do the themes interact with or support each other? Support your response with textual evidence.

Reading & Writing Companion

ON MONSIEUR'S DEPARTURE

POETRY
Elizabeth I
1582

INTRODUCTION

Elizabeth I was the queen of England from 1558 until her death in 1603. Her reign was known as the Elizabethan era, which is famous for the emergence of the English Renaissance. While serving as queen, the well-educated Elizabeth I wrote numerous poems that seem to be about her life, including "On Monsieur's Departure," in which the speaker expresses the pain of unrequited love.

"I love, and yet am forced to seem to hate..."

  FIRST READ

1 I grieve and dare not show my **discontent;**
2 I love, and yet am forced to seem to hate;
3 I do, yet dare not say I ever meant;
4 I seem **stark mute,** but inwardly do prate.
5 I am, and not; I freeze and yet am burned,
6 Since from myself another self I turned.

7 My care is like my shadow in the sun—
8 Follows me flying, flies when I pursue it,
9 Stands, and lies by me, doth what I have done;
10 His too familiar care doth make me **rue** it.
11 No means I find to rid him from my breast,
12 Till by the end of things it be **supprest**.

13 Some gentler passion slide into my mind,
14 For I am soft, and made of melting snow;
15 Or be more cruel, Love, and so be kind.
16 Let me float or sink, be high or low;
17 Or let me live with some more sweet content,
18 Or die, and so forget what love e'er meant.

THINK QUESTIONS

1. What contrasts does the speaker set up in the first stanza? What is the effect of these contrasts? Cite textual evidence to support your response.

2. In the second stanza, to what does the speaker compare her feelings? What feeling does this stanza give the reader? Support your response with textual evidence.

3. What is the speaker asking for in the third stanza? Support your answer with evidence from the text.

4. The word *prate* as used in the poem means "chatter." Knowing that and the structure of the first stanza, what does the word **mute** mean as it is used in "On Monsieur's Departure"? Write your definition of *mute* and tell how you got it.

5. Remembering that the prefix *dis-* means "not" or "opposite of," use the context clues provided in the passage to determine the meaning of **discontent**. Write your definition of *discontent*, and explain how you found it.

Please note that excerpts and passages in the StudySync® library and this workbook are intended as touchstones to generate interest in an author's work. The excerpts and passages do not substitute for the reading of entire texts, and StudySync® strongly recommends that students seek out and purchase the whole literary or informational work in order to experience it as the author intended. Links to online resellers are available in our digital library. In addition, complete works may be ordered through an authorized reseller by filling out and returning to StudySync® the order form enclosed in this workbook.

Reading & Writing
Companion

133

CLOSE READ

Reread the poem "On Monsieur's Departure." As you reread, complete the Focus Questions below. Then use your answers and annotations from the questions to help you complete the Writing Prompt.

FOCUS QUESTIONS

1. Examine the speaker's use of similes and metaphors in the poem. What does the speaker compare using these figures of speech? What purpose do they serve? Highlight similes and metaphors in the text and make annotations to explain their purpose.

2. What point does the speaker make using the hyperbole in the second stanza? How is that different from the point she makes at the end of the third stanza? Highlight your evidence and annotate to explain your ideas.

3. Compare the third stanza with the first stanza. What inference can you make about the speaker's changing state of mind? Highlight your evidence and annotate to explain your ideas.

4. To whom is the speaker addressing in the poem? What inference can be made about the speaker based on this information? Highlight your evidence and make annotations to explain your choices.

5. What option does the speaker leave out of the third stanza? What does this tell the reader about the speaker? What does it reveal about the complexity of being human? Highlight evidence from the text that will help support your ideas.

WRITING PROMPT

What can you infer about the speaker based on what is not said in the poem? How do the figures of speech shape your view of the speaker? What do the emotions of the speaker tell you about the human condition? Support your writing with textual evidence.

SPEECH TO THE TROOPS AT TILBURY

NON-FICTION
Elizabeth I
1588

INTRODUCTION

n August, 1588, King Philip II of Spain sent the huge fleet of warships known as the Spanish Armada to attack and invade England. As ground troops and others assembled at Tilbury, on the bank of the Thames River, in preparation for the expected attack, Elizabeth I, the queen of England, delivered this speech. The Armada was ultimately defeated at sea and never reached England's shores.

"Let tyrants fear."

FIRST READ

NOTES

1   My loving people,

2   We have been persuaded by some that are careful of our safety, to take heed how we commit ourselves to armed multitudes, for fear of **treachery;** but I assure you I do not desire to live to distrust my faithful and loving people.

3   Let **tyrants** fear. I have always so behaved myself that, under God, I have placed my chiefest strength and safeguard in the loyal hearts and good-will of my subjects; and therefore I am come amongst you, as you see, at this time, not for my recreation and **disport,** but being resolved, in the midst and heat of the battle, to live and die amongst you all; to lay down for my God, and for my kingdom, and my people, my honour and my blood, even in the dust.

4   I know I have the body of a weak, feeble woman; but I have the heart and stomach of a king, and of a king of England too, and think foul scorn that Parma or Spain, or any prince of Europe, should dare to invade the borders of my realm; to which rather than any dishonour shall grow by me, I myself will take up arms, I myself will be your general, judge, and rewarder of every one of your virtues in the field.

5   I know already, for your forwardness you have deserved rewards and crowns; and We do assure you on a word of a prince, they shall be duly paid. In the mean time, my lieutenant general shall be in my stead, than whom never prince commanded a more noble or worthy subject; not doubting but by your obedience to my general, by your **concord** in the camp, and your **valour** in the field, we shall shortly have a famous victory over these enemies of my God, of my kingdom, and of my people.

THINK QUESTIONS

1. Who is Queen Elizabeth addressing with this text? How do you know? Support your response with textual evidence.

2. What reason would Queen Elizabeth have for saying that she does not fear for her safety? Support your response with textual evidence.

3. What does Queen Elizabeth promise to her audience? What reason would she have for making such a promise? Cite textual evidence to support your answer.

4. Use context as a clue to the meaning of the word **disport** as it is used in "Speech to the Troops at Tilbury." Then look up *disport* in a print or online dictionary to verify your definition and explain how you found it.

5. Use context to determine the meaning of **tyrants** as used in "Speech to the Troops at Tilbury." Write your definition of *tyrants* and tell how you found it.

CLOSE READ

Reread the text "Speech to the Troops at Tilbury." Then use your answers and annotations from the questions to help you complete the Writing Prompt.

FOCUS QUESTIONS

1. In the second paragraph of her speech, why does Elizabeth say, "Let tyrants fear"? How does this statement support her purpose for the speech? Highlight evidence in the text that shows why Elizabeth uses this phrase, and make annotations to explain her purpose.

2. Why does Elizabeth call out her gender in paragraph 3 of the speech? What purpose does it serve? Highlight evidence and write annotations to support and explain your ideas.

3. What qualities does Elizabeth praise her soldiers for having? How will those qualities bring victory for the English army? What rhetorical device does Elizabeth use in praising her soldiers? Highlight your evidence and annotate to explain your ideas.

4. In the Unit 2 Introduction "The English Renaissance," you read that Elizabeth supported the Protestant Reformation. Using this knowledge, what purpose does Elizabeth's invocations of God in the speech serve? What phrase does Elizabeth use with her references to God to strengthen this purpose? Highlight your evidence and make annotations to explain your choices.

5. Use your understanding of point of view and rhetoric to determine Elizabeth's overall purpose in this speech. Highlight evidence from the text that will help support your ideas.

6. Recall the unit's Essential Question: How do we express the complexities of being human? What complexities about herself does Elizabeth reveal in the speech? How does discussing these complexities aid her purpose? Support your response with textual evidence.

WRITING PROMPT

How does Elizabeth's point of view in "Speech to the Troops at Tilbury" support her purpose for giving the speech? How does she use rhetorical devices to show her point of view and reveal her purpose? Support your writing with textual evidence.

THE PASSIONATE SHEPHERD TO HIS LOVE

POETRY
Christopher Marlowe
1599

INTRODUCTION

Considered by many critics to be the father of English drama, Christopher Marlowe not only had an illustrious literary career as a playwright and poet, he also engaged in covert and dangerous political operations. Marlowe's plays called attention to corruption of those in power, the danger of greed, the darkness of individual suffering, and the need for social responsibility. In contrast to those themes, Marlowe's pastoral poem "The Passionate Shepherd to His Love"

"Come live with me and be my love..."

FIRST READ

1 Come live with me and be my love,
2 And we will all the pleasures prove
3 That valleys, groves, hills, and fields,
4 Woods, or steepy mountain yields.

5 And we will sit upon the rocks,
6 Seeing the shepherds feed their flocks
7 By shallow rivers to whose falls
8 **Melodious** birds sing **madrigals.**

9 And I will make thee beds of roses
10 And a thousand fragrant posies;
11 A cap of flowers and a **kirtle**
12 Embroidered all with leaves of **myrtle;**

13 A gown made of the finest wool
14 Which from our pretty lambs we pull;
15 Fair lined slippers for the cold,
16 With buckles of the purest gold;

17 A belt of straw and ivy buds,
18 With coral clasps and amber studs.
19 And if these pleasures may thee move,
20 Come live with me, and be my Love.

21 The shepherds' **swains** shall dance and sing
22 For thy delight each May morning.
23 If these delights thy mind may move,
24 Then live with me and be my Love.

THINK QUESTIONS

1. What does the shepherd promise to give his love? What do these promises tell you about the speaker? Support your response with textual evidence.

2. What is the speaker's goal in this poem? Do his promises seem realistic? Why or why not? Support your answer with textual evidence.

3. What words or phrases are repeated in the poem? What effect does this repetition have?

4. Use context to determine the meaning of the word **madrigals** as it is used in "The Passionate Shepherd to His Love." Write your definition of *madrigals* and tell how you found it.

Please note that excerpts and passages in the StudySync® library and this workbook are intended as touchstones to generate interest in an author's work. The excerpts and passages do not substitute for the reading of entire texts, and StudySync® strongly recommends that students seek out and purchase the whole literary or informational work in order to experience it as the author intended. Links to online resellers are available in our digital library. In addition, complete works may be ordered through an authorized reseller by filling out and returning to StudySync® the order form enclosed in this workbook.

Reading & Writing
Companion   **141**

CLOSE READ

Reread the poem "The Passionate Shepherd to His Love." As you reread, complete the Focus Questions below. Then use your answers and annotations from the questions to help you complete the Writing Prompt.

FOCUS QUESTIONS

1. What types of figurative language do the first two stanzas contain? What is the effect of this language on the opening of the poem? Highlight evidence in the text and make annotations to explain the language's effect.

2. In what way is the imagery in stanzas 3–5 different from the imagery in the rest of the poem? What effect does this change have? Highlight evidence and write annotations to support your ideas.

3. What message does the alliteration in the final lines of the fifth and sixth stanzas convey to the reader? Highlight your evidence and annotate to explain your ideas.

4. What symbolic meaning might the poem's repeated references to flowers, shepherds, and the month of May represent? Highlight your evidence and make annotations to explain your ideas.

5. Use your understanding of figurative language to identify the central message, or theme, of the poem. Highlight evidence from the text that will help support your ideas.

6. Recall the unit's Essential Question: How do we express the complexities of being human? Does the speaker of "The Passionate Shepherd to His Love" express the complexities of being human? If so, how? If not, what purpose might that serve? Support your response with textual evidence.

WRITING PROMPT

How does the speaker of "The Passionate Shepherd to His Love" use figurative language and hyperbole to attempt to convince his beloved to run away with him? What message does the speaker send about love and his beloved? Support your writing with textual evidence.

THE NYMPH'S REPLY TO THE SHEPHERD

POETRY
Sir Walter Raleigh
1596

INTRODUCTION

Sir Walter Raleigh was an English poet, writer, soldier, politician and explorer—perhaps the best example of a Renaissance man to emerge from the Elizabethan Age. He was described as "the most romantic figure of the most romantic age in the annals of English history" by biographer Hugh de Selincourt. Raleigh's poem "The Nymph's Reply to the Shepherd" was a response to Christopher Marlowe's pastoral "The Passionate Shepherd to His Love."

"All these in me no means can move..."

 FIRST READ

NOTES

1 If all the world and love were young,
2 And truth in every shepherd's tongue,
3 These pretty pleasures might me move
4 To live with thee and be thy Love.

5 But Time drives flocks from field to fold;
6 When rivers rage and rocks grow cold;
7 And **Philomel** becometh dumb;
8 The rest complains of cares to come.

9 The flowers do fade, and **wanton** fields
10 To wayward Winter reckoning yields;
11 A honey tongue, a heart of **gall,**
12 In fancy's spring, but sorrow's fall.

13 Thy gowns, thy shoes, thy beds of roses,
14 Thy cap, thy kirtle, and thy posies,
15 Soon break, soon **wither**—soon forgotten,
16 In folly ripe, in reason rotten.

17 Thy belt of straw and ivy-buds,
18 Thy coral clasps and amber studs,—
19 All these in me no means can move
20 To come to thee and be thy Love.

21 But could youth last, and love still breed,
22 Had joys no date, nor age no need,
23 Then these delights my mind might move
24 To live with thee, and be thy Love.

THINK QUESTIONS

1. What hypothetical situation ("if-then") does the speaker set up in the first stanza and build throughout the poem? Support your answer with textual evidence.

2. Identify two or three ways the speaker badmouths the offerings from "The Passionate Shepherd to His Love." Support your answer with textual evidence.

3. How does the poem end? Does the speaker give a definite answer to the shepherd's advances? Support your answer with evidence from the poem.

4. Use context to determine the meaning of the word **gall** as it is used in "The Nymph's Reply to the Shepherd." Write your definition of *gall* and tell how you found it.

5. Use context to determine the meaning of the word **wither** as it is used in "The Nymph's Reply to the Shepherd." Write your definition of *wither* and tell how you got it.

Please note that excerpts and passages in the StudySync® library and this workbook are intended as touchstones to generate interest in an author's work. The excerpts and passages do not substitute for the reading of entire texts, and StudySync® strongly recommends that students seek out and purchase the whole literary or informational work in order to experience it as the author intended. Links to online resellers are available in our digital library. In addition, complete works may be ordered through an authorized reseller by filling out and returning to StudySync® the order form enclosed in this workbook.

Reading & Writing Companion **145**

CLOSE READ

Reread the poem "The Nymph's Reply to the Shepherd." As you reread, complete the Focus Questions below. Then use your answers and annotations from the questions to help you complete the Writing Prompt.

FOCUS QUESTIONS

1. The speaker—the nymph—begins and ends the poem with a conditional "If." What could the shepherd do or change to get the nymph to come live with him? What can you infer about the nymph based on her request? Highlight evidence in the text and make annotations to explain your answer.

2. The lines "In fancy's spring, but sorrow's fall" and "In folly ripe, in reason rotten" sound almost like idioms or common sayings. Why might the nymph use language that sounds like an idiom? Why is the placement of these lines important? Highlight evidence to support your ideas.

3. Look back at "The Passionate Shepherd to His Love." How is the imagery in Marlowe's poem different from the imagery in Raleigh's reply? Highlight your evidence and make annotations to explain your choices.

4. Look back at "The Passionate Shepherd to His Love." Compare stanzas 3–5 from that poem with stanzas 3–5 of "The Nymph's Reply to the Shepherd." What is the tone of each section of the poem? What key point does each make? Highlight your evidence and annotate to explain your ideas.

5. What is the theme, or central message, of "The Nymph's Reply to the Shepherd"? Highlight evidence from the poem that will help support your ideas.

6. Recall the unit's Essential Question: How do we express the complexities of being human? Who more accurately expresses the complexities of being human, the nymph in Raleigh's poem or the shepherd in "The Passionate Shepherd to His Love"? Highlight textual evidence to support your response.

WRITING PROMPT

Analyze how Christopher Marlowe and Sir Walter Raleigh created different interpretations of the same story in each of their poems. How does Raleigh's poem challenge the meaning and tone of Marlowe's poem? Evaluate which poem is a more effective interpretation. Support your writing with textual evidence from both poems.

UTOPIA

FICTION
Sir Thomas More
1516

INTRODUCTION

Originally published in Latin, *Utopia* is a work of political philosophy by Thomas More, a sixteenth-century English politician and lawyer greatly influenced by the ideas of Renaissance humanism. The book describes a fictional island society called Utopia, where all customs and policies are based on humanistic and rational thought. While the residents of Utopia enjoy communal property, lack of class distinctions and poverty, religious tolerance, and strict control over crime and immoral behavior, the narrative also presents the absurdities in such a near-perfect society. Most scholars view More's depiction of Utopia as a criticism of the social ills of sixteenth-century Europe.

"...those that relapse after they are once pardoned are punished with death."

FIRST READ

Excerpt from: Of Their Slaves, and of Their Marriages

1   Their women are not married before eighteen nor their men before two-and-twenty, and if any of them run into forbidden embraces before marriage they are severely punished, and the privilege of marriage is denied them unless they can obtain a special warrant from the Prince. Such disorders cast a great reproach upon the master and mistress of the family in which they happen, for it is supposed that they have failed in their duty. The reason of punishing this so severely is, because they think that if they were not strictly restrained from all vagrant appetites, very few would engage in a state in which they venture the quiet of their whole lives, by being confined to one person, and are obliged to endure all the inconveniences with which it is accompanied. In choosing their wives they use a method that would appear to us very absurd and ridiculous, but it is constantly observed among them, and is accounted perfectly consistent with wisdom. Before marriage some grave matron presents the bride, naked, whether she is a virgin or a widow, to the bridegroom, and after that some grave man presents the bridegroom, naked, to the bride. We, indeed, both laughed at this, and condemned it as very indecent. But they, on the other hand, wondered at the folly of the men of all other nations, who, if they are but to buy a horse of a small value, are so cautious that they will see every part of him, and take off both his saddle and all his other tackle, that there may be no secret ulcer hid under any of them, and that yet in the choice of a wife, on which depends the happiness or unhappiness of the rest of his life, a man should venture upon trust, and only see about a handsbreadth of the face, all the rest of the body being covered, under which may lie hid what may be contagious as well as loathsome. All men are not so wise as to choose a woman only for her good qualities, and even wise men consider the body as that which adds not a little to the mind, and it is certain there may be some such deformity covered with clothes as may totally **alienate** a man from his wife, when it is too late to part with her; if such a thing is discovered after marriage a man has no remedy but patience;

they, therefore, think it is reasonable that there should be good provision made against such mischievous frauds.

2   There was so much the more reason for them to make a regulation in this matter, because they are the only people of those parts that neither allow of **polygamy** nor of divorces, except in the case of adultery or insufferable **perverseness,** for in these cases the Senate dissolves the marriage and grants the injured person leave to marry again; but the guilty are made infamous and are never allowed the privilege of a second marriage. None are suffered to put away their wives against their wills, from any great **calamity** that may have fallen on their persons, for they look on it as the height of cruelty and treachery to abandon either of the married persons when they need most the tender care of their consort, and that chiefly in the case of old age, which, as it carries many diseases along with it, so it is a disease of itself. But it frequently falls out that when a married couple do not well agree, they, by mutual consent, separate, and find out other persons with whom they hope they may live more happily; yet this is not done without obtaining leave of the Senate, which never admits of a divorce but upon a strict **inquiry** made, both by the senators and their wives, into the grounds upon which it is desired, and even when they are satisfied concerning the reasons of it they go on but slowly, for they imagine that too great easiness in granting leave for new marriages would very much shake the kindness of married people. They punish severely those that defile the marriage bed; if both parties are married they are divorced, and the injured persons may marry one another, or whom they please, but the adulterer and the adulteress are condemned to slavery, yet if either of the injured persons cannot shake off the love of the married person they may live with them still in that state, but they must follow them to that labour to which the slaves are condemned, and sometimes the repentance of the condemned, together with the unshaken kindness of the innocent and injured person, has prevailed so far with the Prince that he has taken off the sentence; but those that relapse after they are once pardoned are punished with death.

THINK QUESTIONS

1. More's *Utopia* describes the social rules of a perfect society. What is the purpose of this excerpt from *Utopia*? Support your answer with evidence from the text.

2. To what does the writer compare the process of examining the bodies of the bride and bridegroom before marriage? What does this comparison reveal about the author and the society? Support your answer with evidence from the text.

3. When a married couple in Utopia wishes to divorce by mutual consent, who makes an inquiry into the matter? What does this tell you about the author's view of the role of women in society? Support your answer with evidence from the text.

4. Remembering that the suffix -*y* can refer to the instance of an action, use context to determine the meaning of the word **inquiry** as used in *Utopia*. Write your definition of *inquiry* and tell how you found it.

5. Remembering that the Middle English prefix *poly-* means "many," and the Greek verb *gamos* means "marriage," consult a dictionary to determine the meaning of the word **polygamy.**

CLOSE READ

Reread the excerpt from the text *Utopia*. As you reread, complete the Focus Questions below. Then use your answers and annotations from the questions to help you complete the Writing Prompt.

FOCUS QUESTIONS

1. What topics related to marriage are discussed in the excerpt from *Utopia*? Highlight evidence to support each topic you identify and make annotations to explain your choices.

2. Verbal irony is when a person says one thing and means another. There is verbal irony in the rules of Utopia involving marriage. The rules are very strict, yet many of the rules have exceptions. Highlight one strict rule that has an exception in the passage. Explain both the rule and the exception using annotations.

3. In the Unit 2 introduction "The English Renaissance," you read about humanism, an intellectual movement that emphasized the ability of individuals to think and act independently, without guidance from higher authorities. Which actions of the leaders of Utopia in this excerpt might have been frowned on by European religious authorities of the time?

4. What goals might the leaders of Utopia have in mind with these rules involving marriage? What sort of society might they be trying to create? Highlight evidence that supports your answers.

5. Recall the unit's Essential Question: How do we express the complexities of being human? What do the strict rules regarding marriage suggest about the complexities of human relationships? Highlight textual evidence to support your answer.

WRITING PROMPT

The word *inquiry* refers to the process of gathering information by asking questions. Write a narrative in which the Senate in Utopia conducts an inquiry into a divorce for two spouses who are not able to get along. Include questions from both the senators and their wives, as well as answers from the people seeking the divorce. Use the excerpt from *Utopia* to inform your understanding of the country's laws about marriage and divorce. Include an example of verbal irony and an example of situational irony in your narrative.

BRAVE NEW WORLD

FICTION
Aldous Huxley
1932

INTRODUCTION

English author and philosopher Aldous Huxley is considered one of the premier intellectuals of his time, and was nominated seven times for the Nobel Prize in Literature. His dystopian page-turner *Brave New World* is more than literature—it's a warning about what the future might hold. In this excerpt, the Director of Hatcheries and Conditioning proudly explains Bokanovsky's Process, which creates up to 96 clones from a single egg.

"The principle of mass production at last applied to biology."

 FIRST READ

Excerpt from Chapter 1

1   A squat grey building of only thirty-four stories. Over the main entrance the words, Central London Hatchery and Conditioning Centre, and, in a shield, the World State's motto, Community, Identity, Stability.

2   The enormous room on the ground floor faced towards the north. Cold for all the summer beyond the panes, for all the tropical heat of the room itself, a harsh thin light glared through the windows, hungrily seeking some draped lay figure, some **pallid** shape of academic goose-flesh, but finding only the glass and nickel and bleakly shining porcelain of a laboratory. Wintriness responded to wintriness. The overalls of the workers were white, their hands gloved with a pale corpse-coloured rubber. The light was frozen, dead, a ghost. Only from the yellow barrels of the microscopes did it borrow a certain rich and living substance, lying along the polished tubes like butter, streak after luscious streak in long recession down the work tables.

3   "And this," said the Director opening the door, "is the Fertilizing Room."

4   Bent over their instruments, three hundred Fertilizers were plunged, as the Director of Hatcheries and Conditioning entered the room, in the scarcely breathing silence, the absentminded, **soliloquizing** hum or whistle, of absorbed concentration. A troop of newly arrived students, very young, pink and **callow,** followed nervously, rather abjectly, at the Director's heels. Each of them carried a note-book, in which, whenever the great man spoke, he desperately scribbled. Straight from the horse's mouth. It was a rare privilege. The DHC for Central London always made a point of personally conducting his new students round the various departments.

5   "Just to give you a general idea," he would explain to them. For of course some sort of general idea they must have, if they were to do their work

intelligently—though as little of one, if they were to be good and happy members of society, as possible. For particulars, as everyone knows, make for virtue and happiness; generalities are intellectually necessary evils. Not philosophers, but fret-sawyers and stamp collectors compose the backbone of society.

6 "Tomorrow," he would add, smiling at them with a slightly menacing geniality, "you'll be settling down to serious work. You won't have time for generalities. Meanwhile . . ."

7 Meanwhile, it was a privilege. Straight from the horse's mouth into the note-book. The boys scribbled like mad.

8 Tall and rather thin but upright, the Director advanced into the room. He had a long chin and big, rather prominent teeth, just covered, when he was not talking, by his full, floridly curved lips. Old, young? Thirty? fifty? fifty-five? It was hard to say. And anyhow the question didn't arise; in this year of stability, a.f. 632, it didn't occur to you to ask it.

9 "I shall begin at the beginning," said the DHC, and the more zealous students recorded his intention in their note-books: Begin at the beginning. "These," he waved his hand, "are the incubators." And opening an insulated door he showed them racks upon racks of numbered test-tubes. "The week's supply of ova. Kept," he explained, "at blood heat; whereas the male gametes," and here he opened another door, "they have to be kept at thirty-five instead of thirty-seven. Full blood heat sterilizes." Rams wrapped in thermogene beget no lambs.

10 Still leaning against the incubators he gave them, while the pencils scurried illegibly across the pages, a brief description of the modern fertilizing process; spoke first, of course, of its surgical introduction — "the operation undergone voluntarily for the good of Society, not to mention the fact that it carries a bonus amounting to six months' salary"; continued with some account of the technique for preserving the excised ovary alive and actively developing; passed on to a consideration of optimum temperature, salinity, viscosity; referred to the liquor in which the detached and ripened eggs were kept; and, leading his charges to the work tables, actually showed them how the liquor was drawn off from the test-tubes; how it was let out drop by drop on to the specially warmed slides of the microscopes; how the eggs which it contained were inspected for abnormalities, counted and transferred to a porous receptacle; how (and he now took them to watch the operation) this receptacle was immersed in a warm bouillon containing free-swimming spermatozoa—at a minimum concentration of one hundred thousand per cubic centimetre, he insisted; and how, after ten minutes, the container was lifted out of the liquor and its contents re-examined; how, if any of the eggs remained unfertilized, it was again immersed, and, if necessary, yet again;

how the fertilized ova went back to the incubators; where the Alphas and Betas remained until definitely bottled; while the Gammas, Deltas and Epsilons were brought out again, after only thirty-six hours, to under-go Bokanovsky's Process.

11 "Bokanovsky's Process," repeated the Director, and the students underlined the words in their little note-books.

12 One egg, one embryo, one adult—normality. But a bokanovskified egg will bud, will **proliferate,** will divide. From eight to ninety-six buds, and every bud will grow into a perfectly formed embryo, and every embryo into a full-sized adult. Making ninety-six human beings grow where only one grew before. Progress.

13 "Essentially," the DHC concluded, "bokanovskification consists of a series of arrests of development. We check the normal growth and, paradoxically enough, the egg responds by budding."

14 Responds by budding. The pencils were busy.

15 He pointed. On a very slowly moving band a rack-full of test-tubes was entering a large metal box, another rack-full was emerging. Machinery faintly purred. It took eight minutes for the tubes to go through, he told them. Eight minutes of hard X-rays being about as much as an egg can stand. A few died; of the rest, the least susceptible divided into two; most put out four buds; some eight; all were returned to the incubators, where the buds began to develop; then, after two days, were suddenly chilled, chilled and checked. Two, four, eight, the buds in their turn budded; and having budded were dosed almost to death with alcohol; consequently burgeoned again and having budded—bud out of bud out of bud were thereafter—further arrest being generally fatal—left to develop in peace. By which time the original egg was in a fair way to becoming anything from eight to ninety-six embryos—a **prodigious** improvement, you will agree, on nature. Identical twins—but not in piddling twos and threes as in the old viviparous days, when an egg would sometimes accidentally divide; actually by dozens, by scores at a time.

16 "Scores," the Director repeated and flung out his arms, as though he were distributing **largesse**. "Scores."

17 But one of the students was fool enough to ask where the advantage lay.

18 "My good boy!" The Director wheeled sharply round on him. "Can't you see? Can't you see?" He raised a hand; his expression was solemn. "Bokanovsky's Process is one of the major instruments of social stability!"

19 Major instruments of social stability.

NOTES

20 Standard men and women; in uniform batches. The whole of a small factory staffed with the products of a single bokanovskified egg.

21 "Ninety-six identical twins working ninety-six identical machines!" The voice was almost tremulous with enthusiasm.

22 "You really know where you are. For the first time in history." He quoted the planetary motto. "Community, Identity, Stability." Grand words. "If we could bokanovskify indefinitely the whole problem would be solved."

23 Solved by standard Gammas, unvarying Deltas, uniform Epsilons. Millions of identical twins. The principle of mass production at last applied to biology.

Excerpted from *Brave New World* by Aldous Huxley, published by HarperCollins Publishers.

THINK QUESTIONS

1. Describe the setting of the first chapter of *Brave New World*. Remember that setting includes details such as the time period, not just the physical locations. Support your response with textual evidence.

2. What happens in the Fertilizing Room shown on the tour? What does this room tell you about the world in which *Brave New World* is set? Cite textual evidence to support your answer.

3. What is Bokanovsky's Process? Why does the Hatchery and Conditioning Centre use this process? How is the process related to the World State's motto? Support your response with textual evidence.

4. The Latin root *sol* means "alone." Use that information and the context clues provided in the passage to determine the meaning of **soliloquizing.** Write your definition of *soliloquizing* and explain how you found it.

5. Use the context clues provided in the passage to determine the meaning of **proliferate.** Write your definition of *proliferate* and explain how you arrived at it.

CLOSE READ

Reread the excerpt from *Brave New World*. As you reread, complete the Focus Questions below. Then use your answers and annotations from the questions to help you complete the Writing Prompt.

FOCUS QUESTIONS

1. As you reread the excerpt from the first chapter of *Brave New World,* pay attention to the characterization, or the descriptions, of the workers in the Central London Hatchery and Conditioning Centre and the characterization of the new students touring the facility. How is each group described? How are the descriptions different, and what might that difference imply? Highlight evidence in the text and make annotations to explain the meaning of these differences.

2. In paragraph 5, the author explains the difference between knowing "particulars" and knowing "generalities." What difference does the author set up? What does this distinction say about the World State's priorities? Highlight evidence and write annotations to explain your ideas.

3. Irony is when an author writes one thing but means another. What is the World State's motto? Based on the description of the work at the Central London Hatchery and Conditioning Centre, how is this motto ironic? What other examples of irony does this excerpt contain? Highlight your evidence and annotate to explain your ideas.

4. Much of the excerpt is a detailed explanation of how human eggs are fertilized and of Bokanovsky's Process. What is the role of the technical language and long descriptions of this process? What does it tell the reader about the World State? Highlight your evidence and make annotations to explain your ideas.

5. Chapter 1 contains several references to animals. What purpose do these elements serve? How do they support the development of story elements? Highlight evidence from the text that will help support your ideas.

6. The Essential Question for this unit is "How do we express the complexities of being human?" How does the society in *Brave New World* view complexity in people? What is ironic, in light of this view, about the students' treatment of the Director? Highlight textual evidence from the selection to support your ideas.

WRITING PROMPT

Analyze how Huxley's choices regarding setting and characterization affect the reader's experience with *Brave New World*. How are characters introduced and described? How does Huxley use description to relate the setting to the characters? How do these story elements contribute to the overall message, or theme, of the selection? Explain any use of irony in Huxley's development of theme. Support your writing with textual evidence.

Please note that excerpts and passages in the StudySync® library and this workbook are intended as touchstones to generate interest in an author's work. The excerpts and passages do not substitute for the reading of entire texts, and StudySync® strongly recommends that students seek out and purchase the whole literary or informational work in order to experience it as the author intended. Links to online resellers are available in our digital library. In addition, complete works may be ordered through an authorized reseller by filling out and returning to StudySync® the order form enclosed in this workbook.

Reading & Writing Companion   **157**

A VALEDICTION FORBIDDING MOURNING

POETRY
John Donne
1633

INTRODUCTION

Born in **1572**, English clergyman John Donne is considered to be the leader of the metaphysical school of poetry, which is known in part for its use of complex and unusual metaphors to meld the sensory and the abstract. Donne's poem "A Valediction Forbidding Mourning" relies on one ingenious simile—that of the drafting compass—to beautifully evoke the sense of two people separated physically but deeply connected emotionally.

"Care less, eyes, lips, and hands to miss."

FIRST READ

1   As virtuous men pass mildly away,
2   And whisper to their souls to go,
3   Whilst some of their sad friends do say
4   The breath goes now, and some say, no;

5   So let us melt, and make no noise,
6   No tear floods, nor sigh-**tempests** move,
7   'Twere **profanation** of our joys
8   To tell the **laity** our love.

9   Moving of th' earth brings harms and fears,
10   Men reckon what it did and meant;
11   But trepidation of the spheres,
12   Though greater far, is innocent.

13   Dull sublunary lovers' love
14   (Whose soul is sense) cannot admit
15   Absence, because it doth remove
16   Those things which elemented it.

17   But we by a love so much refined
18   That our selves know not what it is,
19   Inter-assured of the mind,
20   Care less, eyes, lips, and hands to miss.

21   Our two souls therefore, which are one,
22   Though I must go, endure not yet
23   A **breach,** but an expansion,
24   Like gold to airy thinness beat.

NOTES

25　If they be two, they are two so
26　As stiff twin compasses are two;
27　Thy soul, the fixed foot, makes no show
28　To move, but doth, if th' other do.

29　And though it in the center sit,
30　Yet when the other far doth roam,
31　It leans and hearkens after it,
32　And grows erect, as that comes home.

33　Such wilt thou be to me, who must
34　Like th' other foot, **obliquely** run.
35　Thy firmness makes my circle just,
36　And makes me end where I begun.

THINK QUESTIONS

1.　"A Valediction Forbidding Mourning" consists of a series of comparisons. What is the first comparison, which appears in lines 1–8? Support your answer with textual evidence.

2.　The second comparison in lines 9–16 equates earthquakes with "sublunary lovers" and planetary movements with the speaker's relationship. How is this connected with physical love and spiritual love?

3.　Why might the speaker be concerned about the future of the relationship with the beloved? Support your answer with textual evidence.

4.　Use context to determine the meaning of the word **breach** as it is used in "A Valediction Forbidding Mourning." Write your definition of *breach* and tell how you got it.

5.　Remembering that the Middle English suffix *-ly* is used to create adverbs, look for context clues provided in "A Valediction Forbidding Mourning" to determine the meaning of **obliquely**. Write your definition of *obliquely* and explain how you found it.

CLOSE READ

Reread the poem "A Valediction Forbidding Mourning." As you reread, complete the Focus Questions below. Then use your answers and annotations from the questions to help you complete the Writing Prompt.

FOCUS QUESTIONS

1. As you reread the text of "A Valediction Forbidding Mourning," think about the ways in which the poem is structured as an argument. The speaker is trying to convince the speaker's beloved that they can continue to feel close to each other even when they are far apart. Summarize the sections of the argument, and explain how the sections are related.

2. Two themes in the poem are separation and spirituality. Which theme do you think is more prominent? Highlight textual evidence to support your answer and use the annotations to record your ideas.

3. Although Donne's poem is highly structured and formal in tone, he is still able to instill powerful feelings and musical language in these lines of verse. How can a poem with a formal structure avoid being emotionless and dull? Cite textual evidence to support your statements.

4. How does Donne's word choice contribute to the formal tone of the poem? Use annotations to highlight evidence from the text, taking into account other words he might have chosen.

5. One of the themes in "A Valediction Forbidding Mourning" is the pain of one person going away from another person. How does Donne use this theme to explore the complexities of being human? Cite textual evidence to support your statements.

WRITING PROMPT

How would the impact of "A Valediction Forbidding Mourning" be affected if Donne rewrote it with an open form? Which aspects of the original poem would be difficult to retain, and which would be easy to retain? Use your understanding of poetic structure and figurative language to support your analysis. Support your response with textual evidence.

TO LUCASTA, GOING TO THE WARS

POETRY
Richard Lovelace
1649

INTRODUCTION

Born into a distinguished military and legal family, the cavalier poet Richard Lovelace embroiled himself in the political affairs of 17th century England and was twice thrown in prison. While incarcerated, Lovelace wrote his most acclaimed poetry, including "To Lucasta, Going to the Wars." Some scholars believe that the "Lucasta" of the poem refers to Lucy Sacherevell, who after wrongly hearing that Lovelace had died of wounds in battle, married another man.

"To war and arms I fly."

 FIRST READ

1   Tell me not, Sweet, I am unkind,
2   That from the **nunnery**
3   Of thy **chaste** breast and quiet mind
4   To war and arms I fly.

5   True, a new **mistress** now I chase,
6   The first **foe** in the field;
7   And with a stronger faith embrace
8   A sword, a horse, a shield.

9   Yet this **inconstancy** is such
10   As you too shall adore;
11 I could not love thee, Dear, so much,
12   Loved I not Honor more.

THINK QUESTIONS

1. In "To Lucasta, Going to the Wars," where is the speaker starting from, and where is he going? Support your answer with evidence from the text.

2. What does the speaker mean by the phrase in Stanza 1, "That from the nunnery/of thy chaste breast and quiet mind"?

3. What does the speaker hope to accomplish in the poem? Use textual evidence to support your response.

4. Use context to determine the meaning of the word **chaste** as it is used in the first stanza of "To Lucasta, Going to the Wars." Write your definition of *chaste* and explain how you arrived at this definition.

5. Use the context to identify the meaning of **mistress** as it is used in Stanza 3 of "To Lucasta, Going to the Wars." Then use a dictionary to check your definition and explain how you arrived at this definition.

Please note that excerpts and passages in the StudySync® library and this workbook are intended as touchstones to generate interest in an author's work. The excerpts and passages do not substitute for the reading of entire texts, and StudySync® strongly recommends that students seek out and purchase the whole literary or informational work in order to experience it as the author intended. Links to online resellers are available in our digital library. In addition, complete works may be ordered through an authorized reseller by filling out and returning to StudySync® the order form enclosed in this workbook.

Reading & Writing
Companion
163

CLOSE READ

Reread the poem "To Lucasta, Going to the Wars." As you reread, complete the Focus Questions below. Then use your answers and annotations from the questions to help you complete the Writing Prompt.

FOCUS QUESTIONS

1. Remember that in any poem, the poet uses language economically to pack as much meaning as he can into his words. This is especially true of a short poem like "To Lucasta, Going to the Wars," where every word counts. As you look back at the text, identify words that are particularly vivid or meaningful. Highlight any unfamiliar words and look them up in the dictionary. Use annotations to note the effect of your selected words.

2. Write a short summary of what is happening in Stanza 1. Identify the connotation evoked by words like "sweet," "chaste," and "quiet." How do these words influence the theme and tone of the stanza? Use annotations to record your response.

3. How does the poet use the words "Sweet" and "Dear" in the poem? What are the dictionary definitions—denotations—of these words, and how do those definitions compare to their connotative meanings? What prior knowledge do you have that allows you to understand the emotional context of these terms?

4. Recall that paradox is a figure of speech in which a statement appears to contradict itself yet expresses a truth. Identify the paradox in lines 11–12. How do denotation and connotation work to create the paradox?

5. Use your understanding of connotation, denotation, and figurative language, such as paradox, to identify the theme and deeper meaning of the poem. Highlight evidence from the poem that will help support your ideas and use annotations to record your response.

6. Recall the unit's Essential Question: How do we express the complexities of being human? How does the speaker of "To Lucasta, Going to the Wars" express the complexity of having to choose between love and duty? Highlight evidence from the poem that supports your ideas.

WRITING PROMPT

Using the events and emotions of the poem as a guide, write a letter from the speaker of "To Lucasta, Going to the Wars" to Lucasta. Assume that the speaker has now left for the war and is writing about his experiences. Compare the realities of battle to the speaker's expectations of what "war and arms" would be like. Remember to clearly describe the setting and the speaker's emotions using vivid language with precise connotations. Conclude the letter with the speaker's hopes about the future of their relationship.

2:40 PM

app.studysync.com

ASSIGNMENTS   REVIEW   BINDER   BLASTS   LIBRARY

ysync

WRITE

ED WRITING PROJECT
LITERARY ANALYSIS

Extended Writing Project:
Literary Analysis
by StudySync

1   WRITE

Extended Writing Project Prompt and Directions:

Recall the Essential Question: How do we express th

Choose two or three selections from the unit and wr

the author uses figurative language and figures of sp

speaker or character's feelings and actions. Explain h

language to reveal aspects of the human condition.

Your essay should include:

- an introduction with a clear thesis statement
- body paragraphs with thorough analysis supported by relevant reaso
- a conclusion that effectively wraps up your essay

Font ▾   Size ▾   **B** *I* I̶ₓ A ▾ U ↶

The

I'm

Q W E R T Y U I O

A S D F G H J K L

Z X C V B N M

LITERARY ANALYSIS

WRITING PROMPT

Recall the Essential Question: How do we express the complexities of being human? Choose two or three selections from the unit and write a literary analysis focused on how the author uses figurative language and figures of speech to help readers understand a speaker or character's feelings and actions. Explain how each author uses figurative language to reveal aspects of the human condition.

Your essay should include:

- An introduction with a clear thesis statement
- Body paragraphs with thorough analysis supported by relevant reasons and evidence
- A conclusion that effectively wraps up your essay

Literary analysis is a form of **argumentative writing**. There are different purposes for argumentative writing. For example, an argument might intend to change the readers' perspective, sway them into taking action, or convince readers to accept the writer's ideas and beliefs. In a literary analysis essay, a writer makes claims about the meaning or the value of a literary work and analyzes separate parts of a text to support a conclusion about or interpretation of the work using textual evidence.

To build a strong literary analysis, writers introduce a thesis statement that makes a specific claim or interpretation about a text. They will then support their assertion with relevant evidence from literature. All quotations should be introduced and explained. The writing should stay focused on the main idea and use transition words to help create flow and make connections between supporting details as they build their argument.

The features of literary analysis writing include the following:

- An introduction with a clear thesis statement that makes a claim
- Supporting details and relevant evidence from texts
- A logical organizational structure
- Cohesive and clear relationships between ideas that build an argument or interpretation
- Citations and sources
- A conclusion

As you continue with this extended writing project, you'll receive more instructions and practice to help you craft each of the elements of literary analysis writing in your own essay.

 ## STUDENT MODEL

Before you get started on your own literary analysis essay, begin by reading this essay that one student wrote in response to the writing prompt. As you read this student model, highlight and annotate the features of literary analysis that the student included in her essay.

Feelings Hidden under Trappings and Suits:
Figurative Language in *Hamlet* and "On Monsieur's Departure"

The "human condition" encompasses the unique mental features and behaviors that separate humans from animals. Falling in love, missing a friend, or feeling self-doubt all represent parts of the human condition. In addition, mixed emotions and feelings of inner conflict play a key role in the human condition. In William Shakespeare's play *The Tragedy of Hamlet, Prince of Denmark*, readers experience the inner thoughts of a young prince in turmoil as expressed through his soliloquies. Early in the play, Hamlet's depression and grief overwhelm his private thoughts, but he must put a brave face forward if he is to avenge his father's murder. Queen Elizabeth I's poem "On Monsieur's Departure" describes the sadness felt by a speaker whose beloved abandoned her. Both Shakespeare and Elizabeth I use figures of speech to help readers understand and relate to the experience of holding intense feelings inside, hidden from public display. This act of hiding makes characters human and reveals an important aspect of the human condition.

Elizabeth I was queen of England from 1558 to 1603 ("Elizabeth I"). During her long rule she never married, despite calls from her court to find a king and produce an heir. In her poem "On Monsieur's Departure," the speaker struggles to keep her true feelings hidden. The speaker of the poem is not necessarily Elizabeth, but she would have undoubtedly understood the importance of cultivating a public image. In addition, literary scholars believe the poem was inspired by the breakup of marriage negotiations with Francis, Duke of Anjou, a one-time suitor to Elizabeth (Abrams 998). The speaker sets up her dilemma in the first line: "I...dare not show my discontent." The use of the verb "dare" implies that a strong force keeps her from showing her grief. She continues the use of strong language in the second line: "I love, and yet am forced to seem to hate." Here the speaker clarifies her problem—she is in love with someone, but the outside world "forces" her to "seem to hate." The use of the word "seem" is important. No one can actually force her to hate a person, but she can pretend. The whole stanza comprises a list of paradoxes—figures of speech that seem to be contradictions but actually reveal truth. The truth in this case is that the feelings projected on the outside of a person may be entirely different from what he or she is actually feeling inside.

Like Elizabeth's speaker, Hamlet is torn between his true, inner feelings and the image he needs to project in public. In Act I, scene ii, when Hamlet sees his uncle Claudius a month after his father's death, Claudius addresses Hamlet's grief: "How is it that the clouds still hang on you?" (Shakespeare). Hamlet replies that what they see is only the tip of the iceberg. He hangs on his mother's use of the word "seem"—much like Elizabeth's speaker—when he says:

> Seems, madam? Nay, it is, I know not "seems."
> 'Tis not alone my inky cloak, good mother,
> Nor customary suits of solemn black,
> Nor windy suspiration of forc'd breath,
> No, nor the fruitful river in the eye, . . .
> Together with all forms, moods, shapes of grief,
> That can denote me truly. These indeed seem,
> For they are actions that a man might play,
> But I have that within which passes show,
> These but the trappings and the suits of woe.

Here, Shakespeare uses figurative and descriptive language to convey Hamlet's hidden emotions. Hamlet may be dressed in mourning ("customary suits of solemn black"), sighing ("windy suspiration of forc'd breath"), and crying ("fruitful river in the eye"), but his true grief is on a deeper level inside. The "windy suspiration" is an example of hyperbole. The exaggeration gives the feeling that Hamlet's sighs are bigger and more poignant than the sighs of other people. The metaphor of crying as a "fruitful river" shows Hamlet's grief as endless and rushing, like a river. Later in the speech, Hamlet uses a metaphor to compare himself to an actor, saying what his family sees is "actions that a man might play." Anyone can "play" at grief by doing what Hamlet describes, but he has "that within which passes show"—something hidden and abstract, yet real. Later in the scene, Hamlet realizes he needs to better conceal his emotions, and he ends his first soliloquy with the metaphor "But break my heart, for I must hold my tongue." It is the first indication that Hamlet will "hold his tongue" and avoid taking his revenge, or that he might not act at all.

In Act II, scene ii, Hamlet again compares himself to an actor. In a soliloquy, Shakespeare uses hyperbole to describe how an actor would behave had he experienced a real tragedy: "He would drown the stage with tears, / And cleave the general ear with horrid speech." Hamlet wants to express himself in this way, but he cannot. Comparing oneself to another is an aspect of the human condition. Hamlet wonders if he is a "coward," and then he says he is "pigeon-liver'd" and lacks "gall." This implies that the actor represents the opposite—a brave man with guts. The speaker of "On Monsieur's Departure" also insults herself when she says: "For I am soft, and made of melting snow." Using this metaphor, the speaker admits her own weakness. Some readers may think that the speaker describes herself as "soft" to garner sympathy, because women, especially in Elizabeth's time, were expected to be weak. But, on closer examination, the line is really another connection to the paradoxes of the first stanza. Melting snow is neither water nor snow. It stands in between phases, which is what the speaker wants to be out of, as she says later: "Let me float or sink, be high or low." It is the feeling of being stuck in between that is so painful to the speaker.

Many people, especially those in high places—say a queen or a prince—need to cultivate a public persona to avoid appearing weak. This limit on behavior develops from the complications of human social structures. Literature such as "On Monsieur's Departure" and *The Tragedy of Hamlet, Prince of Denmark* use

Please note that excerpts and passages in the StudySync® library and this workbook are intended as touchstones to generate interest in an author's work. The excerpts and passages do not substitute for the reading of entire texts, and StudySync® strongly recommends that students seek out and purchase the whole literary or informational work in order to experience it as the author intended. Links to online resellers are available in our digital library. In addition, complete works may be ordered through an authorized reseller by filling out and returning to StudySync® the order form enclosed in this workbook.

Reading & Writing Companion **169**

NOTES

figurative language to explore the line all people have to walk between the expression and concealment of feelings. What society deems acceptable plays a central role in what people determine to share or conceal. Deciding what to share or keep hidden inside during social interactions forms an essential part—and challenge—of what make humans human. The use of figurative language in these works gives resonating, tangible expression to these unsaid, intangible feelings.

Works Cited

Abrams, M. H., ed. *The Norton Anthology of English Literature,* Sixth Edition. New York: W. W. Norton & Company, 1993. Print.

"Elizabeth I." *Encyclopædia Britannica.* Encyclopædia Britannica Online. Encyclopædia Britannica Inc., 2014. Web. 27 Aug. 2014.

Elizabeth I. "On Monsieur's Departure." *StudySync.* BookheadEd Learning, LLC., 2015. Web. 4 May 2015.

Shakespeare, William. *The Tragedy of Hamlet, Prince of Denmark. StudySync.* BookheadEd Learning, LLC., 2015. Web. 4 May 2015.

 THINK QUESTIONS

1. Which sentence from the first paragraph states the main idea of the essay?

2. What point does the writer make about Hamlet's outward signs of mourning? How does she support this idea?

3. What comparison between the two texts does the author make in the fourth paragraph? How does this comparison support the writer's thesis statement?

4. Thinking about the writing prompt, which selections or other resources would you like to use to create your own literary analysis essay? What are some ideas that you may want to develop into your own piece?

5. 5. Based on what you have read, listened to, or researched, how would you answer the question: *How do we express the complexities of being human?* What are some ways authors in this unit have expressed what it's like to be human?

NOTES

EXTENDED WRITING PROJECT
PREWRITE

PREWRITE

WRITING PROMPT

Recall the Essential Question: How do we express the complexities of being human? Choose two or three selections from the unit and write a literary analysis focused on how the author uses figurative language and figures of speech to help readers understand a speaker or character's feelings and actions. Explain how each author uses figurative language to reveal aspects of the human condition.

Your essay should include:

- An introduction with a clear thesis statement
- Body paragraphs with thorough analysis supported by relevant reasons and evidence
- A conclusion that effectively wraps up your essay

As you prewrite your literary analysis, think back to the texts you've read so far in this unit. Which texts have vivid figurative language or figures of speech? Do any examples of figurative language stick out in your mind as particularly fresh or beautiful? What new ideas about the human condition do these texts include? Do any of the texts make you think about the human condition in a new way?

Make a list of the answers as you brainstorm these questions for two or three texts. As you write down your ideas, look for patterns that begin to emerge. Which two or three texts have similar ideas? What claim about the human condition can you make based on the texts? What relevant evidence can you gather to support that claim? Answering these questions may help you solidify the ideas you want to discuss in your essay. Use this model to help you get started with your own prewriting:

Text: "On Monsieur's Departure"
Figurative Language: "For I am soft, and made of melting snow" (metaphor)
Comment on the human condition: It is painful to be in an in-between state.

SKILL:
THESIS
STATEMENT

 **DEFINE**

In a literary analysis essay, the thesis statement introduces the writer's interpretation of the literary text to be analyzed. The thesis statement expresses the writer's central or main idea about that text, a position the writer will develop in the body of the essay. A vague, obvious truth does not make a good thesis statement; a thesis statement should be specific and clearly answer the prompt. The thesis statement usually appears in the essay's introductory paragraph and is often the introduction's last sentence. The rest of the paragraphs in the essay all support the thesis statement with facts, evidence, and examples.

 IDENTIFICATION AND APPLICATION

In a literary analysis essay, a thesis statement

- provides the key idea of the writer's interpretation of a text or texts.
- is a precise interpretation or claim based on relevant textual evidence.
- lets the reader know what to expect in the body of the essay.
- sets up the essay so that the reader has a clear idea where the analysis is heading.
- appears in the first paragraph.

 MODEL

The writer of the student model literary analysis essay "Feelings Hidden under Trappings and Suits" puts the thesis statement near the end of the first paragraph. The writer sets the stage for this thesis by tying the unit's essential question to two works to be discussed in the analysis, thus answering the prompt:

Copyright © BookheadEd Learning, LLC

The "human condition" encompasses the unique mental features and behaviors that separate humans from animals. Falling in love, missing a friend, or feeling self-doubt all represent parts of the human condition. In addition, mixed emotions and feelings of inner conflict play a key role in the human condition. In William Shakespeare's play *The Tragedy of Hamlet, Prince of Denmark,* readers experience the inner thoughts of a young prince in turmoil as expressed through his soliloquies. Early in the play, Hamlet's depression and grief overwhelm his private thoughts, but he must put a brave face forward if he is to avenge his father's murder. Queen Elizabeth I's poem "On Monsieur's Departure" describes the sadness felt by a speaker whose beloved abandoned her. **Both Shakespeare and Elizabeth I use figures of speech to help readers understand and relate to the experience of holding intense feelings inside, hidden from public display.** This act of hiding makes characters human and reveals an important aspect of the human condition.

Notice the bold-faced thesis statement. The student's thesis statement focuses on the figurative language used in the play and the poem that she will analyze in the essay. The thesis explains the writer's interpretation of the figurative language: it serves to help readers understand the characters' experiences with hidden feelings. The interpretation in the thesis involves connecting figures of speech and the theme.

The thesis statement is strong in that it shows the reader what direction the essay will take. The reader can expect to learn how each text treats hidden feelings and how figures of speech emphasize this theme.

PRACTICE

Write a thesis statement for your literary analysis that articulates your main idea or claim in relation to the essay prompt. When you are finished, trade with a partner and offer each other feedback. How clear was the writer's main point or claim? Is it obvious what this essay will focus on? Does it specifically address the prompt? Offer each other suggestions, and remember that they are most helpful when they are constructive.

Please note that excerpts and passages in the StudySync® library and this workbook are intended as touchstones to generate interest in an author's work. The excerpts and passages do not substitute for the reading of entire texts, and StudySync® strongly recommends that students seek out and purchase the whole literary or informational work in order to experience it as the author intended. Links to online resellers are available in our digital library. In addition, complete works may be ordered through an authorized reseller by filling out and returning to StudySync® the order form enclosed in this workbook.

Reading & Writing Companion **173**

SKILL:
ORGANIZE
INFORMATIONAL
WRITING

 DEFINE

There are many choices available for **organizing informational writing**. All of them share one common goal: to structure the analysis, explanation, or process in a clear and logical fashion appropriate to the task or purpose for writing. This will allow the writer to better understand how the relevant information should fall into place within the article or essay. If the purpose is to depict a series of historical events, a **chronological or time-order structure** might work best. If the purpose is to describe steps in a process, a **sequential structure** might be more appropriate to the task. If the purpose is to show how these events build upon one another, a **cause-and-effect structure,** which can be quite similar to the chronological structure, might be more effective. If two or more texts or ideas are being analyzed together, a **compare-and-contrast** structure would help the reader mentally form one related group of ideas and information to determine how they relate to another group of ideas and information.

IDENTIFICATION AND APPLICATION

To answer a writing prompt involving literary analysis, the writer should choose an organizational structure that addresses the requirements of the prompt. The prompt for Unit 2 requires the following: (1) the writer chooses two to three selections from Unit 2, (2) the writer analyzes figurative language to show a speaker's or character's feelings and actions and (3) the writer chooses figurative language that reveals aspects of the human condition.

An organizational plan for addressing the prompt might have the following compare and contrast structure:

- The introduction includes a clear thesis statement. The thesis must significantly address an aspect of the human condition. The introduction also indicates which literary texts the writer will be analyzing.

Copyright © BookheadEd Learning, LLC

- For each literary text that is analyzed, there is at least one paragraph providing examples of figurative language from that text that help a reader understand the character or speaker's thoughts and feelings, and that help reveal an aspect of the human condition.
- Body paragraphs also identify similarities and differences between the ways the various texts' characters or speakers comment on the human condition.
- Transitional words and phrases help show how ideas are connected.
- A conclusion revisits the thesis and summarizes its importance.

 MODEL

The author of the student model literary analysis "Feelings Hidden under Trappings and Suits" chose to discuss the Unit 2 texts *The Tragedy of Hamlet* and "On Monsieur's Departure."

The writer reread the selections and found examples of figurative language that seemed to answer the prompt. Then she used the following table to organize ideas generated during prewriting. The table helps the writer organize the body of the essay and ensure that all ideas support the thesis statement and answer the prompt.

LITERARY TEXT	FIGURATIVE LANGUAGE	INTERPRETATION AND CONNECTION TO HUMAN CONDITION
"On Monsieur's Departure"	"'I love, and yet am forced to seem to hate'"	The feelings projected on the outside of a person may be entirely different from what he or she is actually feeling inside.
Hamlet	"'But I have that within which passes show, These but the trappings and the suits of woe.'"	His true grief is on a deeper level inside.

The information in the second row of the table serves as a key idea in the first body paragraph of the essay. The third row serves as a point of organization for the second and third body paragraphs.

 PRACTICE

Fill out a version of the three-column chart from the model using your chosen selections from the unit.

 DEFINE

In informative and argumentative writing, a writer develops the thesis statement with relevant information, called **supporting details**. Relevant information consists of any fact, definition, detail, example, or quotation that is important to the reader's understanding of the topic and is closely related to the thesis or claim. Supporting details can be found in a variety of places, but to be relevant they must provide support for the thesis. Relevant supporting details include the following:

- Facts important to understanding ideas
- Research related to the thesis
- Quotations from experts or other authoritative sources
- Conclusions of scientific findings and studies
- Excerpts from a literary text

Writers can choose supporting details from many sources. Reference books, articles in scholarly journals, news accounts, graphs, biographies, critical reviews, and authoritative websites can all provide relevant information for source material. The writer must be careful to evaluate the quality of information to determine which sources are most important and most closely related to the thesis. If the information doesn't relate to the topic or if the information doesn't strengthen the thesis, it is not relevant.

IDENTIFICATION AND APPLICATION

Step 1:

Review your thesis statement. To identify relevant supporting details, ask this question: What is my key interpretation for this literary analysis? Here is the thesis statement from the student model:

Please note that excerpts and passages in the StudySync® library and this workbook are intended as touchstones to generate interest in an author's work. The excerpts and passages do not substitute for the reading of entire texts, and StudySync® strongly recommends that students seek out and purchase the whole literary or informational work in order to experience it as the author intended. Links to online resellers are available in our digital library. In addition, complete works may be ordered through an authorized reseller by filling out and returning to StudySync® the order form enclosed in this workbook.

Reading & Writing Companion   **177**

Both Shakespeare and Elizabeth I use figures of speech to help readers understand and relate to the experience of holding intense feelings inside, hidden from public display.

The key interpretation is that the two authors are revealing an aspect of the human condition by using figures of speech to show how people sometimes keep their true emotions hidden inside.

Step 2:

When answering the extended writing prompt, you need to ask yourself which passages in your chosen texts would best support your key interpretation, or claim. The writer of the student model chose a poem and a play. The writer needed to find strong support in both texts to craft an effective literary analysis.

Here is a quotation that the writer chose from "On Monsieur's Departure" to support her thesis:

> **I love, and yet am forced to seem to hate.**

This is a figure of speech called a paradox: it seems like a contradiction but it actually reveals truth. The speaker feels forced to hide her feelings by showing the opposite. Notice how well this connects with the thesis above.

The other text that the student chose to analyze in the literary analysis essay is *Hamlet*. Here is one of the quotations the writer chose to use as supporting evidence:

> **But break my heart, for I must hold my tongue.**

"Hold my tongue" is a figure of speech that means not talking when you want to say something. This is another way of holding in feelings, so it connects with the interpretation in the thesis.

 MODEL

Sometimes a longer quotation serves as a supporting detail in a literary analysis. Authors rarely sum up ideas in one or two nice sentences. The relevant evidence may be spread across several sentences or lines and require the reader to use inference skills. The writer of the student model found some strong supporting evidence in a group of lines spoken by Hamlet. The writer uses some introductory sentences to show how the quotation is relevant to the thesis and to draw a connection to the other text in the analysis:

In Act I, scene ii, when Hamlet sees his uncle Claudius a month after his father's death, Claudius addresses Hamlet's grief: "How is it that the clouds still hang on you?" Hamlet replies that what they see is only the tip of the iceberg. He hangs on his mother's use of the word "seem"—much like Elizabeth's speaker—when he says:

> Seems, madam? Nay, it is, I know not "seems."
> 'Tis not alone my inky cloak, good mother,
> Nor customary suits of solemn black,
> Nor windy suspiration of forc'd breath,
> No, nor the fruitful river in the eye, . . .
> Together with all forms, moods, shapes of grief,
> That can denote me truly. These indeed seem,
> For they are actions that a man might play,
> But I have that within which passes show,
> These but the trappings and the suits of woe.

The key line is the next-to-last one: "But I have that within which passes show." This means Hamlet is holding something inside. The previous lines of the quotation provide the context for the reader to infer what is being held "within": negative emotions such as grief. Hamlet indicates that the emotions hidden inside him are much worse than the gloom he is showing on the outside, "the trappings and the suits of woe." Indeed, words from this line of the quotation are used in the title of the literary analysis.

Please note that excerpts and passages in the StudySync® library and this workbook are intended as touchstones to generate interest in an author's work. The excerpts and passages do not substitute for the reading of entire texts, and StudySync® strongly recommends that students seek out and purchase the whole literary or informational work in order to experience it as the author intended. Links to online resellers are available in our digital library. In addition, complete works may be ordered through an authorized reseller by filling out and returning to StudySync® the order form enclosed in this workbook.

Reading & Writing Companion

179

PLAN

WRITING PROMPT

Recall the Essential Question: How do we express the complexities of being human? Choose two or three selections from the unit and write a literary analysis focused on how the author uses figurative language and figures of speech to help readers understand a speaker or character's feelings and actions. Explain how each author uses figurative language to reveal aspects of the human condition.

Your essay should include:

- An introduction with a clear thesis statement
- Body paragraphs with thorough analysis supported by relevant reasons and evidence
- A conclusion that effectively wraps up your essay

Review the information you listed in your three-column chart listing two to three selections, figurative language examples, and an interpretation about the human condition. Review your preliminary thesis from the Thesis lesson. This organized information and your thesis statement will help you create a road map to use for writing your essay.

Consider the following questions as you create the road map you'll use to develop your main paragraph topics and their supporting details:

- What vivid examples of figurative language do your chosen selections have?
- How do you interpret these instances of figurative language?
- What does the figurative language show about the character or speaker?
- How does your interpretation of the figurative language connect to the human condition?

Copyright © BookheadEd Learning, LLC

 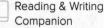

- What aspects about the human condition does the author reveal through the figurative language used in the text?

Use this model to get started with your road map:

Thesis statement: Both Shakespeare and Elizabeth I use figures of speech to help readers understand and relate to the experience of holding intense feelings inside, hidden from public display.

Paragraph 1 Topic: How figurative language in "On Monsieur's Departure" reveals an aspect of the human condition
 Supporting Detail #1: Quote containing figurative language
 Supporting Detail #2: Interpretation

Paragraph 2 Topic: How figurative language in *Hamlet* reveals an aspect of the human condition
 Supporting Detail #1: Quote containing figurative language
 Supporting Detail #2: Interpretation

Paragraph 3 Topic: *Hamlet* and "On Monsieur's Departure"
 Supporting Detail #1: Quotations
 Supporting Detail #2: Interpretations

SKILL: INTRODUCTIONS

⭐ DEFINE

The **introduction** to an argumentative text usually states the **main idea** or **claim** that will be examined or argued in the subsequent paragraphs. In addition, the writer may try to engage or "hook" the reader with an interesting piece of relevant information that sets up the significance of the analysis or the process to be described. For example, a scientific article might pique the reader's interest by promising to explain how an archeological discovery relates to our current understanding of backaches, or a recipe will entice the reader with pictures of a luscious chocolate cake and a teasing line about how it looks rich but costs next-to-nothing to make. The introduction may also set forth the basic structure of the text that will follow, providing readers with a roadmap of sorts before the trip officially begins.

••• IDENTIFICATION AND APPLICATION

- In argumentative writing, the introduction should indicate what type of claim the writer will be making. The writing might be in the form of a report, a news article, or an interpretation of literature.

- The introduction should clearly indicate the **topic** of the essay and state the **thesis statement**, or claim, that the author will be supporting. The thesis should be specific and not be an obvious truth that everyone agrees with.

- A strongly stated thesis engages readers' attention and makes them more likely to read the whole analysis. A dull thesis with generic language may cause readers to stop at the end of the introduction.

STUDYSYNC LIBRARY | Extended Writing Project

- It is customary to build interest in the topic by beginning the introduction with a **"hook,"** or a way to grab the reader's attention. This awakens the reader's natural curiosity and encourages him or her to read on. Hooks can ask open-ended questions, make connections to the reader or to life, or introduce a surprising fact.

- In a literary analysis, the introduction should give information about the literary text being analyzed. It should also provide some background information about the text to provide context for the reader.

 MODEL

The writer of the student model literary analysis "Feelings Hidden under Trappings and Suits" uses the first paragraph of the essay as the introduction. The writer begins by explaining the topic and then introduces the two texts being analyzed. Then the writer presents the thesis statement.

> **The "human condition" encompasses the unique mental features and behaviors that separate humans from animals.** *Falling in love, missing a friend, or feeling self-doubt all represent parts of the human condition. In addition, mixed emotions and feelings of inner conflict play a key role in the human condition. In* **William Shakespeare's play** *The Tragedy of Hamlet, Prince of Denmark,* *readers experience the inner thoughts of a young prince in turmoil as expressed through his soliloquies. Early in the play, Hamlet's depression and grief overwhelm his private thoughts, but he must put a brave face forward if he is to avenge his father's murder.* **Queen Elizabeth I's poem "On Monsieur's Departure"** *describes the sadness felt by a speaker whose beloved abandoned her.* **Both Shakespeare and Elizabeth I use figures of speech to help readers understand and relate to the experience of holding intense feelings inside, hidden from public display.** *This act of hiding makes characters human and reveals an important aspect of the human condition.*

The topic of the literary analysis essay, as required by the extended writing prompt, is how authors use figurative language to express the human condition. The writer begins the essay by explaining what the phrase "human condition" means. After defining the topic, the writer gives a couple of examples to reinforce the reader's understanding and serve as a hook. Next, the writer indicates that the literary analysis will cover a play by William Shakespeare and a poem by Elizabeth I. The thesis statement is an interpretation that connects a theme that appears in both texts.

Reading & Writing Companion **183**

 PRACTICE

Write an introduction for your literary analysis that includes a hook, the topic, and the thesis statement, or your claim. When you are finished, trade with a partner and offer each other feedback. How convincing is the language of your partner's thesis statement or claim? How clear is the topic? Were you hooked? Offer each other suggestions, and remember that they are most helpful when they are constructive.

SKILL: BODY PARAGRAPHS AND TRANSITIONS

 DEFINE

Body paragraphs are the section of the essay between the introduction and conclusion paragraphs. This is where you support your thesis statement by developing your main points with relevant evidence, or supporting details, from the text and your own analysis. Typically, each body paragraph will focus on one main point or idea to create clarity. The main point of each body paragraph must support the thesis statement or claim.

In each body paragraph, a writer needs to clarify the relationship between his or her ideas and evidence. To make sure the reader follows all the ideas put forth in the essay, a writer needs to provide **clarification**. He or she does this by using **transitions**. Transitions are connecting words and phrases that clarify the relationships among ideas in a text. Transitions work at three different levels: within a sentence, between paragraphs, and to indicate organizational structure. By adding transition words or phrases to the beginning or end of a paragraph, writers guide readers smoothly through the text.

In addition, transition words and phrases help writers make connections between words within a sentence. Conjunctions such as *and, or,* and *but* and prepositions such as *with, beyond,* and *inside* show the relationships between words. Transitions help writers create **cohesion**. In writing, cohesion means having all your sentences closely linked to each other and to the thesis statement.

IDENTIFICATION AND APPLICATION

- Body paragraphs are the section of the essay between the introduction and conclusion paragraphs. The body paragraphs provide the reasons and evidence needed to support the claim a writer makes in his or her thesis statement. Typically, writers develop one main idea per body paragraph.

- A body paragraph could be structured as follows:
  - › **Topic sentence:** The topic sentence is the first sentence of your body paragraph and clearly states the main point of the paragraph. It's important that your topic sentence develops your thesis statement.
  - › **Evidence #1:** Present evidence to support your topic sentence. Evidence can be relevant facts, definitions, concrete details, quotations, or other information and examples.
  - › **Analysis/Explanation #1:** After presenting evidence, you will need to analyze that evidence and explain how it supports your main idea and, in effect, your thesis statement.
  - › **Evidence #2:** Provide a second piece of evidence to further support your main idea.
  - › **Analysis/Explanation #2:** Analyze this second piece of evidence and explain how it supports your topic sentence and, in effect, your thesis statement.
  - › **Concluding sentence:** After presenting your evidence, you need to wrap up your main idea and transition to the next paragraph in your conclusion sentence.

- Transition words help readers understand the flow of ideas and concepts within a paragraph and between paragraphs.
  - › Some of the most useful transitions are words that indicate that the ideas in one paragraph are building on or adding to those in another. Examples include: *furthermore, therefore, in addition, moreover, by extension, in order to,* etc.

- Clarify ideas by varying your syntax, or sentence structure.
  - › Use a combination of simple, complex, and compound sentences.

 MODEL

In the student model essay "Feelings Hidden under Trappings and Suits: Figurative Language in *Hamlet* and 'On Monsieur's Departure,'" the first body paragraph aims to analyze the figurative language in "On Monsieur's Departure." Recall the essay's thesis statement:

> *Both Shakespeare and Elizabeth I use figures of speech to help readers understand and relate to the experience of holding intense feelings inside, hidden from public display. This act of hiding makes characters human and reveals an important aspect of the human condition.*

NOTES

The writer begins the first body paragraph with some background information on the poem. The third sentence is topic sentence, which introduces the paragraph's main idea: "In her poem 'On Monsieur's Departure,' the speaker struggles to keep her true feelings hidden." A few sentences later, the writer introduces her first piece of evidence from the text:

> The speaker sets up her dilemma in the first line: "I . . . dare not show my discontent."

Then the writer begins to analyze and explain why she included this evidence.

> The use of the verb "dare" implies that a strong force keeps her from showing her grief. She continues the use of strong language in the second line: "I love, and yet am forced to seem to hate." Here the speaker clarifies her problem—she is in love with someone, but the outside world "forces" her to "seem to hate." The use of the word "seem" is important. No one can actually force her to hate a person, but she can pretend.

The writer presents a detailed explanation of the vivid language in the first two lines of the poem. While the explanation is not incorrect, it does not support the writer's claim that Elizabeth uses figures of speech to express her intense feelings. The body paragraph then introduces the idea of figures of speech without any evidence:

> The whole stanza comprises a list of paradoxes—figures of speech that seem to be contradictions but actually reveal truth. The truth in this case is that the feelings projected on the outside of a person may be entirely different from what he or she is actually feeling inside.

While this analysis is not incorrect, it is not supported by the evidence presented by the writer. Overall, the paragraph needs to clarify the relationship between the thesis statement and the ideas presented in this body paragraph.

 PRACTICE

Write one body paragraph for your literary analysis that follows the suggested format. When you are finished, trade with a partner and offer each other feedback. How effective is the topic sentence at stating the main point of the paragraph? How strong is the evidence used to support the topic sentence? Are all quotes and paraphrased evidence cited properly? Did the analysis thoroughly support the topic sentence? Offer each other suggestions, and remember that they are most helpful when they are constructive.

SKILL: CONCLUSIONS

⭐ DEFINE

A strong and effective **conclusion** should follow from and support the information or explanation that was presented in the preceding text. It should **restate the central or main idea** in some way and articulate the significance of the topic, noting any interesting or important implications the analysis or explanation may have for the reader. Perhaps most importantly, it should provide the reader with a sense of closure, the satisfying feeling that the central idea has been thoroughly addressed.

••• IDENTIFICATION AND APPLICATION

When your composition is a response to a writing prompt, it is a good idea to use the conclusion to review how your essay has met the requirements of the writing prompt. Recall the extended writing prompt for this unit:

Recall the Essential Question: How do we express the complexities of being human?

Write a literary analysis. Choose two to three selections from the unit and analyze how the author uses figurative language and figures of speech to help readers understand a speaker or character's feelings and actions. Explain how each author uses figurative language to reveal aspects of the human condition.

In a response to this prompt, the writer will include most or all of the following in his or her conclusion:

- The thesis statement/claim
- The aspects of the human condition that the essay touches on
- The literary texts discussed in the prompt
- Types of figurative language used in the texts

NOTES

The order of these elements is not important, except that they should be organized logically and with transitions. Consider examining the conclusion side by side with the introduction, which includes the same information. Remember, the conclusion is the writer's way of referring back to this information in a way that will help the reader remember where they started. Ultimately, a writer will use the conclusion to, in some way, connect his or her ideas to the readers.

 ## MODEL

The author of the student model literary analysis "Feelings Hidden under Trappings and Suits" created a flow chart to outline the conclusion to the analysis.

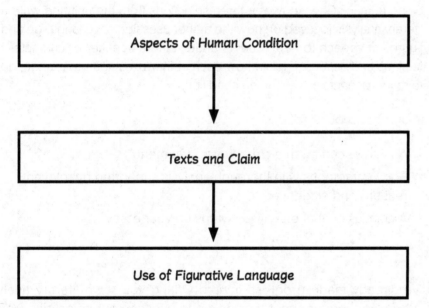

The graphic organizer shows that the conclusion will begin with a review of the ideas about the human condition included in the literary analysis. Then the conclusion will review the texts analyzed and the claim made. It will finish by explaining how the figurative language reveals human complexities.

PRACTICE

Write a conclusion for your literary analysis essay. When you are finished, trade with a partner and offer each other feedback. How effectively did the writer restate the main points of the essay in the conclusion? What final thought did the writer leave you with? Offer each other suggestions, and remember that they are most helpful when they are constructive.

NOTES

EXTENDED WRITING PROJECT
DRAFT

DRAFT

WRITING PROMPT

Recall the Essential Question: How do we express the complexities of being human? Choose two or three selections from the unit and write a literary analysis focused on how the author uses figurative language and figures of speech to help readers understand a speaker or character's feelings and actions. Explain how each author uses figurative language to reveal aspects of the human condition.

Your essay should include:

- An introduction with a clear thesis statement
- Body paragraphs with thorough analysis supported by relevant reasons and evidence
- A conclusion that effectively wraps up your essay

You've already made progress toward writing your own literary analysis essay. You've thought about the topic and chosen your selections. You've identified what you want to claim about how the authors use figurative language to express the human condition in characters. You've decided how to organize information, and gathered supporting details and relevant evidence. Now it's time to write a draft.

When drafting, ask yourself these questions:

- How can I improve my hook to make it more appealing?
- What can I do to clarify my thesis statement?
- Which relevant facts, strong details, and interesting quotations should I include in each body paragraph to support the thesis statement and make it a strong claim?

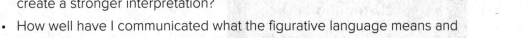

- Would more precise language or different details about these texts create a stronger interpretation?
- How well have I communicated what the figurative language means and what it communicates about the human condition?
- What final thought do I want to leave with my readers?

Using your roadmap and your other prewriting materials, write a draft of your essay. Remember that writing a literary analysis begins with an introduction and presents a thesis statement. Body paragraphs provide supporting details and relevant information. A concluding paragraph restates or reinforces your thesis statement. An effective conclusion can also do more—it can leave a lasting impression on your readers. Before you submit your draft, read it over carefully. You want to be sure that you've responded to all aspects of the prompt.

REVISE

WRITING PROMPT

Recall the Essential Question: How do we express the complexities of being human? Choose two or three selections from the unit and write a literary analysis focused on how the author uses figurative language and figures of speech to help readers understand a speaker or character's feelings and actions. Explain how each author uses figurative language to reveal aspects of the human condition.

Your essay should include:

- An introduction with a clear thesis statement
- Body paragraphs with thorough analysis supported by relevant reasons and evidence
- A conclusion that effectively wraps up your essay

You have written a draft of your literary analysis essay. You have also received input from your peers about how to improve it. Now you are going to revise your draft.

Here are some recommendations to help you revise.

- Review the suggestions made by your peers.
- Focus on maintaining a formal style. A formal style suits your purpose—giving information about a serious topic. It also fits your audience—students, teachers, and other readers interested in learning more about your topic.
  › As you revise, eliminate any slang.
  › Remove any first-person pronouns such as *I, me,* or *mine* and instances of addressing readers as *you*. These are more suitable to a writing style that is informal, personal, and conversational.

NOTES

> If you include your personal opinions, remove them. Your essay should be clear, direct, and unbiased.

- After you have revised elements of style, think about whether there is anything else you can do to improve your essay's information or organization.

  > Do you need to add any new details to your essay? Is there a particularly moving example of figurative language you could add?

  > Do you make any assertions that are not supported by quotations from the selections? Be sure to cite your sources.

  > Can you substitute a more precise word for a word that is general or dull?

  > Consider your organization. Would your essay flow better if you strengthened the transitions between paragraphs?

- As you add new details or change information, check your punctuation.

  > Check that you spelled names and other words correctly.

NOTES

SKILL:
SOURCES AND
CITATIONS

⭐ DEFINE

When writing an informative/explanatory, argumentative, or literary analysis essay, writers cannot simply make up information or rely on their own subjective experiences or opinions. To thoroughly support the treatment and analysis of their topics, writers need to include information from relevant, accurate, and reliable sources and cite, or acknowledge, them properly. Writers should keep track of these sources as they research and plan their work. When it comes time to write, they can use this information to acknowledge the sources when necessary within the text. If they don't, authors can be accused of **plagiarism,** or stealing someone else's words and ideas. In some academic texts, writers may be asked to provide sources and citations in **footnotes** or **endnotes,** which link specific references within the essay to the correlating pages or chapters in an outside source. In addition to internal citations, writers may also need to provide a full list of sources in a **Works Cited** section or standard **bibliography**.

That means any facts, quotations, statistics, or statements you include that are not common knowledge. **Sources** are the documents and information that an author uses to research his or her writing.

Some sources are **primary sources**. A primary source is a firsthand account of thoughts or events by the individual who experienced them. Examples of primary sources include letters, photographs, official documents, diaries or journals, autobiographies or memoirs, eyewitness accounts and interviews, audio recordings and radio broadcasts, and works of art.

Other sources are **secondary sources**. A secondary source analyzes and interprets primary sources. Some examples of secondary sources include encyclopedia articles, textbooks, commentary or criticisms, histories, documentary films, and news analyses.

Citations are notes that give information about the sources an author used in his or her writing. Citations are required whenever authors quote others' words or refer to others' ideas in their writing. Citations let readers know who originally came up with those words and ideas.

 IDENTIFICATION AND APPLICATION

- All sources must be **credible** and **accurate**. When writing a literary analysis, look for sources from experts in the topic you are writing about.
  - › When researching online, look for URLs that contain ".gov" (government agencies), ".edu" (colleges and universities) and ".org" (museums and other non-profit organizations).
  - › Don't neglect respected print sources. Most scholars do not publish online.

- Include a citation to give credit to any source, whether primary or secondary, that is quoted exactly. Make sure the quotation is presented in quotation marks. There are several different ways to cite a source.
  - › If the author's name is mentioned in the essay, include the page number where the quotation can be located: Shakespeare uses an allusion to a classical myth: "For Hecuba? / What's Hecuba to him, or he to Hecuba, / That he should weep for her? " (83).
  - › If the author's name does not appear in the text, include the author's name and the page number in parentheses at the end of the sentence in which the quote appears: The allusion to a classical myth makes readers think of crying widows: "For Hecuba? / What's Hecuba to him, or he to Hecuba, / That he should weep for her? " (Shakespeare 83).
  - › If there is no author, use the title of the work: Elizabeth I was born in 1533 to King Henry VIII's second wife, Anne Boleyn ("Elizabeth I").
  - › For online sources, as with the online encyclopedia above, no page number is needed.

- Citations are also necessary when a writer borrows ideas or takes facts from another source, even if the writer paraphrases, or puts those ideas in his or her own words. Follow the same citation rules as for exact quotations.

- At the end of the essay, include a Works Cited list with full bibliographical information on each source cited, formatted correctly in MLA style.

 MODEL

The writer of the student model essay "Feelings Hidden under Trappings and Suits: Figurative Language in *Hamlet* and 'On Monsieur's Departure'" used four sources in writing the literary analysis essay. In addition to the two texts she chose to analyze, the writer found background information in two reference sources: a literature anthology and an online encyclopedia.

The writer included the two reference sources in the second paragraph:

> Elizabeth I was queen of England from 1558 to 1603 (**"Elizabeth I"**). During her long rule she never married, despite calls from her court to find a king and produce an heir. In her poem "On Monsieur's Departure," the speaker struggles to keep her true feelings hidden. The speaker of the poem is not necessarily Elizabeth, but she would have undoubtedly understand the importance of cultivating a public image. In addition, literary scholars believe the poem was inspired by the breakup of marriage negotiations with Francis, Duke of Anjou, a one-time suitor to Elizabeth (**Abrams 998**).

In the first sentence, the writer used a fact from the encyclopedia entry. That information is not common knowledge and needs to be cited. The entry did not have an author, so it is cited by the title of the article. Because the encyclopedia entry is online, she did not include a page number. The second citation in this paragraph is a paraphrase of someone else's ideas. The writer found this information in a literature anthology edited by M. H. Abrams. Because it is a book, it gets a page number. That way any reader can easily find the ideas the writer shared.

Later in the model essay, the writer quotes exactly from *Hamlet*.

> Like Elizabeth's speaker, Hamlet is torn between his true, inner feelings and the image he needs to project in public. In Act I, scene ii, when Hamlet sees his uncle Claudius a month after his father's death, Claudius addresses Hamlet's grief: "How is it that the clouds still hang on you?" (**Shakespeare**).

The writer included the author's name because it was not previously mentioned in the paragraph.

EDIT, PROOFREAD AND PUBLISH

WRITING PROMPT

Recall the Essential Question: How do we express the complexities of being human? Choose two or three selections from the unit and write a literary analysis focused on how the author uses figurative language and figures of speech to help readers understand a speaker or character's feelings and actions. Explain how each author uses figurative language to reveal aspects of the human condition.

Your essay should include:

- An introduction with a clear thesis statement
- Body paragraphs with thorough analysis supported by relevant reasons and evidence
- A conclusion that effectively wraps up your essay

You have revised your literary analysis essay and received input from your peers on that revision. Now it's time to edit and proofread your essay to produce a final version. Have you included all of the valuable suggestions from your peers? Ask yourself: Have I fully developed my thesis statement with strong textual evidence? Have I accurately cited my sources? What more can I do to improve my essay's information and organization?

When you are satisfied with your work, move on to proofread it for errors. For example, check that you have used correct punctuation for quotations and citations. Have you followed hyphenation conventions? Have you corrected any misspelled words?

Once you have made all your corrections, you are ready to publish your work. You can distribute your writing to family and friends, hang it on a bulletin board or post it on your blog. If you publish online, create links to your sources and citations. That way, readers can follow up on what they've learned from your essay and read more on their own.

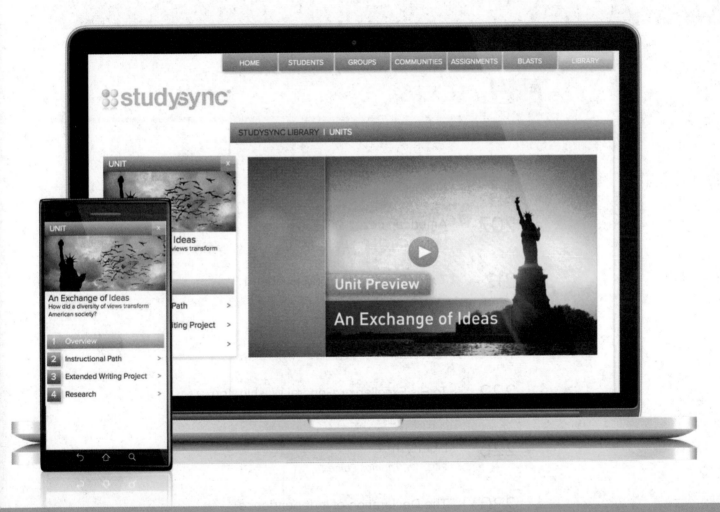

studysync®

Reading & Writing Companion

How did a diversity of views transform American society?

An Exchange of Ideas

An Exchange of Ideas

TEXTS

TEXTS

EXTENDED WRITING PROJECT

453

Text Fulfillment
through
StudySync

A MODEL OF CHRISTIAN CHARITY

NON-FICTION

John Winthrop
1630

INTRODUCTION

In the 1620s, Puritans began to establish communities in America after leaving England to escape what they viewed as corruption in the Church of England. In 1630, English Puritan leader John Winthrop guided 800 followers from England to America and established the Massachusetts Bay Colony, for which Winthrop served 12 years as governor. In his sermon "A Model of Christian Charity," Winthrop tells fellow colonists that they have a God-given responsibility to establish an ideal way of life in America—"a city upon a hill"—and admonishes his followers to do

"Thus stands the cause between God and us."

FIRST READ

NOTES

1   It rests now to make some application of this discourse, by the present design, which gave the occasion of writing of it. Herein are four things to be **propounded**; first the persons, secondly, the work, thirdly the end, fourthly the means.

2   First, for the persons. We are a company professing ourselves fellow members of Christ, in which respect only, though we were absent from each other many miles, and had our employments as far distant, yet we ought to account ourselves knit together by this bond of love and live in the exercise of it, if we would have comfort of our being in Christ. This was notorious in the practice of the Christians in former times; as is testified of the Waldenses, from the mouth of one of the adversaries Aeneas Sylvius "mutuo ament pene antequam norunt"—they use to love any of their own religion even before they were acquainted with them.

3   Secondly for the work we have in hand. It is by a mutual consent, through a special overvaluing **providence** and a more than an ordinary **approbation** of the churches of Christ, to seek out a place of cohabitation and consortship under a due form of government both civil and ecclesiastical. In such cases as this, the care of the public must oversway all private respects, by which, not only conscience, but mere civil policy, doth bind us. For it is a true rule that particular estates cannot subsist in the ruin of the public.

4   Thirdly, the end is to improve our lives to do more service to the Lord; the comfort and increase of the body of Christ, whereof we are members, that ourselves and **posterity** may be the better preserved from the common corruptions of this evil world, to serve the Lord and work out our salvation under the power and purity of his holy ordinances.

5   Fourthly, for the means whereby this must be effected. They are twofold, a conformity with the work and end we aim at. These we see are extraordinary,

therefore we must not content ourselves with usual ordinary means. Whatsoever we did, or ought to have done, when we lived in England, the same must we do, and more also, where we go. That which the most in their churches maintain as truth in profession only, we must bring into familiar and constant practice; as in this duty of love, we must love brotherly without **dissimulation**, we must love one another with a pure heart **fervently**. We must bear one another's burdens. We must not look only on our own things, but also on the things of our brethren.

6   Neither must we think that the Lord will bear with such failings at our hands as he doth from those among whom we have lived; and that for these three reasons:

7   First, in regard of the more near bond of marriage between Him and us, wherein He hath taken us to be His, after a most strict and peculiar manner, which will make Him the more jealous of our love and obedience. So He tells the people of Israel, you only have I known of all the families of the earth, therefore will I punish you for your transgressions.

8   Secondly, because the Lord will be sanctified in them that come near Him. We know that there were many that corrupted the service of the Lord; some setting up altars before his own; others offering both strange fire and strange sacrifices also; yet there came no fire from heaven, or other sudden judgment upon them, as did upon Nadab and Abihu, whom yet we may think did not sin **presumptuously**.

9   Thirdly, when God gives a special commission He looks to have it strictly observed in every article; When He gave Saul a commission to destroy Amaleck, He indented with him upon certain articles, and because he failed in one of the least, and that upon a fair pretense, it lost him the kingdom, which should have been his reward, if he had observed his commission.

10   Thus stands the cause between God and us. We are entered into **covenant** with Him for this work. We have taken out a commission. The Lord hath given us leave to draw our own articles. We have professed to enterprise these and those accounts, upon these and those ends. We have hereupon besought Him of favor and blessing. Now if the Lord shall please to hear us, and bring us in peace to the place we desire, then hath He ratified this covenant and sealed our commission, and will expect a strict performance of the articles contained in it; but if we shall neglect the observation of these articles which are the ends we have propounded, and, dissembling with our God, shall fall to embrace this present world and prosecute our carnal intentions, seeking great things for ourselves and our posterity, the Lord will surely break out in wrath against us, and be revenged of such a people, and make us know the price of the breach of such a covenant.

11 Now the only way to avoid this shipwreck, and to provide for our posterity, is to follow the **counsel** of Micah, to do justly, to love mercy, to walk humbly with our God. For this end, we must be knit together, in this work, as one man. We must entertain each other in brotherly affection. We must be willing to abridge ourselves of our superfluities, for the supply of others' necessities. We must uphold a familiar commerce together in all meekness, gentleness, patience and liberality. We must delight in each other; make others' conditions our own; rejoice together, mourn together, labor and suffer together, always having before our eyes our commission and community in the work, as members of the same body. So shall we keep the unity of the spirit in the bond of peace. The Lord will be our God, and delight to dwell among us, as His own people, and will command a blessing upon us in all our ways, so that we shall see much more of His wisdom, power, goodness and truth, than formerly we have been acquainted with. We shall find that the God of Israel is among us, when ten of us shall be able to resist a thousand of our enemies; when He shall make us a praise and glory that men shall say of succeeding plantations, "may the Lord make it like that of New England." For we must consider that we shall be as a city upon a hill. The eyes of all people are upon us. So that if we shall deal falsely with our God in this work we have undertaken, and so cause Him to withdraw His present help from us, we shall be made a story and a by-word through the world. We shall open the mouths of enemies to speak evil of the ways of God, and all professors for God's sake. We shall shame the faces of many of God's worthy servants, and cause their prayers to be turned into curses upon us till we be consumed out of the good land whither we are going.

THINK QUESTIONS

1. What is the connection among the persons to whom Winthrop is speaking? Why did these people come to America?

2. Use details from the text to show that Winthrop believes his people have a special relationship with the Lord.

3. In the first paragraph, Winthrop speaks of "end" and "means." An "end" refers to a goal and "means" refers to the actions that accomplish the goal. In Winthrop's sermon, what is the end and what are the means?

4. Use context to determine the meaning of the word **dissimulation** as it is used in "A Model of Christian Charity." Write your definition of "dissimulation" and explain how you arrived at it.

5. Use context to determine the meaning of the word **covenant** as it is used in "A Model of Christian Charity." Write your definition of "covenant" and explain how you figured it out.

Please note that excerpts and passages in the StudySync® library and this workbook are intended as touchstones to generate interest in an author's work. The excerpts and passages do not substitute for the reading of entire texts, and StudySync® strongly recommends that students seek out and purchase the whole literary or informational work in order to experience it as the author intended. Links to online resellers are available in our digital library. In addition, complete works may be ordered through an authorized reseller by filling out and returning to StudySync® the order form enclosed in this workbook.

Reading & Writing Companion **205**

CLOSE READ

Reread the sermon "A Model of Christian Charity." As you reread, complete the Focus Questions below. Then use your answers and annotations from the questions to help you complete the Writing Prompt.

FOCUS QUESTIONS

1. In the first paragraph Winthrop lists four things to be propounded, or offered for consideration, to his audience of Puritan colonists. Why might he have chosen to list these four things in the order that he does?

2. There is a second list in the middle of the excerpt from "A Model of Christian Charity." What is this second list about, and which of the four topics from the first paragraph is it most closely connected to? Highlight evidence from the text and make annotations to support your explanation.

3. In his sermon, Winthrop includes allusions to the Biblical figures Nadab, Abihu, and Saul. In what way might these allusions give weight to Winthrop's recommendations? Why might he have chosen these particular figures to mention in the sermon?

4. In the final paragraph, Winthrop lists things the colonists must do to please God. Summarize this counsel. What does Winthrop say will result if the colonists follow the counsel? What will result if they reject the counsel? Highlight evidence from the text and make annotations to support your explanation.

5. The part of Winthrop's speech that is most remembered and quoted is the metaphor "a city on a hill." What do you think he means by these words? Cite text evidence to support your idea.

6. The Essential Question for this unit is "How did a diversity of views transform American society?" The first two major English colonies in America were markedly different. The Massachusetts Bay Colony was organized along the lines recommended by John Winthrop. The other colony, located in Jamestown, Virginia, was not founded by a religious group. Rather, it was organized by investors who developed an economy based on growing and exporting tobacco. What would have been the benefits of living in each colony, and how might these benefits have contributed to the growth of American settlements?

WRITING PROMPT

Winthrop's sermon is very unified in structure, containing no irrelevant ideas. He often presents his points in lists, for clarity. In an essay, show how the metaphor of "a city on a hill," the most famous part of his sermon, is related to one of the three lists that appear earlier in the text. Explain the meaning of the phrase, as Winthrop is using it. Then make connections between the phrase and the content of one of the lists. Cite textual evidence to support your analysis.

AMERICAN JEZEBEL

NON-FICTION
Eve LaPlante
2004

INTRODUCTION

Anne Hutchinson emigrated from England to the Massachusetts Bay Colony in 1632. The daughter of a clergyman with independent views, she began organizing weekly meetings to discuss the sermons of the Puritan minister, John Cotton. Initially attended by women, Hutchinson's meetings quickly became popular with men as well. Hutchinson's dynamic approach, investing individuals with the power to interpret Puritan theology, coupled with her growing popularity, constituted a threat to Governor John Winthrop, who put Hutchinson on trial and ultimately had her banished from the colony. Nathaniel Hawthorne is said to have used Hutchinson as a model for the character of Hester Prynne in *The*

"More than a few men in the room, including several of the ministers, considered her a witch."

 FIRST READ

Chapter 1: Enemy of the State

1   "Anne Hutchinson is present," a male voice announced from somewhere in the crowded meetinghouse, momentarily quieting the din that filled its cavernous hall. The meetinghouse of Cambridge, Massachusetts, a square structure of timber and clay with a thatched roof, served as the community's city hall, church, and courthouse—the latter its role this chilly Tuesday in November 1637. Hearing the news that the defendant had arrived, scores of bearded heads in black felt hats turned to find the one woman in the crowd.

2   There was nothing **auspicious** about Anne Hutchinson's appearance as she stood in the doorway alongside several male relatives and supporters, awaiting the start of the trial. She was forty-six years old, of average height and bearing, with an unremarkable face. Her petticoat fell almost to the ground, revealing only the tips of her leather boots. Against the cold she wore a wool mantua, or cloak. A white coif covered her hair, as was the custom of the day. Besides that and her white linen smock and neckerchief, she wore all black. She was a stranger to no one present, having ministered as midwife and nurse to many of their wives and children. All knew her to be an active member of the church of Boston, the wife of the wealthy textile merchant, William Hutchinson, the mother of twelve living children, and the grandmother of one, a five-day-old boy who just that Sunday had been baptized. There was, in short, no outward sign to show she was an enemy of the state.

3   Enemy she was, though, indeed the greatest threat Massachusetts had ever known. More than a few men in the room, including several of the ministers, considered her a witch. Others believed the Devil had taken over her soul. The governor, John Winthrop, who was waiting in an antechamber of the meetinghouse to begin the trial over which he would preside, suspected her

of using her devilish powers to **subjugate** men by establishing "the community of women" to foster "their **abominable** wickedness."

4   Anne Hutchinson's greatest crime, and the source of her power, was the series of public meetings she held at her house to discuss Scripture and theology. At first, in 1635, the evening meetings had been just for women, who then were generally encouraged to gather in small groups to gossip and offer mutual support. Soon scores of women, enchanted by her intelligence and magnetism, flocked to hear her analysis of the week's Scripture reading, which many of them preferred to the ministers' latest interpretation. "Being a woman very helpful in times of childbirth and other occasions of bodily infirmities, [Hutchinson] easily inserted herself into the affections of many," an official observed. Her "pretense was to repeat [the ministers'] sermons," the governor added, "but when that was done, she would comment upon the doctrines, interpret passages at her pleasure, and expound dark places of Scripture, and make it serve her turn," going beyond "wholesome truths" to "set forth her own stuff." One minister, Thomas Weld, reported that her "custom was for her scholars to propound questions and she (gravely sitting in the chair) did make answers thereunto." This was especially grievous in a time when the single chair in every house was for the use of the man alone.

5   Men had begun to accompany their wives to Hutchinson's meetings in 1636, and as her audiences swelled she offered a second session of religious instruction each week, just as the colonial ministers liked to give a Thursday lecture as well as their Sunday sermon. The Reverend Weld lamented that members of her audience, "being tainted, conveyed the infection to others," including "some of the magistrates, some gentlemen, some scholars and men of learning, some Burgesses of our General Court, some of our captains and soldiers, some chief men in towns, and some eminent for religion, parts, and wit." Anne Hutchinson had "stepped out of [her] place," in the **succinct** phrase of the Reverend Hugh Peter, of Salem—she "had rather been a husband than a wife; and a preacher than a hearer; and a magistrate than a subject."

6   It was painfully clear to Governor Winthrop, who had an excellent view of her comings and goings from his house directly across the road from hers in Boston, that Anne Hutchinson possessed the strongest **constituency** of any leader in the colony. She was, he confided in his journal, "a woman of a haughty and fierce carriage, a nimble wit and an active spirit, and a very voluble tongue." Her name was absent (on account of her sex) from every offensive political act and document, he observed, but she was behind them all. "More bold than a man," she was Virgil's *dux foemina facti*, "the woman leading all the action"—the breeder and nourisher of all the county's distempers, the sower of political and religious discord. Before Mistress Hutchinson had arrived in America, in the fall of 1634, all was sweetness and light, he recalled. Now that she was here, all was chaos.

Excerpted from *American Jezebel* by Eve LaPlante, published by HarperCollins Publishers.

 THINK QUESTIONS

1. Who is the defendant in the trial described in the excerpt? Why does the author spend so much time describing her appearance? Cite textual evidence to support your response.

2. Explain how Anne Hutchinson became an "enemy of the state." Support your response with evidence from the text.

3. Using the information presented in the text, make an inference about how women in the Massachusetts Bay Colony were expected to act. Support your inference with textual evidence.

4. Use context to determine the meaning of the word **succinct** as it is used in *American Jezebel*. Write your definition of "succinct" and tell how you arrived at it.

5. Use context to determine the meaning of **constituency** as it is used in *American Jezebel*. Write your definition of "constituency" and tell how you arrived at it.

CLOSE READ

Reread the excerpt from *American Jezebel*. As you reread, complete the Focus Questions below. Then use your answers and annotations from the questions to help you complete the Writing Prompt.

FOCUS QUESTIONS

1. Explain how the author uses the third paragraph to introduce Governor John Winthrop's ideas about Anne Hutchinson. Highlight evidence from the text and make annotations to explain your choices.

2. Paragraph 4 describes how Anne Hutchinson's meetings changed as time went on. According to this paragraph, what about those meetings bothered the ministers and officials of the Massachusetts Bay Colony? Highlight evidence to support your ideas, and write annotations to explain your choices.

3. What inferences about Puritan life can you make based on the details in paragraph 5? Highlight your textual evidence and make annotations to explain your ideas.

4. In the last paragraph, the author reiterates Governor John Winthrop's view of Anne Hutchinson. What does he think of her? What conclusion can you draw about Winthrop based on his reaction to her? Highlight your evidence and make annotations to explain your ideas.

5. How did the views and actions of Anne Hutchinson help to transform early American society? Highlight and annotate textual evidence to support your answer.

WRITING PROMPT

How did conflicting ideas about religion and the role of women help to cause the crisis surrounding Anne Hutchinson? Analyze the sequence of events and interactions that helped contribute to her downfall. End with a statement about what her downfall implies about life in the early American colonies. Cite textual evidence to support your analysis.

TO MY DEAR AND LOVING HUSBAND

POETRY
Anne Bradstreet
1660

INTRODUCTION

Two years after marrying Simon Bradstreet, the son of a Puritan minister, at age 16, Anne Bradstreet came to America in John Winthrop's fleet that brought 700 Puritans from England to the Massachusetts Bay Colony. In 1650, Bradstreet's first book of poetry, *The Tenth Muse Lately Sprung Up in America,* was published in England—the first publication of a female author living in the New World. Her poetry demonstrates a subtle, but passionate, feminism, as in the declaration of love in one of her best-known poems, "To My Dear and

"If ever two were one, then surely we."

FIRST READ

"To My Dear and Loving Husband"

1 If ever two were one, then surely we.
2 If ever man were loved by wife, then thee;
3 If ever wife was happy in a man,
4 Compare with me ye women if you can.

5 I **prize** thy love more than whole mines of gold,
6 Or all the riches that the East doth hold.
7 My love is such that rivers cannot **quench**,
8 Nor ought but love from thee give **recompense**.

9 Thy love is such I can no way repay;
10 The heavens reward thee **manifold**, I pray.
11 Then while we live, in love let's so persever,
12 That when we live no more we may live ever.

THINK QUESTIONS

1. What can readers infer about the relationship between the speaker and her husband? What text evidence in the poem supports this inference?

2. The word *persever* is an outdated form of *persevere,* which means "to continue despite difficulty." In what does the speaker want herself and her husband to persever, and why? Cite text evidence to support your answer.

3. What references does the speaker make to money or wealth? What is the effect of these references?

4. Use context to determine the meaning of the word **prize** as it is used in "To My Dear and Loving Husband." Write your definition of "prize," and tell how you determined it.

5. Use context and your knowledge of word parts to determine the meaning of the word **manifold** as it is used in "To My Dear and Loving Husband." Write your definition of "manifold," and tell how you determined it.

CLOSE READ

Reread the poem "To My Dear and Loving Husband." As you reread, complete the Focus Questions below. Then use your answers and annotations from the questions to help you complete the Writing Prompt.

FOCUS QUESTIONS

1. What are two words you would use to describe the style of "To My Dear and Loving Husband"? Highlight evidence from the text and make annotations to support your choices.

2. How many times does the phrase "If ever" appear in the poem? How does this phrase help develop the meaning of the poem? Highlight evidence from the text and make annotations to explain your response.

3. Who is the speaker addressing in this poem? What is her tone, or attitude, toward the one to whom she is speaking? Identify words and phrases in the poem that support your answers.

4. What makes the line "My love is such that rivers cannot quench" an example of metaphor? What makes the line an example of hyperbole as well? Interpret what the line means. Make annotations to explain your response.

5. Choose from the poem another example of figurative language that you find fresh, engaging, or beautiful. Identify the kind of figurative language it is, and explain the idea it expresses. What does it contribute to the meaning of the poem? Highlight textual evidence and make annotations to explain your interpretation.

6. Recall the Essential Question: How did a diversity of views transform American society? From reading Bradstreet's poem, what can you infer about Puritan colonial women's views of marriage and God? What do you think Bradstreet's fellow (or sister) colonists may have gained from reading her poems? Support your answer.

WRITING PROMPT

Explain how figurative language is used in "To My Dear and Loving Husband" to express the speaker's feelings about her marriage and her thoughts about God and Heaven. Then discuss another element of style that adds to the poem's effectiveness or appeal. Support your ideas with evidence from the text, including specific examples of figurative language.

SECOND TREATISE OF GOVERNMENT

NON-FICTION
John Locke
1689

INTRODUCTION

British political philosopher John Locke was one of the most influential thinkers of the Age of Enlightenment, a cultural movement that began in the late 17th century and emphasized individualism and reason over tradition. Originally published anonymously, *Two Treatises of Government* became one of Locke's most well-known works. In the first treatise, Locke argues against absolute power for the monarchy. The second treatise provides Locke's outline for a better form of government; one that protects the natural rights of citizens and that derives its power from the consent of the governed. This excerpt is taken from the second treatise, which deeply influenced Thomas Jefferson, the principal writer of the Declaration of Independence.

"Must the people then always lay themselves open to the cruelty and rage of tyranny?"

 FIRST READ

NOTES

From Chapter II: Of the State of Nature

1   Sect. 4. To understand political power right, and derive it from its original, we must consider, what state all men are naturally in, and that is, a state of perfect freedom to order their actions, and dispose of their possessions and persons, as they think fit, within the bounds of the law of nature, without asking leave, or depending upon the will of any other man.

2   A state also of equality, wherein all the power and **jurisdiction** is reciprocal, no one having more than another; there being nothing more evident, than that creatures of the same species and rank, **promiscuously** born to all the same advantages of nature, and the use of the same **faculties**, should also be equal one amongst another without subordination or subjection, unless the lord and master of them all should, by any manifest declaration of his will, set one above another, and confer on him, by an evident and clear appointment, an undoubted right to dominion and sovereignty.

....

3   Sect. 6. But though this be a state of liberty, yet it is not a state of licence: though man in that state have an uncontroulable liberty to dispose of his person or possessions, yet he has not liberty to destroy himself, or so much as any creature in his possession, but where some nobler use than its bare preservation calls for it. The state of nature has a law of nature to govern it, which obliges every one: and reason, which is that law, teaches all mankind, who will but consult it, that being all equal and independent, no one ought to harm another in his life, health, liberty, or possessions

From Chapter VIII: Of the Beginning of Political Societies

4 Sect. 95. Men being, as has been said, by nature, all free, equal, and independent, no one can be put out of this estate, and subjected to the political power of another, without his own consent. The only way whereby any one **divests** himself of his natural liberty, and puts on the bonds of civil society, is by agreeing with other men to join and unite into a community for their comfortable, safe, and peaceable living one amongst another, in a secure enjoyment of their properties, and a greater security against any, that are not of it. This any number of men may do, because it injures not the freedom of the rest; they are left as they were in the liberty of the state of nature. When any number of men have so consented to make one community or government, they are thereby presently incorporated, and make one body politic, wherein the majority have a right to act and conclude the rest.

5 Sect. 96. For when any number of men have, by the consent of every individual, made a community, they have thereby made that community one body, with a power to act as one body, which is only by the will and determination of the majority: for that which acts any community, being only the consent of the individuals of it, and it being necessary to that which is one body to move one way; it is necessary the body should move that way whither the greater force carries it, which is the consent of the majority: or else it is impossible it should act or continue one body, one community, which the consent of every individual that united into it, agreed that it should; and so every one is bound by that consent to be concluded by the majority. And therefore we see, that in assemblies, impowered to act by positive laws, where no number is set by that positive law which impowers them, the act of the majority passes for the act of the whole, and of course determines, as having, by the law of nature and reason, the power of the whole.

From Chapter IX: Of the Ends of Political Society and Government

6 Sect. 123. If man in the state of nature be so free, as has been said; if he be absolute lord of his own person and possessions, equal to the greatest, and subject to no body, why will he part with his freedom? why will he give up this empire, and subject himself to the dominion and controul of any other power? To which it is obvious to answer, that though in the state of nature he hath such a right, yet the enjoyment of it is very uncertain, and constantly exposed to the invasion of others: for all being kings as much as he, every man his equal, and the greater part no strict observers of equity and justice, the enjoyment of the property he has in this state is very unsafe, very unsecure. This makes him willing to quit a condition, which, however free, is full of fears and continual dangers: and it is not without reason, that he seeks out, and is willing to join in society with others, who are already united, or have a mind

to unite, for the mutual preservation of their lives, liberties and estates, which I call by the general name, property.

7   Sect. 124. The great and chief end, therefore, of men's uniting into **commonwealths**, and putting themselves under government, is the preservation of their property. To which in the state of nature there are many things wanting.

From Chapter XIX: Of the Dissolution of Government

8   Sect. 232. Whosoever uses force without right, as every one does in society, who does it without law, puts himself into a state of war with those against whom he so uses it; and in that state all former ties are cancelled, all other rights cease, and every one has a right to defend himself, and to resist the aggressor. This is so evident, that Barclay himself, that great assertor of the power and sacredness of kings, is forced to confess, That it is lawful for the people, in some cases, to resist their king; and that too in a chapter, wherein he pretends to shew, that the divine law shuts up the people from all manner of rebellion. Whereby it is evident, even by his own doctrine, that, since they may in some cases resist, all resisting of princes is not rebellion. His words are these....

9   Sect. 233. But if any one should ask, Must the people then always lay themselves open to the cruelty and rage of tyranny? Must they see their cities pillaged, and laid in ashes, their wives and children exposed to the tyrant's lust and fury, and themselves and families reduced by their king to ruin, and all the miseries of want and oppression, and yet sit still? Must men alone be debarred the common privilege of opposing force with force, which nature allows so freely to all other creatures for their preservation from injury? I answer: Self-defence is a part of the law of nature; nor can it be denied the community, even against the king himself: but to revenge themselves upon him, must by no means be allowed them; it being not agreeable to that law. Wherefore if the king shall shew an hatred, not only to some particular persons, but sets himself against the body of the commonwealth, whereof he is the head, and shall, with intolerable ill usage, cruelly tyrannize over the whole, or a considerable part of the people, in this case the people have a right to resist and defend themselves from injury: but it must be with this caution, that they only defend themselves, but do not attack their prince: they may repair the damages received, but must not for any provocation exceed the bounds of due reverence and respect. They may repulse the present attempt, but must not revenge past violences: for it is natural for us to defend life and limb, but that an inferior should punish a superior, is against nature. The mischief which is designed them, the people may prevent before it be done; but when it is done, they must not revenge it on the king, though author of the villany. This therefore is the privilege of the people in general, above

what any private person hath; that particular men are allowed by our adversaries themselves (Buchanan only excepted) to have no other remedy but patience; but the body of the people may with respect resist intolerable tyranny; for when it is but moderate, they ought to endure it.

10   Sect. 234. Thus far that great advocate of monarchical power allows of resistance.

THINK QUESTIONS

1. According to Locke, what is the natural state of human beings? How does this description contribute to Locke's argument? Cite textual evidence to support your response.

2. According to Chapters VIII and IX, how are political societies formed, and what is their function? Support your response with evidence from the text.

3. Using the information presented in the *Second Treatise of Government*, when might it be "lawful" for a group to oppose their king? Support your response with textual evidence.

4. Use context to determine the meaning of the word **divests** as it is used in the *Second Treatise of Government*. Write your definition of "divests" and explain how you arrived at it.

5. Use context to determine the meaning of the word **commonwealths** as it is used in the *Second Treatise of Government*. Write your definition of "commonwealths" and tell how you arrived at it.

CLOSE READ

Reread the excerpt from *Second Treatise of Government*. As you reread, complete the Focus Questions below. Then use your answers and annotations from the questions to help you complete the Writing Prompt.

FOCUS QUESTIONS

1. What textual evidence does Locke give to support the central claim of Chapter II? Highlight evidence in the text and make annotations to explain how the textual evidence you've chosen helps you understand Locke's central ideas.

2. Locke divides the text into chapters and sections. Explain how Sect. 96 builds on ideas Locke puts forth in Sect. 95. Make annotations and highlight evidence in the text to explain your response.

3. Reread Sect. 123, and highlight the definition Locke gives for "property" at the end of the paragraph. Explain this definition. How is Locke's meaning different from the definition of "property" today?

4. Sect. 233 contains a long quotation from William Barclay. What is the main idea of this section? How does the information in this section contribute to Locke's main ideas about the nature of human beings? Highlight your evidence and annotate to explain your ideas.

5. Does Locke support his initial claim that all people are naturally equals throughout the text? Why or why not? Consider evidence from Chapter II and Chapter XIX in your response. Highlight your evidence and annotate to explain your ideas.

6. John Locke was a British philosopher. Yet his ideas influenced the Founding Fathers of the United States. What views regarding the role of government does *Second Treatise of Government* reveal, and how did these views transform American society? Highlight your evidence and annotate to explain your ideas.

WRITING PROMPT

Analyze the author's choices as he develops ideas throughout the *Second Treatise of Government*. What is the central idea of the text? How does Locke use supporting evidence to develop that central idea? Cite textual evidence to support your analysis and to show how Locke's ideas interact throughout the text. Determine the meaning of technical language as necessary.

TO HIS EXCELLENCY, GENERAL WASHINGTON

POETRY
Phillis Wheatley
1775

INTRODUCTION

When she was just seven or eight years old, Phillis Wheatley was captured in Africa by slave traders and brought to America. Recognizing Wheatley's extreme intelligence, her new owners in Boston taught her to read and write. By the time she was twelve, Wheatley was reading Greek and Latin classics and studying difficult passages from the Bible. She soon began writing poetry, and published her first poem when she was only thirteen years old. In 1775, when General George Washington traveled to Boston to assume leadership of the Continental Army, Wheatley wrote this poem about Washington and sent it to him. Washington was so honored by Wheatley's poem that he later

"Proceed, great chief, with virtue on thy side..."

FIRST READ

1   **Celestial** choir! enthron'd in realms of light,
2   Columbia's scenes of glorious toils I write.
3   While freedom's cause her anxious breast alarms,
4   She flashes dreadful in **refulgent** arms.
5   See mother earth her offspring's fate bemoan,
6   And nations gaze at scenes before unknown!
7   See the bright beams of heaven's revolving light
8   Involved in sorrows and the veil of night!

9   The Goddess comes, she moves divinely fair,
10 Olive and laurel binds Her golden hair:
11 Wherever shines this native of the skies,
12 Unnumber'd charms and recent graces rise.

13 Muse! Bow **propitious** while my pen relates
14 How pour her armies through a thousand gates,
15 As when Eolus heaven's fair face deforms,
16 Enwrapp'd in tempest and a night of storms;
17 Astonish'd ocean feels the wild uproar,
18 The **refluent** surges beat the sounding shore;
19 Or think as leaves in Autumn's golden reign,
20 Such, and so many, moves the warrior's train.
21 In bright array they seek the work of war,
22 Where high unfurl'd the **ensign** waves in air.
23 Shall I to Washington their praise recite?
24 Enough thou know'st them in the fields of fight.
25 Thee, first in peace and honors—we demand
26 The grace and glory of thy martial band.
27 Fam'd for thy valour, for thy virtues more,
28 Hear every tongue thy guardian aid implore!

29 One century scarce perform'd its destined round,
30 When Gallic powers Columbia's fury found;
31 And so may you, whoever dares disgrace
32 The land of freedom's heaven-defended race!
33 Fix'd are the eyes of nations on the scales,
34 For in their hopes Columbia's arm prevails.
35 Anon Britannia droops the **pensive** head,
36 While round increase the rising hills of dead.
37 Ah! Cruel blindness to Columbia's state!
38 Lament thy thirst of boundless power too late.

39 Proceed, great chief, with virtue on thy side,
40 Thy ev'ry action let the Goddess guide.
41 A crown, a mansion, and a throne that shine,
42 With gold unfading, WASHINGTON! Be thine.

THINK QUESTIONS

1. Columbia is a name used historically for a personification of the United States. How does the speaker describe Columbia in the first and second stanzas? What does that description imply about the speaker's view of the United States? Cite textual evidence to support your response.

2. What two things does the speaker compare in the first half of the third stanza? What is the effect of this comparison? What impact does this imagery have on the poem's mood? Support your response with textual evidence.

3. To whom is the last stanza addressed? What is the speaker's message to this person? Cite evidence from the poem to support your response.

4. Use context to determine the meaning of the word **refulgent** as it is used in "To His Excellency, General Washington." Write your definition of "refulgent" and explain how you determined it.

5. Use context to determine the meaning of the word **ensign** as it is used in "To His Excellency, General Washington." Write your definition of "ensign" and explain how you determined it.

CLOSE READ

Reread the poem, "To His Excellency, George Washington." As you reread, complete the Focus Questions below. Then use your answers and annotations from the questions to help you complete the Writing Prompt.

FOCUS QUESTIONS

1. What types of figures of speech does Wheatley use in the first stanza to introduce the topic of her poem? Highlight evidence from the text and make annotations to explain the effect of the chosen figures of speech.

2. Recall from the Unit Introduction that the Enlightenment brought a neoclassical revival to philosophy and literature. What do the first ten lines of the third stanza describe? How does Wheatley use neoclassical allusions and similes to enhance the description and add meaning? Support your answer with textual evidence and make annotations to explain your answer.

3. In the second half of the third stanza, Washington is introduced. What words and phrases does the speaker use to describe Washington? What are the connotations of these words? Highlight your textual evidence and make annotations to explain your choices.

4. The fourth stanza contains a lengthy example of personification. What is being personified in this stanza? What is the effect of the author's choice to use personification in this way? Highlight evidence from the text and make annotations to support your explanation.

5. How does the poem end? What key words and phrases does the last stanza include, and what connotations do these words have? What larger ideas do these connotations imply? How do those ideas relate to the title of the poem? Highlight textual evidence and make annotations to explain your ideas.

6. Recall the Essential Question: How did a diversity of views transform American society? What view does the speaker have of America? How do you know? How might an African American poet's views transform society? Highlight evidence to support your answer.

WRITING PROMPT

What themes about freedom or the American Revolution does "To His Excellency, General Washington" contain? How does the use of figures of speech and connotations help Wheatley express these themes? Use your understanding of figurative language to determine themes that emerge in this poem. Support your writing with evidence from the text.

LIBERTY TREE

POETRY
Thomas Paine
1775

INTRODUCTION

Thomas Paine, a political activist and a Founding Father, played a pivotal role in the American independence movement. Born in England, Paine's political theories were greatly influenced by Enlightenment ideas concerning the precedence of human rights. Although he is known more for his informational pamphlets, such as *Common Sense* and *The Crisis*, Paine also wrote the political poem "Liberty Tree," inspired by a famous elm tree that stood near

"From the east to the west blow the trumpet to arms..."

 FIRST READ

1   In a chariot of light from the regions of day,
2   The Goddess of Liberty came;
3   Ten thousand **celestials** directed the way
4   And hither conducted the dame.
5   A fair budding branch from the gardens above,
6   Where millions with millions agree,
7   She brought in her hand as a pledge of her love,
8   And the plant she named *Liberty Tree.*

9   The celestial **exotic** struck deep in the ground,
10   Like a native it flourished and bore;
11   The fame of its fruit drew the nations around,
12   To seek out this peaceable shore.
13   Unmindful of names or distinction they came,
14   For freemen like brothers agree;
15   With one spirit endued, they one friendship pursued,
16   And their temple was *Liberty Tree.*

17   Beneath this fair tree, like the **patriarchs** of old,
18   Their bread in contentment they ate,
19   **Unvexed** with the troubles of silver and gold,
20   The cares of the grand and the great.
21   With timber and tar they Old England supplied,
22   And supported her power on the sea;
23   Her battles they fought, without getting a groat,
24   For the honor of *Liberty Tree.*

25   But hear, O ye swains, 'tis a tale most **profane**,
26   How all the tyrannical powers,
27   Kings, Commons, and Lords, are uniting a main
28   To cut down this guardian of ours;

NOTES

29   From the east to the west blow the trumpet to arms

30   Through the land let the sound of it flee,

31   Let the far and the near, all unite with a cheer,

32   In defence of our *Liberty Tree*.

☁ THINK QUESTIONS

1. Where did the Liberty Tree come from? What inference can you make about the speaker's opinion of liberty based on this information? Support your inference with textual evidence.

2. Explain who the "freemen" in the poem are and what their relationship is to the Liberty Tree. What is their relationship to "Old England"? Support your answer with textual evidence.

3. What changes at the end of the poem? What is the speaker requesting of the reader? Support your answer with textual evidence.

4. Use context to determine the meaning of the word **exotic** as it is used in "Liberty Tree." Write your definition of "exotic" and explain how you arrived at it.

5. Use context to determine the meaning of the word **unvexed** as it is used in "Liberty Tree." Write your definition of "unvexed" and explain how you arrived at it. Then verify its meaning in a dictionary.

CLOSE READ

Reread the poem "Liberty Tree." As you reread, complete the Focus Questions below. Then use your answers and annotations from the questions to help you complete the Writing Prompt.

FOCUS QUESTIONS

1. What is the poem's tone in the first three stanzas? How does the poem's tone change in the final stanza? How does the change in tone emphasize the shift in meaning between the first three stanzas and the final stanza? Highlight words and phrases from the text that express the tone, and make annotations to explain your choices.

2. Part of a poet's style is his or her use of figurative language. Highlight two or three examples of figurative language in the poem. How does the use of figurative language impact the tone? Make annotations to explain your choices.

3. Reread Phillis Wheatley's "To His Excellency, General Washington." How does Wheatley use figurative language? Compare her style with Paine's in "Liberty Tree." Highlight evidence from the text and make annotations to support your explanation.

4. In "Liberty Tree," Thomas Paine uses the central image of the Liberty Tree. In "To His Excellency, General Washington," Wheatley uses the personified Columbia as a central image. Compare and contrast these two images. What is the overall effect of each image? How do the central images support each poem's theme? Highlight textual evidence and make annotations to explain your ideas.

5. What central idea or theme do "Liberty Tree" and "To His Excellency, General Washington" share? How did this view transform America? Highlight textual evidence to support your response.

WRITING PROMPT

Compare and contrast the styles of "Liberty Tree" and "To His Excellency, General Washington." What kinds of tones and figurative language does each poet use? How do these choices help develop the overall theme of each poem? What do the different styles tell you about American literature in the 18th century? Support your writing with evidence from the text.

THE DECLARATION OF INDEPENDENCE

NON-FICTION
Thomas Jefferson
1776

INTRODUCTION

On June 11, 1776, the delegates of the Second Continental Congress had appointed a five-member committee to draft a statement declaring independence from Britain. The committee included Benjamin Franklin, John Adams, and Thomas Jefferson, and Jefferson was called upon to do the writing. Some of his ideas were not new. According to English political philosopher John Locke's theory of "natural law," which Jefferson had studied, human beings are "by nature free, equal and independent." Following Locke, Jefferson stressed that the American Revolution was a struggle for the rights of all people

"We hold these truths to be self-evident, that all men are created equal..."

 FIRST READ

NOTES

In Congress, July 4, 1776

The unanimous Declaration of the thirteen united States of America

1   When in the Course of human events, it becomes necessary for one people to dissolve the political bands which have connected them with another, and to assume, among the Powers of the earth, the separate and equal station to which the Laws of Nature and of Nature's God entitle them, a decent respect to the opinions of mankind requires that they should declare the causes which impel them to the separation.

2   We hold these truths to be self-evident, that all men are created equal, that they are endowed by their Creator with certain unalienable Rights, that among these are Life, Liberty, and the pursuit of Happiness.—That to secure these rights, Governments are instituted among Men, deriving their just powers from the consent of the governed,—That whenever any Form of Government becomes destructive of these ends, it is the Right of the People to alter or to abolish it, and to institute new Government, laying its foundation on such principles and organizing its powers in such form, as to them shall seem most likely to effect their Safety and Happiness. **Prudence**, indeed, will dictate that Governments long established should not be changed for light and transient causes; and accordingly all experience hath shown, that mankind are more disposed to suffer, while evils are sufferable, than to right themselves by abolishing the forms to which they are accustomed. But when a long train of abuses and usurpations, pursuing invariably the same Object evinces a design to reduce them under absolute Despotism, it is their right, it is their duty, to throw off such Government, and to provide new Guards for their future security.—Such has been the patient sufferance of these Colonies; and such is now the necessity which constrains them to alter their former Systems of Government. The history of the present King of Great Britain is a history of repeated injuries and usurpations, all having in direct object the

NOTES

establishment of an absolute Tyranny over these States. To prove this, let Facts be submitted to a candid world.

3   He has refused his Assent to Laws, the most wholesome and necessary for the public good.

4   He has forbidden his Governors to pass Laws of immediate and pressing importance, unless suspended in their operation till his Assent should be obtained; and when so suspended, he has utterly neglected to attend to them.

5   He has refused to pass other Laws for the accommodation of large districts of people, unless those people would relinquish the right of Representation in the Legislature, a right inestimable to them and formidable to tyrants only.

6   He has called together legislative bodies at places unusual, uncomfortable, and distant from the depository of their Public Records, for the sole purpose of fatiguing them into compliance with his measures.

7   He has dissolved Representative Houses repeatedly, for opposing with manly firmness his invasions on the rights of the people.

8   He has refused for a long time, after such dissolutions, to cause others to be elected; whereby the Legislative Powers, incapable of Annihilation, have returned to the People at large for their exercise; the State remaining in the mean time exposed to all the dangers of invasion from without, and convulsions within.

9   He has endeavoured to prevent the population of these States; for that purpose obstructing the Laws of Naturalization of Foreigners; refusing to pass others to encourage their migration hither, and raising the conditions of new Appropriations of Lands.

10   He has obstructed the Administration of Justice, by refusing his Assent to Laws for establishing Judiciary Powers.

11   He has made judges dependent on his Will alone, for the tenure of their offices, and the amount and payment of their salaries.

12   He has erected a multitude of New Offices, and sent hither swarms of Officers to harass our People, and eat out their substance.

13   He has kept among us, in times of peace, Standing Armies without the Consent of our legislatures.

14 He has affected to render the Military independent of and superior to the Civil Power.

15 He has combined with others to subject us to a jurisdiction foreign to our constitution, and unacknowledged by our laws; giving his Assent to their Acts of pretended legislation:

16 For quartering large bodies of armed troops among us:

17 For protecting them, by a mock Trial, from Punishment for any Murders which they should commit on the Inhabitants of these States:

18 For cutting off our Trade with all parts of the world:

19 For imposing taxes on us without our Consent:

20 For depriving us, in many cases, of the benefits of Trial by Jury:

21 For transporting us beyond Seas to be tried for pretended offences:

22 For abolishing the free System of English Laws in a neighbouring Province, establishing therein an Arbitrary government, and enlarging its Boundaries so as to render it at once an example and fit instrument for introducing the same absolute rule into these Colonies:

23 For taking away our Charters, abolishing our most valuable Laws, and altering fundamentally the Forms of our Governments:

24 For suspending our own Legislatures and declaring themselves invested with Power to legislate for us in all cases whatsoever.

25 He has abdicated Government here, by declaring us out of his Protection and waging War against us.

26 He has plundered our seas, ravaged our Coasts, burnt our towns, and destroyed the lives of our people.

27 He is at this time transporting large armies of foreign mercenaries to complete the works of death, desolation and tyranny, already begun with circumstances of Cruelty & **perfidy** scarcely paralleled in the most barbarous ages, and totally unworthy of the Head of a civilized nation.

28 He has constrained our fellow Citizens taken Captive on the high Seas to bear Arms against their Country, to become the executioners of their friends and Brethren, or to fall themselves by their Hands.

NOTES

29   He has excited domestic insurrections amongst us, and has endeavoured to bring on the inhabitants of our frontiers, the merciless Indian Savages, whose known rule of warfare is an undistinguished destruction of all ages, sexes and conditions.

30   In every stage of these Oppressions We have Petitioned for Redress in the most humble terms: Our repeated Petitions have been answered only by repeated injury. A Prince, whose character is thus marked by every act which may define a Tyrant, is unfit to be the ruler of a free People.

31   Nor have We been wanting in attention to our British brethren. We have warned them from time to time of attempts by their legislature to extend an unwarrantable jurisdiction over us. We have reminded them of the circumstances of our emigration and settlement here. We have appealed to their native justice and magnanimity, and we have conjured them by the ties of our common kindred to disavow these usurpations, which would inevitably interrupt our connections and correspondence. They too have been deaf to the voice of justice and of **consanguinity**. We must, therefore, **acquiesce** in the necessity, which denounces our Separation, and hold them, as we hold the rest of mankind, Enemies in War, in Peace Friends.

32   We, therefore, the Representatives of the United States of America, in General Congress, Assembled, appealing to the Supreme Judge of the world for the **rectitude** of our intentions, do, in the Name, and by the Authority of the good People of these Colonies, solemnly publish and declare, That these United Colonies are, and of Right ought to be Free and Independent States; that they are Absolved from all Allegiance to the British Crown, and that all political connection between them and the State of Great Britain, is and ought to be totally dissolved; and that as Free and Independent States, they have full Power to levy War, conclude Peace, contract Alliances, establish Commerce, and to do all other Acts and Things which Independent States may of right do. And for the support of this Declaration, with a firm reliance on the Protection of Divine Providence, we mutually pledge to each other our Lives, our Fortunes and our sacred Honor.

THINK QUESTIONS

1. According to the first paragraph, what is the purpose of the Declaration of Independence beyond simply claiming freedom from British rule? Identify the phrase that states this purpose most clearly and relate it to the rest of the document.

2. In paragraph 2, what does Jefferson say about the treatment of the colonists under the King of Great Britain? According to Jefferson, what justifies a revolt against the existing government? Use evidence from the text to support your response.

3. Where in the document does Jefferson officially declare independence, and how does he define independence for the states? Use evidence from the text to support your response.

4. Consider the Latin root of the word **consanguinity**: *sanguis,* which means "blood." Combine this with the knowledge that the prefix *con-* means "with" to come up with a reasonable definition of the word in the context of this document. Can you find any supporting evidence of your definition within the same paragraph?

5. Consider the meaning of the Latin root *rect-*: "right" or "straight." Use what you know about word roots and affixes to come up with a definition for the word **rectitude**. Then check your prediction of the word's meaning in context. What other words can be made from this Latin root?

CLOSE READ

Reread the text of the Declaration of Independence. As you reread, complete the Focus Questions below. Then use your answers and annotations from the questions to help you complete the Writing Prompt.

FOCUS QUESTIONS

1. Analyze the structure of the three sections of the Declaration of Independence. Annotate where one section ends and another begins. What is the purpose of each section, and how do these purposes represent the logical sequence of an argument?

2. After the introductory section of the Declaration, Jefferson presents a long list of complaints against Great Britain. The first six of these complaints involve the British king's actions toward American legislatures. Why might Jefferson have chosen to place so much emphasis on this aspect of Britain's relations with its American colonies? Highlight evidence from the text and make annotations to support your explanation.

3. When the Declaration of Independence was read aloud in American cities, people responded enthusiastically. Jefferson used literary elements such as hyperbole to make his manifesto more engaging. Highlight examples of hyperbole, and explain its role in persuading readers to take action.

4. In the conclusion, how does Jefferson restate the claim to his argument? What powers does he claim for the new nation, and why might he have chosen those powers? Support your response with textual evidence.

5. The Essential Question for this unit is "How did a diversity of views transform American society?" How does the Declaration of Independence encourage a diversity of views in America? Highlight evidence from the text and make annotations to support your explanation.

WRITING PROMPT

The Unit Introduction "From Puritanism to the Enlightenment" discusses conflicts in England in the 1600s that changed the country's government in a lasting way; these events included a civil war. Write a comparison and contrast essay in which you compare events in England in the 1600s with the situation in the American colonies, as described by Jefferson in the Declaration of Independence. Include in your analysis a discussion of arguments involving the rights of the people and the powers of the monarch. Use textual evidence to support your analysis.

UNITED STATES V. THE AMISTAD

NON-FICTION
U.S. Supreme Court
1841

INTRODUCTION

The *United States* v. *The Amistad* is a famous U.S. Supreme Court case from 1841 in which the Court had to decide whether to grant freedom to Africans who were kidnapped by Spanish slave traders. The Africans led a violent rebellion aboard the Spanish ship *La Amistad*, and were eventually apprehended near Long Island, New York. *Amistad* was a complicated case that involved international parties, including British and Spanish interests. The Spanish owners of the ship demanded their "property" be returned and cited Pinckney's Treaty of 1795, which established friendship between the United States and Spain, as the legal basis for their claim. John Quincy Adams, who served as the sixth President of the United States, argued before the Supreme Court for the freedom of the Africans

"No man has a right to life or liberty, if he has an enemy able to take them from him."

 FIRST READ

From John Quincy Adams' oral argument in favor of the defendants:

1   There is the principle, on which a particular decision is demanded from this Court, by the Official Journal of the Executive, on behalf of the southern states? Is that a principle recognized by this Court? Is it the principle of that Declaration [of Independence]? It is alleged in the Official Journal, that war gives the right to take the life of our enemy, and that this confers a right to make him a slave, on account of having spared his life. Is that the principle on which these United States stand before the world? That Declaration says that every man is "endowed by his Creator with certain inalienable rights," and that among these are "life, liberty, and the pursuit of happiness." If these rights are inalienable, they are incompatible with the rights of the victor to take the life of his enemy in war, or to spare his life and make him a slave. If this principle is sound, it reduces to brute force all the rights of man. It places all the sacred relations of life at the power of the strongest. No man has a right to life or liberty, if he has an enemy able to take them from him. There is the principle. There is the whole argument of this paper. Now I do not deny that the only principle upon which a color of right can be attributed to the condition of slavery is by assuming that the natural state of man is war. The bright intellect of the South, clearly saw, that without this principle for a corner stone, he had no foundation for his argument. He assumes it therefore without a blush, as Hobbes assumed it to prove that government and **despotism** are synonymous words. I will not here discuss the right or the rights of slavery, but I say that the doctrine of Hobbes, that War is the natural state of man, has for ages been exploded, as equally disclaimed and rejected by the philosopher and the Christian. That it is utterly incompatible with any theory of human rights, and especially with the rights which the Declaration of Independence proclaims as self-evident truths. The moment you come, to the Declaration of Independence, that every man has a right to life and liberty, an inalienable right, this case is decided. I ask nothing more in behalf of these unfortunate men, than this Declaration.

NOTES

From the majority opinion of the Court, delivered by Justice Joseph Story:

2   It has been argued on behalf of the United States, that the Court are bound to deliver them up, according to the treaty of 1795, with Spain, which has in this particular been continued in full force, by the treaty of 1819, ratified in 1821. The sixth article of that treaty, seems to have had, principally, in view cases where the property of the subjects of either state had been taken possession of within the territorial jurisdiction of the other, during war. The eighth article provides for cases where the shipping of the inhabitants of either state are forced, through stress of weather, pursuit of pirates, or enemies, or any other urgent necessity, to seek shelter in the ports of the other. There may well be some doubt entertained, whether the present case, in its actual circumstances, falls within the purview of this article. But it does not seem necessary, for reasons hereafter stated, absolutely to decide it. The ninth article provides, "that all ships and merchandise, of what nature soever, which shall be rescued out of the hands of any pirates or robbers, on the high seas, shall be brought into some port of either state, and shall be delivered to the custody of the officers of that port, in order to be taken care of and restored entire to the true **proprietor**, as soon as due and sufficient proof shall be made concerning the property thereof." This is the article on which the main reliance is placed on behalf of the United States, for the restitution of these negroes. To bring the case within the article, it is essential to establish, First, that these negroes, under all the circumstances, fall within the description of merchandise, in the sense of the treaty. Secondly, That there has been a rescue of them on the high seas, out of the hands of the pirates and robbers; which, in the present case, can only be, by showing that they themselves are pirates and robbers; and, Thirdly, that Ruiz and Montez, the asserted proprietors, are the true proprietors, and have established their title by competent proof.

3   If these negroes were, at the time, lawfully held as slaves under the laws of Spain, and recognised by those laws as property capable of being lawfully bought and sold; we see no reason why they may not justly be deemed within the intent of the treaty, to be included under the denomination of merchandise, and, as such, ought to be restored to the claimants: for, upon that point, the laws of Spain would seem to furnish the proper rule of interpretation. But, admitting this, it is clear, in our opinion, that neither of the other essential facts and requisites has been established in proof; and the *onus probandi* of both lies upon the claimants to give rise to the *casus foederis*. It is plain beyond controversy, if we examine the evidence, that these negroes never were the lawful slaves of Ruiz or Montez, or of any other Spanish subjects. They are natives of Africa, and were kidnapped there, and were unlawfully transported to Cuba, in violation of the laws and treaties of Spain, and the most solemn edicts and declarations of that government. By those laws, and treaties, and edicts, the African slave trade is utterly abolished; the dealing in that trade is deemed a **heinous** crime; and the negroes thereby

introduced into the dominions of Spain, are declared to be free. Ruiz and Montez are proved to have made the pretended purchase of these negroes, with a full knowledge of all the circumstances. And so **cogent** and irresistible is the evidence in this respect, that the District Attorney has admitted in open Court, upon the record, that these negroes were native Africans, and recently imported into Cuba, as alleged in their answers to the libels in the case. The supposed proprietary interest of Ruiz and Montez, is completely displaced, if we are at liberty to look at the evidence of the admissions of the District Attorney.

....

4   It is also a most important consideration in the present case, which ought not to be lost sight of, that, supposing these African negroes not to be slaves, but kidnapped, and free negroes, the treaty with Spain cannot be obligatory upon them; and the United States are bound to respect their rights as much as those of Spanish subjects. The conflict of rights between the parties under such circumstances, becomes positive and inevitable, and must be decided upon the eternal principles of justice and international law. If the contest were about any goods on board of this ship, to which American citizens asserted a title, which was denied by the Spanish claimants, there could be no doubt of the right of such American citizens to **litigate** their claims before any competent American tribunal, notwithstanding the treaty with Spain. A fortiori, the doctrine must apply where human life and human liberty are in issue; and constitute the very essence of the controversy. The treaty with Spain never could have intended to take away the equal rights of all foreigners, who should contest their claims before any of our Courts, to equal justice; or to deprive such foreigners of the protection given them by other treaties, or by the general law of nations. Upon the merits of the case, then, there does not seem to us to be any ground for doubt, that these negroes ought to be deemed free; and that the Spanish treaty interposes no obstacle to the just assertion of their rights.

☁ THINK QUESTIONS

1. How does John Quincy Adams argue that principles in the Declaration of Independence overpower claims made by victors in wartime? Support your answer with textual evidence.

2. What three key questions does Justice Joseph Story identify as the test of whether or not the enslaved passengers on the *Amistad* are subject to Pinckney's Treaty of 1795? How do these questions relate to Adams's argument? Support your answer with evidence from the text.

3. In his first paragraph, Justice Story explains the implications of Pinckney's Treaty of 1795. However, in his second and third paragraphs, he highlights the problems with upholding the treaty. Briefly explain his reasons below. How does this relate to Adams's argument, and what can you infer from this opinion about how courts in the United States apply the principle of natural rights?

4. Use context to determine the meaning of the word **proprietor** as it is used in *United States* v. *The Amistad*. Write your definition of proprietor and tell how you arrived at it.

5. The verb **litigate** means "to make a situation the subject of a lawsuit." Adding the suffix --*ion* creates the word "litigation." What does "litigation" mean?

CLOSE READ

Reread the ruling of *United States* v. *The Amistad.* As you reread, complete the Focus Questions below. Then use your answers and annotations from the questions to help you complete the Writing Prompt.

FOCUS QUESTIONS

1. Toward the end of the excerpt from John Quincy Adams's oral argument, he concedes a point to his opposition, the plaintiffs: "Now I do not deny that the only principle upon which a color of right can be attributed to the condition of slavery is by assuming that the natural state of man is war." Explain why Adams may have conceded this point and how this point relates to the larger pattern of reasoning in his argument. Evaluate the contribution of this point to his overall argument.

2. Justice Story's opinion explains legal issues and discusses the various legalities of the issue at hand. Do you think his personal opinion is in line with his legal interpretation? Why or why not? Cite textual evidence for your response.

3. Recall that rhetoric is the art of speaking and writing persuasively. Reread Adams's argument and highlight at least three examples of rhetorical devices. Make annotations to explain the use of rhetoric and how it impacts his argument.

4. Legal writing contains technical terms, often from Latin. Find one such term in Story's opinion. Define the term, explain what it means in the context of the opinion, and write a short answer explaining how it relates to the opinion as a whole.

5. A diversity of views transformed American society, as did a variety of legal decisions. Briefly recap the Supreme Court decision in *United States* v. *The Amistad*, mentioning key, related issues that would continue to provoke debate through the Civil War. What connections can you make between this decision and subsequent issues about equality in the United States through the 20th century?

WRITING PROMPT

While the scope of *United States* v. *The Amistad* is focused narrowly on one group of enslaved passengers (during a time in which many enslaved Africans endured the brutality of the slave trade) and the Supreme Court focused its attention on the legal issues at hand (not the larger, overall issue of the legality of slavery), this case becomes a touchstone for the movement toward equality in the United States. Imagine you are John Quincy Adams. Write a speech that you would give to the media, outside on the courthouse steps, just following the verdict in the case (as indicated in the majority opinion of the Court delivered by Justice Story). Explain the meaning of the verdict, citing textual evidence from both Adams's argument and the majority opinion of the Court, and describe what further legal and social changes need to be made in the United States of the 1840s.

DEMOCRACY IN AMERICA

NON-FICTION

Alexis de Tocqueville
1835

INTRODUCTION

rench political thinker and historian Alexis de Tocqueville spent nine months touring America before publishing *De la Démocratie* en Amerique in 1835. The landmark work about life and institutions in the evolving democracy of 19th century America has been widely quoted since, and remains relevant for any discussion about the American democratic system. In this excerpt, Tocqueville describes what he considers to be the unique Anglo-American combination of

"Religion is no less the companion of liberty..."

 FIRST READ

From Chapter 2: "The Origins of the Anglo-Americans"

1   The remarks I have made will suffice to display the character of Anglo-American civilization in its true light. It is the result (and this should be constantly present to the mind of two distinct elements), which in other places have been in frequent hostility, but which in America have been admirably incorporated and combined with one another. I allude to the spirit of Religion and the spirit of Liberty.

2   The settlers of New England were at the same time **ardent sectarians** and daring innovators. Narrow as the limits of some of their religious opinions were, they were entirely free from political prejudices. Hence arose two tendencies, distinct but not opposite, which are constantly **discernible** in the manners as well as in the laws of the country.

3   It might be imagined that men who sacrificed their friends, their family, and their native land to a religious conviction were absorbed in the pursuit of the intellectual advantages which they purchased at so dear a rate. The energy, however, with which they strove for the acquirement of wealth, moral enjoyment, and the comforts as well as liberties of the world, is scarcely inferior to that with which they devoted themselves to Heaven.

4   Political principles and all human laws and institutions were moulded and altered at their pleasure; the barriers of the society in which they were born were broken down before them; the old principles which had governed the world for ages were no more; a path without a turn and a field without an horizon were opened to the exploring and ardent curiosity of man: but at the limits of the political world he checks his researches, he **discreetly** lays aside the use of his most **formidable** faculties, he no longer consents to doubt or to innovate, but carefully abstaining from raising the curtain of the sanctuary, he yields with submissive respect to truths which he will not discuss. Thus, in

NOTES

the moral world everything is classed, adapted, decided, and foreseen; in the political world everything is **agitated**, uncertain, and disputed: in the one is a passive, though a voluntary, obedience; in the other an independence scornful of experience and jealous of authority.

5 These two tendencies, apparently so **discrepant**, are far from conflicting; they advance together, and mutually support each other. Religion perceives that civil liberty affords a noble exercise to the faculties of man, and that the political world is a field prepared by the Creator for the efforts of the intelligence. Contented with the freedom and the power which it enjoys in its own sphere, and with the place which it occupies, the empire of religion is never more surely established than when it reigns in the hearts of men unsupported by aught beside its native strength.

6 Religion is no less the companion of liberty in all its battles and its triumphs; the cradle of its infancy, and the divine source of its claims. The safeguard of morality is religion, and morality is the best security of law and the surest pledge of freedom.

THINK QUESTIONS

1. Describe the "sectarian" and "innovator" urges of the early settlers of New England, as noted by de Tocqueville. Cite textual evidence to support your response.

2. What is the difference between the moral world and the political world? According to de Tocqueville, how do the two work together? Support your response with textual evidence.

3. Summarize de Tocqueville's views of Anglo-Americans. What unique advantage does the group seem to have? Support your answer with textual evidence.

4. The word **sectarians** comes from the Middle English word *secte,* meaning "group" or "faction." Using this information and the context of the word as it is used in *Democracy in America*, determine the meaning of "sectarians." Write your definition and explain how you arrived at it.

5. Use context to determine the meaning of **agitated** as it is used in *Democracy in America*. Write your definition of "agitated" and explain how you arrived at it.

CLOSE READ

Reread the excerpt from *Democracy in America*. As you reread, complete the Focus Questions below. Then use your answers and annotations from the questions to help you complete the Writing Prompt.

FOCUS QUESTIONS

1. What does de Tocqueville wish to convey in the first paragraph of the chapter? What is its purpose? What ideas does de Tocqueville introduce in the second and third paragraph? Why are the ideas introduced in this order? Support your answer with textual evidence and make annotations to explain your answer.

2. Summarize paragraph 4 of the excerpt. How does de Tocqueville use this paragraph to support his claim about the settlers of New England? Highlight your textual evidence and make annotations to support your ideas.

3. In paragraph 4, de Tocqueville uses a metaphor to explain why the process for setting up a government in New England was special. What is the metaphor, and what does de Tocqueville mean by it? How does this metaphor support his central idea? Highlight textual evidence to support your response.

4. How, in de Tocqueville's view, do religious conviction and political freedom "mutually support each other"? Why did these two attitudes appear in the United States? Highlight evidence from the text and make annotations to support your explanation.

5. According to de Tocqueville, how did the diversity of views in the early New England settlers transform American society? Highlight textual evidence to support your response.

WRITING PROMPT

Evaluate the effectiveness of de Tocqueville's structure in this excerpt from *Democracy in America*. In what order does de Tocqueville present his ideas, and why does this order matter? Does the structure make his argument clear, convincing, and engaging? Make sure your response has a clear claim supported by textual evidence.

A VINDICATION OF THE RIGHTS OF WOMAN

NON-FICTION
Mary Wollstonecraft
1792

INTRODUCTION

Mary Wollstonecraft, a British writer from the 18th century, is considered the mother of the modern feminist movement. Wollstonecraft called for a "revolution in female manners" and for a world in which women were not limited to menial labor and not relegated to the dependent roles of wife, companion, and governess. This excerpt is reproduced from Wollstonecraft's groundbreaking work of feminist philosophy, *A Vindication of the Rights of Woman*.

"I wish to persuade women to endeavour to acquire strength…"

FIRST READ

From the Introduction

1 I have turned over various books written on the subject of education, and patiently observed the conduct of parents and the management of schools; but what has been the result? a profound conviction, that the neglected education of my fellow creatures is the grand source of the misery I deplore; and that women in particular, are rendered weak and wretched by a variety of concurring causes, originating from one hasty conclusion. The conduct and manners of women, in fact, evidently prove, that their minds are not in a healthy state; for, like the flowers that are planted in too rich a soil, strength and usefulness are sacrificed to beauty; and the flaunting leaves, after having pleased a fastidious eye, fade, disregarded on the stalk, long before the season when they ought to have arrived at maturity. One cause of this barren blooming I attribute to a false system of education, gathered from the books written on this subject by men, who, considering females rather as women than human creatures, have been more anxious to make them alluring mistresses than rational wives; and the understanding of the sex has been so bubbled by this **specious** homage, that the civilized women of the present century, with a few exceptions, are only anxious to inspire love, when they ought to cherish a nobler ambition, and by their abilities and virtues exact respect.

....

2 Yet, because I am a woman, I would not lead my readers to suppose, that I mean violently to agitate the contested question respecting the equality and inferiority of the sex; but as the subject lies in my way, and I cannot pass it over without subjecting the main tendency of my reasoning to misconstruction, I shall stop a moment to deliver, in a few words, my opinion. In the government of the physical world, it is observable that the female, in general, is inferior to the male. The male pursues, the female yields—this is the law of nature; and

it does not appear to be suspended or **abrogated** in favour of woman. This physical superiority cannot be denied—and it is a noble prerogative! But not content with this natural pre-eminence, men endeavour to sink us still lower, merely to render us alluring objects for a moment; and women, intoxicated by the adoration which men, under the influence of their senses, pay them, do not seek to obtain a durable interest in their hearts, or to become the friends of the fellow creatures who find amusement in their society.

3   I am aware of an obvious inference: from every quarter have I heard exclamations against masculine women; but where are they to be found? If, by this appellation, men mean to **inveigh** against their ardour in hunting, shooting, and gaming, I shall most cordially join in the cry; but if it be, against the imitation of manly virtues, or, more properly speaking, the attainment of those talents and virtues, the exercise of which ennobles the human character, and which raise females in the scale of animal being, when they are comprehensively termed mankind—all those who view them with a philosophical eye must, I should think, wish with me, that they may every day grow more and more masculine.

....

4   My own sex, I hope, will excuse me, if I treat them like rational creatures, instead of flattering their fascinating graces, and viewing them as if they were in a state of perpetual childhood, unable to stand alone. I earnestly wish to point out in what true dignity and human happiness consists—I wish to persuade women to endeavour to acquire strength, both of mind and body, and to convince them, that the soft phrases, susceptibility of heart, delicacy of sentiment, and refinement of taste, are almost synonymous with epithets of weakness, and that those beings who are only the objects of pity and that kind of love, which has been termed its sister, will soon become objects of contempt.

5   Dismissing then those pretty feminine phrases, which the men condescendingly use to soften our slavish dependence, and despising that weak elegancy of mind, exquisite sensibility, and sweet docility of manners, supposed to be the sexual characteristics of the weaker vessel, I wish to show that elegance is inferior to virtue, that the first object of laudable ambition is to obtain a character as a human being, regardless of the distinction of sex; and that secondary views should be brought to this simple touchstone.

....

6   The education of women has, of late, been more attended to than formerly; yet they are still reckoned a frivolous sex, and ridiculed or pitied by the writers who endeavour by satire or instruction to improve them. It is acknowledged that they spend many of the first years of their lives in acquiring a smattering

of accomplishments: meanwhile, strength of body and mind are sacrificed to libertine notions of beauty, to the desire of establishing themselves, the only way women can rise in the world—by marriage. And this desire making mere animals of them, when they marry, they act as such children may be expected to act: they dress; they paint, and nickname God's creatures. Surely these weak beings are only fit for the seraglio! Can they govern a family, or take care of the poor babes whom they bring into the world?

7   If then it can be fairly deduced from the present conduct of the sex, from the prevalent fondness for pleasure, which takes place of ambition and those nobler passions that open and enlarge the soul; that the instruction which women have received has only tended, with the constitution of civil society, to render them insignificant objects of desire; mere propagators of fools! if it can be proved, that in aiming to accomplish them, without cultivating their understandings, they are taken out of their sphere of duties, and made ridiculous and useless when the short lived bloom of beauty is over, I presume that RATIONAL men will excuse me for endeavouring to persuade them to become more masculine and respectable.

8   Indeed, the word *masculine* is only a **bugbear**. There is little reason to fear that women will acquire too much courage or fortitude, for their apparent inferiority with respect to bodily strength must render them, in some degree, dependent on men in the various relations of life, but why should it be increased by prejudices that give a sex to virtue and confound simple truths with sensual reveries?

From Chapter II: The Prevailing Opinion of a Sexual Character Discussed.

9   Consequently, the most perfect education, in my opinion, is such an exercise of the understanding as is best calculated to strengthen the body and form the heart; or, in other words, to enable the individual to attain such habits of virtue as will render it independent. In fact, it is a farce to call any being virtuous whose virtues do not result from the exercise of its own reason. This was Rousseau's opinion respecting men: I extend it to women, and confidently assert that they have been drawn out of their sphere by false refinement, and not by an endeavour to acquire masculine qualities. Still the regal homage which they receive is so intoxicating, that, till the manners of the times are changed, and formed on more reasonable principles, it may be impossible to convince them that the illegitimate power, which they obtain by degrading themselves, is a curse, and that they must return to nature and equality, if they wish to secure the placid satisfaction that unsophisticated affections impart. ... I may be accused of arrogance; still I must declare, what I firmly believe, that all the writers who have written on the subject of female education and manners, from Rousseau to Dr. Gregory, have contributed to render women

more artificial, weaker characters, than they would otherwise have been; and, consequently, more useless members of society....

10 ...The woman who has only been taught to please, will soon find that her charms are oblique sun-beams, and that they cannot have much effect on her husband's heart when they are seen every day, when the summer is past and gone....

11 Nature has given woman a weaker frame than man; but, to ensure her husband's affections, must a wife, who, by the exercise of her mind and body, whilst she was discharging the duties of a daughter, wife, and mother, has allowed her constitution to retain its natural strength, and her nerves a healthy tone, is she, I say, to condescend, to use art, and feign a sickly delicacy, in order to secure her husband's affection? Weakness may excite tenderness, and gratify the arrogant pride of man; but the lordly caresses of a protector will not gratify a noble mind that pants for and deserves to be respected. Fondness is a poor substitute for friendship!

12 In a **seraglio**, I grant, that all these arts are necessary; the epicure must have his palate tickled, or he will sink into apathy; but have women so little ambition as to be satisfied with such a condition? Can they supinely dream life away in the lap of pleasure, or in the languor of weariness, rather than assert their claim to pursue reasonable pleasures, and render themselves conspicuous, by practising the virtues which dignify mankind? Surely she has not an immortal soul who can loiter life away, merely employed to adorn her person, that she may amuse the languid hours, and soften the cares of a fellow-creature who is willing to be enlivened by her smiles and tricks, when the serious business of life is over.

13 Besides, the woman who strengthens her body and exercises her mind will, by managing her family and practising various virtues, become the friend, and not the humble dependent of her husband; and if she deserves his regard by possessing such substantial qualities, she will not find it necessary to conceal her affection, nor to pretend to an unnatural coldness of constitution to excite her husband's passions. In fact, if we revert to history, we shall find that the women who have distinguished themselves have neither been the most beautiful nor the most gentle of their sex.

14 Nature, or to speak with strict propriety God, has made all things right; but man has sought him out many inventions to mar the work. I now allude to that part of Dr. Gregory's treatise, where he advises a wife never to let her husband know the extent of her sensibility or affection. Voluptuous precaution; and as ineffectual as absurd. Love, from its very nature, must be transitory. To seek for a secret that would render it constant, would be as wild a search as for the philosopher's stone, or the grand panacea; and the discovery would be

equally useless, or rather **pernicious** to mankind. The most holy band of society is friendship. It has been well said, by a shrewd satirist, "that rare as true love is, true friendship is still rarer."

15　This is an obvious truth, and the cause not lying deep, will not elude a slight glance of inquiry.

16　Love, the common passion, in which chance and sensation take place of choice and reason, is in some degree, felt by the mass of mankind; for it is not necessary to speak, at present, of the emotions that rise above or sink below love. This passion, naturally increased by suspense and difficulties, draws the mind out of its accustomed state, and exalts the affections; but the security of marriage, allowing the fever of love to subside, a healthy temperature is thought insipid, only by those who have not sufficient intellect to substitute the calm tenderness of friendship, the confidence of respect, instead of blind admiration, and the sensual emotions of fondness.

17　This is, must be, the course of nature—friendship or indifference inevitably succeeds love. And this constitution seems perfectly to harmonize with the system of government which prevails in the moral world. Passions are spurs to action, and open the mind; but they sink into mere appetites, become a personal momentary gratification, when the object is gained, and the satisfied mind rests in enjoyment. ...

18　But to view the subject in another point of view. Do passive **indolent** women make the best wives? Confining our discussion to the present moment of existence, let us see how such weak creatures perform their part? Do the women who, by the attainment of a few superficial accomplishments, have strengthened the prevailing prejudice, merely contribute to the happiness of their husbands? Do they display their charms merely to amuse them? And have women, who have early imbibed notions of passive obedience, sufficient character to manage a family or educate children? So far from it, that, after surveying the history of woman, I cannot help agreeing with the severest satirist, considering the sex as the weakest as well as the most oppressed half of the species. ...

19　But avoiding, as I have hitherto done, any direct comparison of the two sexes collectively, or frankly acknowledging the inferiority of woman, according to the present appearance of things, I shall only insist, that men have increased that inferiority till women are almost sunk below the standard of rational creatures. Let their faculties have room to unfold, and their virtues to gain strength, and then determine where the whole sex must stand in the intellectual scale. Yet, let it be remembered, that for a small number of distinguished women I do not ask a place.

THINK QUESTIONS

1. Who does Wollstonecraft say has written the books about women's education? Why is this detail important to Wollstonecraft's analysis? What inference can readers make based on this detail? Support your answer with textual evidence.

2. According to Wollstonecraft, what will make women better wives and mothers? What can readers infer about Wollstonecraft's view of marriage based on this idea? Cite textual evidence to support your response.

3. What is a seraglio, and why does Wollstonecraft refer to it in the text? Based on this reference, what can readers infer about Wollstonecraft's ideas about the traditional role of women? Support your response with evidence from the text.

4. Use context to determine the meaning of the word **inveigh** as it is used in *A Vindication of the Rights of Woman*. Write your definition of "inveigh" and explain how you arrived at it.

5. Use context to determine the meaning of the word **indolent** as it is used in *A Vindication of the Rights of Woman*. Write your definition of "indolent" and explain how you arrived at it.

CLOSE READ

Reread the excerpt from *A Vindication on the Rights of Woman*. As you reread, complete the Focus Questions below. Then use your answers and annotations from the questions to help you complete the Writing Prompt.

FOCUS QUESTIONS

1. What are the main ideas of the first paragraph? What textual evidence gives readers clues that help determine the main ideas of the paragraph? Highlight evidence from the text and make annotations to explain your choices.

2. In the Introduction, which words does the writer call attention to with italics or all capital letters? Why are these words important to the central idea the writer conveys in the text? Make annotations marking these words, and make inferences about the text. Support your answer with textual evidence and make annotations to explain your answer choices.

3. In Chapter II, the writer makes references to Rousseau and Dr. Gregory. Why does the writer refer to these men? How do these references help her develop the central idea of the text? Highlight your textual evidence and make annotations to explain your choices.

4. What does the writer say about men's and women's bodies? Why does the writer include these details? How do they help develop the central idea of the text? Highlight evidence from the text and make annotations to support your explanation.

5. In the second to last paragraph, Wollstonecraft writes, "I cannot help agreeing with the severest satirist, considering the sex as the weakest as well as the most oppressed half of the species." Why does Wollstonecraft agree that women are weak? How does this sentence serve as a summary of the central idea of the text? Highlight textual evidence and make annotations to explain your ideas.

6. What is Wollstonecraft's view of marriage? How does it differ from the view of marriage suggested by Anne Bradstreet's poem "To My Dear and Loving Husband"? What do these differing viewpoints suggest about how attitudes about marriage changed from the mid-17th century to the late 18th century? Highlight textual evidence and make annotations to explain your ideas.

WRITING PROMPT

Write an objective summary of the excerpt from Mary Wollstonecraft's *A Vindication of the Rights of Woman*. What is the author's central idea? What supporting ideas and details does the author use to develop her central idea? Remember to use an objective tone and include only the most important details from the text. Include at least one direct quotation to support your summary.

WOMAN IN THE NINETEENTH CENTURY

NON-FICTION
Margaret Fuller
1845

INTRODUCTION

Margaret Fuller was one of the earliest and most vocal supporters of women's rights in the United States. Fuller's book *Woman in the Nineteenth Century* laid the groundwork for the women's suffrage movement, which eventually resulted in the Nineteenth Amendment and women's right to vote. In the excerpt, Fuller focuses on women's social status and concludes that women's issues cannot be advanced unless women are allowed to represent

"We would have every path laid open to Woman as freely as to Man."

FIRST READ

NOTES

From Part I: Woman in the Nineteenth Century

1   Knowing that there exists in the minds of men a tone of feeling toward women as toward slaves, such as is expressed in the common phrase, "Tell that to women and children;" that the infinite soul can only work through them in already ascertained limits; that the gift of reason, Man's highest prerogative, is allotted to them in much lower degree; that they must be kept from mischief and melancholy by being constantly engaged in active labor, which is to be furnished and directed by those better able to think, etc., etc.,—we need not multiply instances, for who can review the experience of last week without recalling words which imply, whether in jest or earnest, these views, or views like these,—knowing this, can we wonder that many reformers think that measures are not likely to be taken in behalf of women, unless their wishes could be publicly represented by women?

2   "That can never be necessary," cry the other side. "All men are privately influenced by women; each has his wife, sister, or female friends, and is too much biased by these relations to fail of representing their interests; and, if this is not enough, let them propose and enforce their wishes with the pen. The beauty of home would be destroyed, the delicacy of the sex be violated, the dignity of halls of legislation degraded, by an attempt to introduce them there. Such duties are inconsistent with those of a mother;" and then we have **ludicrous** pictures of ladies in hysterics at the polls, and senate-chambers filled with cradles.

3   But if, in reply, we admit as truth that Woman seems destined by nature rather for the inner circle, we must add that the arrangements of civilized life have not been, as yet, such as to secure it to her. Her circle, if the duller, is not the quieter. If kept from "excitement," she is not from drudgery. Not only the Indian squaw carries the burdens of the camp, but the favorites of Louis XIV accompany him in his journeys, and the washerwoman stands at her tub, and

carries home her work at all seasons, and in all states of health. Those who think the physical circumstances of Woman would make a part in the affairs of national government unsuitable, are by no means those who think it impossible for negresses to endure field-work, even during pregnancy, or for seamstresses to go through their killing labors.

4   As to the use of the pen, there was quite as much opposition to Woman's possessing herself of that help to free agency as there is now to her seizing on the **rostrum** or the desk; and she is likely to draw, from a permission to plead her cause that way, opposite inferences to what might be wished by those who now grant it.

5   As to the possibility of her filling with grace and dignity any such position, we should think those who had seen the great actresses, and heard the Quaker preachers of modern times, would not doubt that Woman can express publicly the fullness of thought and creation, without losing any of the peculiar beauty of her sex. What can pollute and tarnish is to act thus from any motive except that something needs to be said or done. Woman could take part in the processions, the songs, the dances of old religion; no one fancied her delicacy was impaired by appearing in public for such a cause.

6   As to her home, she is not likely to leave it more than she now does for balls, theatres, meetings for promoting missions, revival meetings, and others to which she flies, in hope of an animation for her existence commensurate with what she sees enjoyed by men. Governors of ladies'-fairs are no less engrossed by such a charge, than the governor of a state by his; presidents of Washingtonian societies no less away from home than presidents of conventions. If men look straitly to it, they will find that, unless their lives are domestic, those of the women will not be. A house is no home unless it contain food and fire for the mind as well as for the body. The female Greek, of our day, is as much in the street as the male to cry, "What news?" We doubt not it was the same in Athens of old. The women, shut out from the market-place, made up for it at the religious festivals. For human beings are not so constituted that they can live without expansion. If they do not get it in one way, they must in another, or perish.

7   As to men's representing women fairly at present, while we hear from men who owe to their wives not only all that is comfortable or graceful, but all that is wise, in the arrangement of their lives, the frequent remark, "You cannot reason with a woman,"—when from those of delicacy, nobleness, and poetic culture, falls the contemptuous phrase "women and children," and that in no light **sally** of the hour, but in works intended to give a permanent statement of the best experiences,—when not one man, in the million, shall I say? no, not in the hundred million, can rise above the belief that Woman was made *for Man,*—when such traits as these are daily forced upon the attention, can

NOTES

we feel that Man will always do justice to the interests of Woman? Can we think that he takes a sufficiently discerning and religious view of her office and destiny *ever* to do her justice, except when prompted by sentiment,— accidentally or transiently, that is, for the sentiment will vary according to the relations in which he is placed? The lover, the poet, the artist, are likely to view her nobly. The father and the philosopher have some chance of liberality; the man of the world, the legislator for expediency, none.

8   Under these circumstances, without attaching importance, in themselves, to the changes demanded by the champions of Woman, we hail them as signs of the times. We would have every **arbitrary** barrier thrown down. We would have every path laid open to Woman as freely as to Man. Were this done, and a slight temporary fermentation allowed to subside, we should see crystallizations more pure and of more various beauty. We believe the divine energy would pervade nature to a degree unknown in the history of former ages, and that no discordant collision, but a ravishing harmony of the spheres, would ensue.

9   Yet, then and only then will mankind be ripe for this, when inward and outward freedom for Woman as much as for Man shall be acknowledged as a right, not yielded as a concession. As the friend of the negro assumes that one man cannot by right hold another in bondage, so should the friend of Woman assume that Man cannot by right lay even well-meant restrictions on Woman. If the negro be a soul, if the woman be a soul, apparelled in flesh, to one Master only are they accountable. There is but one law for souls, and, if there is to be an interpreter of it, he must come not as man, or son of man, but as son of God.

10   Were thought and feeling once so far elevated that Man should esteem himself the brother and friend, but nowise the lord and tutor, of Woman,— were he really bound with her in equal worship,—arrangements as to function and employment would be of no consequence. What Woman needs is not as a woman to act or rule, but as a nature to grow, as an intellect to discern, as a soul to live freely and unimpeded, to unfold such powers as were given her when we left our common home. If fewer talents were given her, yet if allowed the free and full employment of these, so that she may render back to the giver his own with **usury**, she will not complain; nay, I dare to say she will bless and rejoice in her earthly birth-place, her earthly lot. Let us consider what obstructions impede this good era, and what signs give reason to hope that it draws near.

11   I was talking on this subject with Miranda, a woman, who, if any in the world could, might speak without heat and bitterness of the position of her sex. Her father was a man who cherished no sentimental reverence for Woman, but a firm belief in the equality of the sexes. She was his eldest child, and came to

Please note that excerpts and passages in the StudySync® library and this workbook are intended as touchstones to generate interest in an author's work. The excerpts and passages do not substitute for the reading of entire texts, and StudySync® strongly recommends that students seek out and purchase the whole literary or informational work in order to experience it as the author intended. Links to online resellers are available in our digital library. In addition, complete works may be ordered through an authorized reseller by filling out and returning to StudySync® the order form enclosed in this workbook.

Reading & Writing Companion   **259**

him at an age when he needed a companion. From the time she could speak and go alone, he addressed her not as a plaything, but as a living mind. Among the few verses he ever wrote was a copy addressed to this child, when the first locks were cut from her head; and the reverence expressed on this occasion for that cherished head, he never belied. It was to him the temple of immortal intellect. He respected his child, however, too much to be an indulgent parent. He called on her for clear judgment, for courage, for honor and fidelity; in short, for such virtues as he knew. In so far as he possessed the keys to the wonders of this universe, he allowed free use of them to her, and, by the incentive of a high expectation, he forbade, so far as possible, that she should let the privilege lie idle.

12   Thus this child was early led to feel herself a child of the spirit. She took her place easily, not only in the world of organized being, but in the world of mind. A dignified sense of self-dependence was given as all her portion, and she found it a sure anchor. Herself securely anchored, her relations with others were established with equal security. She was fortunate in a total absence of those charms which might have drawn to her bewildering flatteries, and in a strong electric nature, which repelled those who did not belong to her, and attracted those who did. With men and women her relations were noble,—affectionate without passion, intellectual without coldness. The world was free to her, and she lived freely in it. Outward adversity came, and inward conflict; but that faith and self-respect had early been awakened which must always lead, at last, to an outward serenity and an inward peace.

13   Of Miranda I had always thought as an example, that the restraints upon the sex were **insuperable** only to those who think them so, or who noisily strive to break them. She had taken a course of her own, and no man stood in her way. Many of her acts had been unusual, but excited no uproar. Few helped, but none checked her; and the many men who knew her mind and her life, showed to her confidence as to a brother, gentleness as to a sister. And not only refined, but very coarse men approved and aided one in whom they saw resolution and clearness of design. Her mind was often the leading one, always effective.

 THINK QUESTIONS

1. Why does Fuller draw a comparison between women and slaves? What can readers infer about women's rights in the nineteenth century based on this comparison? Cite textual evidence to support your response.

2. What locations does Fuller list in paragraph 6? Why does she list these places? What can readers infer about the perception of women in the nineteenth century based on the information in this paragraph? Support your inference with evidence from the text.

3. Who is Miranda? What words and phrases does Fuller use to describe her? How does Miranda relate to the main ideas of the text? Support your response with evidence from the text.

4. Use context to determine the meaning of the word **rostrum** as it is used in *Woman in the Nineteenth Century*. Write your definition of "rostrum" and explain how you arrived at it.

5. Use context to determine the meaning of the word **sally** as it is used in *Woman in the Nineteenth Century*. Write your definition of "sally" and tell how you arrived at it.

CLOSE READ

Reread the excerpt from *Woman in the Nineteenth Century.* As you reread, complete the Focus Questions below. Then use your answers and annotations from the questions to help you complete the Writing Prompt.

FOCUS QUESTIONS

1. How does Fuller's argumentative tone and distinct point of view help make paragraphs 1 and 2 especially powerful? Highlight evidence from the text and make annotations to explain your response.

2. Fuller begins paragraphs 4–7 with the words "As to." Why? What points of view are revealed by this choice? Highlight your textual evidence and make annotations to explain your reasoning.

3. What point of view is advanced in paragraphs 8–10? How is it different from the point of view that Fuller reveals earlier in the text? Highlight your textual evidence and make annotations to explain your response.

4. What is Fuller's point of view in paragraphs 11–13 regarding the upbringing and education of young girls? What is the purpose of discussing Miranda? Highlight evidence from the text and make annotations to support your explanation.

5. Fuller's text argues one strong point of view and also explains the claims belonging to those who oppose her. Why does Fuller present both sides of the issue? How did the diversity of views shown in this text affect American society during this time period? Highlight textual evidence and make annotations to explain your answer.

WRITING PROMPT

Margaret Fuller's *Woman in the Nineteenth Century* presents counterclaims to many anti-suffrage views of the time. In a short compare-and-contrast essay, identify some of the anti-suffrage points of view against which the author argues. Then discuss how she makes use of counterclaims to advance her own point of view. Support your writing with evidence from the text.

GULLIVER'S TRAVELS

FICTION
Jonathan Swift
1726

INTRODUCTION

Jonathan Swift's *Gulliver's Travels* is considered a masterpiece of satire, critiquing 18th century Enlightenment thinking that reason alone can advance human society and arguing for the importance of religion and compassion in the guidance of human affairs. In this excerpt from Part I, Swift offers satirical commentary on 18th century English politics. Lilliput, an island of miniature people engaged in ridiculous conflicts, is said to symbolize the Kingdom of England, with the two major political parties of England, the Tories and Whigs, represented by Lilliput's High Heels and Low Heels. Rival island Blefuscu

"I found my arms and legs were strongly fastened on each side to the ground..."

 FIRST READ

From Part I: A Voyage to Lilliput, Chapter I

1   What became of my companions in the boat, as well as of those who escaped on the rock, or were left in the vessel, I cannot tell; but conclude they were all lost. For my own part, I swam as fortune directed me, and was pushed forward by wind and tide. I often let my legs drop, and could feel no bottom; but when I was almost gone, and able to struggle no longer, I found myself within my depth; and by this time the storm was much **abated**. The declivity was so small, that I walked near a mile before I got to the shore, which I **conjectured** was about eight o'clock in the evening. I then advanced forward near half a mile, but could not discover any sign of houses or inhabitants; at least I was in so weak a condition, that I did not observe them. I was extremely tired, and with that, and the heat of the weather, and about half a pint of brandy that I drank as I left the ship, I found myself much inclined to sleep. I lay down on the grass, which was very short and soft, where I slept sounder than ever I remembered to have done in my life, and, as I reckoned, about nine hours; for when I awaked, it was just day-light. I attempted to rise, but was not able to stir: for, as I happened to lie on my back, I found my arms and legs were strongly fastened on each side to the ground; and my hair, which was long and thick, tied down in the same manner. I likewise felt several slender **ligatures** across my body, from my arm-pits to my thighs. I could only look upwards; the sun began to grow hot, and the light offended my eyes. I heard a confused noise about me; but in the posture I lay, could see nothing except the sky.

2   In a little time I felt something alive moving on my left leg, which advancing gently forward over my breast, came almost up to my chin; when, bending my eyes downwards as much as I could, I perceived it to be a human creature not six inches high, with a bow and arrow in his hands, and a quiver at his back. In the mean time, I felt at least forty more of the same kind (as I conjectured) following the first. I was in the utmost astonishment, and roared

so loud, that they all ran back in a fright; and some of them, as I was afterwards told, were hurt with the falls they got by leaping from my sides upon the ground. However, they soon returned, and one of them, who ventured so far as to get a full sight of my face, lifting up his hands and eyes by way of admiration, cried out in a shrill but distinct voice, *Hekinah degul*: the others repeated the same words several times, but then I knew not what they meant. I lay all this while, as the reader may believe, in great uneasiness.

3   At length, struggling to get loose, I had the fortune to break the strings, and wrench out the pegs that fastened my left arm to the ground; for, by lifting it up to my face, I discovered the methods they had taken to bind me, and at the same time with a violent pull, which gave me excessive pain, I a little loosened the strings that tied down my hair on the left side, so that I was just able to turn my head about two inches. But the creatures ran off a second time, before I could seize them; whereupon there was a great shout in a very shrill accent, and after it ceased I heard one of them cry aloud *Tolgo phonac*; when in an instant I felt above a hundred arrows discharged on my left hand, which, pricked me like so many needles; and besides, they shot another flight into the air, as we do bombs in Europe, whereof many, I suppose, fell on my body, (though I felt them not), and some on my face, which I immediately covered with my left hand. When this shower of arrows was over, I fell a groaning with grief and pain; and then striving again to get loose, they discharged another volley larger than the first, and some of them attempted with spears to stick me in the sides; but by good luck I had on a buff **jerkin**, which they could not pierce.

4   I thought it the most prudent method to lie still, and my design was to continue so till night, when, my left hand being already loose, I could easily free myself: and as for the inhabitants, I had reason to believe I might be a match for the greatest army they could bring against me, if they were all of the same size with him that I saw. But fortune disposed otherwise of me. When the people observed I was quiet, they discharged no more arrows; but, by the noise I heard, I knew their numbers increased; and about four yards from me, over against my right ear, I heard a knocking for above an hour, like that of people at work; when turning my head that way, as well as the pegs and strings would permit me, I saw a stage erected about a foot and a half from the ground, capable of holding four of the inhabitants, with two or three ladders to mount it: from whence one of them, who seemed to be a person of quality, made me a long speech, whereof I understood not one syllable. But I should have mentioned, that before the principal person began his oration, he cried out three times, *Langro dehul san* (these words and the former were afterwards repeated and explained to me); whereupon, immediately, about fifty of the inhabitants came and cut the strings that fastened the left side of my head, which gave me the liberty of turning it to the right, and of observing the person and gesture of him that was to speak. He appeared to be of a

NOTES

middle age, and taller than any of the other three who attended him, whereof one was a page that held up his train, and seemed to be somewhat longer than my middle finger; the other two stood one on each side to support him. He acted every part of an orator, and I could observe many periods of threatenings, and others of promises, pity, and kindness.

5   I answered in a few words, but in the most submissive manner, lifting up my left hand, and both my eyes to the sun, as calling him for a witness; and being almost famished with hunger, having not eaten a morsel for some hours before I left the ship, I found the demands of nature so strong upon me, that I could not forbear showing my impatience (perhaps against the strict rules of decency) by putting my finger frequently to my mouth, to signify that I wanted food. The *hurgo* (for so they call a great lord, as I afterwards learnt) understood me very well. He descended from the stage, and commanded that several ladders should be applied to my sides, on which above a hundred of the inhabitants mounted and walked towards my mouth, laden with baskets full of meat, which had been provided and sent thither by the king's orders, upon the first intelligence he received of me. I observed there was the flesh of several animals, but could not distinguish them by the taste. There were shoulders, legs, and loins, shaped like those of mutton, and very well dressed, but smaller than the wings of a lark. I ate them by two or three at a mouthful, and took three loaves at a time, about the bigness of musket bullets.

....

6   It seems, that upon the first moment I was discovered sleeping on the ground, after my landing, the emperor had early notice of it by an express; and determined in council, that I should be tied in the manner I have related, (which was done in the night while I slept;) that plenty of meat and drink should be sent to me, and a machine prepared to carry me to the capital city.

7   This resolution perhaps may appear very bold and dangerous, and I am confident would not be imitated by any prince in Europe on the like occasion. However, in my opinion, it was extremely prudent, as well as generous: for, supposing these people had endeavoured to kill me with their spears and arrows, while I was asleep, I should certainly have awaked with the first sense of smart, which might so far have roused my rage and strength, as to have enabled me to break the strings wherewith I was tied; after which, as they were not able to make resistance, so they could expect no mercy.

From Part I: A Voyage to Lilliput, Chapter IV

8   One morning, about a **fortnight** after I had obtained my liberty, Reldresal, principal secretary (as they style him) for private affairs, came to my house attended only by one servant. He ordered his coach to wait at a distance, and desired I would give him an hours audience; which I readily consented to, on

account of his quality and personal merits, as well as of the many good offices he had done me during my solicitations at court. I offered to lie down that he might the more conveniently reach my ear, but he chose rather to let me hold him in my hand during our conversation.

9   He began with compliments on my liberty; said "he might pretend to some merit in it;" but, however, added, "that if it had not been for the present situation of things at court, perhaps I might not have obtained it so soon. For," said he, "as **flourishing** a condition as we may appear to be in to foreigners, we labour under two mighty evils: a violent faction at home, and the danger of an invasion, by a most potent enemy, from abroad.

10   As to the first, you are to understand, that for about seventy moons past there have been two struggling parties in this empire, under the names of *Tramecksan* and *Slamecksan,* from the high and low heels of their shoes, by which they distinguish themselves. It is alleged, indeed, that the high heels are most agreeable to our ancient constitution; but, however this be, his majesty has determined to make use only of low heels in the administration of the government, and all offices in the gift of the crown, as you cannot but observe; and particularly that his majesty's imperial heels are lower at least by a *drurr* than any of his court (*drurr* is a measure about the fourteenth part of an inch). The **animosities** between these two parties run so high, that they will neither eat, nor drink, nor talk with each other. We compute the *Tramecksan,* or high heels, to exceed us in number; but the power is wholly on our side. We apprehend his imperial highness, the heir to the crown, to have some tendency towards the high heels; at least we can plainly discover that one of his heels is higher than the other, which gives him a hobble in his gait.

11   Now, in the midst of these intestine disquiets, we are threatened with an invasion from the island of Blefuscu, which is the other great empire of the universe, almost as large and powerful as this of his majesty. For as to what we have heard you affirm, that there are other kingdoms and states in the world inhabited by human creatures as large as yourself, our philosophers are in much doubt, and would rather conjecture that you dropped from the moon, or one of the stars; because it is certain, that a hundred mortals of your bulk would in a short time destroy all the fruits and cattle of his majesty's dominions: besides, our histories of six thousand moons make no mention of any other regions than the two great empires of Lilliput and Blefuscu. Which two mighty powers have, as I was going to tell you, been engaged in a most obstinate war for six-and-thirty moons past.

12   It began upon the following occasion. It is allowed on all hands, that the primitive way of breaking eggs, before we eat them, was upon the larger end; but his present majesty's grandfather, while he was a boy, going to eat an egg, and breaking it according to the ancient practice, happened to cut one

of his fingers. Whereupon the emperor his father published an edict, commanding all his subjects, upon great penalties, to break the smaller end of their eggs. The people so highly resented this law, that our histories tell us, there have been six rebellions raised on that account; wherein one emperor lost his life, and another his crown.

13   These civil commotions were constantly **fomented** by the monarchs of Blefuscu; and when they were **quelled**, the exiles always fled for refuge to that empire. It is computed that eleven thousand persons have at several times suffered death, rather than submit to break their eggs at the smaller end. Many hundred large volumes have been published upon this controversy: but the books of the Big-endians have been long forbidden, and the whole party rendered incapable by law of holding employments. During the course of these troubles, the emperors of Blefuscu did frequently **expostulate** by their ambassadors, accusing us of making a schism in religion, by offending against a fundamental doctrine of our great prophet Lustrog, in the fifty-fourth chapter of the Blundecral (which is their Alcoran).

14   This, however, is thought to be a mere strain upon the text; for the words are these: 'that all true believers break their eggs at the convenient end.' And which is the convenient end, seems, in my humble opinion to be left to every man's conscience, or at least in the power of the chief magistrate to determine. Now, the Big-endian exiles have found so much credit in the emperor of Blefuscu's court, and so much private assistance and encouragement from their party here at home, that a bloody war has been carried on between the two empires for six-and-thirty moons, with various success; during which time we have lost forty capital ships, and a much a greater number of smaller vessels, together with thirty thousand of our best seamen and soldiers; and the damage received by the enemy is reckoned to be somewhat greater than ours. However, they have now equipped a numerous fleet, and are just preparing to make a descent upon us; and his imperial majesty, placing great confidence in your valour and strength, has commanded me to lay this account of his affairs before you."

15   I desired the secretary to present my humble duty to the emperor; and to let him know, "that I thought it would not become me, who was a foreigner, to interfere with parties; but I was ready, with the hazard of my life, to defend his person and state against all invaders."

THINK QUESTIONS

1. Why did the small people of Lilliput first try to attack Gulliver but then provide him with food? Use textual details to support your inference.

2. Write two or three sentences describing the two political parties in Lilliput; include details from the text.

3. Use details from the text to write two or three sentences describing why Reldresal believes that his people face "the danger of an invasion."

4. Use context to determine the meaning of the word **ligatures** as it is used in the excerpt from *Gulliver's Travels*. Write your definition of "ligatures" and tell how you arrived at it.

5. Use the context clues provided in the passage to determine the meaning of **animosities.** Write your definition of "animosities" and tell how you arrived at it.

CLOSE READ

Reread the excerpt from *Gulliver's Travels*. As you reread, complete the Focus Questions below. Then use your answers and annotations from the questions to help you complete the Writing Prompt.

FOCUS QUESTIONS

1. In Chapter I of *Gulliver's Travels*, the narrator exhibits a variety of emotions. Describe these changes in emotion and why they occur. How does the point of view chosen for Gulliver help us to understand his emotions? Highlight evidence from the text and make annotations to explain your choices.

2. In paragraphs 3 and 4, the Lilliputians attack Gulliver with arrows and spears but then stop their attack. Make an inference about why they likely attacked Gulliver and why they stopped. Support your answer with textual evidence and make annotations to explain your answer choices.

3. Reldresal quotes a statement by the prophet Lustrog, "that all true believers break their eggs at the convenient end." He adds his own comment that determining which end is convenient should "be left to every man's conscience." How does this comment connect with ideas in fundamental American documents, such as the Declaration of Independence? Support your opinion with examples and details.

4. One reason that writers during Swift's era used satire to criticize government leaders is that the writers were unlikely to be punished for their work if they approached it in this way. Why would it be difficult to prove that Swift is criticizing the rulers of Britain in *Gulliver's Travels*? Support your answer with textual evidence.

5. In Chapter IV, Gulliver listens to Reldresal describe the two political parties in Lilliput. What makes this description a satire? The Essential Question for this unit is about a "diversity of views." What message do you think Swift is sending to his readers about the diversity of views among British politicians? Highlight evidence from the text and make annotations to explain your choices.

WRITING PROMPT

Literary critics view *Gulliver's Travels* as a satire on the human condition as well as a satire on European politics. Analyze how Swift uses Gulliver's point of view to promote his own ideas. What kinds of human behavior is Swift satirizing? Name at least two. Support your writing with evidence from the text.

REMARKS CONCERNING THE SAVAGES OF NORTH AMERICA

NON-FICTION
Benjamin Franklin
1784

INTRODUCTION

Benjamin Franklin, a widely admired historical figure, was an author, printer, scientist, inventor and statesman, in addition to being one of the Founding Fathers of the United States. Among his many accomplishments, Franklin also wrote humorous satirical works. In this essay, he defends the Native Americans, and offers biting commentary about the uncivil behavior of American colonists,

"Our laborious manner of Life, compared with theirs, they esteem slavish and base."

 FIRST READ

1   SAVAGES we call them, because their manners differ from ours, which we think the perfection of civility; they think the same of theirs.

2   Perhaps, if we could examine the manners of different nations with Impartiality, we should find no People so rude, as to be without any Rules of Politeness; nor any so polite, as not to have some remains of Rudeness.

3   The Indian Men, when young, are Hunters and Warriors; when old, Counselors; for all their Government is by Counsel, or Advice, of the sages; there is no Force, there are no Prisons, no Officers to compel Obedience, or inflict punishment. Hence they generally study **Oratory**; the best speaker having the most Influence. The Indian Women till the Ground, dress the Food, nurse and bring up the Children, and preserve and hand down to posterity the Memory of Public Transactions. These Employments of Men and Women are accounted natural and honorable. Having few Artificial Wants, they have abundance of Leisure for Improvement by Conversation. Our laborious manner of Life, compared with theirs, they esteem slavish and base; and the Learning, on which we value ourselves, they regard as frivolous and useless. An instance of this occurred at the Treaty of Lancaster, in Pennsylvania, 1744, between the Government of Virginia and the Six Nations. After the principal Business was settled, the commissioners from Virginia acquainted the Indians by a Speech, that there was at Williamsburg a College, with a Fund for Educating Indian Youth; and that, if the Six Nations would send down half a dozen of their sons to that College, the government would take Care that they should be well provided for, and instructed in all the Learning of the white People. It is one of the Indian Rules of Politeness not to answer a public Proposition the same day that it is made; they think it would be treating it as a light Matter; and that they show it Respect by taking time to consider it, as of a Matter important. They therefore deferred their Answer till the day following; when their Speaker began by expressing their deep Sense of the kindness of the Virginia Government, in making them that Offer; for we know,

says he, that you highly esteem the kind of Learning taught in those Colleges, and that the Maintenance of our Young men, while with you, would be very expensive to you. We are convinced, therefore, that you mean to do us good by your Proposal, and we thank you heartily. But who are wise, must know that different Nations have different Conceptions of things; and you will therefore not take it amiss, if our Ideas of this Kind of Education happen not to be the same with yours. We have had some Experience of it: Several of our Young People were formerly brought up at the Colleges of the Northern Provinces; they were instructed in all your sciences; but when they came back to us, they were bad runners, **ignorant** of every means of living in the Woods, unable to bear either Cold or Hunger, knew neither how to build a Cabin, take a Deer, or kill an Enemy, spoke our Language imperfectly; were therefore neither fit for Hunters, Warriors, or Counselors; they were totally good for nothing. We are however not the less obliged by your kind Offer, though we decline accepting it; and to show our grateful Sense of it, if the gentlemen of Virginia will send us a dozen of their Sons, we will take great Care of their Education, instruct them in all we know, and make *Men* of them.

4   Having frequent occasions to hold public Councils, they have acquired great Order and Decency in conducting them. The old Men sit in the foremost Ranks, the warriors in the next, and the Women and Children in the hindmost. The business of the Women is to take exact notice of what passes, Imprint it in their memories, for they have no Writing, and communicate it to their children. They are the Records of the Council, and they preserve traditions of the Stipulations in Treaties a hundred Years back, which when we compare with our Writings we always find exact. He that would speak, rises. The rest observe a profound Silence. When he has finished and sits down, they leave him five or six Minutes to recollect, that if he has omitted anything he intended to say, or has anything to add, he may rise again and deliver it. To interrupt another, even in common conversation, is reckoned highly indecent. How different this is from the Conduct of a polite British House of Commons, where scarce a Day passes without some Confusion, that makes the speaker hoarse in calling *to order*; and how different from the mode of Conversation in many polite Companies of Europe, where if you do not deliver your Sentence with great rapidity, you are cut off in the middle of it by the impatient **Loquacity** of those you converse with, and never suffer'd to finish it.

5   The politeness of these savages in conversation is indeed carried to excess, since it does not permit them to contradict or deny the Truth of what is asserted in their Presence. By this means they indeed avoid Disputes, but then it becomes difficult to know their Minds, or what Impression you make upon them. The Missionaries who have attempted to convert them to Christianity, all complain of this as one of the great Difficulties of their Mission. The Indians hear with Patience the Truths of the Gospel explained to them,

and give their usual Tokens of **assent** and Approbation: you would think they were convinced. No such Matter. It is mere Civility.

6   A Swedish Minister, having assembled the Chiefs of the Susquehanah Indians, made a Sermon to them, acquainting them with the principal historical Facts on which our Religion is founded, such as the Fall of our first Parents by Eating an Apple, the Coming of Christ to repair the Mischief, his Miracles and Suffering, etc. When he had finished, an Indian Orator stood up to thank him. What you have told us, says he, is all very good. It is indeed bad to eat Apples. It is better to make them all into Cyder. We are much obliged by your Kindness in coming so far to tell us those things which you have heard from your Mothers. In Return, I will tell you some of those we have heard from ours.

7   In the Beginning, our Fathers had only the Flesh of Animals to subsist on, and if their hunting was unsuccessful, they were starving. Two of our young Hunters, having killed a Deer, made a Fire in the Woods to broil some Part of it. When they were about to satisfy their Hunger, they beheld a beautiful young Woman descend from the clouds, and seat herself on that Hill which you see yonder among the blue Mountains. They said to each other, it is a Spirit that perhaps has smelt our broiling Venison and wishes to eat of it: let us offer some to her. They presented her with the Tongue: She was pleased with the taste of it, and said, your Kindness shall be rewarded. Come to this Place after thirteen Moons, and you shall find something that will be of great Benefit in nourishing you and your Children to the latest Generations. They did so, and, to their Surprise, found Plants they had never seen before, but which from that ancient time have been constantly cultivated among us to our great Advantage. Where her right Hand had touch'd the Ground, they found Maize; where her left Hand had touch'd it, they found Kidney-beans; and where her backside had sat on it, they found Tobacco. The good missionary, disgusted with this idle Tale, said, what I delivered to you were sacred truths; but what you tell me is mere Fable, Fiction, and Falsehood. The Indian, offended, repli'd My Brother, it seems your Friends have not done you Justice in your Education; they have not well instructed you in the Rules of common Civility. You saw that we who understand and practice those Rules, believed all your Stories; you refuse to believe ours?

8   When any of them come into our Towns, our People are apt to crowd round them, gaze upon them, and **incommode** them where they desire to be private; this they esteem great Rudeness, and the Effect of the **want** of Instruction in the Rules of Civility and good Manners. We have, say they, as much Curiosity as you, and when you come into our towns we wish for Opportunities of looking at you; but for this purpose we hide ourselves behind Bushes, where you are to pass, and never intrude ourselves into Company.

9   Their Manner of entering one anothers Village has likewise its Rules. It is reckon'd uncivil in traveling Strangers to enter a Village abruptly, without giving Notice of their Approach. Therefore as soon as they arrive within hearing, they stop and hollow, remaining there till invited to enter. Two old Men usually come out to them, and lead them in. There is in every Village a vacant Dwelling, called the Strangers House. Here they are placed, while the old men go round from Hut to Hut, acquainting the Inhabitants, that Strangers are arrived, who are probably hungry and weary; and every one sends them what he can spare of Victuals and Skins to repose on. When the Strangers are refresh'd, Pipes & Tobacco are brought; and then, but not before, conversation begins, with Enquiries who they are, whither bound, what news, &c. and it usually ends with Offers of service, if the Strangers have Occasion of Guides, or any necessaries for continuing their Journey; and nothing is exacted for the Entertainment.

10   The same Hospitality, esteemed among them as a principal Virtue, is practiced by private Persons; of which *Conrad Weiser,* our Interpreter, gave the following Instances. He had been naturaliz'd among the Six-Nations, and spoke well the Mohawk Language. In going thro' the Indian Country, to carry a message from our Governor to the Council at *Onondaga,* he called at the Habitation of Canassetego, an old Acquaintance, who embraced him, spread Furs for him to sit on, placed before him some boiled Beans and Venison, and mixed some Rum and Water for his drink. When he was well refresh'd, and had lit his Pipe, Canassetego began to converse with him, ask'd how he had fared the many Years since they had seen each other, whence he then came, what occasioned the journey, etc.

11   Conrad answered all his Questions; and when the Discourse began to flag the Indian, to continue it, said, "Conrad, you have lived long among the white People, and know something of their Customs; I have been sometimes at Albany, and have observed, that once in seven Days, they shut up their Shops and assemble all in the great house; tell me, what it is for? what do they do there? They meet there, says Conrad, to hear & learn *good things.* I do not doubt, says the Indian, that they tell you so; they have told me the same; but I doubt the Truth of what they say; & I will tell you my Reasons. I went lately to Albany to sell my Skins, & buy Blankets, Knives, Powder, Rum, &c. You know I used generally to deal with Hans Hanson; but I was a little inclined this time to try some other Merchants. However, I called first upon Hans, and ask'd him what he would give for Beaver; He said he could not give any more than four Shillings a Pound; but, says he, I cannot talk on Business now; this is the Day when we meet together to learn *good things,* and I am going to the Meeting. So I thought to myself, since we cannot do any Business to day, I may as well go to the Meeting too; and I went with him.

12   There stood up a Man in black, and began to talk to the People very angrily. I did not understand what he said; but, perceiving that he looked much at me & at Hanson, I imagined he was angry at seeing me there; so I went out, sat down near the House, struck Fire & lit my Pipe; waiting till the Meeting should break up. I thought too, that the Man had mentioned something of Beaver, and I suspected it might be the Subject of their Meeting. So when they came out I accosted any merchant; well, Hans, says I, I hope you have agreed to give more than four shillings a pound. No, says he, I cannot give so much. I cannot give more than three Shillings and six Pence. I then spoke to several other Dealers, but they all sung the same song, three & six Pence, three & six Pence. This made it clear to me that my Suspicion was right; and that whatever they pretended of Meeting to learn *good things,* the real Purpose was to consult how to cheat Indians in the Price of Beaver.

13   Consider but a little, Conrad, and you must be of my Opinion. If they met so often to learn *good things,* they would certainly have learned some before this time. But they are still ignorant. You know our Practice. If a white man, in traveling thro' our Country, enters one of our Cabins, we all treat him as I treat you; we dry him if he is wet, we warm him if he is cold, and give him Meat & Drink that he may allay his Thirst and Hunger, & we spread soft Furs for him to rest & sleep on: We demand nothing in return.

14   But if I go into a White man's House at Albany, and ask for Victuals and Drink, they say, Where is your Money? and if I have none they say, Get out, you Indian Dog. You see they have not yet learnt those little *good things,* that we need no Meetings to be instructed in, because our Mothers taught them to us when we were Children. And therefore it is impossible their Meetings should be as they say for any such Purpose, or have any such Effect; they are only to contrive *the Cheating of Indians in the Price of Beaver.*

THINK QUESTIONS

1. Based on information in paragraph 3, how and why are Native Americans and American colonists educated differently? Cite textual evidence to support your response.

2. According to paragraph 8, why do Native Americans hide when white people approach? Is this the real reason? How do you know? Cite textual evidence to support your response.

3. What are the "Meeting" and "good things" that Canassetego discusses in paragraphs 11–14? What inference can readers make based on this description? Support your inference with textual evidence.

4. Use context to determine the meaning of the word **ignorant** as it is used in "Remarks Concerning the Savages of North America." Write your definition of "ignorant" and explain how you arrived at it.

5. Use context to determine the meaning of the word **incommode** as it is used in "Remarks Concerning the Savages of North America." Write your definition of "incommode" and tell how you arrived at it.

CLOSE READ

Reread the essay "Remarks Concerning the Savages of North America." As you reread, complete the Focus Questions below. Then use your answers and annotations from the questions to help you complete the Writing Prompt.

FOCUS QUESTIONS

1. Explain how the first paragraph sets up the comparison-and-contrast structure of the text. Highlight evidence from the text and make annotations to explain your answer.

2. How does Benjamin Franklin use reasoning in paragraph 3 to show why the Native Americans did not want to accept the offer to send some young men to Willamsburg College? Support your answer with textual evidence and make annotations to explain your response.

3. What point(s) of view does Franklin use in the text? How does the point of view change throughout the text? Consider Franklin's use of pronouns. Highlight your textual evidence and make annotations to explain your choices.

4. In paragraphs 6–8 Franklin includes anecdotes of conversations between Native Americans and Christian missionaries. How do these anecdotes contribute to the overall structure of the text? How does this structure help Franklin make his points clearly? Highlight evidence from the text and make annotations to support your explanation.

5. Does the structure of the text help Franklin make his points effectively? Why or why not? Cite examples that are especially effective. Highlight textual evidence and make annotations to explain your ideas.

6. What two points of view does Franklin's text reveal? How are these points of view alike? How are they different? What do these distinct points of view suggest about American society in the late 18th century? Highlight textual evidence and make annotations to support your inferences.

WRITING PROMPT

Is Franklin's argument in "Remarks Concerning the Savages of North America" convincing? Why or why not? Consider how text structure, point of view, and logical reasoning work together to help readers understand the author's main points. Begin by identifying the text structure, and explain how it helps the writer advance his argument. Support your writing with evidence from the text.

EXTENDED WRITING PROJECT

ysync

WRITE

x

ED WRITING PROJECT
GUMENTATIVE WRITING

Extended Writing Project:
Argumentative Writing
by StudySync

1 WRITE

Extended Writing Project Prompt and Directions:
Think about the key ideals of the United States today, su
individuality, and so on. Focus on one Ideal and choose
the Ideal. Argue why your chosen text is the best embod
the text matters today. Support your statements about co
outside research. Cite evidence from your chosen text in y

Your argumentative essay should include:

- an introduction with a clear claim explaining your chosen idea
  best represents it
- clear and cohesive body paragraphs with analysis supported by relevant reasons and
  evidence
- a conclusion that effectively wraps up your essay

Font   Size   B I I Iₓ A U

The

I'm

ARGUMENTATIVE WRITING

WRITING PROMPT

Think about the key ideals of the United States today, such as equality, self-sufficiency, individuality, and so on. Focus on one ideal and choose a text from the unit that best embodies the ideal. Argue why your chosen text is the best embodiment of the ideal, and explain why the text matters today. Support your statements about contemporary American society with outside research. Cite evidence from your chosen text in your response.

Your argumentative essay should include:

- an introduction with a clear claim explaining your chosen ideal and how your chosen text best represents it
- clear and cohesive body paragraphs with analysis supported by relevant reasons and evidence
- a conclusion that effectively wraps up your essay

Argumentative writing asks you to make a claim or take a position on a topic and then to identify, evaluate, and provide textual evidence that offers reasonable support for the claim. Some examples of argumentative writing include editorials, opinion pieces, and some forms of literary analysis.

Strong argumentative writing begins with an introductory paragraph that provides a general context for the topic and then presents a reasonably narrow thesis statement that explicitly states the writer's claim, or position on the topic. The body paragraphs of an argumentative essay focus on providing relevant reasons and evidence that support the thesis. Argumentative essays often contain direct quotations, or citations, submitted as evidence. All quotations should be introduced and explained. Argumentative essays develop a writer's claim through transition words that create cohesion and that make connections between reasons and citations. Strong argumentative essays end with a conclusion that revisits the main point of the thesis statement and synthesizes the evidence that has been provided in support of the writer's claim.

The features of argumentative writing include:

- clear and logical organizational structure
- an introduction with a clear thesis statement that makes a claim
- body paragraphs that develop and support the claim with reasons and relevant evidence
- precise language and domain-specific vocabulary
- citations of sources
- a concluding paragraph that summarizes the argument and restates the thesis statement

As you continue with this extended writing project, you'll receive more instructions and practice to help you craft each of the elements of argumentative writing in your own essay.

STUDENT MODEL

Before you get started on your own argumentative essay, begin by reading this essay that one student wrote in response to the writing prompt. As you read this student model, highlight and annotate the features of argumentative writing that the student included in her essay.

"Every Path Laid Open":
Equality and Woman in the Nineteenth Century

"All men are created equal." That's the promise made to every American. Equality is a key ideal of the United States. As a country, we like to think that everyone, regardless of gender, race, or social class, is equal in the eyes of the law and has equal opportunities to live his or her best life. Margaret Fuller's Woman in the Nineteenth Century best embodies the American ideal of equality because she powerfully argues for rights for a long-oppressed group: women. The text still matters today because American society has made great strides in gender equality but total equality has still not been achieved.

In 1776, the Declaration of Independence set forth the ideal of equality: "all men are created equal, that they are endowed by their Creator with certain unalienable Rights, that among these are Life, Liberty, and the pursuit of Happiness." Notice, however, Jefferson's choice of words. All *men*, not *people*, are created equal and have rights. Women were left out. The Constitution begins with the words "We the People," a phrase rooted in populism, but really meaning white land-owning men. Almost one hundred years later, after the Civil War, that wording changed slightly. The Fourteenth Amendment to the Constitution, approved in 1868, declares, "All persons born or naturalized in the United States . . . are citizens of the United States" (amend. XIV, sec. 1). The Fourteenth Amendment seemed to be a victory for women because it promised "equal protection of the laws." Those words have been the basis for most gender and racial discrimination lawsuits ever since. In practice, though, only men were considered citizens. The Fifteenth Amendment made no mention of women at all: "The right of citizens of the United States to vote shall not be denied or abridged by the United States or by any state on account of race, color, or previous condition of servitude" (amend. XV, sec. 1). It would be another half century before women could vote.

Margaret Fuller's *Woman in the Nineteenth Century* was published in 1845, years before the Fourteenth and Fifteenth Amendments were added to the Constitution. At the time, women clearly did not have "equal protection of the laws." Unmarried women had some rights, such as the right to own property, but a woman lost those rights to her husband as soon as she got married (Salmon). Women were expected to stay home, and few were educated. Fuller sees this life as one of "drudgery." In her book, Fuller argues for women to be granted the same rights and opportunities as men. Fuller says that men do not want women to be educated because they are likely to draw "opposite inferences to what might be wished by those who now grant it"—in other words, to have ideas different from those of the men currently in power, which would undermine their authority. In addition, Fuller argues that women must be granted the opportunity to discover their talents for themselves outside of the home:

> What Woman needs is not as a woman to act or rule, but as a nature to grow, as an intellect to discern, as a soul to live freely and unimpeded, to unfold such powers as were given her when we left our common home.

Fuller does not want men to grant these freedoms to women in the same way they indulge a child. She calls for "inward and outward freedom for Woman as much as for Man shall be acknowledged as a *right*, not yielded as a concession." That is an important distinction to be made, that women have rights that should be granted and that women should be in control of their own rights and lives.

Some may argue that in all of Fuller's arguments about equality, she does leave out an important subset of women: that of the lower class. The rights and privileges Fuller calls for would apply only to upper-class women. In the early 1800s, only upper-class people were educated. Many states at the time of Fuller's writing still required men to be property owners in order to vote, and people of color were still restricted from voting in most states (Mintz). The women in Fuller's text attend "balls, theatres, meetings for promoting missions, revival meetings." Those are not activities of the lower classes. Fuller, however, seems to acknowledge that her argument is for wealthy women. She cites working-class women in support of her argument that women are as capable as men:

> Not only the Indian squaw carries the burdens of the camp, but the favorites of Louis XIV accompany him in his journeys, and the washerwoman stands at her tub, and carries home her work at all seasons, and in all states of health. Those who think the physical circumstances of Woman would make a part in the affairs of national government unsuitable, are by no means those who think it impossible for negresses to endure field-work, even during pregnancy, or for seamstresses to go through their killing labors.

Fuller's choice of words in this passage is important. The fact that she holds up these women as evidence to her critic's counterclaim shows that she admires working women's strength and perseverance. (Fuller's use of racially charged language such as "squaw" and "negresses" is more a sign of the time period than racism on her part.) Fuller would grant all women the same opportunities.

It has been almost 170 years since Fuller wrote *Woman in the Nineteenth Century*, but some of her ideas are still too relevant. In good news, women in 2014 comprised 53 percent of voters, which is about equivalent to women's population (Liasson). In 2012, women overwhelmingly supported President Barack Obama, a key reason for his win (Abdullah). Fuller would likely celebrate the direct influence of women on politics, and she'd be glad to know there were no "ladies in hysterics at the polls." But women still do not have equal representation in Congress. In 2014, there were 99 women in Congress. It seems like a lot, but that is only

19 percent of total seats—nowhere near the 53 percent share of women in the electorate ("Women in the U.S. Congress 2014 Fact Sheet"). As Fuller wrote, "Can we think that he takes a sufficiently discerning and religious view of her office and destiny *ever* to do her justice, except when prompted by sentiment,—accidentally or transiently, that is, for the sentiment will vary according to the relations in which he is placed?" Some men may represent women fairly, but they can't "do justice to the interests of Woman." Women need to be present in Congress to represent their interests.

When Fuller was writing *Woman in the Nineteenth Century*, it was only a few generations after the Founding Fathers. The Civil War was still twenty years off; the Nineteenth Amendment was 75 years away. Her ideas may not have immediately changed the state of women in the United States, but her ideas were ahead of her time. Her arguments in favor of gender equality reflect both the American ideal of equality and the patriotic value of fighting for what you believe in. In short, Fuller's "mind was often the leading one, always effective."

THINK QUESTIONS

1. What is the central or main idea of this essay? How do you know? Cite textual evidence to support your response.

2. What context does the writer provide about equality in the United States? How does this information support the writer's central idea?

3. What details does the writer provide in support of her statements about the contemporary relevance of *Woman in the Nineteenth Century*? What makes it persuasive?

4. Thinking about the writing prompt, which selections, Blasts, or other resources would you like to use to create your own argumentative essay? What are some ideas that you may want to develop into your own piece?

5. Based on what you have read, listened to, or researched, how would you answer the question: *How did a diversity of views transform American society?* How have these views contributed to modern ideals in the United States?

PREWRITE

WRITING PROMPT

Think about the key ideals of the United States today, such as equality, self-sufficiency, individuality, and so on. Focus on one ideal and choose a text from the unit that best embodies the ideal. Argue why your chosen text is the best embodiment of the ideal, and explain why the text matters today. Support your statements about contemporary American society with outside research. Cite evidence from your chosen text in your response.

Your argumentative essay should include:

- an introduction with a clear claim explaining your chosen ideal and how your chosen text best represents it
- clear and cohesive body paragraphs with analysis supported by relevant reasons and evidence
- a conclusion that effectively wraps up your essay

As you prewrite your argumentative essay, first think about the key ideals of the United States. What adjectives would you use to describe the goals of the United States? Remember that ideals are positive attributes that may not have been achieved yet. Start to make a list of these ideals.

Then think about the texts you've read so far in this unit. Do any of these texts contain ideas that match an ideal from your list? You may want to add to your list as you recall the central ideas of the texts from the unit. What do these texts have to say about these ideals? How might that text or the ideas in that text have contributed to American society? What claim about American ideals or society could you make based on these texts? What quotations or evidence could you pull from these texts to support a claim? Answering these questions may help you solidify the ideas you want to discuss in your essay.

SKILL:
THESIS
STATEMENT

⭐ DEFINE

In an argument, the thesis statement introduces what the writer will argue in the essay. The thesis statement expresses the writer's central or main claim, or the position the writer will develop in the body of the essay. A vague, obvious truth does not make a good thesis statement; an argumentative thesis statement should be a precise, knowledgeable claim that is clearly related to the prompt. The thesis statement usually appears in the essay's introductory paragraph and is often the introduction's last sentence. The rest of the paragraphs in the essay all support the thesis statement with facts, evidence, and examples.

⋯ IDENTIFICATION AND APPLICATION

In an argumentative essay, a thesis statement:

- clearly states the writer's central claim
- is a precise, knowledgeable claim based on textual evidence, not the writer's personal opinions
- lets the reader know what to expect in the body of the essay
- sets up the essay so that the reader has a clear idea of what the writer is trying to prove
- appears in the first paragraph

↻ MODEL

The writer of the student model argumentative essay "Every Path Laid Open" puts the thesis statement near the end of the first paragraph. The writer leads up to the thesis statement by first identifying the key ideal he or she will be writing about and then considering which text from the unit best embodies that ideal, thus tying together both parts of the prompt:

NOTES

"All men are created equal." That's the promise made to every American. Equality is a key ideal of the United States. As a country, we like to think that everyone, regardless of gender, race, or social class, is equal in the eyes of the law and has equal opportunities to live his or her best life. **Margaret Fuller's** *Woman in the Nineteenth Century* **best embodies the American ideal of equality because she powerfully argues for rights for a long-oppressed group: women. The text still matters today because American society has made great strides in gender equality but total equality has still not been achieved.**

The writer's thesis is strong because it makes a decisive and text-based claim. After reading these sentences, readers know they can expect the writer to offer textual evidence to prove these ideas. Most thesis statements are made of a single sentence. There is one part of the prompt, however, that is missing from the first bold sentence that makes up the thesis statement. This sentence does not address why the text is still important today. The writer includes this information in the sentence that follows, making this a two-sentence thesis statement. Sometimes, as in essays like this that have long or complicated claims, it is better to split the thesis into two sentences than to risk putting too much information into an unclear or run-on sentence.

 PRACTICE

Refer to the list you created in the prewrite part of the process of American ideals and the texts that embody them. Write a thesis statement for your argumentative essay that states your main idea or claim in relation to the essay prompt. When you are finished, trade with a partner and offer each other feedback. How clear was the writer's main point or claim? Is it obvious what ideal this essay will focus on? Does the thesis specifically address all the requirements of the prompt? Offer each other suggestions, and remember that they are most helpful when they are constructive.

NOTES

SKILL: REASONS AND RELEVANT EVIDENCE

⭐ DEFINE

Before beginning to write an argumentative essay, writers must plan what they are going to say. The most important part of the plan is an explanation of the reasoning behind their argument. Reasons support the writer's thesis statement and seek to convince readers of the writer's point of view. To support their reasoning, writers need to present credible, provable evidence in the form of facts, quotations, and other documented research. Textual evidence is the information that supports the writer's claim in an argument. Strong textual evidence may be in the form of quotations from experts, facts, statistics, or references to other credible sources. Weaker textual evidence cannot always be proven to be true. It may be in the form of opinions, personal beliefs, or emotional appeals. In addition to explaining their own reasons, good writers use reasoning and relevant evidence to develop and address counterclaims, or opposing claims, that state the opposite position or point of view. To hold readers' interest, writers must also establish the significance of their claims. In other words, they need to let readers know why their argumentative essay is worth reading.

••• IDENTIFICATION AND APPLICATION

Step 1:

Review your thesis statement. To identify relevant supporting details, ask yourself, "What is my main idea or central claim about this topic?" For example, here is the thesis statement from the student model:

> Margaret Fuller's *Woman in the Nineteenth Century* best embodies the American ideal of equality because she powerfully argues for rights for a long-oppressed group: women. The text still matters today because American society has made great strides in gender equality but total equality has still not been achieved.

Step 2:

Ask what a reader needs to know about the topic (for example, why equality is a key American ideal or how women have been "long-oppressed") in order to understand the main idea. A writer may draw on facts or quotations from credible sources to explain ideas readers need to know.

> In 1776, the Declaration of Independence set forth the ideal of equality: "all men are created equal, that they are endowed by their Creator with certain unalienable Rights, that among these are Life, Liberty, and the pursuit of Happiness."

A writer might add another detail to develop and strengthen the claim further in the continued hopes of convincing the reader:

> All *men*, not *people*, are created equal and have rights. Women were left out.

In this case, the writer builds his or her claim by first drawing upon a credible foundational document, the Declaration of Independence, to establish equality as an American ideal and then by analyzing the quotation to show that women have not always been considered equal under the law.

Step 3:

Look for other related facts, quotations, details, and statistics. These will strengthen your thesis statement. Keep in mind that identifying and gathering supporting details is a building process. In an essay, one sentence often builds on another and guides the reader forward. Unrelated details, however, can stop readers in their tracks and leave them confused. Ask yourself:

- Is this information necessary to the reader's understanding?
- Does this information help to develop and prove my point?
- Does this information relate closely to my thesis statement?
- Can I find stronger evidence to support my argument?

 MODEL

The writer of the student model argumentative essay "Every Path Laid Open" chose Margaret Fuller's *Woman in the Nineteenth Century* as the text that best embodies the ideal of equality. However, the writer also draws textual evidence from other foundational documents to support the claims made in the essay.

The writer found examples of textual evidence that explain why equality is a key ideal in the United States. Then he or she used the following chart to organize ideas generated during prewriting. Such a chart helps the writer organize the body of the essay and ensure that all claims are supported and help develop the thesis statement.

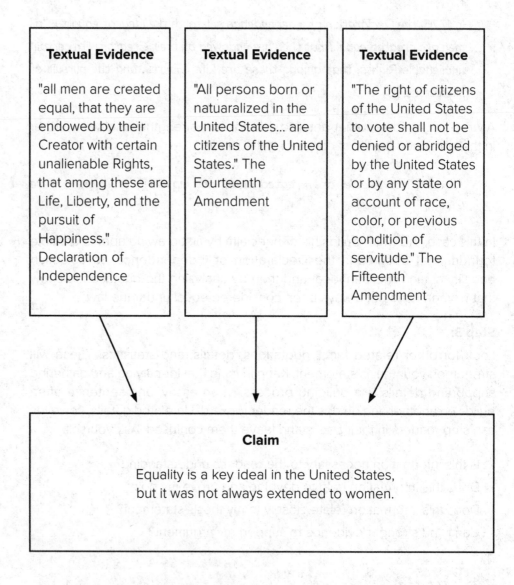

Textual Evidence

"all men are created equal, that they are endowed by their Creator with certain unalienable Rights, that among these are Life, Liberty, and the pursuit of Happiness." Declaration of Independence

Textual Evidence

"All persons born or natuaralized in the United States... are citizens of the United States." The Fourteenth Amendment

Textual Evidence

"The right of citizens of the United States to vote shall not be denied or abridged by the United States or by any state on account of race, color, or previous condition of servitude." The Fifteenth Amendment

Claim

Equality is a key ideal in the United States, but it was not always extended to women.

The information in the top three boxes provides textual evidence the writer uses to build the first body paragraph of the essay. The bottom box contains a claim that helps develop the writer's thesis statement.

 PRACTICE

Fill out a textual evidence chart using the textual evidence you will use to support your thesis statement in your argumentative essay. List as many quotations or facts in the boxes as necessary. Complete additional charts to develop supporting claims as needed.

NOTES

Organize
ARGUMENTATIVE
WRITING

sync skills

SKILL:
ORGANIZE
ARGUMENTATIVE
WRITING

⭐ DEFINE

Writers of persuasive or argumentative essays intend to convince readers of their position or point of view on a subject. In order to be successful, they need to build a clear **organizational structure** that shows how their reasons and relevant evidence relate to and support their claims, or arguments. The writer's central claim is stated in an argumentative thesis statement, which is usually found at the end of the **introduction.** Writers include supporting evidence in the **body paragraphs** that follow. In addition to presenting evidence to support their claims in the body paragraphs, writers must also distinguish their claims from counterclaims and any alternate claims that may be similar to their own.

Informational/explanatory texts often use sequential, chronological, problem-and-solution, comparison-and-contrast, or cause-and-effect text structures, but writers of argumentative texts do not always rely on these structures to build their arguments. The general structure of an argumentative essay contains an introduction, body paragraphs, and a **conclusion.** The body paragraphs might appear in an order that begins with the writer's most important point and leads to the least important or in an ascending sequence that builds up to the writer's central claim and supporting evidence. Alternatively, body paragraphs may appear in chronological or sequential order reflecting the development of cultural or historical ideas. In an argumentative essay, the writer is free to organize information in whatever way he or she finds most effective.

IDENTIFICATION AND APPLICATION

- An argumentative essay is made up of an introduction, body paragraphs, and a conclusion.

- In the introduction, the writer takes a position on the topic and states a claim in a precise, knowledgeable thesis statement.

- The body of the essay contains facts, quotations, statistics, or other factual data and uses logical reasoning to develop the writer's thesis statement.

- One or more body paragraphs may be devoted to acknowledging counterclaims or alternative claims, but the majority of the information in the body should support and develop the writer's thesis statement.

- An argumentative essay should be organized in a way that is both clear and effective in order to convince the reader of the writer's point of view on the topic.

- The conclusion wraps up the writer's ideas and restates the central claim in a way that follows from and supports the rest of the essay.

- Writers may consider writing an outline to help organize the claims, counterclaims, and evidence they will use to develop their argument.

 MODEL

Writers of argumentative essays are charged with the task of organizing information in a way that will be convincing to readers. The writer of "Every Path Laid Open" does not follow a single organizational text structure, but rather combines several in order to make the central argument of the essay clear to readers. The first body paragraph uses a chronological structure to establish historical context for the writer's argument, tracing the evolution of American citizenship from the Declaration of Independence through the Fifteenth Amendment to the Constitution:

> In 1776, the Declaration of Independence set forth the ideal of equality: "all men are created equal, that they are endowed by their Creator with certain unalienable Rights, that among these are Life, Liberty, and the pursuit of Happiness." ... The Fourteenth Amendment to the Constitution, approved in 1868, declares, "All persons born or naturalized in the United States ... are citizens of the United States" (amend. XIV, sec. 1). ... The Fifteenth Amendment made no mention of women at all: "The right of citizens of the United States to vote shall not be denied or abridged by the United States or by any state on account of race, color, or previous condition of servitude" (amend. XV, sec. 1).

Once this historical context has been established, the writer moves to an ascending text structure, culminating in the main point that Fuller's text embodies the ideal of equality because her arguments are still valid today. Women today still suffer from under-representation in American government:

Please note that excerpts and passages in the StudySync® library and this workbook are intended as touchstones to generate interest in an author's work. The excerpts and passages do not substitute for the reading of entire texts, and StudySync® strongly recommends that students seek out and purchase the whole literary or informational work in order to experience it as the author intended. Links to online resellers are available in our digital library. In addition, complete works may be ordered through an authorized reseller by filling out and returning to StudySync® the order form enclosed in this workbook.

Reading & Writing
Companion

293

[W]omen still do not have equal representation in Congress. In 2014, there were 99 women in Congress. It seems like a lot, but that is only 19 percent of total seats ... As Fuller wrote, "Can we think that he takes a sufficiently discerning and religious view of her office and destiny *ever* to do her justice, except when prompted by sentiment,—accidentally or transiently, that is, for the sentiment will vary according to the relations in which he is placed?" Some men may represent women fairly, but they can't "do justice to the interests of Woman." Women need to be present in Congress to represent their interests.

The essay would not have been as effective if the writer had placed the historical context after this final body paragraph. This ascending text structure is especially effective because it first seeks to persuade readers that equality is an important ideal and then argues that women today still fall short of being true equals in American society. By concluding with this strong claim, the writer invites readers to follow a line of reasoning in the hope that they will arrive at the same conclusion.

EXTENDED WRITING PROJECT
PLAN

PLAN

WRITING PROMPT

Think about the key ideals of the United States today, such as equality, self-sufficiency, individuality, and so on. Focus on one ideal and choose a text from the unit that best embodies the ideal. Argue why your chosen text is the best embodiment of the ideal, and explain why the text matters today. Support your statements about contemporary American society with outside research. Cite evidence from your chosen text in your response.

Your argumentative essay should include:

- an introduction with a clear claim explaining your chosen ideal and how your chosen text best represents it
- clear and cohesive body paragraphs with analysis supported by relevant reasons and evidence
- a conclusion that effectively wraps up your essay

Review the information you listed in your *Reasons and Relevant Evidence* Textual Evidence Chart, including the textual evidence that you will use to support your central claim. Review your preliminary thesis from the Thesis Statement lesson. This organized information and your thesis will help you to create a road map to use for writing your essay.

Consider the following questions as you develop the reasoning of your main paragraphs and their textual evidence in the road map:
- Does your thesis statement present a precise claim that can be argued over the course of several paragraphs?
- How does your text reflect the American ideal you chose?

NOTES

- What does your textual evidence suggest about the writer of the text? What does it suggest about the United States at the time the text was written?

- What other texts reflect the ideal you chose? Do they make any counterclaims you need to address? Any alternate claims?

- Why is the text you chose still important to the United States today?

Use this road map model to help you navigate through writing your argumentative essay:

Essay Road Map
Thesis statement (Claim):
Paragraph 1 (Reason):
Textual Evidence #1:
Textual Evidence #2:
Paragraph 2 (Reason):
Textual Evidence #1:
Textual Evidence #2:
Paragraph 3 (Reason):
Textual Evidence #1:
Textual Evidence #2:

SKILL: INTRODUCTIONS

 ## DEFINE

The **introduction** is the opening paragraph or section of a nonfiction text. In an argumentative essay, the introduction sets forth a precise and knowledgeable **claim** by introducing the **topic** and stating the **thesis** that will be developed and supported in the body of the text. The introduction of some argumentative texts may also acknowledge an **alternate or opposing claim** that the writer may disprove over the course of the essay. A strong introduction also generates interest in the topic by inserting a **"hook"** that engages readers in an interesting or unexpected way.

 ## IDENTIFICATION AND APPLICATION

- In argumentative writing, the introduction identifies the topic of the essay by explicitly stating what the text will be about. The writer may also use the introduction to provide some necessary background information about the topic to help the reader understand the argument that he or she is about the make.

- In addition to the topic, the introduction includes the main, or most important, claim that the writer will develop in the text. This main idea is the thesis. It should indicate the point the writer will make and the source materials he or she will discuss. It will often be at the end of the introduction. Note that a thesis is not always stated explicitly within the text. In the introduction, a writer might instead hint at the thesis through details and ideas that help the reader make an inference.

- In the introduction, the writer may also distinguish his or her argument from opposing views by establishing its relative importance or significance to those views.

- It is customary to build interest in the topic by beginning the introduction with a "hook," or a way to grab the reader's attention. This awakens the reader's natural curiosity and encourages him or her to read on. Hooks can ask open-ended questions, make connections to the reader or to life, or introduce a surprising fact.

MODEL

Here is the first paragraph of the introduction of the student model essay "Every Path Laid Open":

> **"All men are created equal."** That's the promise made to every American. **Equality is a key ideal of the United States.** As a country, we like to think that everyone, regardless of gender, race, or social class, is equal in the eyes of the law and has equal opportunities to live his or her best life. **Margaret Fuller's** *Woman in the Nineteenth Century* **best embodies the American ideal of equality because she powerfully argues for rights for a long-oppressed group: women.** The text still matters today because American society has made great strides in gender equality but **total equality has still not been achieved.**

In the opening sentence, the writer gets right at the topic of the paper: equality. The writer also uses a quotation as a strong hook to draw readers' attention. (The source of the quotation is given in the second paragraph of the student model.) The second sentence serves as a sort of counterclaim, as it states an idea the writer seeks to disprove in the essay. The third sentence explains the importance of the argument: Equality is a core principle of the United States. Note that the writer uses the term "ideal," which implies that the "promise" of equality may not be delivered in reality.

The claim of the student model begins in the middle of the first paragraph. The paper will focus on a work by Margaret Fuller that argues in favor of equality for women. The writer uses vivid language to engage readers, claiming that women are a "long-oppressed group," and states a precise claim that he or she will develop in the body paragraphs of the essay.

In the last sentence of the first paragraph, the writer gives a strong statement that emphasizes the significance of the topic: Fuller's text is still relevant today. The sentence has the additional advantage of adding an element of irony to the paragraph. The statement "[a]ll men are created equal" can be taken literally to mean that women are not treated as equals to men. The introduction is an effective one because it uses powerful language to state a clear claim and to motivate readers to keep reading.

PRACTICE

Write an introduction for your essay that includes your thesis statement and a hook to capture your readers' interest. Trade with a peer review partner when you are finished and offer feedback on each other's introductions. How strong is the language of your partner's thesis statement? How clear is the topic? What is the claim he or she is trying to make? Were you hooked? Offer each other suggestions, and remember that they are most helpful when they are constructive.

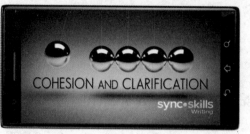

SKILL: COHESION AND CLARIFICATION

 DEFINE

Readers need guideposts to follow an argument and to connect or group information as they read. The connection of ideas and information to form a complete or whole piece of writing is called **cohesion.** A writer uses language to construct sentences, relate ideas, and connect information to make his or her writing clear and understandable. **Clarification,** or the process of explaining ideas as clearly as possible, is key to ensuring that readers will understand what a writer is trying to say. One way writers achieve cohesion and clarification is by linking major sections of a text through the use of phrases and clauses, transitions, and parallel structure.

●●● IDENTIFICATION AND APPLICATION

- Writers of argumentative essays use cohesion in their language to clarify their claims and counterclaims and to construct clear relationships between the reasons and evidence of their argument.
- Writers use signal words to show direct relationships between ideas:
  › "cause and effect" signal words: *since, because, therefore, thus, consequently*
  › "compare and contrast" signal words: *similarly, in comparison, however, yet, despite, and, or*
  › "problem and solution" signal words: *problem, solution, so that, in order to, because*
- Introductory phrases and clauses, which begin a sentence and end in a comma, help create connections between ideas:
  › *Because of these events, As the results show, or According to experts*
- Writers use conjunctions to connect words, clauses, or sentences:
  › *and, or, but, nor, yet, so, because, although, since, until*

- Using parallel structure shows readers that one or more ideas have equal importance:
  › gerunds: *walking, reading, swimming*
  › infinitives: *to play, to practice, to achieve*
  › prepositional phrases (all): *at work, at the beach, and at home*
  › prepositional phrases (one, with multiple objects): *at work, the beach, and home*

MODEL

The writer of the student model argumentative essay "Every Path Laid Open" creates coherence and clarity with a variety of constructions.

> Margaret Fuller's *Woman in the Nineteenth Century* was published in 1845, years before the Fourteenth and Fifteenth Amendments were added to the Constitution. **At the time,** women clearly did not have "equal protection of the laws." Unmarried women had some rights, such as the right to own property, **but** a woman lost those rights to her husband as soon as she got married (Salmon). Women were expected to stay home, **and** few were educated. Fuller sees this life as one of "drudgery." **In her book,** Fuller argues for women **to be granted** the same rights and opportunities as men. Fuller says that men do not want women **to be educated** because they are likely **to draw** "opposite inferences to what might be wished by those who now grant it"—in other words, **to have** ideas different from those of the men currently in power, which would undermine their authority. In addition, Fuller argues that women must be granted the opportunity **to discover** their talents for themselves outside of the home:

In this paragraph, the writer uses the introductory prepositional phrases "At the time" and "In her book" to clarify connections to more general points that she makes. "At the time" creates a connection to the historical background she provides in the previous sentence. "In her book" provides a connection between the writer's idea and Fuller's text.

The writer also uses conjunctions to connect ideas. The conjunction "but" contrasts two pieces of information regarding women's rights in the mid-1800s. In the sentence that follows, the conjunction "and" connects two ways women were oppressed during the time period.

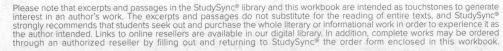

NOTES

In the second half of the paragraph, the writer uses a series of infinitives that creates a parallel structure: "to be educated," "to draw," "to have" and "to discover." This structure provides a cohesive discussion of what Fuller believes women should be allowed to do.

In the next section, the writer discusses another section of Fuller's text:

> Fuller does not want men to grant these freedoms to women in the same way they indulge a child. She calls for "inward and outward freedom for Woman as much as for Man shall be acknowledged as a *right,* not yielded as a concession." **That is an important distinction to be made,** that women have rights that should be granted and that women should be in control of their own rights and lives.
>
> Some may argue that in all of Fuller's arguments about equality, she does leave out an important subset of women: that of the **lower class.** The rights and privileges Fuller calls for would apply only to **upper-class** women. In the early 1800s, only **upper-class** people were educated. Many states at the time of Fuller's writing still required men to be property owners in order to vote, and people of color were still restricted from voting in most states (Mintz). The women in Fuller's text attend "balls, theatres, meetings for promoting missions, revival meetings." Those are not activities of the **lower classes.** Fuller, **however,** seems to acknowledge that her argument is for wealthy women. ...

In the first paragraph, the highlighted introductory clause clarifies that the previous sentence contains one of the key points in the essay. The second paragraph has a comparison-and-contrast structure. The use of the compound words "lower class" and "upper-class" help to create a parallel structure that provides clarity for the comparison. In the last sentence, the word "however" signals a contrast.

 PRACTICE

Write a clear and cohesive body paragraph for your argumentative essay. When you are finished, trade with a partner and offer each other feedback. How well did the writer use signal words or introductory phrases to show the relationship between ideas? Does the writer use parallel structure to create cohesion? Did the writer make his or her argument as clearly as possible? How well does the writer support his or her ideas? What other support could the writer have included? Offer each other suggestions, and remember that they are most helpful when they are constructive.

302 Reading & Writing Companion

SKILL: CONCLUSIONS

 DEFINE

A strong and effective **conclusion** should follow from and support the argument that was presented in the rest of the text. It should **restate the claim or thesis** in some way and articulate the significance of the topic, noting the most important examples and evidence. Perhaps most importantly, a conclusion should provide the reader with a sense of **closure** and the satisfying feeling that the claim has been thoroughly supported.

⋯ IDENTIFICATION AND APPLICATION

- A strong argumentative essay should follow a logical and effective sequence, and its conclusion should feel like the essay's clear stopping point.

- An effective conclusion to an argumentative essay reinforces the thesis statement (or central claim) and why it is significant or worth considering.

- An effective argumentative conclusion briefly mentions or reviews the strongest supporting details or evidence. This reminds readers of the most relevant information and evidence in the essay.

- The conclusion leaves the reader with a final thought. In argumentative writing, this final thought may:

  › Answer a question posed by the introduction
  › Issue a call to action to address the issue under discussion
  › Present a last, compelling example
  › Recommend other authors or texts that extend the argument
  › Spark curiosity and encourage readers to learn more

Please note that excerpts and passages in the StudySync® library and this workbook are intended as touchstones to generate interest in an author's work. The excerpts and passages do not substitute for the reading of entire texts, and StudySync® strongly recommends that students seek out and purchase the whole literary or informational work in order to experience it as the author intended. Links to online resellers are available in our digital library. In addition, complete works may be ordered through an authorized reseller by filling out and returning to StudySync® the order form enclosed in this workbook.

Reading & Writing Companion   **303**

 MODEL

When your composition is a response to a writing prompt, it is a good idea to use the conclusion to review how your essay has met the requirements of the assignment. Recall the extended writing prompt for this unit:

WRITING PROMPT

Think about the key ideals of the United States today, such as equality, self-sufficiency, individuality, and so on. Focus on one ideal and choose a text from the unit that best embodies the ideal. Argue why your chosen text is the best embodiment of the ideal, and explain why the text matters today. Support your statements about contemporary American society with outside research. Cite textual evidence from your chosen text in your response.

In a response to this prompt, the writer will include most or all of the following in his or her conclusion:

- The ideal of the United States that the essay touches on
- The thesis statement/claim
- The literary text discussed in the prompt and why it best embodies the ideal
- Why the text matters today

Now look at the conclusion for the model essay "Every Path Laid Open":

When Fuller was writing ***Woman in the Nineteenth Century,*** it was only a few generations after the Founding Fathers. The Civil War was still twenty years off; the Nineteenth Amendment was 75 years away. Her ideas may not have immediately changed the state of women in the United States, **but her ideas were ahead of her time. Her arguments in favor of gender equality reflect both the American ideal of equality and the patriotic value of fighting for what you believe in.** In short, Fuller's "mind was often the leading one, always effective."

NOTES

In this short paragraph, the writer hits almost all of the main requirements of the assignment. The conclusion restates that the writer has identified "equality" as an American ideal and that he or she has chosen *Woman in the Nineteenth Century* as a text that embodies this ideal. The writer also restates the main idea of the thesis in a new and interesting way: "[Fuller's] arguments in favor of gender equality reflect both the American ideal of equality and the patriotic value of fighting for what you believe in." The conclusion does not explicitly restate the significance of the text, but by saying that "her ideas were ahead of her time," the writer implies that Fuller's text is still significant today.

 PRACTICE

Create a three-circles graphic organizer for the elements you plan to include in the conclusion to your argumentative essay. In the large center circle, list the text you have chosen, and explain why it embodies an idea. In the smaller top circle, list the American ideal you have chosen. In the smaller left circle, restate your thesis. In the smaller right circle, explain why the text is still significant today. When you have finished, think about this question: What do you hope readers will take away from your essay? Write down ideas for the final thought you would like to leave with them. Save these notes for the Draft stage of your Extended Writing Project.

DRAFT

WRITING PROMPT

Think about the key ideals of the United States today, such as equality, self-sufficiency, individuality, and so on. Focus on one ideal and choose a text from the unit that best embodies the ideal. Argue why your chosen text is the best embodiment of the ideal, and explain why the text matters today. Support your statements about contemporary American society with outside research. Cite evidence from your chosen text in your response.

Your argumentative essay should include:

- an introduction with a clear claim explaining your chosen ideal and how your chosen text best represents it
- clear and cohesive body paragraphs with analysis supported by relevant reasons and evidence
- a conclusion that effectively wraps up your essay

You've already made progress toward writing your own argumentative text. You've thought about the topic and chosen an American ideal and the text you think best embodies it. You've identified textual evidence and thought about how you can organize it effectively. You've decided what to include in your introduction and conclusion. Now it's time to write a draft.

When drafting, ask yourself these questions:

- What can I do to clarify my thesis statement?
- How can I improve my hook to make it more engaging?
- Which relevant facts, strong details, and interesting quotations in each body paragraph will best support the thesis statement?
- How well have I communicated how the text embodies the American ideal?

- How well have I explained why this text is still relevant to American society today?
- Would more precise language or different details about the text and its significance make the text more convincing?
- What final thought do I want to leave with my readers?

Using your graphic organizers and your other prewriting notes, write a draft of your essay. Remember that argumentative writing begins with an introduction and presents a clear and precise claim in the thesis statement. Body paragraphs provide relevant quotations and other textual evidence to support your claim. A concluding paragraph restates or reinforces your thesis statement in a new and interesting way and leaves a lasting impression on your readers. Before you submit your draft, read it over carefully. You want to be sure that you've responded to all aspects of the prompt.

REVISE

WRITING PROMPT

Think about the key ideals of the United States today, such as equality, self-sufficiency, individuality, and so on. Focus on one ideal and choose a text from the unit that best embodies the ideal. Argue why your chosen text is the best embodiment of the ideal, and explain why the text matters today. Support your statements about contemporary American society with outside research. Cite evidence from your chosen text in your response.

Your argumentative essay should include:

- an introduction with a clear claim explaining your chosen ideal and how your chosen text best represents it
- clear and cohesive body paragraphs with analysis supported by relevant reasons and evidence
- a conclusion that effectively wraps up your essay

You have written a draft of your argumentative essay. You have also received input from your peers about how to improve it. Now you are going to revise your draft.

Here are some recommendations to help you revise.

- Review the suggestions made by your peers.
- Focus on maintaining a formal style. A formal style suits your purpose—giving information about a serious topic. It also fits your audience—students, teachers, and other readers interested in learning more about your topic.
  - › As you revise, eliminate any slang.

NOTES

> Remove any first-person pronouns, such as "I," "me," or "my," and any instances of addressing readers as "you." These are more suitable to a writing style that is informal, personal, and conversational.

> If you include your personal opinions, remove them. Your essay should be clear, direct, and unbiased.

- After you have revised elements of style, think about whether there is anything else you can do to improve your essay's information or organization.

  > Do you need to add any new details to your essay? Is there a particularly interesting quotation you could add?

  > Do you need to add any new evidence to your essay? Do you make any claims that are not supported by reasons and evidence?

  > Can you substitute a more precise word for a word that is general or dull?

  > Consider your organization. Would your essay flow better if you strengthened the transitions between paragraphs?

- As you add new details or change information, check your punctuation.

  > Check that you spelled names and titles of texts correctly.

Please note that excerpts and passages in the StudySync® library and this workbook are intended as touchstones to generate interest in an author's work. The excerpts and passages do not substitute for the reading of entire texts, and StudySync® strongly recommends that students seek out and purchase the whole literary or informational work in order to experience it as the author intended. Links to online resellers are available in our digital library. In addition, complete works may be ordered through an authorized reseller by filling out and returning to StudySync® the order form enclosed in this workbook.

Reading & Writing
Companion

309

SKILL: SOURCES AND CITATIONS

⭐ DEFINE

When writing an argumentative essay, writers cannot simply make up information or rely on their own subjective experiences or opinions. To thoroughly support the treatment and analysis of their topics, writers need to include information from relevant, accurate, and reliable sources and cite, or acknowledge, them properly. **Sources** are the documents and information that a writer uses to research his or her writing.

There are two basic types of sources: primary and secondary. A **primary source** is a first-hand account of thoughts or events by the individual who experienced them. Examples of primary sources include letters, photographs, official documents, diaries or journals, autobiographies or memoirs, eyewitness accounts and interviews, audio recordings and radio broadcasts, and works of art.

A **secondary source** analyzes and interprets primary sources. Some examples of secondary sources include encyclopedia articles, textbooks, commentary or criticisms, histories, documentary films, and news analyses.

Writers should keep track of these sources as they research and plan their work. When it comes time to write, they can use this information to support any claims made within the text. Any facts, quotations, statistics, or statements included that are not common knowledge need to be cited. **Citations** are notes that give information about the sources a writer uses in his or her writing. Citations are required whenever writers quote others' words or refer to others' ideas in their writing. If writers don't include citations, they can be accused of **plagiarism,** or stealing someone else's words and ideas. In some academic texts, writers may be asked to provide sources and citations in **footnotes** or **endnotes,** which link specific references within the essay to the correlating pages or chapters in an outside source. In addition to internal citations, writers may also need to provide a full list of sources in a **Works Cited** section or standard **bibliography.**

Read the following tips for effectively citing sources:

- All sources must be credible and accurate. Look for sources from experts in the topic you are writing about.

  › When researching online, look for URLs that contain ".gov" (government agencies), ".edu" (colleges and universities), and ".org" (museums and other non-profit organizations).

  › Don't neglect respected print sources. Most scholars do not publish online.

- Include a citation to give credit to any source, whether primary or secondary, that is quoted exactly. Make sure the quotation is presented in quotation marks. There are several different ways to cite a source.

  › If the author's name is mentioned in the essay, include the page number where the quotation can be located:

    Fuller sees this life as one of "drudgery" (20).

  › If the author's name does not appear in the text, include the author's name and the page number in parentheses at the end of the sentence in which the quote appears:

    The life of a woman of that time was filled with "drudgery" (Fuller 20).

- Citations are also necessary when a writer borrows ideas or takes facts from another source, even if the writer paraphrases, or puts those ideas in his or her own words. Follow the same citation rules as for exact quotations.

  › If there is no author, use the title of the work:

    It seems like a lot, but that is only 19 percent of total seats--nowhere near the 53 percent share of women in the electorate ("Women in the U.S. Congress 2014 Fact Sheet").

  › For online sources, as with the fact sheet above, no page number is needed.

- At the end of the essay, include a Works Cited list with full bibliographical information on each source cited, formatted correctly in MLA style.

MODEL

The writer of the student argumentative essay "Every Path Laid Open" used seven sources in gathering her evidence. In addition to the text that she chose to analyze, the writer found background information in news articles, a fact sheet, histories, and a foundational document.

In the second paragraph, the writer quotes from the US Constitution:

> Almost one hundred years later, after the Civil War, that wording changed slightly. The Fourteenth Amendment to the Constitution, approved in 1868, declares, "All persons born or naturalized in the United States ... are citizens of the United States" **(amend. XIV, sec. 1)**.

Because the writer quotes from a text directly, she needs to provide an in-line **citation** for that quotation. The Constitution does not have page numbers, so MLA style requires that writers include the article or amendment and section numbers, as the writer did here. That makes the information easy to find in a long document.

In the fourth paragraph, the writer of this argumentative essay introduces many facts and ideas that are not common knowledge:

> In good news, women in 2014 comprised 53 percent of voters, which is about equivalent to women's population **(Liasson)**. In 2012, women overwhelmingly supported President Barack Obama, a key reason for his win **(Abdullah)**. Fuller would likely celebrate the direct influence of women on politics, and she'd be glad to know there were no "ladies in hysterics at the polls." But women still do not have equal representation in Congress. In 2014, there were 99 women in Congress. It seems like a lot, but that is only 19 percent of total seats—nowhere near the 53 percent share of women in the electorate **("Women in the U.S. Congress 2014 Fact Sheet")**.

The first two sources cited in this paragraph "(Liasson)" and "(Abdullah)" come from online news sources and thus do not require page numbers. In the Works Cited list, a reader can see that the more detailed information about female voters in 2012 comes from a CNN article titled "How women ruled the 2012 election and where the GOP went wrong" by Halimah Abdullah. If the reader wants to learn more or check the writer's facts, he or she can find that article easily.

The last fact, about the number of women in Congress, is also not common knowledge and needs to be cited. The source for that number does not have a clear author, so the writer included the title of the work in the citation: "("Women in the U.S. Congress 2014 Fact Sheet")." The fact sheet is an online source and does not require a page number.

PRACTICE

Write citations for quoted information in your argumentative essay. When you are finished, trade with a partner and offer feedback. How well did he or she cite sources in the essay? How varied were the types of sources cited? Offer each other suggestions, and remember that they are most helpful when they are constructive.

EDIT, PROOFREAD, AND PUBLISH

WRITING PROMPT

Think about the key ideals of the United States today, such as equality, self-sufficiency, individuality, and so on. Focus on one ideal and choose a text from the unit that best embodies the ideal. Argue why your chosen text is the best embodiment of the ideal, and explain why the text matters today. Support your statements about contemporary American society with outside research. Cite evidence from your chosen text in your response.

Your argumentative essay should include:

- an introduction with a clear claim explaining your chosen ideal and how your chosen text best represents it
- clear and cohesive body paragraphs with analysis supported by relevant reasons and evidence
- a conclusion that effectively wraps up your essay

You have revised your argumentative essay and received input from your peers on that revision. Now it's time to edit and proofread your essay to produce a final version. Have you included all the valuable suggestions from your peers? Ask yourself: Have I fully developed my thesis statement with strong textual evidence? Have I accurately cited my sources? What more can I do to improve my essay's support and organization?

When you are satisfied with your work, move on to proofread it for errors. For example, check that you have used correct punctuation for quotations and citations. Have you used hyphens correctly? Have you corrected any misspelled words?

Once you have made all your corrections, you are ready to submit and publish your work. You can distribute your writing to family and friends, hang it on a bulletin board, or post it on your blog. If you publish online, create links to your sources and citations. That way, readers can follow-up on what they've learned from your essay and read more on their own.

studysync®

Reading & Writing Companion

How have the literary movements of the last two centuries affected us?

Emotional Currents

Emotional Currents

TEXTS

TEXTS

EXTENDED WRITING PROJECT

453

Text Fulfillment
through
StudySync

THE RIME OF THE ANCIENT MARINER

POETRY
Samuel Taylor Coleridge
1798

INTRODUCTION

Samuel Taylor Coleridge's "The Rime of the Ancient Mariner" was published in *Lyrical Ballads*, a collection of poems that helped launch the Romanticism movement. In the poem, an old sailor detains a reluctant wedding guest and relates a strange, cautionary tale of what happens to those who don't heed

"Water, water, everywhere,
Nor any drop to drink."

FIRST READ

Part I

1 It is an ancient mariner
2 And he stoppeth one of three.
3 —"By thy long grey beard and glittering eye,
4 Now wherefore stoppest thou me?

5 The bridegroom's doors are opened wide,
6 And I am next of kin;
7 The guests are met, the feast is set:
8 May'st hear the merry din."

9 He holds him with his skinny hand,
10 "There was a ship," quoth he.
11 "Hold off! unhand me, grey-beard loon!"
12 Eftsoons his hand dropped he.

13 He holds him with his glittering eye—
14 The wedding-guest stood still,
15 And listens like a three-years' child:
16 The mariner hath his will.

17 The wedding-guest sat on a stone:
18 He cannot choose but hear;
19 And thus spake on that ancient man,
20 The bright-eyed mariner.

21 "The ship was cheered, the harbour cleared,
22 Merrily did we drop
23 Below the kirk, below the hill,
24 Below the lighthouse top.

25 The sun came up upon the left,
26 Out of the sea came he!
27 And he shone bright, and on the right
28 Went down into the sea.

29 Higher and higher every day,
30 Till over the mast at noon—"
31 The wedding-guest here beat his breast,
32 For he heard the loud bassoon.

33 The bride hath paced into the hall,
34 Red as a rose is she;
35 Nodding their heads before her goes
36 The merry minstrelsy.

37 The wedding-guest he beat his breast,
38 Yet he cannot choose but hear;
39 And thus spake on that ancient man,
40 The bright-eyed mariner.

41 "And now the storm-blast came, and he
42 Was tyrannous and strong;
43 He struck with his o'ertaking wings,
44 And chased us south along.

45 With sloping masts and dipping prow,
46 As who pursued with yell and blow
47 Still treads the shadow of his foe,
48 And forward bends his head,
49 The ship drove fast, loud roared the blast,
50 And southward aye we fled.

51 Listen, stranger! Mist and snow,
52 And it grew wondrous cold:
53 And ice mast-high came floating by,
54 As green as emerald.

55 And through the drifts the snowy clifts
56 Did send a dismal sheen:
57 Nor shapes of men nor beasts we ken—
58 The ice was all between.

59 The ice was here, the ice was there,
60 The ice was all around:
61 It cracked and growled, and roared and howled,
62 Like noises in a swound!

63 At length did cross an **albatross,**

64 Thorough the fog it came;

65 As if it had been a Christian soul,

66 We hailed it in God's name.

67 It ate the food it ne'er had eat,

68 And round and round it flew.

69 The ice did split with a thunder-fit;

70 The helmsman steered us through!

71 And a good south wind sprung up behind;

72 The albatross did follow,

73 And every day, for food or play,

74 Came to the mariners' hollo!

75 In mist or cloud, on mast or shroud,

76 It perched for **vespers** nine;

77 Whiles all the night, through fog-smoke white,

78 Glimmered the white moon-shine."

79 "God save thee, ancient mariner!

80 From the fiends, that plague thee thus!—

81 Why lookst thou so?" "With my crossbow

82 I shot the albatross.

Part II

83 The sun now rose upon the right:

84 Out of the sea came he,

85 Still hid in mist, and on the left

86 Went down into the sea.

87 And the good south wind still blew behind,

88 But no sweet bird did follow,

89 Nor any day for food or play

90 Came to the mariners' hollo!

91 And I had done an hellish thing,

92 And it would work 'em woe:

93 For all averred, I had killed the bird

94 That made the breeze to blow.

95 Ah wretch! said they, the bird to slay,

96 That made the breeze to blow!

NOTES

97   Nor dim nor red, like God's own head,
98   The glorious sun uprist:
99   Then all averred, I had killed the bird
100 That brought the fog and mist.
101 'Twas right, said they, such birds to slay,
102 That bring the fog and mist.

103 The fair breeze blew, the white foam flew,
104 The furrow followed free;
105 We were the first that ever burst
106 Into that silent sea.

107 Down dropped the breeze, the sails dropped down,
108 'Twas sad as sad could be;
109 And we did speak only to break
110 The silence of the sea!

111 All in a hot and copper sky,
112 The bloody sun, at noon,
113 Right up above the mast did stand,
114 No bigger than the moon.

115 Day after day, day after day,
116 We stuck, nor breath nor motion;
117 As idle as a painted ship
118 Upon a painted ocean.

119 Water, water, everywhere,
120 And all the boards did shrink;
121 Water, water, everywhere,
122 Nor any drop to drink.

123 The very deeps did rot: O Christ!
124 That ever this should be!
125 Yea, slimy things did crawl with legs
126 Upon the slimy sea.

127 About, about, in reel and rout
128 The death-fires danced at night;
129 The water, like a witch's oils,
130 Burnt green, and blue and white.

131 And some in dreams assured were
132 Of the spirit that plagued us so;
133 Nine fathom deep he had followed us
134 From the land of mist and snow.

135 And every tongue, through utter drought,
136 Was withered at the root;
137 We could not speak, no more than if
138 We had been choked with soot.

139 Ah! wel-a-day! what evil looks
140 Had I from old and young!
141 Instead of the cross, the albatross
142 About my neck was hung.

Part III

143 There passed a weary time. Each throat
144 Was parched, and glazed each eye.
145 A weary time! A weary time!
146 How glazed each weary eye,
147 When looking westward, I beheld
148 A something in the sky.

149 At first it seemed a little speck,
150 And then it seemed a mist;
151 It moved and moved, and took at last
152 A certain shape, I wist.

153 A speck, a mist, a shape, I wist!
154 And still it neared and neared:
155 As if it dodged a water sprite,
156 It plunged and tacked and veered.

157 With throats unslaked, with black lips baked,
158 We could nor laugh nor wail;
159 Through utter drouth all dumb we stood!
160 I bit my arm, I sucked the blood,
161 And cried, A sail! a sail!

162 With throats unslaked, with black lips baked,
163 Agape they heard me call:
164 Gramercy! they for joy did grin,
165 And all at once their breath drew in,
166 As they were drinking all.

167 See! see! (I cried) she tacks no more!
168 Hither to work us weal;
169 Without a breeze, without a tide,
170 She steadies with upright keel!

Reading & Writing
Companion **325**

171 The western wave was all aflame.
172 The day was well nigh done!
173 Almost upon the western wave
174 Rested the broad bright sun;
175 When that strange shape drove suddenly
176 Betwixt us and the sun.

177 And straight the sun was flecked with bars,
178 (Heaven's mother send us grace!)
179 As if through a dungeon grate he peered
180 With broad and burning face.

181 Alas! (thought I, and my heart beat loud)
182 How fast she nears and nears!
183 Are those her sails that glance in the sun,
184 Like restless gossameres?

185 Are those her ribs through which the sun
186 Did peer, as through a grate?
187 And is that woman all her crew?
188 Is that a Death? and are there two?
189 Is Death that woman's mate?

190 Her lips were red, her looks were free,
191 Her locks were yellow as gold:
192 Her skin was as white as leprosy,
193 The nightmare Life-in-Death was she,
194 Who thicks man's blood with cold.

195 The naked hulk alongside came,
196 And the twain were casting dice;
197 'The game is done! I've won! I've won!'
198 Quoth she, and whistles thrice.

199 The sun's rim dips; the stars rush out:
200 At one stride comes the dark;
201 With far-heard whisper, o'er the sea,
202 Off shot the spectre bark.

203 We listened and looked sideways up!
204 Fear at my heart, as at a cup,
205 My lifeblood seemed to sip!
206 The stars were dim, and thick the night,
207 The steersman's face by his lamp gleamed white;
208 From the sails the dews did drip—

209   Till clomb above the eastern bar
210   The horned moon, with one bright star
211   Within the nether tip.

212   One after one, by the star-dogged moon,
213   Too quick for groan or sigh,
214   Each turned his face with ghastly pang,
215   And cursed me with his eye.

216   Four times fifty living men,
217   (And I heard nor sigh nor groan)
218   With heavy thump, a lifeless lump,
219   They dropped down one by one.

220   Their souls did from their bodies fly—
221   They fled to bliss or woe!
222   And every soul, it passed me by,
223   Like the whizz of my crossbow!"

Part IV

224   "I fear thee, ancient mariner!
225   I fear thy skinny hand!
226   And thou art long, and lank, and brown,
227   As is the ribbed sea-sand.

228   I fear thee and thy glittering eye,
229   And thy skinny hand, so brown."—
230   "Fear not, fear not, thou wedding-guest!
231   This body dropped not down.

232   Alone, alone, all, all alone,
233   Alone on a wide wide sea!
234   And never a saint took pity on
235   My soul in agony.

236   The many men, so beautiful!
237   And they all dead did lie:
238   And a thousand thousand slimy things
239   Lived on; and so did I.

240   I looked upon the rotting sea,
241   And drew my eyes away;
242   I looked upon the rotting deck,
243   And there the dead men lay.

244 I looked to heaven, and tried to pray;
245 But or ever a prayer had gushed,
246 A wicked whisper came, and made
247 My heart as dry as dust.

248 I closed my lids, and kept them close,
249 Till the balls like pulses beat;
250 For the sky and the sea, and the sea and the sky
251 Lay like a load on my weary eye,
252 And the dead were at my feet.

253 The cold sweat melted from their limbs,
254 Nor rot nor reek did they:
255 The look with which they looked on me
256 Had never passed away.

257 An orphan's curse would drag to hell
258 A spirit from on high;
259 But oh! more horrible than that
260 Is the curse in a dead man's eye!
261 Seven days, seven nights, I saw that curse,
262 And yet I could not die.

263 The moving moon went up the sky,
264 And nowhere did abide:
265 Softly she was going up,
266 And a star or two beside—

267 Her beams bemocked the sultry main,
268 Like April hoar-frost spread;
269 But where the ship's huge shadow lay,
270 The charmed water burnt alway
271 A still and awful red.

272 Beyond the shadow of the ship,
273 I watched the water snakes:
274 They moved in tracks of shining white,
275 And when they reared, the elfish light
276 Fell off in hoary flakes.

277 Within the shadow of the ship
278 I watched their rich attire:
279 Blue, glossy green, and velvet black,
280 They coiled and swam; and every track
281 Was a flash of golden fire.

282 O happy living things! No tongue
283 Their beauty might declare:
284 A spring of love gushed from my heart,
285 And I blessed them unaware:
286 Sure my kind saint took pity on me,
287 And I blessed them unaware.

288 The selfsame moment I could pray;
289 And from my neck so free
290 The albatross fell off, and sank
291 Like lead into the sea.

Part V

292 Oh sleep! it is a gentle thing,
293 Beloved from pole to pole!
294 To Mary-Queen the praise be given!
295 She sent the gentle sleep from heaven,
296 That slid into my soul.

297 The silly buckets on the deck,
298 That had so long remained,
299 I dreamt that they were filled with dew;
300 And when I awoke, it rained.

301 My lips were wet, my throat was cold,
302 My garments all were dank;
303 Sure I had drunken in my dreams,
304 And still my body drank.

305 I moved, and could not feel my limbs:
306 I was so light—almost
307 I thought that I had died in sleep,
308 And was a blessed ghost.

309 And soon I heard a roaring wind:
310 It did not come anear;
311 But with its sound it shook the sails,
312 That were so thin and sere.

313 The upper air bursts into life!
314 And a hundred fire-flags sheen,
315 To and fro they were hurried about!
316 And to and fro, and in and out,
317 The wan stars danced between.

NOTES

318 And the coming wind did roar more loud,
319 And the sails did sigh like sedge;
320 And the rain poured down from one black cloud;
321 The moon was at its edge.

322 The thick black cloud was cleft, and still
323 The moon was at its side:
324 Like waters shot from some high crag,
325 The lightning fell with never a jag,
326 A river steep and wide.

327 The loud wind never reached the ship,
328 Yet now the ship moved on!
329 Beneath the lightning and the moon
330 The dead men gave a groan.

331 They groaned, they stirred, they all uprose,
332 Nor spake, nor moved their eyes;
333 It had been strange, even in a dream,
334 To have seen those dead men rise.

335 The helmsman steered, the ship moved on;
336 Yet never a breeze up-blew;
337 The mariners all 'gan work the ropes,
338 Where they were wont to do;
339 They raised their limbs like lifeless tools—
340 We were a ghastly crew.

341 The body of my brother's son
342 Stood by me, knee to knee:
343 The body and I pulled at one rope,
344 But he said nought to me."

345 "I fear thee, ancient mariner!"
346 "Be calm, thou wedding-guest!
347 'Twas not those souls that fled in pain,
348 Which to their corses came again,
349 But a troop of spirits blessed.

350 For when it dawned—they dropped their arms,
351 And clustered round the mast;
352 Sweet sounds rose slowly through their mouths,
353 And from their bodies passed.

354 Around, around, flew each sweet sound,
355 Then darted to the sun;
356 Slowly the sounds came back again,
357 Now mixed, now one by one.

358 Sometimes a-dropping from the sky
359 I heard the skylark sing;
360 Sometimes all little birds that are,
361 How they seemed to fill the sea and air
362 With their sweet jargoning!

363 And now 'twas like all instruments,
364 Now like a lonely flute;
365 And now it is an angel's song,
366 That makes the heavens be mute.

367 It ceased; yet still the sails made on
368 A pleasant noise till noon,
369 A noise like of a hidden brook
370 In the leafy month of June,
371 That to the sleeping woods all night
372 Singeth a quiet tune.

373 Till noon we silently sailed on,
374 Yet never a breeze did breathe:
375 Slowly and smoothly went the ship,
376 Moved onward from beneath.

377 Under the keel nine fathom deep,
378 From the land of mist and snow,
379 The spirit slid: and it was he
380 That made the ship to go.
381 The sails at noon left off their tune,
382 And the ship stood still also.

383 The sun, right up above the mast,
384 Had fixed her to the ocean:
385 But in a minute she 'gan stir,
386 With a short uneasy motion—
387 Backwards and forwards half her length
388 With a short uneasy motion.

389 Then like a pawing horse let go,
390 She made a sudden bound:
391 It flung the blood into my head,
392 And I fell down in a swound.

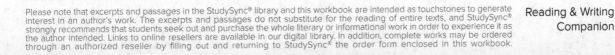

Reading & Writing
Companion

331

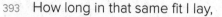

NOTES

393 How long in that same fit I lay,
394 I have not to declare;
395 But ere my living life returned,
396 I heard and in my soul discerned
397 Two voices in the air.

398 'Is it he?' quoth one, 'Is this the man?
399 By him who died on cross,
400 With his cruel bow he laid full low
401 The harmless albatross.

402 The spirit who bideth by himself
403 In the land of mist and snow,
404 He loved the bird that loved the man
405 Who shot him with his bow.'

406 The other was a softer voice,
407 As soft as honeydew:
408 Quoth he, 'The man hath **penance** done,
409 And penance more will do.'

Part VI

FIRST VOICE

410 'But tell me, tell me! speak again,
411 Thy soft response renewing—
412 What makes that ship drive on so fast?
413 What is the ocean doing?'

SECOND VOICE

414 'Still as a slave before his lord,
415 The ocean hath no blast;
416 His great bright eye most silently
417 Up to the moon is cast—

418 If he may know which way to go;
419 For she guides him smooth or grim.
420 See, brother, see! how graciously
421 She looketh down on him.'

FIRST VOICE

422 'But why drives on that ship so fast,
423 Without or wave or wind?'

NOTES

SECOND VOICE

424 'The air is cut away before,
425 And closes from behind.

426 Fly, brother, fly! more high, more high!
427 Or we shall be belated:
428 For slow and slow that ship will go,
429 When the mariner's trance is abated.'

430 I woke, and we were sailing on
431 As in a gentle weather:
432 'Twas night, calm night, the moon was high;
433 The dead men stood together.

434 All stood together on the deck,
435 For a charnel-dungeon fitter:
436 All fixed on me their stony eyes,
437 That in the moon did glitter.

438 The pang, the curse, with which they died,
439 Had never passed away:
440 I could not draw my eyes from theirs,
441 Nor turn them up to pray.

442 And now this spell was snapped: once more
443 I viewed the ocean green,
444 And looked far forth, yet little saw
445 Of what had else been seen—

446 Like one, that on a lonesome road
447 Doth walk in fear and dread,
448 And having once turned round walks on,
449 And turns no more his head;
450 Because he knows a frightful fiend
451 Doth close behind him tread.

452 But soon there breathed a wind on me,
453 Nor sound nor motion made:
454 Its path was not upon the sea,
455 In ripple or in shade.

456 It raised my hair, it fanned my cheek
457 Like a meadow-gale of spring—
458 It mingled strangely with my fears,
459 Yet it felt like a welcoming.

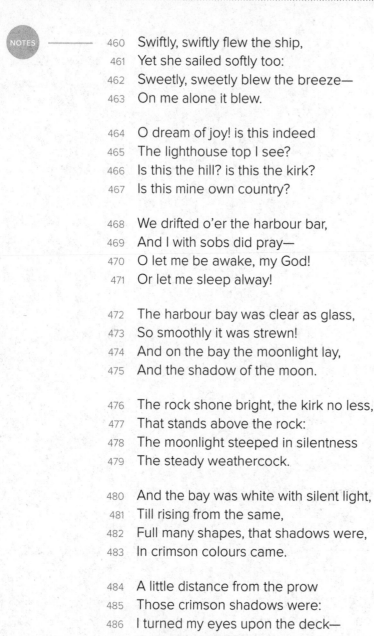

NOTES

460 Swiftly, swiftly flew the ship,
461 Yet she sailed softly too:
462 Sweetly, sweetly blew the breeze—
463 On me alone it blew.

464 O dream of joy! is this indeed
465 The lighthouse top I see?
466 Is this the hill? is this the kirk?
467 Is this mine own country?

468 We drifted o'er the harbour bar,
469 And I with sobs did pray—
470 O let me be awake, my God!
471 Or let me sleep alway!

472 The harbour bay was clear as glass,
473 So smoothly it was strewn!
474 And on the bay the moonlight lay,
475 And the shadow of the moon.

476 The rock shone bright, the kirk no less,
477 That stands above the rock:
478 The moonlight steeped in silentness
479 The steady weathercock.

480 And the bay was white with silent light,
481 Till rising from the same,
482 Full many shapes, that shadows were,
483 In crimson colours came.

484 A little distance from the prow
485 Those crimson shadows were:
486 I turned my eyes upon the deck—
487 O Christ! what saw I there!

488 Each corse lay flat, lifeless and flat,
489 And, by the holy rood!
490 A man all light, a **seraph** man,
491 On every corse there stood.

492 This seraph band, each waved his hand:
493 It was a heavenly sight!
494 They stood as signals to the land,
495 Each one a lovely light;

496 This seraph band, each waved his hand,
497 No voice did they impart—
498 No voice; but oh! the silence sank
499 Like music on my heart.

500 But soon I heard the dash of oars,
501 I heard the pilot's cheer;
502 My head was turned perforce away
503 And I saw a boat appear.

504 The pilot and the pilot's boy,
505 I heard them coming fast:
506 Dear Lord in heaven! it was a joy
507 The dead men could not blast.

508 I saw a third—I heard his voice:
509 It is the hermit good!
510 He singeth loud his godly hymns
511 That he makes in the wood.
512 He'll **shrieve** my soul, he'll wash away
513 The albatross's blood.

Part VII

514 This hermit good lives in that wood
515 Which slopes down to the sea.
516 How loudly his sweet voice he rears!
517 He loves to talk with mariners
518 That come from a far country.

519 He kneels at morn, and noon, and eve—
520 He hath a cushion plump:
521 It is the moss that wholly hides
522 The rotted old oak stump.

523 The skiff boat neared: I heard them talk,
524 'Why, this is strange, I trow!
525 Where are those lights so many and fair,
526 That signal made but now?'

527 'Strange, by my faith!' the hermit said—
528 'And they answered not our cheer!
529 The planks look warped! and see those sails,
530 How thin they are and sere!
531 I never saw aught like to them,
532 Unless perchance it were

NOTES

533 Brown skeletons of leaves that lag
534 My forest-brook along;
535 When the ivy tod is heavy with snow,
536 And the owlet whoops to the wolf below,
537 That eats the she-wolf's young.'

538 'Dear Lord! it hath a fiendish look,'
539 The pilot made reply,
540 'I am a-feared'—'Push on, push on!'
541 Said the hermit cheerily.

542 The boat came closer to the ship,
543 But I nor spake nor stirred;
544 The boat came close beneath the ship,
545 And straight a sound was heard.

546 Under the water it rumbled on,
547 Still louder and more dread:
548 It reached the ship, it split the bay;
549 The ship went down like lead.

550 Stunned by that loud and dreadful sound,
551 Which sky and ocean smote
552 Like one that hath been seven days drowned
553 My body lay afloat;
554 But swift as dreams, myself I found
555 Within the pilot's boat.

556 Upon the whirl, where sank the ship,
557 The boat spun round and round;
558 And all was still, save that the hill
559 Was telling of the sound.

560 I moved my lips—the pilot shrieked
561 And fell down in a fit;
562 The holy hermit raised his eyes,
563 And prayed where he did sit.

564 I took the oars: the pilot's boy,
565 Who now doth crazy go,
566 Laughed loud and long, and all the while
567 His eyes went to and fro.
568 'Ha! ha!' quoth he, 'full plain I see,
569 The devil knows how to row.'

570 And now, all in my own country,
571 I stood on the firm land!
572 The hermit stepped forth from the boat,
573 And scarcely he could stand.

574 'Oh shrieve me, shrieve me, holy man!'
575 The hermit crossed his brow.
576 'Say quick,' quoth he, 'I bid thee say—
577 What manner of man art thou?'

578 Forthwith this frame of mine was wrenched
579 With a woeful agony,
580 Which forced me to begin my tale;
581 And then it left me free.

582 Since then, at an uncertain hour,
583 That agony returns:
584 And till my ghastly tale is told,
585 This heart within me burns.

586 I pass, like night, from land to land;
587 I have strange power of speech;
588 The moment that his face I see,
589 I know the man that must hear me:
590 To him my tale I teach.

591 What loud uproar bursts from that door!
592 The wedding-guests are there:
593 But in the garden-bower the bride
594 And bridemaids singing are:
595 And hark the little vesper bell,
596 Which biddeth me to prayer!

597 O wedding-guest! This soul hath been
598 Alone on a wide wide sea:
599 So lonely 'twas, that God himself
600 Scarce seemed there to be.

601 Oh sweeter than the marriage feast,
602 'Tis sweeter far to me,
603 To walk together to the kirk
604 With a goodly company!—

605 To walk together to the kirk,
606 And all together pray,
607 While each to his great Father bends,

NOTES

608   Old men, and babes, and loving friends
609   And youths and maidens gay!

610   Farewell, farewell! but this I tell
611   To thee, thou wedding-guest!
612   He prayeth well, who loveth well
613   Both man and bird and beast.

614   He prayeth best, who loveth best
615   All things both great and small;
616   For the dear God who loveth us,
617   He made and loveth all."

618   The mariner, whose eye is bright,
619   Whose beard with age is hoar,
620   Is gone: and now the wedding-guest
621   Turned from the bridegroom's door.

622   He went like one that hath been stunned,
623   And is of sense forlorn:
624   A sadder and a wiser man,
625   He rose the morrow morn.

THINK QUESTIONS

1. To whom does the Ancient Mariner tell his story? Why does he choose this person? What compels the person to listen? Support your response with textual evidence.

2. What happens to the ship after the "storm-blast" comes? Where does the ship end up? What problems do the sailors face there? Cite textual evidence to support your response.

3. Describe the sailors' experience with the albatross. What do the sailors first think of the bird? How do their feelings change over time? Describe how the albatross dies and how the sailors believe they are affected by his death. Support your answer with textual evidence.

4. Who are the passengers on the skeleton ship that appears in Part III? What do the passengers do? What happens to the mariner's fellow sailors after the skeleton ship appears? Support your answer with textual evidence.

5. Describe what happens in Parts IV through VII. How does the mariner begin to break his curse? What happens on the ship after the curse is broken? What happens to the mariner upon his return to land? Cite textual evidence to support your response.

6. Use context to determine the meaning of the word **seraph** as it is used in "The Rime of the Ancient Mariner." Write your definition of "seraph" and tell how you arrived at it.

7. Use context to determine the meaning of the word **shrieve** as it is used in "The Rime of the Ancient Mariner." Write your definition of "shrieve" and tell how you arrived at it.

CLOSE READ

Reread the poem "The Rime of the Ancient Mariner." As you reread, complete the Focus Questions below. Then use your answers and annotations from the questions to help you complete the Writing Prompt.

FOCUS QUESTIONS

1. "The Rime of the Ancient Mariner" contains many supernatural elements. Choose one supernatural happening in the poem and analyze its tone, including word choice and figurative language. What is the author's attitude toward supernatural elements? Highlight your chosen section from the poem and make annotations to analyze its tone.

2. What is the basic structure and rhyme scheme of the poem? Where does Coleridge break from this pattern, and what is the effect of these breaks? Highlight your textual evidence and make annotations to explain the effects.

3. Explain the role of the sun and the moon in the poem. At what key moments does the mariner refer to the sun and the moon? Why might the sun and the moon be important to the sailors? How do the descriptions of the sun and the moon contribute to the poem's tone? Highlight textual evidence to support your response.

4. Determine one or more themes in the poem and explain how theme is developed throughout the poem. Highlight textual evidence to support your response, and make annotations to explain your choices.

5. This unit's Essential Question asks, "How have the literary movements of the last two centuries affected us?" The phrase "an albatross around one's neck," a reference to "The Rime of the Ancient Mariner," has become a common allusion. Based on your reading of the poem, what does this expression mean? What purpose do literary allusions serve? Cite textual evidence to support your response.

WRITING PROMPT

Write at least 300 words explaining why the mariner is compelled to repeat his story. What is he trying to release by retelling it? Will he succeed? In your answer, cite examples of tone that support your explanation. Also touch on the role of the wedding guest.

YOUNG GOODMAN BROWN

FICTION
Nathaniel Hawthorne
1835

INTRODUCTION

I n Nathaniel Hawthorne's short story "Young Goodman Brown," the title character dismisses his wife Faith's trepidation and sets out on an undisclosed mission into the forest—the domain of the devil. There he meets up with a mysterious old man carrying a serpentine walking stick—the devil himself—who claims to be well-acquainted with several men and women seemingly above reproach, including the pious Goody Cloyse, also out walking in the woods.

"With heaven above and Faith below, I will yet stand firm against the devil!"

NOTES

FIRST READ

1 Young Goodman Brown came forth at sunset into the street at Salem village; but put his head back, after crossing the **threshold**, to exchange a parting kiss with his young wife. And Faith, as the wife was aptly named, thrust her own pretty head into the street, letting the wind play with the pink ribbons of her cap while she called to Goodman Brown.

2 "Dearest heart," whispered she, softly and rather sadly, when her lips were close to his ear, "prithee put off your journey until sunrise and sleep in your own bed to-night. A lone woman is troubled with such dreams and such thoughts that she's afeard of herself sometimes. Pray tarry with me this night, dear husband, of all nights in the year."

3 "My love and my Faith," replied young Goodman Brown, "of all nights in the year, this one night must I tarry away from thee. My journey, as thou callest it, forth and back again, must needs be done 'twixt now and sunrise. What, my sweet, pretty wife, dost thou doubt me already, and we but three months married?"

4 "Then God bless you!" said Faith, with the pink ribbons; "and may you find all well when you come back."

5 "Amen!" cried Goodman Brown. "Say thy prayers, dear Faith, and go to bed at dusk, and no harm will come to thee."

6 So they parted; and the young man pursued his way until, being about to turn the corner by the meeting-house, he looked back and saw the head of Faith still peeping after him with a melancholy air, in spite of her pink ribbons.

7 "Poor little Faith!" thought he, for his heart smote him. "What a wretch am I to leave her on such an errand! She talks of dreams, too. Methought as she spoke there was trouble in her face, as if a dream had warned her what work is to be done tonight. But no, no; 't would kill her to think it. Well, she's a

blessed angel on earth; and after this one night I'll cling to her skirts and follow her to heaven."

8   With this excellent resolve for the future, Goodman Brown felt himself justified in making more haste on his present evil purpose. He had taken a dreary road, darkened by all the gloomiest trees of the forest, which barely stood aside to let the narrow path creep through, and closed immediately behind. It was all as lonely as could be; and there is this peculiarity in such a solitude, that the traveler knows not who may be concealed by the innumerable trunks and the thick boughs overhead; so that with lonely footsteps he may yet be passing through an unseen multitude.

9   "There may be a devilish Indian behind every tree," said Goodman Brown to himself; and he glanced fearfully behind him as he added, "What if the devil himself should be at my very elbow!"

10   His head being turned back, he passed a crook of the road, and, looking forward again, beheld the figure of a man, in grave and decent attire, seated at the foot of an old tree. He arose at Goodman Brown's approach and walked onward side by side with him.

11   "You are late, Goodman Brown," said he. "The clock of the Old South was striking as I came through Boston, and that is full fifteen minutes agone."

12   "Faith kept me back a while," replied the young man, with a tremor in his voice, caused by the sudden appearance of his companion, though not wholly unexpected.

13   It was now deep dusk in the forest, and deepest in that part of it where these two were journeying. As nearly as could be **discerned**, the second traveler was about fifty years old, apparently in the same rank of life as Goodman Brown, and bearing a considerable resemblance to him, though perhaps more in expression than features. Still they might have been taken for father and son. And yet, though the elder person was as simply clad as the younger, and as simple in manner too, he had an indescribable air of one who knew the world, and who would not have felt **abashed** at the governor's dinner table or in King William's court, were it possible that his affairs should call him thither. But the only thing about him that could be fixed upon as remarkable was his staff, which bore the likeness of a great black snake, so curiously wrought that it might almost be seen to twist and wriggle itself like a living serpent. This, of course, must have been an **ocular** deception, assisted by the uncertain light.

14   "Come, Goodman Brown," cried his fellow-traveler, "this is a dull pace for the beginning of a journey. Take my staff, if you are so soon weary."

15 "Friend," said the other, exchanging his slow pace for a full stop, "having kept covenant by meeting thee here, it is my purpose now to return whence I came. I have scruples touching the matter thou wot'st of."

16 "Sayest thou so?" replied he of the serpent, smiling apart. "Let us walk on, nevertheless, reasoning as we go; and if I convince thee not thou shalt turn back. We are but a little way in the forest yet."

17 "Too far! too far!" exclaimed the goodman, unconsciously resuming his walk. "My father never went into the woods on such an errand, nor his father before him. We have been a race of honest men and good Christians since the days of the martyrs; and shall I be the first of the name of Brown that ever took this path and kept—"

18 "Such company, thou wouldst say," observed the elder person, interpreting his pause. "Well said, Goodman Brown! I have been as well acquainted with your family as with ever a one among the Puritans; and that's no trifle to say. I helped your grandfather, the constable, when he lashed the Quaker woman so smartly through the streets of Salem; and it was I that brought your father a pitch-pine knot, kindled at my own hearth, to set fire to an Indian village, in King Philip's war. They were my good friends, both; and many a pleasant walk have we had along this path, and returned merrily after midnight. I would fain be friends with you for their sake."

19 "If it be as thou sayest," replied Goodman Brown, "I marvel they never spoke of these matters; or, verily, I marvel not, seeing that the least rumor of the sort would have driven them from New England. We are a people of prayer, and good works to boot, and abide no such wickedness."

20 "Wickedness or not," said the traveler with the twisted staff, "I have a very general acquaintance here in New England. The deacons of many a church have drunk the communion wine with me; the selectmen of divers towns make me their chairman; and a majority of the Great and General Court are firm supporters of my interest. The governor and I, too—But these are state secrets."

21 "Can this be so?" cried Goodman Brown, with a stare of amazement at his undisturbed companion. "Howbeit, I have nothing to do with the governor and council; they have their own ways, and are no rule for a simple husbandman like me. But, were I to go on with thee, how should I meet the eye of that good old man, our minister, at Salem village? Oh, his voice would make me tremble both Sabbath day and lecture day."

22 Thus far the elder traveler had listened with due gravity; but now burst into a fit of **irrepressible** mirth, shaking himself so violently that his snake-like staff actually seemed to wriggle in sympathy.

23 "Ha! ha! ha!" shouted he again and again; then composing himself, "Well, go on, Goodman Brown, go on; but, prithee, don't kill me with laughing."

24 "Well, then, to end the matter at once," said Goodman Brown, considerably nettled, "there is my wife, Faith. It would break her dear little heart; and I'd rather break my own."

25 "Nay, if that be the case," answered the other, "e'en go thy ways, Goodman Brown. I would not for twenty old women like the one hobbling before us that Faith should come to any harm."

26 As he spoke he pointed his staff at a female figure on the path, in whom Goodman Brown recognized a very pious and exemplary dame, who had taught him his catechism in youth, and was still his moral and spiritual adviser, jointly with the minister and Deacon Gookin.

27 "A marvel, truly, that Goody Cloyse should be so far in the wilderness at nightfall," said he. "But with your leave, friend, I shall take a cut through the woods until we have left this Christian woman behind. Being a stranger to you, she might ask whom I was consorting with and whither I was going."

28 "Be it so," said his fellow-traveler. "Betake you to the woods, and let me keep the path."

29 Accordingly the young man turned aside, but took care to watch his companion, who advanced softly along the road until he had come within a staff's length of the old dame. She, meanwhile, was making the best of her way, with singular speed for so aged a woman, and mumbling some indistinct words—a prayer, doubtless—as she went. The traveler put forth his staff and touched her withered neck with what seemed the serpent's tail.

30 "The devil!" screamed the pious old lady.

31 "Then Goody Cloyse knows her old friend?" observed the traveler, confronting her and leaning on his writhing stick.

32 "Ah, forsooth, and is it your worship indeed?" cried the good dame. "Yea, truly is it, and in the very image of my old gossip, Goodman Brown, the grandfather of the silly fellow that now is. But—would your worship believe it?—my broomstick hath strangely disappeared, stolen, as I suspect, by that unhanged witch, Goody Cory, and that, too, when I was all anointed with the juice of smallage, and cinquefoil, and wolf's bane."

33 "Mingled with fine wheat and the fat of a new-born babe," said the shape of old Goodman Brown.

34 "Ah, your worship knows the recipe," cried the old lady, cackling aloud. "So, as I was saying, being all ready for the meeting, and no horse to ride on, I made up my mind to foot it; for they tell me there is a nice young man to be taken into communion to-night. But now your good worship will lend me your arm, and we shall be there in a twinkling."

35 "That can hardly be," answered her friend. "I may not spare you my arm, Goody Cloyse; but here is my staff, if you will."

36 So saying, he threw it down at her feet, where, perhaps, it assumed life, being one of the rods which its owner had formerly lent to the Egyptian magi. Of this fact, however, Goodman Brown could not take cognizance. He had cast up his eyes in astonishment, and, looking down again, beheld neither Goody Cloyse nor the serpentine staff, but his fellow-traveler alone, who waited for him as calmly as if nothing had happened.

37 "That old woman taught me my catechism," said the young man; and there was a world of meaning in this simple comment.

38 They continued to walk onward, while the elder traveler **exhorted** his companion to make good speed and persevere in the path, discoursing so aptly that his arguments seemed rather to spring up in the bosom of his auditor than to be suggested by himself. As they went, he plucked a branch of maple to serve for a walking stick, and began to strip it of the twigs and little boughs, which were wet with evening dew. The moment his fingers touched them they became strangely withered and dried up as with a week's sunshine. Thus the pair proceeded, at a good free pace, until suddenly, in a gloomy hollow of the road, Goodman Brown sat himself down on the stump of a tree and refused to go any farther.

39 "Friend," said he, stubbornly, "my mind is made up. Not another step will I budge on this errand. What if a wretched old woman do choose to go to the devil when I thought she was going to heaven: is that any reason why I should quit my dear Faith and go after her?"

40 "You will think better of this by and by," said his acquaintance, composedly. "Sit here and rest yourself a while; and when you feel like moving again, there is my staff to help you along."

41 Without more words, he threw his companion the maple stick, and was as speedily out of sight as if he had vanished into the deepening gloom. The young man sat a few moments by the roadside, applauding himself greatly, and thinking with how clear a conscience he should meet the minister in his morning walk, nor shrink from the eye of good old Deacon Gookin. And what calm sleep would be his that very night, which was to have been spent so wickedly, but so purely and sweetly now, in the arms of Faith! Amidst these

pleasant and praiseworthy meditations, Goodman Brown heard the tramp of horses along the road, and deemed it advisable to conceal himself within the verge of the forest, conscious of the guilty purpose that had brought him thither, though now so happily turned from it.

42   On came the hoof tramps and the voices of the riders, two grave old voices, conversing soberly as they drew near. These mingled sounds appeared to pass along the road, within a few yards of the young man's hiding-place; but, owing doubtless to the depth of the gloom at that particular spot, neither the travelers nor their steeds were visible. Though their figures brushed the small boughs by the wayside, it could not be seen that they intercepted, even for a moment, the faint gleam from the strip of bright sky athwart which they must have passed. Goodman Brown alternately crouched and stood on tiptoe, pulling aside the branches and thrusting forth his head as far as he durst without discerning so much as a shadow. It vexed him the more, because he could have sworn, were such a thing possible, that he recognized the voices of the minister and Deacon Gookin, jogging along quietly, as they were wont to do, when bound to some ordination or ecclesiastical council. While yet within hearing, one of the riders stopped to pluck a switch.

43   "Of the two, reverend sir," said the voice like the deacon's, "I had rather miss an ordination dinner than to-night's meeting. They tell me that some of our community are to be here from Falmouth and beyond, and others from Connecticut and Rhode Island, besides several of the Indian powwows, who, after their fashion, know almost as much deviltry as the best of us. Moreover, there is a goodly young woman to be taken into communion."

44   "Mighty well, Deacon Gookin!" replied the solemn old tones of the minister. "Spur up, or we shall be late. Nothing can be done, you know, until I get on the ground."

45   The hoofs clattered again; and the voices, talking so strangely in the empty air, passed on through the forest, where no church had ever been gathered or solitary Christian prayed. Whither, then, could these holy men be journeying so deep into the heathen wilderness? Young Goodman Brown caught hold of a tree for support, being ready to sink down on the ground, faint and overburdened with the heavy sickness of his heart. He looked up to the sky, doubting whether there really was a heaven above him. Yet there was the blue arch, and the stars brightening in it.

46   "With heaven above and Faith below, I will yet stand firm against the devil!" cried Goodman Brown.

47   While he still gazed upward into the deep arch of the **firmament** and had lifted his hands to pray, a cloud, though no wind was stirring, hurried across the zenith and hid the brightening stars. The blue sky was still visible, except

Please note that excerpts and passages in the StudySync® library and this workbook are intended as touchstones to generate interest in an author's work. The excerpts and passages do not substitute for the reading of entire texts, and StudySync® strongly recommends that students seek out and purchase the whole literary or informational work in order to experience it as the author intended. Links to online resellers are available in our digital library. In addition, complete works may be ordered through an authorized reseller by filling out and returning to StudySync® the order form enclosed in this workbook.

Reading & Writing Companion   **347**

directly overhead, where this black mass of cloud was sweeping swiftly northward. Aloft in the air, as if from the depths of the cloud, came a confused and doubtful sound of voices. Once the listener fancied that he could distinguish the accents of towns-people of his own, men and women, both pious and ungodly, many of whom he had met at the communion table, and had seen others rioting at the tavern. The next moment, so indistinct were the sounds, he doubted whether he had heard aught but the murmur of the old forest, whispering without a wind. Then came a stronger swell of those familiar tones, heard daily in the sunshine at Salem village, but never until now from a cloud of night There was one voice of a young woman, uttering lamentations, yet with an uncertain sorrow, and entreating for some favor, which, perhaps, it would grieve her to obtain; and all the unseen multitude, both saints and sinners, seemed to encourage her onward.

48 "Faith!" shouted Goodman Brown, in a voice of agony and desperation; and the echoes of the forest mocked him, crying, "Faith! Faith!" as if bewildered wretches were seeking her all through the wilderness.

49 The cry of grief, rage, and terror was yet piercing the night, when the unhappy husband held his breath for a response. There was a scream, drowned immediately in a louder murmur of voices, fading into far-off laughter, as the dark cloud swept away, leaving the clear and silent sky above Goodman Brown. But something fluttered lightly down through the air and caught on the branch of a tree. The young man seized it, and beheld a pink ribbon.

50 "My Faith is gone!" cried he, after one stupefied moment. "There is no good on earth; and sin is but a name. Come, devil; for to thee is this world given."

51 And, maddened with despair, so that he laughed loud and long, did Goodman Brown grasp his staff and set forth again, at such a rate that he seemed to fly along the forest path rather than to walk or run. The road grew wilder and drearier and more faintly traced, and vanished at length, leaving him in the heart of the dark wilderness, still rushing onward with the instinct that guides mortal man to evil. The whole forest was peopled with frightful sounds—the creaking of the trees, the howling of wild beasts, and the yell of Indians; while sometimes the wind tolled like a distant church bell, and sometimes gave a broad roar around the traveler, as if all Nature were laughing him to scorn. But he was himself the chief horror of the scene, and shrank not from its other horrors.

52 "Ha! ha! ha!" roared Goodman Brown when the wind laughed at him.

53 "Let us hear which will laugh loudest. Think not to frighten me with your deviltry. Come witch, come wizard, come Indian powwow, come devil himself, and here comes Goodman Brown. You may as well fear him as he fear you."

54   In truth, all through the haunted forest there could be nothing more frightful than the figure of Goodman Brown. On he flew among the black pines, brandishing his staff with frenzied gestures, now giving vent to an inspiration of horrid **blasphemy,** and now shouting forth such laughter as set all the echoes of the forest laughing like demons around him. The fiend in his own shape is less hideous than when he rages in the breast of man. Thus sped the demoniac on his course, until, quivering among the trees, he saw a red light before him, as when the felled trunks and branches of a clearing have been set on fire, and throw up their lurid blaze against the sky, at the hour of midnight. He paused, in a lull of the tempest that had driven him onward, and heard the swell of what seemed a hymn, rolling solemnly from a distance with the weight of many voices. He knew the tune; it was a familiar one in the choir of the village meeting-house. The verse died heavily away, and was lengthened by a chorus, not of human voices, but of all the sounds of the benighted wilderness pealing in awful harmony together. Goodman Brown cried out, and his cry was lost to his own ear by its unison with the cry of the desert.

55   In the interval of silence he stole forward until the light glared full upon his eyes. At one extremity of an open space, hemmed in by the dark wall of the forest, arose a rock, bearing some rude, natural resemblance either to an altar or a pulpit, and surrounded by four blazing pines, their tops aflame, their stems untouched, like candles at an evening meeting. The mass of foliage that had overgrown the summit of the rock was all on fire, blazing high into the night and fitfully illuminating the whole field. Each pendent twig and leafy festoon was in a blaze. As the red light arose and fell, a numerous congregation alternately shone forth, then disappeared in shadow, and again grew, as it were, out of the darkness, peopling the heart of the solitary woods at once.

56   "A grave and dark-clad company," quoth Goodman Brown.

57   In truth they were such. Among them, quivering to and fro between gloom and splendor, appeared faces that would be seen next day at the council board of the province, and others which, Sabbath after Sabbath, looked devoutly heavenward, and benignantly over the crowded pews, from the holiest pulpits in the land. Some affirm that the lady of the governor was there. At least there were high dames well known to her, and wives of honored husbands, and widows, a great multitude, and ancient maidens, all of excellent repute, and fair young girls, who trembled lest their mothers should espy them. Either the sudden gleams of light flashing over the obscure field bedazzled Goodman Brown, or he recognized a score of the church members of Salem village famous for their especial sanctity. Good old Deacon Gookin had arrived, and waited at the skirts of that venerable saint, his revered pastor. But, irreverently consorting with these grave, reputable, and pious people, these elders of the church, these chaste dames and dewy virgins, there were

men of dissolute lives and women of spotted fame, wretches given over to all mean and filthy vice, and suspected even of horrid crimes. It was strange to see that the good shrank not from the wicked, nor were the sinners abashed by the saints. Scattered also among their pale-faced enemies were the Indian priests, or powwows, who had often scared their native forest with more hideous incantations than any known to English witchcraft.

58 "But where is Faith?" thought Goodman Brown; and, as hope came into his heart, he trembled.

59 Another verse of the hymn arose, a slow and mournful strain, such as the pious love, but joined to words which expressed all that our nature can conceive of sin, and darkly hinted at far more. **Unfathomable** to mere mortals is the lore of fiends. Verse after verse was sung; and still the chorus of the desert swelled between like the deepest tone of a mighty organ; and with the final peal of that dreadful anthem there came a sound, as if the roaring wind, the rushing streams, the howling beasts, and every other voice of the unconcerted wilderness were mingling and according with the voice of guilty man in homage to the prince of all. The four blazing pines threw up a loftier flame, and obscurely discovered shapes and visages of horror on the smoke wreaths above the impious assembly. At the same moment the fire on the rock shot redly forth and formed a glowing arch above its base, where now appeared a figure. With reverence be it spoken, the figure bore no slight similitude, both in garb and manner, to some grave divine of the New England churches.

60 "Bring forth the converts!" cried a voice that echoed through the field and rolled into the forest.

61 At the word, Goodman Brown stepped forth from the shadow of the trees and approached the congregation, with whom he felt a loathful brotherhood by the sympathy of all that was wicked in his heart. He could have well-nigh sworn that the shape of his own dead father beckoned him to advance, looking downward from a smoke wreath, while a woman, with dim features of despair, threw out her hand to warn him back. Was it his mother? But he had no power to retreat one step, nor to resist, even in thought, when the minister and good old Deacon Gookin seized his arms and led him to the blazing rock. Thither came also the slender form of a veiled female, led between Goody Cloyse, that pious teacher of the catechism, and Martha Carrier, who had received the devil's promise to be queen of hell. A rampant hag was she. And there stood the proselytes beneath the canopy of fire.

62 "Welcome, my children," said the dark figure, "to the communion of your race. Ye have found thus young your nature and your destiny. My children, look behind you!"

63   They turned; and flashing forth, as it were, in a sheet of flame, the fiend worshippers were seen; the smile of welcome gleamed darkly on every visage.

64   "There," resumed the sable form, "are all whom ye have reverenced from youth. Ye deemed them holier than yourselves, and shrank from your own sin, contrasting it with their lives of righteousness and prayerful aspirations heavenward. Yet here are they all in my worshipping assembly. This night it shall be granted you to know their secret deeds: how hoary-bearded elders of the church have whispered wanton words to the young maids of their households; how many a woman, eager for widows' weeds, has given her husband a drink at bedtime and let him sleep his last sleep in her bosom; how beardless youths have made haste to inherit their fathers' wealth; and how fair damsels—blush not, sweet ones—have dug little graves in the garden, and bidden me, the sole guest to an infant's funeral. By the sympathy of your human hearts for sin ye shall scent out all the places—whether in church, bedchamber, street, field, or forest—where crime has been committed, and shall exult to behold the whole earth one stain of guilt, one mighty blood spot. Far more than this. It shall be yours to penetrate, in every bosom, the deep mystery of sin, the fountain of all wicked arts, and which inexhaustibly supplies more evil impulses than human power—than my power at its utmost—can make manifest in deeds. And now, my children, look upon each other."

65   They did so; and, by the blaze of the hell-kindled torches, the wretched man beheld his Faith, and the wife her husband, trembling before that unhallowed altar.

66   "Lo, there ye stand, my children," said the figure, in a deep and solemn tone, almost sad with its despairing awfulness, as if his once angelic nature could yet mourn for our miserable race. "Depending upon one another's hearts, ye had still hoped that virtue were not all a dream. Now are ye undeceived. Evil is the nature of mankind. Evil must be your only happiness. Welcome again, my children, to the communion of your race."

67   "Welcome," repeated the fiend worshippers, in one cry of despair and triumph.

68   And there they stood, the only pair, as it seemed, who were yet hesitating on the verge of wickedness in this dark world. A basin was hollowed, naturally, in the rock. Did it contain water, reddened by the lurid light? or was it blood? or, perchance, a liquid flame? Herein did the shape of evil dip his hand and prepare to lay the mark of baptism upon their foreheads, that they might be partakers of the mystery of sin, more conscious of the secret guilt of others, both in deed and thought, than they could now be of their own. The husband cast one look at his pale wife, and Faith at him. What polluted wretches would

Please note that excerpts and passages in the StudySync® library and this workbook are intended as touchstones to generate interest in an author's work. The excerpts and passages do not substitute for the reading of entire texts, and StudySync® strongly recommends that students seek out and purchase the whole literary or informational work in order to experience it as the author intended. Links to online resellers are available in our digital library. In addition, complete works may be ordered through an authorized reseller by filling out and returning to StudySync® the order form enclosed in this workbook.

Reading & Writing Companion   **351**

the next glance show them to each other, shuddering alike at what they disclosed and what they saw!

69   "Faith! Faith!" cried the husband, "look up to heaven, and resist the wicked one."

70   Whether Faith obeyed he knew not. Hardly had he spoken when he found himself amid calm night and solitude, listening to a roar of the wind which died heavily away through the forest. He staggered against the rock, and felt it chill and damp; while a hanging twig, that had been all on fire, besprinkled his cheek with the coldest dew.

71   The next morning young Goodman Brown came slowly into the street of Salem village, staring around him like a bewildered man. The good old minister was taking a walk along the graveyard to get an appetite for breakfast and meditate his sermon, and bestowed a blessing, as he passed, on Goodman Brown. He shrank from the venerable saint as if to avoid an anathema. Old Deacon Gookin was at domestic worship, and the holy words of his prayer were heard through the open window. "What God doth the wizard pray to?" quoth Goodman Brown. Goody Cloyse, that excellent old Christian, stood in the early sunshine at her own lattice, catechizing a little girl who had brought her a pint of morning's milk. Goodman Brown snatched away the child as from the grasp of the fiend himself. Turning the corner by the meeting-house, he spied the head of Faith, with the pink ribbons, gazing anxiously forth, and bursting into such joy at sight of him that she skipped along the street and almost kissed her husband before the whole village. But Goodman Brown looked sternly and sadly into her face, and passed on without a greeting.

72   Had Goodman Brown fallen asleep in the forest and only dreamed a wild dream of a witch-meeting?

73   Be it so if you will; but, alas! it was a dream of evil omen for young Goodman Brown. A stern, a sad, a darkly meditative, a distrustful, if not a desperate man did he become from the night of that fearful dream. On the Sabbath day, when the congregation were singing a holy psalm, he could not listen because an anthem of sin rushed loudly upon his ear and drowned all the blessed strain. When the minister spoke from the pulpit with power and **fervid** eloquence, and, with his hand on the open Bible, of the sacred truths of our religion, and of saint-like lives and triumphant deaths, and of future bliss or misery unutterable, then did Goodman Brown turn pale, dreading lest the roof should thunder down upon the gray blasphemer and his hearers. Often, waking suddenly at midnight, he shrank from the bosom of Faith; and at morning or eventide, when the family knelt down at prayer, he scowled and muttered to himself, and gazed sternly at his wife, and turned away. And when

he had lived long, and was borne to his grave a hoary corpse, followed by Faith, an aged woman, and children and grandchildren, a goodly procession, besides neighbors not a few, they carved no hopeful verse upon his tombstone, for his dying hour was gloom.

THINK QUESTIONS

1. Who is Young Goodman Brown, and why does he go for a walk into a wooded area outside a village? What happens when he first enters the woods? Support your answer with textual evidence.

2. Describe three things that Goodman Brown sees during the night that astonish him. Cite textual evidence to support your answer.

3. How does Goodman Brown change after his night in the woods? Support your answer with textual evidence.

4. Use context to determine the meaning of the word **threshold** as it is used in "Young Goodman Brown." Write your definition of "threshold" and tell how you arrived at it.

5. Remembering that the prefix *ir-* is a variant of the Latin prefix *in-,* meaning "not," and the Latin adjective suffix *-ible* means "capable of," use the context clues provided in the passage to determine the meaning of **irrepressible**. Write your definition of "irrepressible" and tell how you arrived at it.

CLOSE READ

Reread the short story "Young Goodman Brown." As you reread, complete the Focus Questions below. Then use your answers and annotations from the questions to help you complete the Writing Prompt.

FOCUS QUESTIONS

1. Identify those aspects of the setting that Young Goodman Brown perceives to be realistic and those aspects that he perceives to be magical or otherwise peculiar. Why do you think the two are intermixed in the same story? How do they relate to the plot? Highlight evidence from the text and make annotations to explain your answers.

2. Analyze the role of trees as part of the setting of the story. Consider how Hawthorne describes them in various paragraphs. What might the trees represent, and what might the forest as a whole stand for? Support your answer with textual evidence and make annotations to explain your answer choices.

3. Compare and contrast Goodman Brown's attitude and behavior when he is in Salem village at the start of the story with his attitude and behavior in the forest in the paragraphs that follow. Highlight evidence from the text and make annotations to explain your response.

4. Discuss how the setting in "Young Goodman Brown" helps to create the mood of the story and how the setting affects the protagonist. Support your answer with textual evidence and make annotations to explain your answer choices.

5. Recall the unit's Essential Question: "How have the literary movements of the last two centuries affected us?" In what kinds of contemporary stories do we typically see a struggle between good and evil, similar to the one in "Young Goodman Brown"? How does the setting help develop this struggle, in both "Young Goodman Brown" and these contemporary stories? Highlight elements in Hawthorne's story that compare to elements of these contemporary books or movies, and make annotations to explain your responses.

WRITING PROMPT

Discuss how Hawthorne uses descriptions of the setting to create an increasingly frightening mood in "Young Goodman Brown," up until the last three paragraphs of the story. Support your writing with at least five pieces of evidence from the text.

THE MASQUE OF THE RED DEATH

FICTION

Edgar Allan Poe

1842

INTRODUCTION

Gothic master Edgar Allen Poe was one of America's earliest practitioners of the short story, famous for his tales of mystery and macabre. In this story, the "Red Death" is raging, and people are dying. Prince Prospero invites a thousand friends into his castle and locks out the rest of the world. Inside, he and his friends believe that they are safe from the plague that has killed so many, but everything changes the night the prince holds a masquerade ball.

"There was a sharp cry— and the dagger dropped gleaming upon the sable carpet…"

FIRST READ

1   The "Red Death" had long devastated the country. No **pestilence** had ever been so fatal, or so hideous. Blood was its Avatar and its seal—the redness and the horror of blood. There were sharp pains, and sudden dizziness, and then profuse bleeding at the pores, with dissolution. The scarlet stains upon the body and especially upon the face of the victim, were the pest ban which shut him out from the aid and from the sympathy of his fellow-men. And the whole seizure, progress and termination of the disease, were the incidents of half an hour.

2   But the Prince Prospero was happy and dauntless and sagacious. When his **dominions** were half depopulated, he summoned to his presence a thousand hale and light-hearted friends from among the knights and dames of his court, and with these retired to the deep seclusion of one of his castellated abbeys. This was an extensive and magnificent structure, the creation of the prince's own eccentric yet **august** taste. A strong and lofty wall girdled it in. This wall had gates of iron. The courtiers, having entered, brought furnaces and massy hammers and welded the bolts. They resolved to leave means neither of ingress nor egress to the sudden impulses of despair or of frenzy from within. The abbey was amply provisioned. With such precautions the courtiers might bid defiance to contagion. The external world could take care of itself. In the meantime it was folly to grieve, or to think. The prince had provided all the appliances of pleasure. There were buffoons, there were improvisatori, there were ballet-dancers, there were musicians, there was Beauty, there was wine. All these and security were within. Without was the "Red Death."

3   It was towards the close of the fifth or sixth month of his seclusion, and while the pestilence raged most furiously abroad, that the Prince Prospero entertained his thousand friends at a masked ball of the most unusual magnificence.

4   It was a voluptuous scene, that masquerade. But first let me tell of the rooms in which it was held. These were seven—an imperial suite. In many palaces,

Copyright © BookheadEd Learning, LLC

NOTES

however, such suites form a long and straight vista, while the folding doors slide back nearly to the walls on either hand, so that the view of the whole extent is scarcely impeded. Here the case was very different, as might have been expected from the duke's love of the *bizarre*. The apartments were so irregularly disposed that the vision embraced but little more than one at a time. There was a sharp turn at every twenty or thirty yards, and at each turn a novel effect. To the right and left, in the middle of each wall, a tall and narrow Gothic window looked out upon a closed corridor which pursued the windings of the suite. These windows were of stained glass whose colour varied in accordance with the prevailing hue of the decorations of the chamber into which it opened. That at the eastern extremity was hung, for example in blue—and vividly blue were its windows. The second chamber was purple in its ornaments and tapestries, and here the panes were purple. The third was green throughout, and so were the casements. The fourth was furnished and lighted with orange—the fifth with white—the sixth with violet. The seventh apartment was closely shrouded in black velvet tapestries that hung all over the ceiling and down the walls, falling in heavy folds upon a carpet of the same material and hue. But in this chamber only, the colour of the windows failed to correspond with the decorations. The panes here were scarlet—a deep blood colour. Now in no one of the seven apartments was there any lamp or candelabrum, amid the profusion of golden ornaments that lay scattered to and fro or depended from the roof. There was no light of any kind emanating from lamp or candle within the suite of chambers. But in the corridors that followed the suite, there stood, opposite to each window, a heavy tripod, bearing a brazier of fire, that projected its rays through the tinted glass and so glaringly illumined the room. And thus were produced a multitude of gaudy and fantastic appearances. But in the western or black chamber the effect of the fire-light that streamed upon the dark hangings through the blood-tinted panes, was ghastly in the extreme, and produced so wild a look upon the countenances of those who entered, that there were few of the company bold enough to set foot within its precincts at all.

5   It was in this apartment, also, that there stood against the western wall, a gigantic clock of ebony. Its pendulum swung to and fro with a dull, heavy, monotonous clang; and when the minute-hand made the circuit of the face, and the hour was to be stricken, there came from the brazen lungs of the clock a sound which was clear and loud and deep and exceedingly musical, but of so peculiar a note and emphasis that, at each lapse of an hour, the musicians of the orchestra were constrained to pause, momentarily, in their performance, to harken to the sound; and thus the waltzers perforce ceased their evolutions; and there was a brief disconcert of the whole gay company; and, while the chimes of the clock yet rang, it was observed that the giddiest grew pale, and the more aged and sedate passed their hands over their brows as if in confused revery or meditation. But when the echoes had fully ceased, a light laughter at once pervaded the assembly; the musicians looked

at each other and smiled as if at their own nervousness and folly, and made whispering vows, each to the other, that the next chiming of the clock should produce in them no similar emotion; and then, after the lapse of sixty minutes, (which embrace three thousand and six hundred seconds of the Time that flies,) there came yet another chiming of the clock, and then were the same disconcert and **tremulousness** and meditation as before.

6   But, in spite of these things, it was a gay and magnificent revel. The tastes of the duke were peculiar. He had a fine eye for colours and effects. He disregarded the *decora* of mere fashion. His plans were bold and fiery, and his conceptions glowed with barbaric lustre. There are some who would have thought him mad. His followers felt that he was not. It was necessary to hear and see and touch him to be *sure* that he was not.

7   He had directed, in great part, the movable embellishments of the seven chambers, upon occasion of this great *fête*; and it was his own guiding taste which had given character to the masqueraders. Be sure they were grotesque. There were much glare and glitter and piquancy and phantasm—much of what has been since seen in "Hernani". There were arabesque figures with unsuited limbs and appointments. There were delirious fancies such as the madman fashions. There were much of the beautiful, much of the wanton, much of the *bizarre*, something of the terrible, and not a little of that which might have excited disgust. To and fro in the seven chambers there stalked, in fact, a multitude of dreams. And these—the dreams—writhed in and about taking hue from the rooms, and causing the wild music of the orchestra to seem as the echo of their steps. And, anon, there strikes the ebony clock which stands in the hall of the velvet. And then, for a moment, all is still, and all is silent save the voice of the clock. The dreams are stiff-frozen as they stand. But the echoes of the chime die away—they have endured but an instant—and a light, half-subdued laughter floats after them as they depart. And now again the music swells, and the dreams live, and writhe to and fro more merrily than ever, taking hue from the many tinted windows through which stream the rays from the tripods. But to the chamber which lies most westwardly of the seven, there are now none of the maskers who venture; for the night is **waning** away; and there flows a ruddier light through the blood-coloured panes; and the blackness of the sable drapery appals; and to him whose foot falls upon the sable carpet, there comes from the near clock of ebony a muffled peal more solemnly emphatic than any which reaches *their* ears who indulged in the more remote gaieties of the other apartments.

8   But these other apartments were densely crowded, and in them beat feverishly the heart of life. And the revel went whirlingly on, until at length there commenced the sounding of midnight upon the clock. And then the music ceased, as I have told; and the evolutions of the waltzers were quieted; and there was an uneasy cessation of all things as before. But now there

were twelve strokes to be sounded by the bell of the clock; and thus it happened, perhaps, that more of thought crept, with more of time, into the meditations of the thoughtful among those who revelled. And thus too, it happened, perhaps, that before the last echoes of the last chime had utterly sunk into silence, there were many individuals in the crowd who had found leisure to become aware of the presence of a masked figure which had arrested the attention of no single individual before. And the rumour of this new presence having spread itself whisperingly around, there arose at length from the whole company a buzz, or murmur, expressive of disapprobation and surprise—then, finally, of terror, of horror, and of disgust.

9   In an assembly of phantasms such as I have painted, it may well be supposed that no ordinary appearance could have excited such sensation. In truth the masquerade licence of the night was nearly unlimited; but the figure in question had out-Heroded Herod, and gone beyond the bounds of even the prince's indefinite decorum. There are chords in the hearts of the most reckless which cannot be touched without emotion. Even with the utterly lost, to whom life and death are equally jests, there are matters of which no jest can be made. The whole company, indeed, seemed now deeply to feel that in the costume and bearing of the stranger neither wit nor propriety existed. The figure was tall and gaunt, and shrouded from head to foot in the habiliments of the grave. The mask which concealed the visage was made so nearly to resemble the countenance of a stiffened corpse that the closest scrutiny must have had difficulty in detecting the cheat. And yet all this might have been endured, if not approved, by the mad revellers around. But the mummer had gone so far as to assume the type of the Red Death. His vesture was dabbled in blood—and his broad brow, with all the features of the face, was besprinkled with the scarlet horror.

10 When the eyes of the Prince Prospero fell upon this **spectral** image (which, with a slow and solemn movement, as if more fully to sustain its role, stalked to and fro among the waltzers) he was seen to be convulsed, in the first moment with a strong shudder either of terror or distaste; but, in the next, his brow reddened with rage.

11 "Who dares,"—he demanded hoarsely of the courtiers who stood near him— "who dares insult us with this blasphemous mockery? Seize him and unmask him—that we may know whom we have to hang, at sunrise, from the battlements!"

12 It was in the eastern or blue chamber in which stood the Prince Prospero as he uttered these words. They rang throughout the seven rooms loudly and clearly, for the prince was a bold and robust man, and the music had become hushed at the waving of his hand.

13   It was in the blue room where stood the prince, with a group of pale courtiers by his side. At first, as he spoke, there was a slight rushing movement of this group in the direction of the intruder, who at the moment was also near at hand, and now, with deliberate and stately step, made closer approach to the speaker. But from a certain nameless awe with which the mad assumptions of the mummer had inspired the whole party, there were found none who put forth hand to seize him; so that, unimpeded, he passed within a yard of the prince's person; and, while the vast assembly, as if with one impulse, shrank from the centres of the rooms to the walls, he made his way uninterruptedly, but with the same solemn and measured step which had distinguished him from the first, through the blue chamber to the purple—through the purple to the green—through the green to the orange—through this again to the white—and even thence to the violet, ere a decided movement had been made to arrest him. It was then, however, that the Prince Prospero, maddening with rage and the shame of his own momentary cowardice, rushed hurriedly through the six chambers, while none followed him on account of a deadly terror that had seized upon all. He bore aloft a drawn dagger, and had approached, in rapid impetuosity, to within three or four feet of the retreating figure, when the latter, having attained the extremity of the velvet apartment, turned suddenly and confronted his pursuer. There was a sharp cry—and the dagger dropped gleaming upon the sable carpet, upon which, instantly afterwards, fell prostrate in death the Prince Prospero. Then, summoning the wild courage of despair, a throng of the revellers at once threw themselves into the black apartment, and, seizing the mummer, whose tall figure stood erect and motionless within the shadow of the ebony clock, gasped in unutterable horror at finding the grave cerements and corpse-like mask, which they handled with so violent a rudeness, untenanted by any tangible form.

14   And now was acknowledged the presence of the Red Death. He had come like a thief in the night. And one by one dropped the revellers in the blood-bedewed halls of their revel, and died each in the despairing posture of his fall. And the life of the ebony clock went out with that of the last of the gay. And the flames of the tripods expired. And Darkness and Decay and the Red Death held illimitable dominion over all.

THINK QUESTIONS

1. Why does Prince Prospero invite a thousand of his friends to an abbey and have the doors welded shut? Support your answer with evidence from the text.

2. What big event does the prince organize after the people have been in seclusion for five to six months? What is unique about the rooms used for this event? Include details from the text in your answers.

3. How do the people in the abbey meet a tragic end during the event? Support your answer with evidence from the text.

4. Use context to determine the meaning of the word **pestilence** as it is used in "The Masque of the Red Death." Write your definition of "pestilence" and tell how you arrived at it.

5. Use context to determine the meaning of the word **waning** as it is used in "The Masque of the Red Death." Write your definition of "waning" and tell how you arrived at it.

CLOSE READ

Reread the short story "The Masque of the Red Death." As you reread, complete the Focus Questions below. Then use your answers and annotations from the questions to help you complete the Writing Prompt.

FOCUS QUESTIONS

1. When Prince Prospero confronts the bloody intruder at his ball, he says, "Seize him and unmask him—that we may know whom we have to hang, at sunrise. . . ." Explain why this quotation is an example of situational irony. Highlight your textual evidence and make annotations to explain your choices.

2. Reread the description of the mysterious stranger who attended the masquerade ball. What does the description suggest to readers about the masked stranger, and how might his appearance at the ball be an example of dramatic irony? Highlight your textual evidence and make annotations to explain your choices.

3. A common theme in Gothic literature involves the inability of people to escape their fate. Analyze how this theme applies to "The Masque of the Red Death." Highlight your textual evidence and make annotations to explain your answer choices.

4. Analyze Prince Prospero's character. How is he depicted in the story? Is he a heroic character? Why is his death ironic? Highlight your textual evidence and make annotations to explain your answer choices.

5. The Essential Question for this unit asks, "How have the literary movements of the last two centuries affected us?" "The Masque of the Red Death" is part of the Gothic tradition, which falls under romanticism. Recall that romantics focused on nature, extreme emotions, the exotic, the monstrous, and the influence of folklore and medieval history. How well does "The Masque of the Red Death" fit into this category? Why might readers today still be drawn to stories like this one? Highlight elements of the story related to romanticism and explain why you found them particularly captivating.

WRITING PROMPT

Both "The Masque of the Red Death" and "Young Goodman Brown" can be seen as allegories, or stories that use characters and plot as symbols for larger ideas about the nature of humanity. How are these stories alike and different? You might consider the stories' symbols, settings, characters, use of language, and so on. What larger idea about the nature of humanity does each present? Support your writing with evidence from the text.

PRIDE AND PREJUDICE

FICTION
Jane Austen
1813

INTRODUCTION

Over the course of the novel *Pride and Prejudice*, Jane Austen presents British-regency-era polite society and reveals its preoccupation with marriage and money through her portrayal of the Bennet family. In the following excerpt from the opening chapter of the book, Austin sets the scene, introducing readers to the personalities of the Bennets.

"The business of her life was to get her daughters married..."

FIRST READ

From Chapter 1

1   It is a truth universally acknowledged that a single man in possession of a good fortune must be in want of a wife.

2   However little known the feelings or views of such a man may be on his first entering a neighbourhood, this truth is so well fixed in the minds of the surrounding families that he is considered as the rightful property of someone or other of their daughters.

3   "My dear Mr. Bennet," said his lady to him one day, "have you heard that Netherfield Park is let at last?"

4   Mr. Bennet replied that he had not.

5   "But it is," returned she; "for Mrs. Long has just been here, and she told me all about it."

6   Mr. Bennet made no answer.

7   "Do not you want to know who has taken it?" cried his wife impatiently.

8   "You want to tell me, and I have no objection to hearing it."

9   This was invitation enough.

10 "Why, my dear, you must know, Mrs. Long says that Netherfield is taken by a young man of large fortune from the north of England; that he came down on Monday in a chaise and four to see the place, and was so much delighted with it, that he agreed with Mr. Morris immediately; that he is to take possession before Michaelmas, and some of his servants are to be in the house by the end of next week."

NOTES

11 "What is his name?"

12 "Bingley."

13 "Is he married or single?"

14 "Oh! single, my dear, to be sure! A single man of large fortune; four or five thousand a year. What a fine thing for our girls!"

15 "How so? how can it affect them?"

16 "My dear Mr. Bennet," replied his wife, "how can you be so **tiresome!** You must know that I am thinking of his marrying one of them."

17 "Is that his design in settling here?"

18 "Design! Nonsense, how can you talk so! But it is very likely that he may fall in love with one of them, and therefore you must visit him as soon as he comes."

19 "I see no occasion for that. You and the girls may go, or you may send them by themselves, which perhaps will be still better, for as you are as handsome as any of them, Mr. Bingley might like you the best of the party."

20 "My dear, you flatter me. I certainly have had my share of beauty, but I do not pretend to be anything extraordinary now. When a woman has five grown-up daughters she ought to give over thinking of her own beauty."

21 "In such cases a woman has not often much beauty to think of."

22 "But, my dear, you must indeed go and see Mr. Bingley when he comes into the neighbourhood."

23 "It is more than I engage for, I assure you."

24 "But consider your daughters. Only think what an establishment it would be for one of them. Sir William and Lady Lucas are determined to go, merely on that account, for in general, you know, they visit no new-comers. Indeed you must go, for it will be impossible for us to visit him if you do not."

25 "You are **over-scrupulous** surely. I dare say Mr. Bingley will be very glad to see you; and I will send a few lines by you to assure him of my hearty consent to his marrying whichever he chooses of the girls: though I must throw in a good word for my little Lizzy."

NOTES

26 "I desire you will do no such thing. Lizzy is not a bit better than the others; and I am sure she is not half so handsome as Jane, nor half so good-humoured as Lydia. But you are always giving her the preference."

27 "They have none of them much to recommend them," replied he; "they are all silly and ignorant, like other girls; but Lizzy has something more of quickness than her sisters."

28 "Mr. Bennet, how can you abuse your own children in such a way! You take delight in vexing me. You have no compassion on my poor nerves."

29 "You mistake me, my dear. I have a high respect for your nerves. They are my old friends. I have heard you mention them with consideration these twenty years at least."

30 "Ah! you do not know what I suffer."

31 "But I hope you will get over it, and live to see many young men of four thousand a year come into the neighbourhood."

32 "It will be no use to us if twenty such should come, since you will not visit them."

33 "Depend upon it, my dear, that when there are twenty, I will visit them all."

34 Mr. Bennet was so odd a mixture of quick parts, sarcastic humour, reserve, and **caprice,** that the experience of three-and-twenty years had been insufficient to make his wife understand his character. Her mind was less difficult to develop. She was a woman of mean understanding, little information, and uncertain temper. When she was **discontented** she fancied herself nervous. The business of her life was to get her daughters married; its **solace** was visiting and news.

THINK QUESTIONS

1. What event has Mrs. Bennet so excited at the beginning of the excerpt and why? What does she want Mr. Bennet to do in response to this event? Cite textual evidence to support your response.

2. Describe the relationship between Mr. and Mrs. Bennet. What inferences can you make about each parent's relationships with their daughters? Support your response with textual evidence.

3. What inferences can you make about the role of women in English society in the early nineteenth century based on the excerpt? Support your response with evidence from the text.

4. Use context to determine the meaning of the word **tiresome** as it is used in *Pride and Prejudice*. Write your definition of "tiresome" and tell how you arrived at it. Then, use a dictionary to verify your definition.

5. Remembering that the prefix *-dis* means "not," use the context clues provided in the passage to determine the meaning of **discontented.** Write your definition of "discontented" and tell how you arrived at it.

CLOSE READ

Reread the excerpt from *Pride and Prejudice*. As you reread, complete the Focus Questions below. Then use your answers and annotations from the questions to help you complete the Writing Prompt.

FOCUS QUESTIONS

1. Describe Mr. Bennet's character using your own words, and support your description with evidence from Austen's text. Why is he so difficult for Mrs. Bennet to understand, and what does this difficulty reveal about her character? Highlight your textual evidence and make annotations to explain your choices.

2. Identify three examples of Mr. Bennet's "sarcastic humour." Make annotations to distinguish what he says from what he really means. What is the effect of this sarcasm on Mrs. Bennet? Highlight evidence to support your response.

3. Remember that irony is used to contrast what is said with what is meant, or what happens with what was expected. Identify examples of irony in Mrs. Bennet's dialogue. What is the difference between Mrs. Bennet's irony and Mr. Bennet's sarcasm? Highlight examples of irony and make annotations to note the differences.

4. What details about the Bennets' daughters are revealed in this excerpt? What does the discussion of the girls reveal about the characters of Mr. and Mrs. Bennet? Highlight your evidence and make annotations to explain your response.

5. How is Austen's use of dialogue to illuminate her characters similar to contemporary media, such as television and movies? How is it different? Highlight your evidence and make annotations to explain your ideas.

WRITING PROMPT

Which character do you think Austen wants her readers to prefer, and why? In explaining your answer, note how Jane Austen uses dialogue to characterize Mr. and Mrs. Bennet in the first chapter of *Pride and Prejudice,* and explore the roles that irony and sarcasm play in this characterization. Use your understanding of direct and indirect characterization to support your analysis. Cite textual evidence from the excerpt to support your response.

WUTHERING HEIGHTS

FICTION
Emily Brontë
1847

INTRODUCTION

Heathcliff, a homeless boy brought into the Wuthering Heights estate, and Catherine, its young mistress, strike up a fast friendship that turns to romantic love, but it is a love that is not to be. In these excerpts, Catherine tells her maid Nelly of her plan to create a future with Heathcliff and then suffers

"If I've done wrong, I'm dying for it. It is enough!

NOTES

FIRST READ

Excerpt from Chapter 9

1   "Nelly, do you never dream **queer** dreams?" she said, suddenly, after some minutes' reflection.

2   "Yes, now and then," I answered.

3   "And so do I. I've dreamt in my life dreams that have stayed with me ever after, and changed my ideas: they've gone through and through me, like wine through water, and altered the colour of my mind. And this is one: I'm going to tell it—but take care not to smile at any part of it."

4   "Oh! don't, Miss Catherine!" I cried. . . I was superstitious about dreams then, and am still; and Catherine had an unusual gloom in her **aspect,** that made me dread something from which I might shape a prophecy, and foresee a fearful catastrophe. . . .

5   "If I were in heaven, Nelly, I should be extremely miserable."

6   "Because you are not fit to go there," I answered. . . .

7   "But it is not for that. I dreamt once that I was there."

8   "I tell you I won't hearken to your dreams, Miss Catherine! I'll go to bed," I interrupted again.

9   She laughed, and held me down; for I made a motion to leave my chair.

10 "This is nothing," cried she: "I was only going to say that heaven did not seem to be my home; and I broke my heart with weeping to come back to earth; and the angels were so angry that they flung me out into the middle of the heath on the top of Wuthering Heights; where I woke sobbing for joy. That will do to explain my secret, as well as the other. I've no more business to marry

Edgar Linton than I have to be in heaven; and if the wicked [Hindley] had not brought Heathcliff so low, I shouldn't have thought of it. It would **degrade** me to marry Heathcliff now; so he shall never know how I love him: and that, not because he's handsome,

11   Nelly, but because he's more myself than I am. Whatever our souls are made of, his and mine are the same; and Linton's is as different as a moonbeam from lightning, or frost from fire."

12   Ere this speech ended I became sensible of Heathcliff's presence. Having noticed a slight movement, I turned my head, and saw him rise from the bench, and steal out noiselessly. He had listened till he heard Catherine say it would degrade her to marry him, and then he stayed to hear no further. My companion, sitting on the ground, was prevented by the back of the settle from remarking his presence or departure; but I started, and bade her hush!

. . .

13   "Nelly, I see now you think me a selfish wretch; but did it never strike you that if Heathcliff and I married, we should be beggars? Whereas, if I marry Linton I can aid Heathcliff to rise, and place him out of my brother's power."

14   "With your husband's money, Miss Catherine?" I asked. "You'll find him not so pliable as you calculate upon: and, though I'm hardly a judge, I think that's the worst motive you've given yet for being the wife of young Linton."

From Chapter 15

15   *[After overhearing Catherine, Heathcliff leaves Wuthering Heights; no one knows where he has gone. Catherine marries Edgar Linton. A few years later, Heathcliff returns from his unexplained absence with a fortune and marries Edgar's sister. In this chapter he visits Catherine while she is dying; Nelly has arranged for the visit to take place while Edgar is out.]*

16   With straining eagerness Catherine gazed towards the entrance of her chamber. [Heathcliff] did not hit the right room directly: she motioned me to admit him, but he found it out ere I could reach the door, and in a stride or two was at her side, and had her grasped in his arms. . . .

17   "You and Edgar have broken my heart, Heathcliff! And you both come to bewail the deed to me, as if *you* were the people to be pitied! I shall not pity you, not I. You have killed me—and thriven on it, I think. How strong you are! How many years do you mean to live after I am gone?"

18   Heathcliff had knelt on one knee to embrace her; he attempted to rise, but she seized his hair, and kept him down.

19   "I wish I could hold you," she continued, bitterly, "till we were both dead! I shouldn't care what you suffered. I care nothing for your sufferings. Why shouldn't you suffer? I do! Will you forget me? Will you be happy when I am in the earth? Will you say twenty years hence, 'That's the grave of Catherine Earnshaw? I loved her long ago, and was wretched to lose her; but it is past. I've loved many others since: my children are dearer to me than she was; and, at death, I shall not rejoice that I am going to her: I shall be sorry that I must leave them!' Will you say so, Heathcliff?"

20   "Don't torture me till I'm as mad as yourself," cried he, wrenching his head free, and grinding his teeth.

21   The two, to a cool spectator, made a strange and fearful picture. . . . Her present **countenance** had a wild vindictiveness in its white cheek, and a bloodless lip and scintillating eye; and she retained in her closed fingers a portion of the locks she had been grasping. As to her companion, while raising himself with one hand, he had taken her arm with the other; and so inadequate was his stock of gentleness to the requirements of her condition, that on his letting go I saw four distinct impressions left blue in the colourless skin.

22   "Are you possessed with a devil," he pursued, savagely, "to talk in that manner to me when you are dying? Do you reflect that all those words will be branded in my memory, and eating deeper eternally after you have left me? You know you lie to say I have killed you: and, Catherine, you know that I could as soon forget you as my existence! Is it not sufficient for your infernal selfishness, that while you are at peace I shall writhe in the torments of hell?"

23   . . . An instant they held asunder, and then how they met I hardly saw, but Catherine made a spring, and he caught her, and they were locked in an embrace from which I thought my mistress would never be released alive: in fact, to my eyes, she seemed directly insensible. He flung himself into the nearest seat, and on my approaching hurriedly to ascertain if she had fainted, he gnashed at me, and foamed like a mad dog, and gathered her to him with greedy jealousy. I did not feel as if I were in the company of a creature of my own species: it appeared that he would not understand, though I spoke to him; so I stood off, and held my tongue, in great perplexity.

24   A movement of Catherine's relieved me a little presently: she put up her hand to clasp his neck, and bring her cheek to his as he held her; while he, in return, covering her with frantic caresses, said wildly—"You teach me now how cruel you've been—cruel and false. *Why* did you despise me? *Why* did you betray your own heart, Cathy? I have not one word of comfort. You deserve this. You have killed yourself. Yes, you may kiss me, and cry; and wring out my kisses and tears: they'll blight you—they'll damn you. You loved

NOTES

me—then what *right* had you to leave me? What right—answer me—for the poor fancy you felt for Linton?

25 Because misery and degradation, and death, and nothing that God or Satan could inflict would have parted us, you, of your own will, did it. I have not broken your heart—*you* have broken it; and in breaking it, you have broken mine. So much the worse for me that I am strong. Do I want to live? What kind of living will it be when you—oh, God! Would *you* like to live with your soul in the grave?"

26 "Let me alone. Let me alone," sobbed Catherine. "If I've done wrong, I'm dying for it. It is enough! You left me too: but I won't upbraid you! I forgive you. Forgive me!"

27 "It is hard to forgive, and to look at those eyes, and feel those wasted hands," he answered. "Kiss me again; and don't let me see your eyes! I forgive what you have done to me. I love *my* murderer—but yours! How can I?"

28 They were silent—their faces hid against each other, and washed by each other's tears. . . .

From Chapter 16

29 [*Heathcliff leaves the house begrudgingly at Nelly's urging because Edgar is returning home. Heathcliff waits outside in the garden for Nelly to bring him word when he can see Catherine once more before she dies*].

30 . . . [Heathcliff] would probably be aware, from the lights flitting to and fro, and the opening and shutting of the outer doors, that all was not right within. I wished, yet feared, to find him. I felt the terrible news must be told, and I longed to get it over; but how to do it I did not know. He was there—at least, a few yards further in the park; leant against an old ash-tree, his hat off, and his hair soaked with the dew that had gathered on the budded branches . . . he raised his eyes [to me] and spoke: "She's dead!" he said; "I've not waited for you to learn that. Put your handkerchief away—don't snivel before me. Damn you all! She wants none of your tears!"

31 . . ."Yes, she's dead!" I answered, checking my sobs and drying my cheeks.

32 "Gone to heaven, I hope; where we may, every one, join her, if we take due warning and leave our evil ways to follow good!"

33 "Did *she* take due warning, then?" asked Heathcliff, attempting a sneer. "Did she die like a saint? Come, give me a true history of the event. How did—?"

34 He endeavoured to pronounce the name [Edgar], but could not manage it; and compressing his mouth he held a silent combat with his inward agony, defying, meanwhile, my sympathy with an unflinching, ferocious stare. "How

did she die?" he resumed, at last—fain, notwithstanding his hardihood, to have a support behind him; for, after the struggle, he trembled, in spite of himself, to his very finger-ends. . . .

35 "Quietly as a lamb!" I answered, aloud. "She drew a sigh, and stretched herself, like a child reviving, and sinking again to sleep; and five minutes after I felt one little pulse at her heart, and nothing more!"

36 "And—did she ever mention me?" he asked, hesitating, as if he dreaded the answer to his question would introduce details that he could not bear to hear.

37 "Her senses never returned: she recognised nobody from the time you left her," I said. "She lies with a sweet smile on her face; and her latest ideas wandered back to pleasant early days. Her life closed in a gentle dream—may she wake as kindly in the other world!"

38 "May she wake in torment!" he cried, with frightful vehemence, stamping his foot, and groaning in a sudden **paroxysm** of ungovernable passion. "Why, she's a liar to the end! Where is she? Not there—not in heaven—not perished—where? Oh! You said you cared nothing for my sufferings! And I pray one prayer—I repeat it till my tongue stiffens—Catherine Earnshaw, may you not rest as long as I am living; you said I killed you—haunt me, then! The murdered do haunt their murderers, I believe. I know that ghosts *have* wandered on earth. Be with me always—take any form—drive me mad! Only do *not* leave me in this abyss, where I cannot find you! Oh, God! It is unutterable! I *cannot* live without my life! I *cannot* live without my soul!"

39 He dashed his head against the knotted trunk; and, lifting up his eyes, howled, not like a man, but like a savage beast being goaded to death with knives and spears. I observed several splashes of blood about the bark of the tree, and his hand and forehead were both stained; probably the scene I witnessed was a repetition of others acted during the night.

40 . . . The place of Catherine's interment, to the surprise of the villagers, was neither in the chapel under the carved monument of the Lintons, nor yet by the tombs of her own relations, outside. It was dug on a green slope in a corner of the kirk-yard, where the wall is so low that heath and bilberry-plants have climbed over it from the moor; and peat-mould almost buries it.

THINK QUESTIONS

1. Why doesn't Nelly want to hear about Catherine's dream? What can readers infer about Nelly's relationships with the other characters based on the reason for her refusal? Support your response with evidence from the text.

2. Why does Catherine marry Edgar Linton instead of Heathcliff? What inference can readers make about Catherine's feelings for Heathcliff based on her reasons? Use evidence from the text to support your inference.

3. In the excerpt from Chapter 15, why is Catherine so angry with Heathcliff? Based on their conversation, what can you infer about how the relationship between these characters has changed since the events of Chapter 9? Support your inference with evidence from the text.

4. Use context to determine the meaning of the word **queer** as it is used in *Wuthering Heights*. Write your definition of "queer" and tell how you arrived at it.

5. Use context to determine the meaning of the word **paroxysm** as it is used in *Wuthering Heights*. Write your definition of "paroxysm" and tell how you arrived at it.

CLOSE READ

Reread the excerpt from *Wuthering Heights*. As you reread, complete the Focus Questions below. Then use your answers and annotations from the questions to help you complete the Writing Prompt.

FOCUS QUESTIONS

1. Write a brief summary of the excerpt from Chapter 9 of Wuthering Heights. Remember to include only the most important details and to maintain an objective tone. Highlight key details from the text that belong in a summary.

2. Consider Brontë's choice to have Heathcliff overhear only part of Catherine's plan. How does this choice help move the plot along, and how does it affect character development? Highlight your textual evidence and make annotations to explain your choices.

3. Compare and contrast the depiction of Catherine in Chapter 9 with how she is presented in Chapter 15. What does her development as a character suggest about the theme of the text? Support your answer with textual evidence and make annotations to explain your answer choices.

4. How does Nelly contribute to the development of theme in the text? Consider her roles both as a character who interacts with Heathcliff and Catherine and as the novel's narrator. Highlight evidence from the text and make annotations to support your explanation.

5. Recall the Essential Question for this unit: "How have the literary movements of the last two centuries affected us?" Trace the elements of romanticism in Wuthering Heights, including its focus on emotion over reason and an interest in the supernatural. How does romanticism shape the text and affect your experience of reading it as a 21st-century reader? Highlight evidence from the text and make annotations to support your explanation.

WRITING PROMPT

Determine two or more themes in Wuthering Heights and analyze how they are developed over the course of the excerpt. How does Brontë use characterization and dialogue to develop theme in the text? How do the themes interact with or build on each other? Support your response with textual evidence.

THE HOUSE OF MIRTH

FICTION

Edith Wharton

1905

INTRODUCTION

Born during the Civil War, American author Edith Wharton combined irony, wit, and a familiarity with privileged classes of society to produce humorous, insightful works of fiction. Her fourth novel, *The House of Mirth*, tells the story of Lily Bart, a well-born but subsequently penniless woman attempting to maintain social standing in New York City of the 1890's. The excerpt here from the book's third chapter hints at the odious expectations placed on Lily in her bid for acceptance by New York's high society.

"Lily could not recall the time when there had been money enough..."

NOTES

FIRST READ

Excerpt from Chapter III

1   A world in which such things could be seemed a miserable place to Lily Bart; but then she had never been able to understand the laws of a universe which was so ready to leave her out of its calculations.

2   She began to undress without ringing for her maid, whom she had sent to bed. She had been long enough in bondage to other people's pleasure to be considerate of those who depended on hers, and in her bitter moods it sometimes struck her that she and her maid were in the same position, except that the latter received her wages more regularly.

3   As she sat before the mirror brushing her hair, her face looked hollow and pale, and she was frightened by two little lines near her mouth, faint flaws in the smooth curve of the cheek.

4   "Oh, I must stop worrying!" she exclaimed. "Unless it's the electric light—" she reflected, springing up from her seat and lighting the candles on the dressing-table.

5   She turned out the wall-lights, and peered at herself between the candle-flames. The white oval of her face swam out waveringly from a background of shadows, the uncertain light blurring it like a haze; but the two lines about the mouth remained.

6   Lily rose and undressed in haste.

7   "It is only because I am tired and have such **odious** things to think about," she kept repeating; and it seemed an added injustice that petty cares should leave a trace on the beauty which was her only defence against them.

Reading & Writing Companion

8   But the odious things were there, and remained with her. She returned wearily to the thought of Percy Gryce, as a wayfarer picks up a heavy load and toils on after a brief rest. She was almost sure she had "landed" him: a few days' work and she would win her reward. But the reward itself seemed unpalatable just then: she could get no zest from the thought of victory. It would be a rest from worry, no more—and how little that would have seemed to her a few years earlier! Her ambitions had shrunk gradually in the **desiccating** air of failure. But why had she failed? Was it her own fault or that of destiny?

9   She remembered how her mother, after they had lost their money, used to say to her with a kind of fierce vindictiveness: "But you'll get it all back—you'll get it all back, with your face.". . . . The remembrance roused a whole train of association, and she lay in the darkness reconstructing the past out of which her present had grown.

10   A house in which no one ever dined at home unless there was "company"; a door-bell perpetually ringing; a hall-table showered with square envelopes which were opened in haste, and oblong envelopes which were allowed to gather dust in the depths of a bronze jar; a series of French and English maids giving warning amid a chaos of hurriedly-ransacked wardrobes and dress-closets; an equally changing dynasty of nurses and footmen; quarrels in the pantry, the kitchen and the drawing-room; **precipitate** trips to Europe, and returns with gorged trunks and days of interminable unpacking; semi-annual discussions as to where the summer should be spent, grey interludes of economy and brilliant reactions of expense—such was the setting of Lily Bart's first memories.

11   Ruling the turbulent element called home was the vigorous and determined figure of a mother still young enough to dance her ball-dresses to rags, while the hazy outline of a neutral-tinted father filled an intermediate space between the butler and the man who came to wind the clocks. Even to the eyes of infancy, Mrs. Hudson Bart had appeared young; but Lily could not recall the time when her father had not been bald and slightly stooping, with streaks of grey in his hair, and a tired walk. It was a shock to her to learn afterward that he was but two years older than her mother.

12   Lily seldom saw her father by daylight. All day he was "down town"; and in winter it was long after nightfall when she heard his fagged step on the stairs and his hand on the school-room door. He would kiss her in silence, and ask one or two questions of the nurse or the governess; then Mrs. Bart's maid would come to remind him that he was dining out, and he would hurry away with a nod to Lily. In summer, when he joined them for a Sunday at Newport or Southampton, he was even more **effaced** and silent than in winter. It seemed to tire him to rest, and he would sit for hours staring at the sea-line from a quiet corner of the verandah, while the clatter of his wife's existence

went on unheeded a few feet off. Generally, however, Mrs. Bart and Lily went to Europe for the summer, and before the steamer was half way over Mr. Bart had dipped below the horizon. Sometimes his daughter heard him denounced for having neglected to forward Mrs. Bart's remittances; but for the most part he was never mentioned or thought of till his patient stooping figure presented itself on the New York dock as a buffer between the magnitude of his wife's luggage and the restrictions of the American custom-house.

13   In this desultory yet agitated fashion life went on through Lily's teens: a zig-zag broken course down which the family craft glided on a rapid current of amusement, tugged at by the underflow of a perpetual need—the need of more money. Lily could not recall the time when there had been money enough, and in some vague way her father seemed always to blame for the deficiency. It could certainly not be the fault of Mrs. Bart, who was spoken of by her friends as a "wonderful manager." Mrs. Bart was famous for the unlimited effect she produced on limited means; and to the lady and her acquaintants there was something heroic in living as though one were much richer than one's bank-book denoted.

14   Lily was naturally proud of her mother's aptitude in this line: she had been brought up in the faith that, whatever it cost, one must have a good cook, and be what Mrs. Bart called "decently dressed." Mrs. Bart's worst reproach to her husband was to ask him if he expected her to "live like a pig"; and his replying in the negative was always regarded as a justification for cabling to Paris for an extra dress or two, and telephoning to the jeweller that he might, after all, send home the turquoise bracelet which Mrs. Bart had looked at that morning.

15   Lily knew people who "lived like pigs," and their appearance and surroundings justified her mother's **repugnance** to that form of existence. They were mostly cousins, who inhabited dingy houses with engravings from Cole's Voyage of Life on the drawing-room walls, and **slatternly** parlour-maids who said "I'll go and see" to visitors calling at an hour when all right-minded persons are conventionally if not actually out. The disgusting part of it was that many of these cousins were rich, so that Lily imbibed the idea that if people lived like pigs it was from choice, and through the lack of any proper standard of conduct. This gave her a sense of reflected superiority, and she did not need Mrs. Bart's comments on the family frumps and misers to foster her naturally lively taste for splendour.

16   Lily was nineteen when circumstances caused her to revise her view of the universe.

☁ THINK QUESTIONS

1. At the beginning of the excerpt, why is Lily Bart distressed by the lines on her face? What inference can you make about her situation and about the position of women in the 1890s based on this information? Cite textual evidence to support your answer.

2. What does Lily mean when she says she almost "landed" Percy Gryce? What inference can you make about Lily's history based on her thoughts about Percy? Support your answer with textual evidence.

3. Describe Lily's childhood. What kind of parents did she have? What effect does her upbringing and past have on her current situation? Cite textual evidence to support your answer.

4. Use context to determine the meaning of the word **odious** as it is used in *The House of Mirth*. Write your definition of "odious" and tell how you arrived at it.

5. Use context to determine the meaning of the word **repugnance** as it is used in *The House of Mirth*. Write your definition of "repugnance" and tell how you arrived at it.

CLOSE READ

Reread the excerpt from *The House of Mirth*. As you reread, complete the Focus Questions below. Then use your answers and annotations from the questions to help you complete the Writing Prompt.

FOCUS QUESTIONS

1. Describe Lily Bart's character as she is presented in this excerpt. How do outside forces influence Lily's character and actions? Highlight character traits and make annotations to explain the effects of outside forces.

2. What do readers learn about Mrs. Bart's character in this excerpt? What irony is revealed in Mrs. Bart's—and by extension, Lily's—attitude toward money? Highlight evidence in the text to support your response.

3. Early in the excerpt, Lily wonders, "But why had she failed? Was it her own fault or that of destiny?" How might Mr. and Mrs. Bart's marriage have influenced Lily's views on marriage and money? What did Mr. and Mrs. Bart's roles in the family teach Lily about societal roles for men and women? Highlight textual evidence and make annotations to explain your response.

4. What is Mrs. Bart's role in Lily's life, both during her childhood and when Lily is an adult? How has Mrs. Bart influenced Lily's perceptions of money and of Mr. Bart? Highlight textual evidence and make annotations to explain your choices.

5. Recall the unit's Essential Question: "How have the literary movements of the last two centuries affected us?" Realistic novels often focus on ideas of money and class. What themes about class does the excerpt from *The House of Mirth* suggest? How are these themes presented in the excerpt, and how is that different from what would be expected in a similar novel today? Highlight evidence to support your response.

WRITING PROMPT

Does Lily truly want wealth and a rich husband, or does she want something else? Use your understanding of character and make inferences based on Lily's childhood and the society in which she lives to form your claim. Support your claim with textual evidence.

O PIONEERS!

FICTION
Willa Cather
1913

INTRODUCTION

Willa Cather's 1913 novel, *O Pioneers!*, captures the American experience at the end of the 19th Century, the western migration of settlers and immigrants to the harsh Nebraska prairie. After her father's death, Alexandra Bergson inherits the family farm, a choice unconventional for its time considering that she had two older brothers. The homestead was entrusted to her because her father recognized she represented the family's best chance for survival. Facing the challenges of farming under unforgiving conditions, Alexandra prospers as a result of her determination, drawing her family together and adopting many technological innovations of the time. A friend, Carl Linstrum, left Nebraska after his family lost their farm and has now returned for a visit. His farm now belongs to Marie Shabata and her husband Frank. Alexandra's younger brother Emil is home from college. *O Pioneers!* beautifully and dramatically chronicles the trials of life on the prairie at a pivotal time in America's move west.

"A pioneer should have imagination..."

FIRST READ

From Part I, Chapter IV

1   The whole country was discouraged. Farmers who were already in debt had to give up their land. A few **foreclosures demoralized** the country. The settlers sat about on the wooden sidewalks in the little town and told each other that the country was never meant for men to live in; the thing to do was to get back to Iowa, to Illinois, to any place that had been proved **habitable**. The Bergson boys, certainly, would have been happier with their uncle Otto, in the bakery shop in Chicago. Like most of their neighbors, they were meant to follow in paths already marked out for them, not to break trails in a new country. A steady job, a few holidays, nothing to think about, and they would have been very happy. It was no fault of theirs that they had been dragged into the wilderness when they were little boys. A pioneer should have imagination, should be able to enjoy the idea of things more than the things themselves.

From Part II, Chapter V

2   The dawn in the east looked like the light from some great fire that was burning under the edge of the world. The color was reflected in the **globules** of dew that sheathed the short gray pasture grass. Carl walked rapidly until he came to the crest of the second hill, where the Bergson pasture joined the one that had belonged to his father. There he sat down and waited for the sun to rise. It was just there that he and Alexandra used to do their milking together, he on his side of the fence, she on hers. He could remember exactly how she looked when she came over the close-cropped grass, her skirts pinned up, her head bare, a bright tin pail in either hand, and the milky light of the early morning all about her. Even as a boy he used to feel, when he saw her coming with her free step, her upright head and calm shoulders, that she looked as if she had walked straight out of the morning itself. Since then, when he had happened to see the sun come up in the country or on the

water, he had often remembered the young Swedish girl and her milking pails.

3   Carl sat musing until the sun leaped above the prairie, and in the grass about him all the small creatures of day began to tune their tiny instruments. Birds and insects without number began to chirp, to twitter, to snap and whistle, to make all manner of fresh shrill noises. The pasture was flooded with light; every clump of ironweed and snow-on-the-mountain threw a long shadow, and the golden light seemed to be rippling through the curly grass like the tide racing in.

4   He crossed the fence into the pasture that was now the Shabatas' and continued his walk toward the pond. He had not gone far, however, when he discovered that he was not the only person abroad. In the draw below, his gun in his hands, was Emil, advancing cautiously, with a young woman beside him. They were moving softly, keeping close together, and Carl knew that they expected to find ducks on the pond. At the moment when they came in sight of the bright spot of water, he heard a whirr of wings and the ducks shot up into the air. There was a sharp crack from the gun, and five of the birds fell to the ground. Emil and his companion laughed delightedly, and Emil ran to pick them up. When he came back, dangling the ducks by their feet, Marie held her apron and he dropped them into it. As she stood looking down at them, her face changed. She took up one of the birds, a rumpled ball of feathers with the blood dripping slowly from its mouth, and looked at the live color that still burned on its plumage.

5   As she let it fall, she cried in distress, "Oh, Emil, why did you?"

6   "I like that!" the boy exclaimed **indignantly.** "Why, Marie, you asked me to come yourself."

7   "Yes, yes, I know," she said tearfully, "but I didn't think. I hate to see them when they are first shot. They were having such a good time, and we've spoiled it all for them."

8   Emil gave a rather sore laugh. "I should say we had! I'm not going hunting with you any more. You're as bad as Ivar. Here, let me take them." He snatched the ducks out of her apron.

9   "Don't be cross, Emil. Only—Ivar's right about wild things. They're too happy to kill. You can tell just how they felt when they flew up. They were scared, but they didn't really think anything could hurt them. No, we won't do that any more."

10   "All right," Emil **assented.** "I'm sorry I made you feel bad." As he looked down into her tearful eyes, there was a curious, sharp young bitterness in his own.

NOTES

11 Carl watched them as they moved slowly down the draw. They had not seen him at all. He had not overheard much of their dialogue, but he felt the import of it. It made him, somehow, unreasonably mournful to find two young things abroad in the pasture in the early morning. He decided that he needed his breakfast.

THINK QUESTIONS

1. Highlight and annotate pieces of textual evidence from Part I, Chapter IV that suggest many settlers wished they hadn't moved west. Do these details support the inference that no one should have moved to the frontier? Why or why not?

2. Based on details in Part II, Chapter V, what can readers infer about the relationship between Carl and Alexandra? Cite textual evidence in your response.

3. How does his observation of Marie and Emil make Carl feel? Considering Carl's remembrances of Alexandra, why might his observation of Marie and Emil make him feel this way? Support your response with textual evidence.

4. Use context to determine the meaning of **demoralized** as it is used in *O Pioneers!* Write your definition of "demoralized" and tell how you arrived at it.

5. Use context to determine the meaning of **indignantly** as it is used in *O Pioneers!* Write your definition of "indignantly" and tell how you arrived at it.

CLOSE READ

Reread the excerpt from *O Pioneers!*. As you reread, complete the Focus Questions below. Then use your answers and annotations from the questions to help you complete the Writing Prompt.

FOCUS QUESTIONS

1. In the excerpt from Part I, Chapter IV, how does the image of the men sitting on wooden sidewalks contrast with the concluding statement of this excerpt? What conclusion can you draw about Cather's attitude toward the setting based on this comparison? Highlight textual evidence and make annotations to explain your choices.

2. How does sound add a layer of meaning on top of the imagery in Part II, Chapter V? Highlight three examples of sound and make annotations to analyze the effect of the imagery.

3. Analyze how the setting relates to plot and theme. What is the significance of the dawn in Part II, Chapter V? Highlight textual evidence and make annotations to explain your choices.

4. Compare and contrast the role of women in *O Pioneers!* and *The House of Mirth*. What daily tasks are women expected to do? How do the men in their lives treat them? Highlight textual evidence to support your response.

5. Recall the unit's Essential Question: "How have the literary movements of the last two centuries affected us?" Willa Cather's realistic novels of the Nebraska prairie experience introduce readers to a place and time and make them feel as if they were there, experiencing firsthand both the place and the strivings of the characters who inhabit it. Highlight details from the excerpt that helped you imagine what it was like to live on the Nebraska frontier in the 19th century. Do contemporary authors paint as clear of a picture of what life is like today? Why or why not?

WRITING PROMPT

Write an argument in which you state whether the Bergson boys should stay on the prairie or leave for Chicago. Support your writing with the arguments for and against life on the prairie that are expressed in the selection, and use your understanding of setting to formulate your claim. Cite textual evidence in your response.

MRS. DALLOWAY

FICTION

Virginia Woolf

1925

INTRODUCTION

One of the earliest novels of the Modern movement in English literature, Virginia Woolf's portrait of a single day in the life of Clarissa Dalloway is a study in inner consciousness, with the reader experiencing shifting points of view through the minds of Mrs. Dalloway and other characters. In this passage from the opening of the novel, Mrs. Dalloway is preparing to host a party

"Mrs. Dalloway said she would buy the flowers herself."

 ## FIRST READ

NOTES

1 Mrs. Dalloway said she would buy the flowers herself.

2 For Lucy had her work cut out for her. The doors would be taken off their hinges; Rumpelmayer's men were coming. And then, thought Clarissa Dalloway, what a morning—fresh as if issued to children on a beach.

3 What a lark! What a plunge! For so it had always seemed to her, when, with a little squeak of the hinges, which she could hear now, she had burst open the French windows and plunged at Bourton into the open air. How fresh, how calm, stiller than this of course, the air was in the early morning; like the flap of a wave; the kiss of a wave; chill and sharp and yet (for a girl of eighteen as she then was) solemn, feeling as she did, standing there at the open window, that something awful was about to happen; looking at the flowers, at the trees with the smoke winding off them and the rooks rising, falling; standing and looking until Peter Walsh said, "**Musing** among the vegetables?"—was that it?—"I prefer men to cauliflowers"—was that it? He must have said it at breakfast one morning when she had gone out on to the terrace—Peter Walsh. He would be back from India one of these days, June or July, she forgot which, for his letters were awfully dull; it was his sayings one remembered; his eyes, his pocket-knife, his smile, his grumpiness and, when millions of things had utterly vanished—how strange it was!—a few sayings like this about cabbages.

4 She stiffened a little on the kerb, waiting for Durtnall's van to pass. A charming woman, Scrope Purvis thought her (knowing her as one does know people who live next door to one in Westminster); a touch of the bird about her, of the jay, blue-green, light, vivacious, though she was over fifty, and grown very white since her illness. There she perched, never seeing him, waiting to cross, very upright.

Please note that excerpts and passages in the StudySync® library and this workbook are intended as touchstones to generate interest in an author's work. The excerpts and passages do not substitute for the reading of entire texts, and StudySync® strongly recommends that students seek out and purchase the whole literary or informational work in order to experience it as the author intended. Links to online resellers are available in our digital library. In addition, complete works may be ordered through an authorized reseller by filling out and returning to StudySync® the order form enclosed in this workbook.

Reading & Writing Companion   389

5   For having lived in Westminster—how many years now? over twenty,—one feels even in the midst of the traffic, or waking at night, Clarissa was positive, a particular hush, or solemnity; an indescribable pause; a suspense (but that might be her heart, affected, they said, by influenza) before Big Ben strikes. There! Out it boomed. First a warning, musical; then the hour, irrevocable. The leaden circles dissolved in the air. Such fools we are, she thought, crossing Victoria Street. For Heaven only knows why one loves it so, how one sees it so, making it up, building it round one, tumbling it, creating it every moment afresh; but the veriest frumps, the most dejected of miseries sitting on doorsteps (drink their downfall) do the same; can't be dealt with, she felt positive, by Acts of Parliament for that very reason: they love life. In people's eyes, in the swing, tramp, and **trudge;** in the bellow and the uproar; the carriages, motor cars, omnibuses, vans, sandwich men shuffling and swinging; brass bands; barrel organs; in the triumph and the jingle and the strange high singing of some aeroplane overhead was what she loved; life; London; this moment of June.

6   For it was the middle of June. The War was over, except for some one like Mrs. Foxcroft at the Embassy last night eating her heart out because that nice boy was killed and now the old Manor House must go to a cousin; or Lady Bexborough who opened a bazaar, they said, with the telegram in her hand, John, her favourite, killed; but it was over; thank Heaven—over. It was June. The King and Queen were at the Palace. And everywhere, though it was still so early, there was a beating, a stirring of galloping ponies, tapping of cricket bats; Lords, Ascot, Ranelagh and all the rest of it; wrapped in the soft mesh of the grey-blue morning air, which, as the day wore on, would unwind them, and set down on their lawns and pitches the bouncing ponies, whose forefeet just struck the ground and up they sprung, the whirling young men, and laughing girls in their transparent **muslins** who, even now, after dancing all night, were taking their absurd woolly dogs for a run; and even now, at this hour, discreet old **dowagers** were shooting out in their motor cars on errands of mystery; and the shopkeepers were fidgeting in their windows with their paste and diamonds, their lovely old sea- green brooches in eighteenth-century settings to tempt Americans (but one must economise, not buy things rashly for Elizabeth), and she, too, loving it as she did with an absurd and faithful passion, being part of it, since her people were courtiers once in the time of the Georges, she, too, was going that very night to kindle and illuminate; to give her party. But how strange, on entering the Park, the silence; the mist; the hum; the slow-swimming happy ducks; the pouched birds waddling; and who should be coming along with his back against the Government buildings, most appropriately, carrying a despatch box stamped with the Royal Arms, who but Hugh Whitbread; her old friend Hugh—the admirable Hugh!

7   "Good-morning to you, Clarissa!" said Hugh, rather extravagantly, for they had known each other as children. "Where are you off to?"

8   "I love walking in London," said Mrs. Dalloway. "Really it's better than walking in the country."

9   They had just come up—unfortunately—to see doctors. Other people came to see pictures; go to the opera; take their daughters out; the Whitbreads came "to see doctors." Times without number Clarissa had visited Evelyn Whitbread in a nursing home. Was Evelyn ill again? Evelyn was a good deal out of sorts, said Hugh, intimating by a kind of pout or swell of his very well-covered, manly, extremely handsome, perfectly upholstered body (he was almost too well dressed always, but presumably had to be, with his little job at Court) that his wife had some internal ailment, nothing serious, which, as an old friend, Clarissa Dalloway would quite understand without requiring him to specify.

 THINK QUESTIONS

1. Read the first sentence of *Mrs. Dalloway*. What can readers infer about Mrs. Dalloway based on this statement? Use text evidence to support your inference.

2. Who is Scrope Purvis, and what words and phrases does he use to describe Mrs. Dalloway? What does this description reveal about Mrs. Dalloway? Cite textual evidence to support your response.

3. What kinds of details does the author use to describe Westminster? Why are these details important to the text? Support your answer with textual evidence.

4. Use context to determine the meaning of the word **lark** as it is used in *Mrs. Dalloway*. Write your definition of "lark" and tell how you arrived at it.

5. Use context to determine the meaning of the word **musing** as it is used in *Mrs. Dalloway*. Write your definition of "musing" and tell how you arrived at it.

CLOSE READ

Reread the excerpt from *Mrs. Dalloway.* As you reread, complete the Focus Questions below. Then use your answers and annotations from the questions to help you complete the Writing Prompt.

FOCUS QUESTIONS

1. How does Woolf use sentence structure to establish meaning and tone? Choose one example sentence, describe its structure, and explain how it suggests a specific tone or meaning. Highlight evidence from the text and make annotations to explain your choices.

2. How does Woolf use description to draw readers into the text? Choose at least one example of language that is particularly fresh, engaging, or beautiful, and explain how it impacts the meaning and tone. Support your answer with textual evidence and make annotations to explain your choice.

3. Consider the city of London as another character in the text. How does Mrs. Dalloway feel about the city? What does her relationship to the city suggest about her? Highlight textual evidence and make annotations to explain your response.

4. How does Woolf use dialogue to develop the story? What do the brief instances of spoken dialogue suggest about the characters and plot? Consider Mrs. Dalloway's exchanges with both Peter Walsh and Hugh Whitbread. Highlight evidence from the text and make annotations to support your explanation.

5. The Essential Question for this unit asks, "How have the literary movements of the last two centuries affected us?" Two characteristics of modernism are a tendency toward experimentation and an interest in psychology. How are these characteristics present in *Mrs. Dalloway,* and how does this knowledge of modernism help you better understand the text? Highlight evidence from the text and make annotations to support your explanation.

WRITING PROMPT

How does the tone of *Mrs. Dalloway* help readers better understand the thoughts and actions of Mrs. Dalloway and the other characters in the novel? How does the author use tone to convey different points of view? Use your understanding of tone, point of view, and characterization to analyze the excerpt. Support your writing with evidence from the text.

THE STAR-SPANGLED BANNER

POETRY
Francis Scott Key
1814

INTRODUCTION

"The Star-Spangled Banner" is the national anthem of the United States. The lyrics come from a poem entitled "Defence of Fort McHenry," which Francis Scott Key wrote from Baltimore Harbor after watching the bombardment of the fort by British ships during the War of 1812. Renamed and set to the tune of a popular British song, it soon became a well known American patriotic song. In 1931, after more than 100 years of widespread popularity, a congressional resolution

"...the bombs bursting in air, Gave proof through the night that our flag was still there."

NOTES

FIRST READ

1   Oh, say can you see by the dawn's early light
2   What so proudly we hailed at the twilight's last gleaming?
3   Whose broad stripes and bright stars thru the **perilous** fight,
4   O'er the **ramparts** we watched were so gallantly streaming?
5   And the rocket's red glare, the bombs bursting in air,
6   Gave proof through the night that our flag was still there.
7   Oh, say does that star-spangled banner yet wave
8   O'er the land of the free and the home of the brave?

9   On the shore, dimly seen through the mists of the deep,
10 Where the foe's **haughty** host in dread silence **reposes,**
11 What is that which the breeze, o'er the towering steep,
12 As it fitfully blows, half conceals, half discloses?
13 Now it catches the gleam of the morning's first beam,
14 In full glory reflected now shines in the stream:
15 'Tis the star-spangled banner! Oh long may it wave
16 O'er the land of the free and the home of the brave!

17 And where is that band who so **vauntingly** swore
18 That the havoc of war and the battle's confusion,
19 A home and a country should leave us no more!
20 Their blood has washed out their foul footsteps' pollution.
21 No refuge could save the **hireling** and slave
22 From the terror of flight, or the gloom of the grave:
23 And the star-spangled banner in triumph doth wave
24 O'er the land of the free and the home of the brave!

25 Oh! thus be it ever, when freemen shall stand
26 Between their loved home and the war's desolation!
27 Blest with victory and peace, may the heav'n rescued land
28 Praise the Power that hath made and preserved us a nation.

29 Then conquer we must, when our cause it is just,
30 And this be our motto: "In God is our trust."
31 And the star-spangled banner in triumph shall wave
32 O'er the land of the free and the home of the brave!

 THINK QUESTIONS

1. What questions does the speaker ask in the first stanza of the song? What is the answer to these questions? Support your response with textual evidence.

2. Summarize the third stanza of the song. How does this stanza provide background information for the rest of the song? Support your response with textual evidence.

3. How does the poet describe the United States's enemy in this battle? Make an inference as to why the poet would have left the name of the enemy uncertain. Support your answer with textual evidence.

4. Use context to determine the meaning of the word **ramparts** as it is used in "The Star-Spangled Banner." Write your definition of "ramparts" and tell how you arrived at it.

5. Remembering that the suffix -*ous* means "full of," use the context clues provided in the song to determine the meaning of **perilous**. Write your definition of "perilous" and tell how you arrived at it.

CLOSE READ

Reread the poem "The Star-Spangled Banner." As you reread, complete the Focus Questions below. Then use your answers and annotations from the questions to help you complete the Writing Prompt.

FOCUS QUESTIONS

1. Describe the song's rhyme scheme. What is the effect of the internal rhyme in some lines? Highlight evidence and make annotations to describe the effects.

2. Identify two or three examples of alliteration and repetition in the song. How does Key use repetition and alliteration to support his purpose? Support your answer with textual evidence and make annotations to explain your answer choices.

3. The last two lines of each stanza are similar, but they are not exactly the same. What differences are there between these final couplets? What purpose might these differences have? Highlight your textual evidence and make annotations to explain your choices.

4. How are the enemies of the United States described in the song? How does this description support Key's purpose? Highlight evidence from the text and make annotations to support your explanation.

5. Recall the Essential Question for this unit: "How have the literary movements of the last two centuries affected us?" What feelings do you have when reading "The Star-Spangled Banner"? What elements of the song impart these feelings? Would your feelings be the same if the song was not the national anthem? Highlight evidence from the text and make annotations to support your response.

WRITING PROMPT

Analyze Key's use of rhetoric in "The Star-Spangled Banner" to determine the theme of the song. In your response, explain how rhetorical devices, including alliteration, repetition, and figurative language, help build the theme. Cite textual evidence to support your response.

BE YE MEN OF VALOUR

NON-FICTION
Winston Churchill
1940

INTRODUCTION

Delivered on May 19, 1940, "Be Ye Men of Valour" was Winston Churchill's first radio address as British prime minister. In the speech, Churchill acknowledges that German military aggression would likely soon be directed at Great Britain, and tells his countrymen not to be intimidated. Instead, he urges, they should prepare to do whatever is necessary to defeat a formidable adversary.

"Our task is not only to win the battle—but to win the war."

 FIRST READ

1   I speak to you for the first time as Prime Minister in a solemn hour for the life of our country, of our empire, of our allies, and, above all, of the cause of freedom. A tremendous battle is raging in France and Flanders. The Germans, by a remarkable combination of air bombing and heavily armored tanks, have broken through the French defenses north of the Maginot Line, and strong columns of their armored vehicles are ravaging the open country, which for the first day or two was without defenders. They have penetrated deeply and spread alarm and confusion in their track. Behind them there are now appearing infantry in lorries, and behind them, again, the large masses are moving forward. The re-groupment of the French armies to make head against, and also to strike at, this intruding wedge has been proceeding for several days, largely assisted by the magnificent efforts of the Royal Air Force.

2   We must not allow ourselves to be intimidated by the presence of these armored vehicles in unexpected places behind our lines. If they are behind our Front, the French are also at many points fighting actively behind theirs. Both sides are therefore in an extremely dangerous position. And if the French Army and our own Army are well handled, as I believe they will be, if the French retain that genius for recovery and counter-attack for which they have so long been famous, and if the British Army shows the dogged endurance and solid fighting power of which there have been so many examples in the past, then a sudden transformation of the scene might spring into being.

3   Now it would be foolish, however, to disguise the gravity of the hour. It would be still more foolish to lose heart and courage or to suppose that well-trained, well-equipped armies numbering three or four millions of men can be overcome in the space of a few weeks, or even months, by a scoop, or raid of mechanized vehicles, however formidable. We may look with confidence to the stabilization of the Front in France, and to the general engagement of the masses, which will enable the qualities of the French and British soldiers

NOTES

to be matched squarely against those of their adversaries. For myself, I have invincible confidence in the French Army and its leaders. Only a very small part of that splendid Army has yet been heavily engaged; and only a very small part of France has yet been invaded. There is a good evidence to show that practically the whole of the specialized and mechanized forces of the enemy have been already thrown into the battle; and we know that very heavy losses have been inflicted upon them. No officer or man, no brigade or division, which grapples at close quarters with the enemy, wherever encountered, can fail to make a worthy contribution to the general result. The Armies must cast away the idea of resisting attack behind concrete lines or natural obstacles, and must realize that mastery can only be regained by furious and unrelenting assault. And this spirit must not only animate the High Command, but must inspire every fighting man.

4 In the air—often at serious odds, often at odds hitherto thought overwhelming— we have been clawing down three or four to one of our enemies; and the relative balance of the British and German Air Forces is now considerably more favorable to us than at the beginning of the battle. In cutting down the German bombers, we are fighting our own battle as well as that of France. My confidence in our ability to fight it out to the finish with the German Air Force has been strengthened by the fierce encounters which have taken place and are taking place. At the same time, our heavy bombers are striking nightly at the tap-root of German mechanized power, and have already inflicted serious damage upon the oil refineries on which the Nazi effort to dominate the world directly depends.

5 We must expect that as soon as stability is reached on the Western Front, the bulk of that hideous apparatus of aggression which gashed Holland into ruin and slavery in a few days will be turned upon us. I am sure I speak for all when I say we are ready to face it, to endure it, and to retaliate against it to any extent that the unwritten laws of war permit. There will be many men and many women in this Island who, when the ordeal comes upon them, as come it will, will feel comfort, and even a pride, that they are sharing the perils of our lads at the Front—soldiers, sailors, and airmen—God bless them—and are drawing away from them a part at least of the onslaught they have to bear. Is not this the appointed time for all to make the utmost exertions in their power? If the battle is to be won, we must provide our men with ever-increasing quantities of the weapons and ammunition they need. We must have, and have quickly, more aeroplanes, more tanks, more shells, more guns. There is **imperious** need for these vital munitions. They increase our strength against the powerfully armed enemy. They replace the wastage of the obstinate struggle—and the knowledge that wastage will speedily be replaced enables us to draw more readily upon our reserves and throw them in now that everything counts so much.

Please note that excerpts and passages in the StudySync® library and this workbook are intended as touchstones to generate interest in an author's work. The excerpts and passages do not substitute for the reading of entire texts, and StudySync® strongly recommends that students seek out and purchase the whole literary or informational work in order to experience it as the author intended. Links to online resellers are available in our digital library. In addition, complete works may be ordered through an authorized reseller by filling out and returning to StudySync® the order form enclosed in this workbook.

Reading & Writing Companion   **399**

6   Our task is not only to win the battle—but to win the war. After this battle in France **abates** its force, there will come the battle for our Island—for all Britain is, and all that Britain means. That will be the struggle. In that supreme emergency we shall not hesitate to take every step, even the most drastic, to call forth from our people the last ounce and the last inch of effort of which they are capable. The interests of property, the hours of labor, are nothing compared to the struggle for life and honor, for right and freedom, to which we have vowed ourselves.

7   I have received from the Chiefs of the French Republic, and in particular from its indomitable Prime Minister, Monsieur Reynaud, the most sacred pledges that whatever happens they will fight to the end, be it bitter or be it glorious. Nay, if we fight to the end, it can only be glorious.

8   Having received His Majesty's commission, I have formed an Administration of men and women of every Party and of almost every point of view. We have differed and quarreled in the past, but now one bond unites us all: to wage war until victory is won, and never to surrender ourselves to servitude and shame, whatever the cost and the agony may be. This is one of the most awe-striking periods in the long history of France and Britain. It is also beyond doubt the most **sublime**. Side by side, unaided except by their kith and kin in the great Dominions and by the wide empires which rest beneath their shield—side by side the British and French peoples have advanced to rescue not only Europe but mankind from the foulest and most soul-destroying tyranny which has ever darkened and stained the pages of history. Behind them, behind us, behind the Armies and Fleets of Britain and France, gather a group of shattered States and bludgeoned races: the Czechs, the Poles, the Norwegians, the Danes, the Dutch, the Belgians—upon all of whom the long night of barbarism will descend, unbroken even by a star of hope, unless we conquer, as conquer we must, as conquer we shall.

9   Today is Trinity Sunday. Centuries ago words were written to be a call and a spur to the faithful servants of truth and justice:

10   Arm yourselves, and be ye men of **valour,** and be in readiness for the conflict; for it is better for us to perish in battle than to look upon the outrage of our nation and our altars. As the will of God is in Heaven, even so let it be.

THINK QUESTIONS

1. What is the current state of the war, and why does Churchill feel such a sense of urgency? Use details from the text to support your inferences.

2. How is what Churchill says about France in Paragraph 1 different from what he says in Paragraph 3? What reaction do you think he hopes to elicit from his audience by making these two points? Support your inferences with evidence from the text.

3. Who are the "group of shattered States and bludgeoned races"? What image of Britain and France does Churchill hope to convey with this reference? Support your answer with textual evidence.

4. Use context to determine the meaning of the word **imperious** as it is used in "Be Ye Men of Valour." Write your definition of "imperious" and tell how you arrived at it.

5. Use context to determine the meaning of the word **sublime** as it is used in "Be Ye Men of Valour." Write your definition of "sublime" and tell how you arrived at it.

Please note that excerpts and passages in the StudySync® library and this workbook are intended as touchstones to generate interest in an author's work. The excerpts and passages do not substitute for the reading of entire texts, and StudySync® strongly recommends that students seek out and purchase the whole literary or informational work in order to experience it as the author intended. Links to online resellers are available in our digital library. In addition, complete works may be ordered through an authorized reseller by filling out and returning to StudySync® the order form enclosed in this workbook.

Reading & Writing Companion   401

CLOSE READ

Reread the speech "Be Ye Men of Valor." As you reread, complete the Focus Questions below. Then use your answers and annotations from the questions to help you complete the Writing Prompt.

FOCUS QUESTIONS

1. Explain how Churchill uses factual information to advance his purpose in the speech. What sorts of information does he include, and what inferences can his audience make based on these facts? Highlight evidence from the text and make annotations to explain your ideas.

2. How does Churchill use rhetoric, or persuasive techniques, to express his point of view? Choose two examples from the text, and explain what makes them particularly convincing or engaging and how they support his purpose. Support your answer with textual evidence and make annotations to explain your choices.

3. Describe the style and tone Churchill uses in the speech. How does his style and tone help his audience understand his purpose and point of view? Highlight your textual evidence and make annotations to explain your ideas.

4. For the conclusion of the speech, Churchill paraphrases a verse from the Bible. How effective is this choice? Does it wrap up his ideas clearly and convincingly? Why or why not? Highlight evidence from the text and make annotations to support your evaluation.

5. The Essential Question for this unit asks, "How have the literary movements of the last two centuries affected us?" Consider the characteristics of romanticism, realism, or modernism, and apply this question to "Be Ye Men of Valour." How did the literary movements of the previous two centuries affect Churchill's writing? Highlight textual evidence and make annotations to explain your ideas.

WRITING PROMPT

Describe Winston Churchill's point of view regarding the role the British should play in World War II. How does he use this point of view to advance his purpose(s) for giving this speech? How does his style or the content of his speech support the persuasiveness of the speech? Support your writing with evidence from the text.

D-DAY PRAYER

NON-FICTION
Franklin D. Roosevelt
1944

INTRODUCTION

Franklin D. Roosevelt was the 32nd president of the United States and was in office throughout World War II. He delivered this short speech on June 6, 1944, a day known in history as D-Day. On that day, more than 160,000 Allied troops landed on the beaches of Normandy, France, to fight Nazi Germany—the largest seaborne military invasion in history. Although the operation contributed significantly to Hitler's defeat, it resulted in a large number of Allied casualties,

"Some will never return. Embrace these, Father, and receive them..."

FIRST READ

1   Last night when I spoke with you about the fall of Rome, I knew at that moment that troops of the United States and our Allies were crossing the Channel in another and greater operation. It has come to pass with success thus far.

2   And so, in this **poignant** hour, I ask you to join with me in prayer:

3   Almighty God: our sons, pride of our Nation, this day have set upon a mighty endeavor, a struggle to preserve our Republic, our religion, and our civilization, and to set free a suffering humanity.

4   Lead them straight and true; give strength to their arms, **stoutness** to their hearts, **steadfastness** in their faith.

5   They will need Thy blessings. Their road will be long and hard. For the enemy is strong. He may hurl back our forces. Success may not come with rushing speed, but we shall return again and again; and we know that by Thy grace, and by the righteousness of our cause, our sons will triumph.

6   They will be sore tried, by night and by day, without rest—until the victory is won. The darkness will be rent by noise and flame. Men's souls will be shaken with the violences of war.

7   For these men are lately drawn from the ways of peace. They fight not for the lust of conquest. They fight to end conquest. They fight to liberate. They fight to let justice arise, and tolerance and good will among all Thy people. They yearn but for the end of battle, for their return to the haven of home.

8   Some will never return. Embrace these, Father, and receive them, Thy heroic servants, into Thy kingdom.

9   And for us at home—fathers, mothers, children, wives, sisters and brothers of brave men overseas—whose thoughts and prayers are ever with them—help

Reading & Writing Companion

NOTES

us, Almighty God, to rededicate ourselves in renewed faith in Thee in this hour of great sacrifice.

10 Many people have urged that I call the Nation into a single day of special prayer. But because the road is long and the desire is great, I ask that our people devote themselves in a continuance of prayer. As we rise to each new day, and again when each day is spent, let words of prayer be on our lips, invoking Thy help to our efforts.

11 Give us strength, too—strength in our daily tasks, to redouble the contributions we make in the physical and the material support of our armed forces.

12 And let our hearts be stout, to wait out the long **travail,** to bear sorrows that may come, to impart our courage unto our sons wheresoever they may be.

13 And, O Lord, give us faith. Give us faith in Thee; faith in our sons; faith in each other; faith in our united crusade. Let not the keenness of our spirit ever be dulled. Let not the impacts of temporary events, of temporal matters of but fleeting moment—let not these **deter** us in our unconquerable purpose.

14 With Thy blessing, we shall prevail over the unholy forces of our enemy. Help us to conquer the apostles of greed and racial arrogancies. Lead us to the saving of our country, and with our sister nations into a world unity that will spell a sure peace—a peace invulnerable to the schemings of unworthy men. And a peace that will let all men live in freedom, reaping the just rewards of their honest toil. Thy will be done, Almighty God. Amen.

 THINK QUESTIONS

1. Why did President Franklin Roosevelt want to lead Americans in prayer during this broadcast? Include textual evidence in your answer.

2. What did Roosevelt ask his audience to do in this speech? Cite textual evidence to support your answer.

3. What did Roosevelt have to say about the difficulty of the D-Day invasion? What does he follow this statement with to garner support for the troops? Support your answer with textual evidence.

4. Use context to determine the meaning of the word **stoutness** as it is used in "D-Day Prayer." Write your definition of "stoutness" and tell how you arrived at it.

5. Use context to determine the meaning of the word **poignant** as it is used in "D-Day Prayer." Write your definition of "poignant" and tell how you arrived at it.

CLOSE READ

Reread Roosevelt's "D-Day Prayer." As you reread, complete the Focus Questions below. Then use your answers and annotations from the questions to help you complete the Writing Prompt.

FOCUS QUESTIONS

1. What is President Roosevelt's purpose in giving the "D-Day Prayer"? How does his choice of style support his purpose? Highlight textual evidence and make annotations to explain how your evidence supports Roosevelt's purpose.

2. Determine the connotations of key words in the seventh paragraph, which begins "For these men. . ." What ideas do these words give to the reader? How do the connotations of the words in this paragraph support Roosevelt's purpose? Highlight key words and make annotations to explain each word's connotation and effect.

3. Analyze how Roosevelt uses the word "faith" throughout "D-Day Prayer." How do the denotation and connotation of "faith" relate to key ideas in the speech? Highlight textual evidence to support your response.

4. Parallelism is the repetition of parallel grammatical structures in a text. Parallel structure is a rhetorical feature that gives texts a clear pattern. President Roosevelt uses parallel grammatical structures in several parts of the prayer. Highlight two instances of parallelism, and make annotations to explain how the rhetorical feature supports Roosevelt's purpose.

5. In the decades after World War I, modernism was the key literary movement for expressing disillusionment with modern war. President Roosevelt gave this speech in 1944, in the middle of another devastating war. In what ways is "D-Day Prayer" a rejection of the ideals of modernism? Highlight textual evidence to support your answer.

WRITING PROMPT

President Roosevelt's "D-Day Prayer" and Winston Churchill's "Be Ye Men of Valour" are two World War II speeches with similar purposes. Compare and contrast the content of the speeches and the rhetorical features each speaker uses to support his purpose. Support your response with textual evidence from both speeches.

app.studysync.com

ASSIGNMENTS   REVIEW   BINDER   BLASTS   LIBRARY

EXTENDED WRITING PROJECT

dysync

WRITE

ED WRITING PROJECT
INFORMATIVE WRITING

Extended Writing Project:
Informative Writing
by StudySync

1   WRITE

Extended Writing Project Prompt and Directions:

Choose one author from this unit whom you'd like to kno
project and write a formal research paper in which you p
life or the time period in which he or she lived, and the li
is associated. Then explain how the author's text from th
period and literary movement as a whole.

- Your essay should include:
- an introduction with a clear thesis
- body paragraphs with relevant evidence from credible source
  support your thesis
- a conclusion paragraph that effectively wraps up your essay

Font   Size   B I I_x A· U

The   I'm

NOTES

EXTENDED WRITING PROJECT
INFORMATIVE WRITING

INFORMATIVE RESEARCH PAPER WRITING

WRITING PROMPT

Choose one author from this unit whom you'd like to know more about. Conduct a research project and write a formal research paper in which you provide information about the author's life or the time period in which he or she lived, and the literary movement with which he or she is associated. Then explain how the author's text from the unit is representative of the time period and literary movement as a whole.

Your essay should include:

- an introduction with a clear thesis
- body paragraphs with relevant evidence from credible sources and thorough analysis to support your thesis
- a conclusion paragraph that effectively wraps up your essay

Informative research papers use textual evidence, including facts, statistics, examples, and details from reliable sources, to give information about a topic. One purpose of informative writing is to convey accurate information to the reader. In addition, informative writing serves to increase readers' knowledge of a subject, to help readers better understand processes, and to enhance readers' comprehension of a certain concept. Informative research papers achieve these goals by using factual information from credible sources.

Outside research is absolutely necessary to a research paper. Research enables writers to not only discover and confirm facts, but also to draw new conclusions about their topic. A strong research paper will use both primary and secondary sources to support the points the writer makes. Primary sources are original documents, such as letters, diaries, speeches, or works of fiction. Secondary sources examine or offer commentary on primary sources. Secondary sources include textbooks, encyclopedias, and works of criticism. For example, Jane Austen's *Pride and Prejudice* is a primary source,

NOTES

and a scholarly article written about the novel is a secondary source. All information taken from primary and secondary sources, including both direct quotations and paraphrases, needs to be accurately and thoroughly cited— that is, referenced and identified using specific guidelines.

However, informational research papers are not just a collection of quotations and paraphrases. Strong informative research papers are based on the writer's own ideas on a topic, which are expressed in a formal thesis statement. The writer then develops his or her thesis, or main idea, with supporting details from his or her research. In a research paper, information, ideas, and examples are organized so that each new element builds on what precedes it in order to create a piece that is unified and whole. The writing stays focused on the main idea, using transition words and phrases to help create flow and make clear connections between supporting details. Although informative writing draws a conclusion to support the thesis, the writing is always objective, unbiased, and free of opinion.

Main features of informative research papers include:

- an introduction with a clear thesis statement
- information from research sources with formal citations
- relevant facts, supporting details, and quotations used to develop the topic
- a clear and logical organizational structure
- precise language and domain-specific vocabulary
- a formal and objective style
- a concluding statement that supports the thesis and summarizes the topic
- a works cited page

As you continue with this Extended Writing Project, you will receive more instructions and practice to help you craft each of the elements of your own informative research paper. You will also learn more about incorporating research into your essay to make and support ideas and claims.

 STUDENT MODEL

Before you get started on your own informative research paper, begin by reading this essay that one student wrote in response to the writing prompt. As you read this student model, highlight and annotate the features of informative research papers that the student included in her essay.

Please note that excerpts and passages in the StudySync® library and this workbook are intended as touchstones to generate interest in an author's work. The excerpts and passages do not substitute for the reading of entire texts, and StudySync® strongly recommends that students seek out and purchase the whole literary or informational work in order to experience it as the author intended. Links to online resellers are available in our digital library. In addition, complete works may be ordered through an authorized reseller by filling out and returning to StudySync® the order form enclosed in this workbook.

Reading & Writing Companion   **409**

NOTES

The Making of Pride and Prejudice:
The Life and Times of Jane Austen

Pride and Prejudice is among the best-loved works of British literature. Written not long after the birth of the British novel, Jane Austen's text examines themes relating to marriage, family relationships, class, and self-knowledge. Austen's keen wit and nuanced depictions of human behavior have won the book generations of admirers. But why do readers love the book so much? A look at Austen's biography and a short overview of literary realism provide helpful context for better understanding this novel.

Jane Austen was born in 1775 and grew up in Steventon, a remote village to the west of London. Her father was the minister of the village church. He also owned a small farm and used his home as a boarding school for several boys (Tomalin 19–20). Jane had six brothers and a sister. Austen's mother wrote humorous poetry, and both parents encouraged their children to spend a great deal of time reading and writing (Tomalin 25). Austen was twice sent to boarding schools, for less than a year in each case. The curricula were not rigorous and consisted mainly of spelling, French, needlework, and dancing (Tomalin 42). Women were not allowed to attend universities at the time (Shields 22). Austen, however, proved to be self-sufficient. Most of her education took place at home; her father had a large library (Tomalin 39). Reading novels was an especially popular pastime in Austen's family. The novel was a relatively new literary form in the late 1700s, and the British especially enjoyed romance novels and adventure novels. Although Austen read many romance novels, the novel that made the greatest impression on her was Samuel Richardson's *The History of Sir Charles Grandison*. This seven-volume work focused on the history of a marriage and was full of scandalous behavior and interesting characters (27). No doubt this book inspired her interest in marriage as a literary subject.

Austen likely found inspiration in her family, too. Austen's only sister, Cassandra, was her best friend. Cassandra was three years older and enjoyed art; she drew the only known portrait of Jane. Cassandra and Jane were so close that Cassandra considered Jane "part of myself" (Tomalin 194). The Bennet family in *Pride and Prejudice,* made up of five daughters, perhaps reflects Austen's bond with her own sister.

During her late teens, Austen attended balls and other social events in her community. And like the Bennet girls, her own family's lack of wealth impeded her chances of finding a suitable suitor. When Austen began to spend time with a young man named Tom Lefroy, his family did not approve of the match. The Lefroy family left the area, and Austen never saw Tom again (Shields 54). She would never marry and would instead spend her life writing about the social conditions that affected matrimony.

The literary scene was in a state of transition at this time. Nineteenth-century Romanticism stressed emotion over reason and offered up improbable stories as a way to inventively pique the imagination of readers (Reuben). Realism, on the other hand, is the exact opposite. Authors of Realism aimed to give readers a realistic, "slice of life" look at the world in which they lived ("The 19th Century"). According to experts, events taking place in nineteenth-century England may have caused this literary shift: "Realism came into being when the romantic view, with its idealized concept of nature, found itself incapable of coming to terms with a new urban reality. Realism portrayed an individual in a changing world confronting personal and communal crises" (Lehan 251). At the turn of the nineteenth century, Great Britain was enjoying an era of prosperity. The onset of the Industrial Revolution saw the weaving industry in Britain growing rapidly, supported by raw materials from India and America. London was one of the world's major centers of trade and industry (Gilbert).

Despite the novel's realism, however, one key element of the real world is missing in *Pride and Prejudice*. During this time England was in the middle of a long war with France, but this conflict does not seem to affect Mrs. Bennet, whose "poor nerves" are rattled only by the idea that her husband will not extend a greeting to their new neighbor (Austen). But that might just be Austen's attempt to keep her novel realistic: "In the days when wars were fought by small professional armies the impact of the fighting on the daily life of people living in small country towns was negligible, and it would have been unrealistic as well as artistically inappropriate for Jane Austen to have expanded her horizon to include discussions of world affairs which were not relevant to the situations she was presenting" (Daiches 745). Instead, Austen focuses on realistic topics that everyone in her audience could relate to: marriage and relationships among family members.

NOTES

In Chapter 1, Mrs. Bennet's focus is on getting her daughters married. She values superficial qualities, such as her daughter Jane's attractiveness and her daughter Lydia's good humor. Mr. Bennet is partial to daughter Lizzy because of her intelligence. This, too, is a marker of realism. Both Mr. and Mrs. Bennet are concerned with their own realities. Pam Morris writes that realism's "emphasis upon the individual apprehension of reality marks a shift from the classical concern with universal truth to a notion of particularity" (77). Yet, Austen's novel presents one tongue-in-cheek "universal truth" in its first line: "It is a truth universally acknowledged that a single man in possession of a good fortune must be in want of a wife" (Austen). This opening remark tells us that, even though the novel is a reflection of realism's focus on the individual, Austen is doing more than just giving readers a realistic depiction of their own world: she is commenting on it as well.

Today, readers can pick up a copy of *Pride and Prejudice* and get a feel for what it was like to live in Jane Austen's England (at least as a member of the upper middle class). We can enjoy the novel for its wit and satire, and we might just see a bit of our own lives in the Bennets' struggles. A large family and life in a small village gave Jane Austen the raw material she needed to write the Bennets' story, and the rise of literary realism helped her turn that story into a masterpiece.

Works Cited

Austen, Jane. "From *Pride and Prejudice*." StudySync. BookheadEd Learning, LLC, 2015. Web. 14 Nov 2014.

Daiches, David. *A Critical History of English Literature.* New York: Ronald Press, 1960. Print.

Gilbert, Bentley Brinkerhoff. "United Kingdom: History." *Encyclopaedia Britannica*. Encyclopaedia Britannica, Inc, 17 Nov. 2014. Web. 14 Nov 2014.

Lehan, Richard. *Realism and Naturalism: The Novel in an Age of Transition.* Madison: U of Wisconsin P, 2005, Print.

Morris, Pam. *Realism.* London: Routledge, 2003. Print.

Reuben, Paul P. "Chapter 3: Early Nineteenth Century and Romanticism—A Brief Introduction." *PAL: Perspectives in American Literature—A Research and Reference Guide.* CSU Stanislaus, 21 June 2014. Web. 14 Nov 2014.

Shields, Carol. *Jane Austen.* New York: Penguin, 2001. Print.

"The 19th Century: Realism and Symbolism." *Norton.* W.W. Norton & Company, 2006. Web. 14 Nov 2014.

Tomalin, Claire. *Jane Austen: A Life.* New York: Knopf, 1997. Print.

 THINK QUESTIONS

1. What is the central or main idea of this research paper? How do you know? Cite textual evidence to support your response.

2. According to the essay, what are some reasons for the enduring popularity of *Pride and Prejudice?* Why is this information relevant to the essay's central idea? Use examples from the text to support your opinion.

3. How is Jane Austen's novel an example of literary Realism? How does this information support the essay's thesis statement? Cite textual evidence to support your response.

4. Thinking about the writing prompt, which selections or other resources would you like to use to create your own informative research paper? What are some ideas that you may want to develop in your own piece?

5. What are some of the literary movements you have learned about in Unit 4? What are the characteristics of these movements??

PREWRITE

WRITING PROMPT

Choose one author from this unit whom you'd like to know more about. Conduct a research project and write a formal research paper in which you provide information about the author's life or the time period in which he or she lived, and the literary movement with which he or she is associated. Then explain how the author's text from the unit is representative of the time period and literary movement as a whole.

Your essay should include:

- an introduction with a clear thesis
- body paragraphs with relevant evidence from credible sources and thorough analysis to support your thesis
- a conclusion paragraph that effectively wraps up your essay

As you prewrite your informative research paper, first think about the various authors whose work you have read in this unit. Which texts stood out to you? Whom would you want to learn more about and why? Why is that author so interesting? Consider any facts you may already know about his or her life, time period, or the literary movement with which his or her work is associated.

Then think about what else you'd like to know about the author you have chosen. What does the author's text from the unit tell you about the time period in which he or she lived? What does it suggest about the author's life? What kinds of source materials could help you find this information? What questions might you ask to jumpstart your research? Remember to ask questions about the author's life, the time period, the literary movement with which he or she is associated, and the text you have read in this unit. Begin prewriting your informative research paper by first making a list of research

Copyright © Bookheaded Learning, LLC

questions and then brainstorming what kinds of sources would help you answer those questions.

Use this model to help you get started with your own prewriting:

Author and Text: Jane Austen; *Pride and Prejudice*

Research Questions:

- When and where did Jane Austen live? What was everyday life like in England during her time?

- Pride and Prejudice focuses on a family. What was Jane Austen's family like? Did she have a big family like the Bennets? Was she a mother herself?

- What historical events were taking place during the time Austen was writing? Are they reflected in the novel?

- How realistic are the events and characters in Pride and Prejudice?

Possible Sources: biography of Jane Austen; encyclopedia entry on English history; history textbook; articles of literary criticism

SKILL:
RESEARCH AND
NOTE-TAKING

⭐ DEFINE

Research is the process of gathering data, such as facts and other information about a topic. Research helps writers narrow or broaden their inquiry into a topic, develop a point of view, and draw conclusions about what information is most relevant to their topic. The information you discover when conducting research will help you solidify your main idea, or thesis, of your informative research paper. Good research will not only help you formulate ideas, but it will also increase your understanding of a topic and strengthen your writing.

Research is the systematic investigation of general and specific factual information from several reliable sources. As you research, it is important to explore a variety of both print and digital resources that specifically relate to your topic. Focusing on only one source can limit your research and give your essay an unintended bias. When conducting research online, for example, you can do an advanced search to find sources that are most relevant to your topic.

It's important to note, however, that not all sources are created equal. Especially when you are looking for digital sources, you need to make sure that the information you find is valid and reliable. Unreliable sources (including collaborative online databases, such as Wikipedia, and works of opinion, such as blogs or personal websites) should never be used in research and note-taking. These sources may or may not be accurate, so they are not reliable. It's best to stick with authoritative sources, such as books, academic journals, university websites, or government databases. You should assess the strengths and weaknesses of each source as you compile your bibliography and take care to find a sufficient number of sources to meet the needs of your task, purpose, and audience.

Information collected from sources must be carefully evaluated to determine if it is accurate and relevant to your topic. Not everything you uncover while researching a topic will support your thesis; you should choose only the most relevant information from each source.

An essential part of the research process is **note-taking.** Note-taking is a systematic method of writing down select pieces of information, either as a paraphrase written in your own words or as direct quotes taken from a source. Good notes can help you keep your topic focused, inspire you to make connections between ideas, and become evidence you cite to support or broaden ideas. Your notes need to include not only information you are going to use, but also details about where and when you found the information. Documenting source information will come in handy when you're compiling your works cited list and help you track it down again later if needed.

When researching and taking notes, you need to choose the method, or combination of methods, that works best for you. Regardless of the method you choose, you must always avoid **plagiarizing,** or taking another person's work and passing it off as your own, whether intentionally or not. There are specific, formal guidelines for including source information that you need to use. You will learn how to do this in the Sources and Citations lesson.

 IDENTIFICATION AND APPLICATION

- Find sources that support and explain your topic; read general and specific information in print books, in academic journals, and on the Internet. Find information that is relevant to your topic and audience. Be sure the sources are reliable.

- Make a bibliographic list of references. Follow any guidelines set forth by the style guide (for example, the *MLA Handbook for Writers of Research Papers*) you need to use for your essay.

- Read information in sources and take notes, being careful to distinguish between paraphrases and direct quotations.

- Create note cards for each source.

- Source cards are note cards that document the author, title, and publication information of each source you plan to use. It is a good idea to number each source card.

- Note cards are paper index cards you can use to keep track of information from each source. Your notes may include key words, phrases, direct quotations, paraphrases, and summaries that specifically relate to the topic. The information on the cards should be relatively short and to the point. Note cards should include the source and a page number, or paragraph number, where the information can be found. Use a new card for each piece of information you want to consider or use. If you use a lot of information from a single source, you might consider having separate note cards for each main topic.

- Online notes can be taken using a word-processing program or a website or application designed specifically for note-taking. Taking notes online may benefit researchers who take a lot of notes since you can only fit so much information on a single note card. An online system also allows you to go back and edit your notes as you narrow or broaden your search.

 MODEL

Take a look at some of the note cards made by the writer of the student model research paper "The Making of *Pride and Prejudice.*"

Source Cards

(Source) (source number) 1	(Source) (source number) 2
Tomalin, Claire. Jane Austen: A life. New York: Knopf, 1997. Print.	*Shields, Carol. Jane Austen.* New York: Penguin, 2001. Print.

The writer wrote her sources in proper MLA style to save time later, but that's not necessary at this stage. A source card only needs to include author, title, and publication information.

Note Cards

(source number) 1	(source number) 2
Austen's education	**More on Austen's education**
• Jane's mother wrote funny poems. "A mother who could make magic with words must have caught all her children's attention" (25).	• Jane and Cassndra were sent to the Abbey School in Reading (22).
• Jane was sent to boarding school at age 7 but was brought home due to illness (33–37).	• Women couldn't attend universities at this time, and "girls' education in Jane Austen's time consisted of what might be called 'accomplishments'" (22).
• By age 8, Austen could "read anything in English on her father's shelves that took her fancy" (39).	• see Tomalin's list of subjects
• The Austen girls were sent to school for a second time in 1785, but only stayed about a year (42–43).	• Mr. Austen brought the girls home in 1786 "perhaps" because he "thought the curriculum at the Abbey School too light" (22).
› studied spelling, needlework, French, and dancing	• Mr. Austen let Jane read whatever she wanted. She loved Samuel Richardson, especially *The History of Sir Charles Grandison,* a seven-volume tome—one million words—which is little read today. . ." (27).

On the note card, the number in the upper right corner matches the source card. That way the writer knows exactly where all that information came from. The writer included page numbers for each piece of information for easy reference.

Next, the writer used these notes to compose the second paragraph of the research paper:

> Jane Austen was born in 1775 and grew up in Steventon, a remote village to the west of London. Her father was the minister of the village church. He also owned a small farm and used his home as a boarding school for several

boys (Tomalin 19–20). Jane had six brothers and a sister. Austen's mother wrote humorous poetry, and both parents encouraged their children to spend a great deal of time reading and writing (Tomalin 25). Austen was twice sent to boarding schools, for less than a year in each case. The curricula were not rigorous and consisted mainly of spelling, French, needlework, and dancing (Tomalin 42). Women were not allowed to attend universities at the time (Shields 22). Austen, however, proved to be self-sufficient. Most of her education took place at home; her father had a large library (Tomalin 39). Reading novels was an especially popular pastime in Austen's family. The novel was a relatively new literary form in the late 1700s, and the British especially enjoyed romance novels and adventure novels. Although Austen read many romance novels, the novel that made the greatest impression on her was Samuel Richardson's *The History of Sir Charles Grandison*. This seven-volume work focused on the history of a marriage and was full of scandalous behavior and interesting characters (27). No doubt this book inspired her interest in marriage as a literary subject.

Notice that the paragraph contains citations in parentheses for each source and the page numbers where the information is found. These citations follow MLA style, although other style guides may dictate the use of footnotes or endnotes.

 PRACTICE

Create four source cards and four note cards that properly record quoted or paraphrased information from four sources. When you are finished, trade with a partner and offer each other feedback. Do the cards contain all of the necessary source information? Do direct quotes appear in quotations? Do the notes make it clear why your peer has included the information? Offer each other suggestions, and remember that they are most helpful when they are constructive.

SKILL:
THESIS
STATEMENT

★ DEFINE

The thesis statement is one of the most important elements in an informative research paper. It introduces what the writer is going to say about the topic of the essay, helps control and focus the information the writer provides, and summarizes the central or main idea. It also gives the reader an overview of the ideas the writer will develop in the body of the essay. Ideas presented in a good thesis statement, although somewhat general, must also be focused on, or specific to, the topic. Words used in the thesis statement should narrow the focus of the topic without giving too many details. For example, a thesis statement that says, "drugs are bad," is too broad and vague. It could be strengthened by a more specific focus on what kinds of drugs are bad, for whom they are bad, and why they may be harmful. The details about the topic will come later in the body of the essay as the writer develops his or her central idea. The thesis statement usually appears near the end of the essay's introductory paragraph. The rest of the paragraphs in the essay will support the thesis statement with facts, evidence, and examples.

••• IDENTIFICATION AND APPLICATION

A thesis statement:

- is a short, focused statement that makes a strong, clear assertion identifying and previewing the writer's central idea.
- lets the reader know the direction the writer will take in the body of the essay, especially what ideas he or she plans to discuss, support, or develop.
- is presented in the introductory paragraph, usually near the end.
- helps the writer focus on relationships among pieces of evidence from multiple sources to support and develop his or her main ideas.
- responds completely and specifically to an essay prompt.

NOTES

MODEL

The introductory paragraph of the student model informative research paper "The Making of *Pride and Prejudice*" concludes with the writer's thesis statement. In this simple statement, the writer addresses the three key parts of the prompt. This sentence identifies the author the writer has chosen to research, the literary movement with which that author is associated, and the historical context he or she will use to develop the paper:

> *Pride and Prejudice is among the best-loved works of British literature. Written not long after the birth of the British novel, Jane Austen's text examines themes relating to marriage, family relationships, class, and self-knowledge. Austen's keen wit and nuanced depictions of human behavior have won the book generations of admirers. But why do readers love the book so much?* **A look at Austen's biography and a short overview of literary realism provide helpful context for better understanding this novel.**

The writer's thesis may address each major part of the prompt, but it does not clearly preview the writer's main ideas. It states that the research paper will take a look at Austen's biography and offer an overview of literary realism, but it falls short of explaining how analyzing such information will help readers better understand *Pride and Prejudice*. A good thesis statement should not only state the kinds of information the writer includes in the paper, but it should also explain how the writer plans to use that information to develop his or her main ideas. A stronger thesis statement for the student model might be as follows: A look at Jane Austen's biography and a short overview of literary realism can give readers insight into characterization in *Pride and Prejudice*.

PRACTICE

Write a thesis statement for your informative research paper that articulates your central idea in relation to the essay prompt. When you are finished, trade with a partner and offer each other feedback. How clear is the writer's main point or idea? Is it obvious what this essay will focus on? Does it specifically address all aspects of the prompt? Offer each other suggestions, and remember that they are most helpful when they are constructive.

SKILL:
ORGANIZE
INFORMATIVE
WRITING

 DEFINE

There are many choices available for **organizing informational writing.** All of them share one common goal: to structure the analysis, explanation, or process in a clear and logical fashion appropriate to the task or purpose for writing. This will allow the writer to better understand how the relevant information should fall into place within the article or essay. If the purpose is to depict a series of historical events, a **chronological or time-order structure** might work best. If the purpose is to describe steps in a process, a **sequential structure** might be more appropriate to the task. If the purpose is to show how these events build upon one another, a **cause-and-effect structure,** which can be quite similar to the chronological structure, might be more effective. If two or more texts or ideas are being analyzed together, a **compare-and-contrast structure** would help the reader mentally form one related group of ideas and information to determine how they relate to another group of ideas and information.

To answer a writing prompt for an informative research paper, the writer should choose an organizational structure that addresses the requirements of the prompt. The prompt for Unit 4 requires the following: (1) the writer chooses an author from Unit 4, (2) the writer gives information about that author's life, time period, and the literary movement with which he or she is associated, and (3) the writer draws a connection between the author's text and the literary movement and/or the time period in which the author lived.

 IDENTIFICATION AND APPLICATION

An organizational plan for addressing the prompt might have the following structure:

- The introduction includes a clear thesis statement. The introduction should indicate the author you've chosen, the title of his or her work, the literary movement you've researched, and a glimpse of the historical context you'll discuss in the body of the paper.

NOTES

- For the body of the research paper, there should be at least one well-developed paragraph devoted to answering each part of the prompt. You might begin with the author's biography, give some information about the time period, and then address the literary movement. Then you might write a final body paragraph that connects this historical context to the text from the unit.

- Body paragraphs should contain the majority of quoted and paraphrased information from your research, along with proper citations.

- Transitional words and phrases help show how your ideas are connected.

- A conclusion revisits the thesis and summarizes your main ideas.

MODEL

Writers of informative research papers need to organize information in a way that is clear and effective. The prompt for this Extended Writing Project requires the writer to provide the reader with a lot of information. Because some of this information relates to historical events, a writer might consider a **chronological or time-order structure.** However, it's possible that not all of the information required by the prompt will be able to be organized along the same chronological timeline. In this case, a blended organizational structure that combines chronology, the **sequence** suggested by the prompt, and both **compare-and-contrast** and **cause-and-effect** analyses may be better to help the writer convey information in a clear and effective manner.

The writer of the student model research paper "The Making of *Pride and Prejudice*" begins with a chronological structure:

> **Jane Austen was born in 1775** and grew up in Steventon, a remote village to the west of London. Her father was the minister of the village church. He also owned a small farm and used his home as a boarding school for several boys (Tomalin 19–20). Jane had six brothers and a sister. Austen's mother wrote humorous poetry, and both parents encouraged their children to spend a great deal of time reading and writing (Tomalin 25). **Austen was twice sent to boarding schools, for less than a year in each case.** The curricula were not rigorous and consisted mainly of spelling, French, needlework, and dancing (Tomalin 42).

The writer signals a chronological structure in the first sentence using a date: "Jane Austen was born in 1775. . ." The date orients the reader in time, provides context in the reader's mind, and answers the part of the prompt that requires a writer to give biographical background information. The rest of the paragraph follows a time-order sequence to give facts about Austen's childhood and education. For example, "Austen was twice sent to boarding schools, for less than a year in each case."

When the writer changes topics to discuss the literary movements of the time period, the text structure changes, too:

> *The literary scene was in a state of transition at this time. Nineteenth-century romanticism stressed emotion over reason and offered up improbable stories as a way to inventively pique the imagination of readers (Reuben).* **Realism, on the other hand, is the exact opposite.** *Authors of realism aimed to give readers a realistic, "slice of life" look at the world in which they lived ("The 19th Century"). According to experts,* **events taking place in nineteenth-century England may have caused this literary shift:** *"Realism came into being when the romantic view, with its idealized concept of nature, found itself incapable of coming to terms with a new urban reality. Realism portrayed an individual in a changing world confronting personal and communal crises" (Lehan 251).*

In this paragraph, the writer uses elements of both compare-and-contrast and cause-and-effect text structures. First, the writer explains the characteristics of romanticism; then he or she uses these details to contrast that movement with realism: "Realism, on the other hand, is the exact opposite." The **transitional phrase** "on the other hand" clues the reader to the shift in topics and tells the reader that the writer is contrasting. Then, in the next sentence, the writer incorporates cause-and-effect structure to suggest a cause for the new interest in realism: "events taking place in nineteenth-century England may have caused this literary shift." This sentence also introduces information about the time period, answering another part of the prompt. In this paragraph, the writer maintains a loose chronology, but elements from other text structures help him or her explain ideas clearly.

NOTES

SKILL:
SUPPORTING
DETAILS

⭐ DEFINE

In informative writing, a writer develops the thesis statement with relevant information called **supporting details.** Relevant information consists of any fact, definition, detail, example, or quotation that is important to the reader's understanding of the topic and is closely related to the thesis or main idea. Supporting details can be found in a variety of places, but to be relevant they must provide support for the thesis. Relevant supporting details include the following:

- Facts important to understanding ideas

- Research related to the thesis

- Quotations from experts or other authoritative sources

- Conclusions of scientific findings and studies

- Excerpts from a literary text

Writers can choose supporting details from many sources. Reference books, articles in scholarly journals, news accounts, graphs, biographies, critical reviews, and authoritative websites can all provide relevant information for source material. The writer must be careful to evaluate the quality of information to determine which sources are most important and most closely related to the thesis. If the information doesn't relate to the topic or strengthen the thesis, it is not relevant.

••• IDENTIFICATION AND APPLICATION

Step 1:

Review your thesis statement. To identify relevant supporting details, ask this question: What information do I need to include to support and develop my thesis statement? Here is the thesis statement from the Student Model:

A look at Austen's biography and a short overview of literary realism provide helpful context for better understanding this novel.

To be fully developed, this thesis requires facts about Austen's life and details about literary realism. It also requires information about the novel *Pride and Prejudice*. This might come in the form of a summary or as quotations from the text.

In those cases when you have difficulty finding strong supporting details for your thesis statement, you should consider revising your thesis so that it fits better with the information you found.

Step 2:

When answering the prompt for the Extended Writing Project, you need to ask yourself which information from your research best supports each element of your thesis. The writer of the student model needed to find facts to connect *Pride and Prejudice* to Austen's biography and the literary movement of realism.

In this paragraph, the writer suggests that Austen may have chosen to write about the difficulties involved with finding a husband because she herself never married:

> *During her late teens, Austen attended balls and other social events in her community. And like the Bennet girls, her own family's lack of wealth impeded her chances of finding a suitable suitor. When Austen began to spend time with a young man named Tom Lefroy, his family did not approve of the match. The Lefroy family left the area, and Austen never saw Tom again (Shields 54).* **She would never marry and would instead spend her life writing about the social conditions that affected matrimony.**

Here the writer uses factual information about Austen's life circumstances to support his or her ideas about the author's writing: "She would never marry and would instead spend her life writing about the social conditions that affected matrimony." Notice how well this idea connects with the thesis above.

NOTES

To develop the entire thesis, the writer must also provide information about realism and connect that literary movement to the novel:

> "In the days when wars were fought by small professional armies the impact of the fighting on the daily life of people living in small country towns was negligible, and it would have been unrealistic as well as artistically inappropriate for Jane Austen to have expanded her horizon to include discussions of world affairs which were not relevant to the situations she was presenting" (Daiches 745). Instead, **Austen focuses on realistic topics that everyone in her audience could relate to: marriage and relationships among family members.**

Here the writer uses a quotation from a credible source to explain why Austen might have chosen to focus on the Bennets' neighborhood instead of the war that was being waged in Europe at the time. Then, the writer points out that Austen's choice makes the novel more relatable to her readers: "Austen focuses on realistic topics that everyone in her audience could relate to: marriage and relationships among family members."

 MODEL

The writer of the student model informative research paper "The Making of *Pride and Prejudice*" used a Textual Evidence Chart to organize the supporting details about realism he or she found during the research process. Such a chart helps the writer organize the body of the essay and ensure that all of the information in the paper helps develop the thesis statement.

Textual Evidence	**Textual Evidence**	**Textual Evidence**
Author of realism aimed to give readers a realistic. "slice of life" look at the world in which they lived ("The 19th century.)"	"Realism came into being when the romantic view, with its idealized concept of nature, found itself incapable of coming to terms with a new urban reality. Realism portrayed an individual in a changing world confronting personal and communal crises" (Lehan 251).	"In the days when wars were fought by small professional armies the impact of the fighting on the daily life of people living in small country towns was negligible, and it would have been unrealistic as well as artistically inappropriate for Jane Austen to have expanded her horizon to include discussions of world affairs which were not relevant to the situations she was presenting" (Daiches 745).

Inference

Mr. and Mrs. Bennet's focus on their own family and the goings on in their neighborhood make the novel realistic, since that is "slice of life: conversation that any married couple might have had at the time.

The information in the top three boxes provides textual evidence from research. The writer used this information to develop the section of the paper that discusses the literary movement with which Jane Austen and *Pride and Prejudice* are associated. The bottom box contains an inference that helps develop the writer's thesis statement. The writer could have used a version of this inference as the conclusion of a paragraph that included the textual evidence.

⚡ PRACTICE

Using a Textual Evidence Chart like the one you have just studied, fill in information you've gathered about your chosen author's biography, time period, or literary movement. Then make an inference based on this information that supports your thesis statement. When you are finished, share your chart with a partner and evaluate each other's inferences. Is the inference logically drawn from the evidence presented? Is there any additional information that the writer could include to strengthen the support for the inference or thesis? Offer each other suggestions, and remember that they are most helpful when they are constructive.

EXTENDED WRITING PROJECT
PLAN

PLAN

WRITING PROMPT

Choose one author from this unit whom you'd like to know more about. Conduct a research project and write a formal research paper in which you provide information about the author's life or the time period in which he or she lived, and the literary movement with which he or she is associated. Then explain how the author's text from the unit is representative of the time period and literary movement as a whole.

Your essay should include:

- an introduction with a clear thesis
- body paragraphs with relevant evidence from credible sources and thorough analysis to support your thesis
- a conclusion paragraph that effectively wraps up your essay

Review the notes you took during the research and note-taking stages, the information you listed in your Textual Evidence Chart, and the inference you made using these supporting details. Then review your thesis statement, and make sure you have gathered enough textual evidence to develop it clearly and thoroughly. This organized information, your thesis statement, and your graphic organizer will help you create a road map to use for writing your essay.

Consider the following questions as you develop your main paragraph topics and organize supporting details in your road map:

- Which author did you choose, and why?
- What did you learn about his or her life and time period?
- What important historical events occurred at this time?

- How does this historical context or information from the author's biography connect to his or her work?
- With which literary movement is the author associated?
- What are some characteristics of that literary movement?
- Is the author's work from the unit representative of that literary movement? Why or why not?
- What textual evidence can you use to draw connections between the author's writing and his or her life, time period, or literary movement?

Use this model to get started with your road map:

Essay Road Map

Thesis statement:

Paragraph 1 Topic:

    Supporting Detail #1:

    Supporting Detail #2:

Paragraph 2 Topic:

    Supporting Detail #1:

    Supporting Detail #2:

Paragraph 3 Topic:

    Supporting Detail #1:

    Supporting Detail #2:

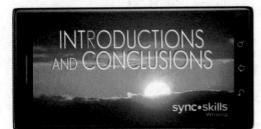

SKILL:
INTRODUCTIONS
AND
CONCLUSIONS

DEFINE

The **introduction** is the opening paragraph or section of a nonfiction text. In a research paper, the introduction sets forth a precise and knowledgeable **thesis** that will be developed and supported in the body of the text and introduces the **topic.** A strong introduction also generates interest in the topic by inserting a **"hook"** that engages readers in an interesting or unexpected way. The hook often tells readers why they should care about the topic.

A strong and effective **conclusion** should follow from and support the information that was presented in the rest of the text. It should **restate the thesis** in some way and articulate the significance of the topic, noting the most important examples and evidence. Perhaps most importantly, a conclusion should provide the reader with a sense of **closure** and the satisfying feeling that the thesis has been thoroughly supported.

IDENTIFICATION AND APPLICATION

- In informational writing, the introduction identifies the topic of the essay by explicitly stating what the text will be about. The writer may also use the introduction to provide some necessary background information about the topic to help the reader understand the thesis statement.

- In addition to the topic, the introduction includes the writer's thesis. It will often be at the end of the introduction. Note that a thesis is not always stated explicitly within the text. In the introduction, a writer might instead hint at the thesis through details and ideas that help the reader make an inference.

- It is customary to build interest in the topic by beginning the introduction with a "hook," or a way to grab the reader's attention. This awakens the reader's natural curiosity and encourages him or her to read on. Hooks

can ask open-ended questions, make connections to the reader or to life, or introduce a surprising fact.

- A strong informational essay should follow a logical and effective sequence, and its conclusion should clearly feel like the essay's stopping point.

- An effective conclusion to an informational essay reinforces the thesis statement and re-emphasizes why it is significant or worth considering.

- The conclusion leaves the reader with a final thought. In informational writing, this final thought may

  › answer a question posed by the introduction.
  › present a last, compelling example.
  › spark curiosity and encourage readers to learn more.

MODEL

The writer of the student model narrative "The Making of *Pride and Prejudice*: The Life and Times of Jane Austen" wrote a strong **introduction** for the essay.

> *Pride and Prejudice* **is among the best-loved works of British literature.** Written not long after the birth of the British novel, Jane Austen's text examines themes relating to marriage, family relationships, class, and self-knowledge. **Austen's keen wit and nuanced depictions of human behavior have won the book generations of admirers. But why do readers love the book so much?**

The essay begins with a simple statement that introduces the **topic** and explains why that topic is important: "*Pride and Prejudice* is among the best-loved works of British literature." The reader knows that the essay is going to talk about *Pride and Prejudice*, and it is going to do so because the book is beloved. Later in the introduction, the author gives one reason why the book is loved: "Austen's keen wit and nuanced depictions of human behavior have won the book generations of admirers." The author follows that statement with a **hook** in the form of an open-ended question to get the reader thinking about what more there might be to the book: "But why do readers love the book so much?"

Finally, the writer ends the introduction with the **thesis statement** for the essay: "A look at Austen's biography and a short overview of literary realism provide helpful context for better understanding this novel." The writer is going to tell readers about Austen's background and the literary movement of which she was a part to increase understanding of the novel.

In the **conclusion,** the writer wraps up the essay:

> **Today, readers can pick up a copy of Pride and Prejudice and get a feel for what it was like to live in Jane Austen's England** (at least as a member of the upper middle class). We can enjoy the novel for its wit and satire, and we might just see a bit of our own lives in the Bennets' struggles. **A large family and life in a small village** gave Jane Austen the raw material she needed to write the Bennets' story, and **the rise of literary realism helped her turn that story into a masterpiece.**

The conclusion begins with a connection to today: "Today, readers can pick up a copy of *Pride and Prejudice* and get a feel for what it was like to live in Jane Austen's England." This might encourage readers who haven't read *Pride and Prejudice* to read it. In the final sentence, the writer reminds readers of evidence presented about Austen's background ("A large family and life in a small village") and the time in which she lived ("the rise of literary realism helped her turn that story into a masterpiece"). This sentence effectively sums up the writer's key points.

 PRACTICE

Write an introduction for your informative research paper that includes a hook, the topic, and the thesis statement. Then write a conclusion that sums up your essay's key points and restates the thesis statement. When you are finished, trade with a partner and offer each other feedback. How strong is the language of your partner's thesis statement? How clear is the topic? Were you hooked? Did the conclusion effectively restate the thesis statement and sum up the writer's ideas? Offer each other suggestions, and remember that they are most helpful when they are constructive.

NOTES

SKILL: BODY PARAGRAPHS AND TRANSITIONS

⭐ DEFINE

Body paragraphs are the section of the essay between the introduction and conclusion paragraphs. This is where you support your thesis statement by developing your main points with relevant evidence, or supporting details, from your research and the text. Typically, each body paragraph will focus on one main point or idea to create clarity. The main point of each body paragraph must support the thesis statement or claim.

In each body paragraph, a writer needs to clarify the relationship between his or her ideas and evidence. To make sure the reader follows all of the ideas put forth in the essay, a writer needs to provide **clarification.** He or she does this by using **transitions.** Transitions are connecting words and phrases that clarify the relationships among ideas in a text. Transitions work at three different levels: within a sentence, between paragraphs, and to indicate organizational structure. By adding transition words or phrases to the beginning or end of a paragraph, writers guide readers smoothly through the text.

In addition, transition words and phrases help writers make connections between words within a sentence. Conjunctions such as *and, or,* and *but* and prepositions such as *with, beyond*, and *inside* show the relationships between words. Transitions help writers create **cohesion.** In writing, cohesion means having all your sentences closely linked to each other and to the thesis statement.

⬤ IDENTIFICATION AND APPLICATION

- Body paragraphs are the section of the essay between the introduction and conclusion paragraphs. The body paragraphs provide the reasons and evidence needed to support the claim a writer makes in his or her thesis statement. Typically, writers develop one main idea per body paragraph.

- A body paragraph could be structured as follows:
  - › **Topic sentence:** The topic sentence is the first sentence of your body paragraph and clearly states the main point of the paragraph. It's important that your topic sentence develops your thesis statement.
  - › **Evidence #1:** Present evidence to support your topic sentence. Evidence can be relevant facts, definitions, concrete details, quotations, or other information and examples.
  - › **Analysis/Explanation #1:** After presenting evidence, you will need to analyze that evidence and explain how it supports your main idea and, in effect, your thesis statement.
  - › **Evidence #2:** Provide a second piece of evidence to further support your main idea.
  - › **Analysis/Explanation #2:** Analyze this second piece of evidence and explain how it supports your topic sentence and, in effect, your thesis statement.
  - › **Concluding sentence:** After presenting your evidence, you need to wrap up your main idea and transition to the next paragraph in your conclusion sentence.

- Transition words and phrases help readers understand the flow of ideas and concepts within a paragraph and between paragraphs.
  - › Some of the most useful transitions are words that indicate that the ideas in one paragraph are building on or adding to those in another. Examples include *furthermore, therefore, in addition, moreover, by extension, in order to,* etc.

- All information that comes from research sources, including direct quotations and your own paraphrases, needs to be cited correctly to avoid plagiarism.

 MODEL

The writer of the student model narrative "The Making of *Pride and Prejudice:* The Life and Times of Jane Austen" wrote a strong **introduction** for the essay.

> **Pride and Prejudice is among the best-loved works of British literature.** Written not long after the birth of the British novel, Jane Austen's text examines themes relating to marriage, family relationships, class, and self-knowledge. Austen's keen wit and nuanced depictions of human behavior have won the book generations of admirers. But why do readers love the book so much?

The essay begins with a simple statement that introduces the **topic** and explains why that topic is important: "*Pride and Prejudice* is among the best-loved works of British literature." The reader knows that the essay is going to talk about *Pride and Prejudice*, and it is going to do so because the book is beloved. Later in the introduction, the author gives one reason why the book is loved: "Austen's keen wit and nuanced depictions of human behavior have won the book generations of admirers." The author follows that statement with a **hook** in the form of an open-ended question to get the reader thinking about what more there might be to the book: "But why do readers love the book so much?"

Finally, the writer ends the introduction with the **thesis statement** for the essay: "A look at Austen's biography and a short overview of literary realism provide helpful context for better understanding this novel." The writer is going to tell readers about Austen's background and the literary movement of which she was a part to increase understanding of the novel.

In the **conclusion,** the writer wraps up the essay:

> **Today, readers can pick up a copy of Pride and Prejudice and get a feel for what it was like to live in Jane Austen's England** (at least as a member of the upper middle class). We can enjoy the novel for its wit and satire, and we might just see a bit of our own lives in the Bennets' struggles. **A large family and life in a small village** gave Jane Austen the raw material she needed to write the Bennets' story, and **the rise of literary realism helped her turn that story into a masterpiece.**

The conclusion begins with a connection to today: "Today, readers can pick up a copy of *Pride and Prejudice* and get a feel for what it was like to live in Jane Austen's England." This might encourage readers who haven't read *Pride and Prejudice* to read it. In the final sentence, the writer reminds readers of evidence presented about Austen's background ("A large family and life in a small village") and the time in which she lived ("the rise of literary realism helped her turn that story into a masterpiece"). This sentence effectively sums up the writer's key points.

PRACTICE

Write one body paragraph for your informative essay that follows the suggested format. When you are finished, trade with a partner and offer each other feedback. How effective is the topic sentence at stating the main point of the paragraph? How strong is the evidence used to support the topic sentence? Are all quotes and paraphrased evidence cited properly? Did the analysis thoroughly support the topic sentence? Offer each other suggestions, and remember that they are most helpful when they are constructive.

DRAFT

WRITING PROMPT

Choose one author from this unit whom you'd like to know more about. Conduct a research project and write a formal research paper in which you provide information about the author's life or the time period in which he or she lived, and the literary movement with which he or she is associated. Then explain how the author's text from the unit is representative of the time period and literary movement as a whole.

Your essay should include:

- an introduction with a clear thesis
- body paragraphs with relevant evidence from credible sources and thorough analysis to support your thesis
- a conclusion paragraph that effectively wraps up your essay

You've already made progress toward writing your own research essay. You've thought about the topic and chosen your author and text. You've identified what you want to say about that author's life and associated literary movement based on research. You've decided how to organize information and gathered supporting details. Now it's time to write a draft.

Using your road map from the Plan lesson and your other prewriting materials, write a draft of your essay. Remember that informative writing begins with an introduction and presents a thesis statement. Body paragraphs provide supporting details and relevant information. A concluding paragraph restates or reinforces your thesis statement. An effective conclusion can also do more—it can leave a lasting impression on your readers.

When drafting, ask yourself these questions:

- How can I improve my hook to make it more appealing?

Copyright © BookheadEd Learning, LLC

- What can I do to clarify my thesis statement?
- What textual evidence—including relevant facts, strong details, and interesting quotations from either research or the literature—supports the thesis statement?
- Would more precise language or different details about the author or time period make the text more exciting and vivid?
- How well have I communicated what this individual experienced and achieved?
- What final thought do I want to leave with my readers?

Before you submit your draft, read it over carefully. You'll want to be sure that you've responded to all aspects of the prompt.

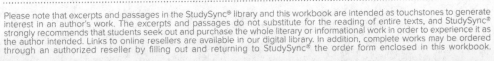

SKILL:
SOURCES AND
CITATIONS

⭐ DEFINE

When writing a research paper, writers cannot simply make up information or rely on their own subjective experiences or opinions. To thoroughly support the treatment and analysis of their topics, writers need to include information from relevant, accurate, and reliable sources and cite, or acknowledge, them properly. **Sources** are the documents and information that a writer uses to research his or her writing.

Writers should keep track of their sources as they research and plan their work. When the time comes to write, they can use this information to support any claims made within the text. Any facts, quotations, statistics, or statements included that are not common knowledge need to be cited. **Citations** are notes that give information about the sources a writer uses in his or her writing. Citations are required whenever writers quote others' words or refer to others' ideas in their writing. If writers don't include citations, they can be accused of **plagiarism,** or stealing someone else's words and ideas.

English papers typically follow MLA style, which calls for **parenthetical citations** in the running text. In some academic texts, writers may be asked to provide sources and citations in **footnotes** or **endnotes,** which link specific references within the essay to the correlating pages or chapters in an outside source. In addition to internal citations, writers may also need to provide a full list of sources in a **Works Cited** section or standard **bibliography.**

⚫⚫⚫ IDENTIFICATION AND APPLICATION

- All sources must be credible and accurate. Look for sources from experts in the topic you are writing about.
  - › When researching online, look for URLs that contain ".gov" (government agencies), ".edu" (colleges and universities), and ".org" (museums and other non-profit organizations).

Copyright © BookheadEd Learning, LLC

NOTES

> › Don't neglect respected print sources. Some scholars do not publish online.

- Include a citation to give credit to any source, whether primary or secondary, that is quoted exactly. Make sure the quotation is presented in quotation marks. There are several different ways to cite a source.

  › If the author's name is mentioned in the essay, include the page number where the quotation can be located:

    - Pam Morris writes that realism's "emphasis upon the individual apprehension of reality marks a shift from the classical concern with universal truth to a notion of particularity" (77).

  › If the author's name does not appear in the text, include the author's name and the page number in parentheses at the end of the sentence in which the quote or paraphrase appears:

    - England may have caused this literary shift: "Realism came into being when the romantic view, with its idealized concept of nature, found itself incapable of coming to terms with a new urban reality. Realism portrayed an individual in a changing world confronting personal and communal crises" (Lehan 251).

- Citations are also necessary when a writer borrows ideas or takes facts from another source, even if the writer paraphrases, or puts those ideas in his or her own words.

  › Follow the same citation rules as for exact quotations:

    - Austen's mother wrote humorous poetry, and both parents encouraged their children to spend a great deal of time reading and writing (Tomalin 25).

  › If there is no author, use the title of the work:

    - Authors of realism aimed to give readers a realistic, "slice of life" look at the world in which they lived ("The 19th Century").

  › For online sources, as with the article above, no page number is needed.

- At the end of the essay, include a Works Cited list with full bibliographical information on each source cited, formatted correctly in MLA style.

MODEL

As with any research paper for an English class, the student model essay "The Making of *Pride and Prejudice*" contains many parenthetical citations.

The literary scene was in a state of transition at this time. Nineteenth-century romanticism stressed emotion over reason and offered up improbable stories as a way to inventively pique the imagination of readers

(Reuben). *Realism, on the other hand, is the exact opposite. Authors of realism aimed to give readers a realistic, "slice of life" look at the world in which they lived* **("The 19th Century").** *According to experts, events taking place in nineteenth-century England may have caused this literary shift: "Realism came into being when the romantic view, with its idealized concept of nature, found itself incapable of coming to terms with a new urban reality. Realism portrayed an individual in a changing world confronting personal and communal crises"* **(Lehan 251).**

In the second sentence in this paragraph, the writer describes the goals of nineteenth-century romanticism. This information is not common knowledge and had to be gained from reading an outside source, so the writer needs to include a citation: (Reuben). The citation is written in parenthesis and comes before the period at the end of the sentence. The source was an online article, which is why the writer does not include a page number.

In the next sentence, the writer gives information about realism from another online source. Because this source does not have a listed author, the writer cites it using the name of the article: ("The 19th Century"). In the final citation in this paragraph, the writer includes a direct quotation from a book about realism. The citation includes the author's name, because the name was not mentioned in the running text, and the page number: (Lehan 251). Notice that the citation appears outside the quotation marks but before the end punctuation.

At the end of the essay, the writer included a Works Cited list with all the sources cited in the paper. Per MLA style, the sources are listed in alphabetical order:

Works Cited

Austen, Jane. "From *Pride and Prejudice*." StudySync. BookheadEd Learning, LLC, 2015. Web. 14 Nov 2014.

Daiches, David. *A Critical History of English Literature*. New York: Ronald Press, 1960. Print.

Gilbert, Bentley Brinkerhoff. "United Kingdom: History." *Encyclopaedia Britannica*. Encyclopaedia Britannica, Inc, 17 Nov. 2014. Web. 14 Nov 2014.

Lehan, Richard. *Realism and Naturalism: The Novel in an Age of Transition*. Madison: U of Wisconsin P, 2005. Print.

NOTES

Morris, Pam. *Realism*. London: Routledge, 2003. Print.

Reuben, Paul P. "Chapter 3: Early Nineteenth Century and Romanticism—A Brief Introduction." *PAL: Perspectives in American Literature—A Research and Reference Guide*. CSU Stanislaus, 21 June 2014. Web. 14 Nov 2014.

Shields, Carol. *Jane Austen*. New York: Penguin, 2001. Print.

"The 19th Century: Realism and Symbolism." *Norton*. W.W. Norton & Company, 2006. Web. 14 Nov 2014.

Tomalin, Claire. *Jane Austen: A Life*. New York: Knopf, 1997. Print.

MLA rules call for the citation to include the type of source, such as Web or Print. Writers do not have to include the URL for online sources. Sources without authors are listed by title. A Works Cited list only includes those works with citations in your paper. Additional sources would be included in a bibliography, if the teacher requested one.

 PRACTICE

Write citations for quoted information in your research paper. When you are finished, trade with a partner and offer feedback. Are all citations done according to MLA style? Is there any information that seems like it came from an outside source that wasn't cited? How varied were the types of sources cited? Offer each other suggestions, and remember that they are most helpful when they are constructive.

Please note that excerpts and passages in the StudySync® library and this workbook are intended as touchstones to generate interest in an author's work. The excerpts and passages do not substitute for the reading of entire texts, and StudySync® strongly recommends that students seek out and purchase the whole literary or informational work in order to experience it as the author intended. Links to online resellers are available in our digital library. In addition, complete works may be ordered through an authorized reseller by filling out and returning to StudySync® the order form enclosed in this workbook.

Reading & Writing Companion **445**

REVISE

WRITING PROMPT

Choose one author from this unit whom you'd like to know more about. Conduct a research project and write a formal research paper in which you provide information about the author's life or the time period in which he or she lived, and the literary movement with which he or she is associated. Then explain how the author's text from the unit is representative of the time period and literary movement as a whole.

Your essay should include:

- an introduction with a clear thesis
- body paragraphs with relevant evidence from credible sources and thorough analysis to support your thesis
- a conclusion paragraph that effectively wraps up your essay

You have written a draft of your research essay. You have also received input from your peers about how to improve it. Now you are going to revise your draft.

Here are some recommendations to help you revise.

- Review the suggestions made by your peers.
- Focus on maintaining a formal style. A formal style suits your purpose—giving information about a serious topic. It also fits your audience—students, teachers, and other readers interested in learning more about your topic.
  › As you revise, eliminate any slang.
  › Remove any first-person pronouns, such as "I," "me," or "mine," or instances of addressing readers as "you." These are more suitable to a writing style that is informal, personal, and conversational.

NOTES

> › If you included your personal opinions, remove them. Your essay should be clear, direct, and unbiased.

- After you have revised elements of style, think about whether there is anything else you can do to improve your essay's information or organization.

  > › Do you need to add any new textual evidence to your essay? Is there a detail about your chosen author's life that readers might find interesting?

  > › Is there a relevant line in the selection that you forgot to quote? Quotations can add life to your essay. Be sure to cite your sources.

  > › Can you substitute a more precise word for a word that is general or dull?

  > › Consider your organization. Would your essay flow better if you strengthened the transitions between paragraphs?

EDIT,
PROOFREAD,
AND PUBLISH

WRITING PROMPT

Choose one author from this unit whom you'd like to know more about. Conduct a research project and write a formal research paper in which you provide information about the author's life or the time period in which he or she lived, and the literary movement with which he or she is associated. Then explain how the author's text from the unit is representative of the time period and literary movement as a whole.

Your essay should include:

- an introduction with a clear thesis
- body paragraphs with relevant evidence from credible sources and thorough analysis to support your thesis
- a conclusion paragraph that effectively wraps up your essay

You have revised your research paper and received input from your peers on that revision. Now it's time to edit and proofread your essay to produce a final version. Have you included all of the valuable suggestions from your peers? Ask yourself: Have I fully developed my thesis statement with strong textual evidence? Have I accurately cited my sources? What more can I do to improve my essay's information and organization?

When you are satisfied with your work, proofread it for errors. Use this list to check for corrections:

- capitalization
- punctuation
- spelling
- grammar
- usage

Copyright © Bookheaded Learning, LLC

Once you have made all your corrections, you are ready to submit and publish your work. You can distribute your writing to family and friends, hang it on a bulletin board, or create an ebook. If you publish online, create links to your sources and citations. That way, readers can follow-up on what they've learned from your essay and read more on their own.

Please note that excerpts and passages in the StudySync® library and this workbook are intended as touchstones to generate interest in an author's work. The excerpts and passages do not substitute for the reading of entire texts, and StudySync® strongly recommends that students seek out and purchase the whole literary or informational work in order to experience it as the author intended. Links to online resellers are available in our digital library. In addition, complete works may be ordered through an authorized reseller by filling out and returning to StudySync® the order form enclosed in this workbook.

Reading & Writing Companion **449**

studysync®
Powered by BookheadEd Learning, LLC

Text Fulfillment
Through StudySync

If you are interested in specific titles, please fill out the form below and we will check availability through our partners.

ORDER DETAILS

Date:

TITLE	AUTHOR	Paperback/ Hardcover	Specific Edition *If Applicable*	Quantity

SHIPPING INFORMATION	BILLING INFORMATION ☐ *SAME AS SHIPPING*
Contact:	Contact:
Title:	Title:
School/District:	School/District:
Address Line 1:	Address Line 1:
Address Line 2:	Address Line 2:
Zip or Postal Code:	Zip or Postal Code:
Phone:	Phone:
Mobile:	Mobile:
Email:	Email:

PAYMENT INFORMATION

☐ CREDIT CARD

Name on Card:

Card Number: Expiration Date: Security Code:

☐ PO

Purchase Order Number:

StudySync Text Fulfillment, BookheadEd Learning, LLC
610 Daniel Young Drive | Sonoma, CA 95476